UNEQUAL DEMOCRACY

UNEQUAL DEMOCRACY

THE POLITICAL ECONOMY OF THE NEW GILDED AGE

Larry M. Bartels

RUSSELL SAGE FOUNDATION • NEW YORK

PRINCETON UNIVERSITY PRESS • PRINCETON AND OXFORD

Published by Princeton University Press, 41 William Street, Princeton, New Jersey 08540

In the United Kingdom: Princeton University Press, 6 Oxford Street, Woodstock, Oxfordshire OX20 1TW

Russell Sage Foundation, 112 East 64th Street, New York, New York 10021

ISBN-13: 978-0-691-13663-9

Library of Congress Cataloging-in-Publication Data

Bartels, Larry M., 1956–
Unequal democracy : the political economy of the new gilded age / Larry M. Bartels.
p.   cm.
Includes bibliographical references and index.
ISBN 978-0-691-13663-9 (hardcover : alk. paper)
1. United States—Economic conditions—1945–   2. Equality—Economic aspects—United States.   3. Political culture—United States—History.   4. Social classes—Political aspects—United States.   5. Power (Social sciences)—Economic aspects—United States.
6. Democracy—Economic aspects—United States.   I. Title.
HC106.5.B347   2008
330.973—dc22   2007044382

British Library Cataloging-in-Publication Data is available

This book has been composed in New Caledonia

Printed on acid-free paper. ∞

press.princeton.edu

Printed in the United States of America

5   7   9   10   8   6   4

For my brother, Thomas Raymond Bartels,
who lived poor and died young

Contents

Preface   ix

1.   The New Gilded Age   1
    Escalating Economic Inequality   6
    Interpreting Inequality   13
    Economic Inequality as a Political Issue   19
    Inequality and American Democracy   23

2.   The Partisan Political Economy   29
    Partisan Patterns of Income Growth   31
    A Partisan Coincidence?   34
    Partisan Differences in Macroeconomic Policy   42
    Macroeconomic Performance and Income Growth   47
    Partisan Policies and Post-Tax Income Growth   54
    Democrats, Republicans, and the Rise of Inequality   61

3.   Class Politics and Partisan Change   64
    In Search of the Working Class   66
    Has the White Working Class Abandoned the
       Democratic Party?   72
    Have Working-Class Whites Become More
       Conservative?   78
    Do "Moral Values" Trump Economics?   83
    Are Religious Voters Distracted from Economic Issues?   90
    Class Politics, Alive and Well   93

4.   Partisan Biases in Economic Accountability   98
    Myopic Voters   99
    The Political Timing of Income Growth   104
    Class Biases in Economic Voting   110
    The Wealthy Give Something Back: Partisan
       Biases in Campaign Spending   116
    Political Consequences of Biased Accountability   120

5.   Do Americans Care about Inequality?   127
    Egalitarian Values   130
    Rich and Poor   136
    Perceptions of Inequality   143
    Facts and Values in the Realm of Inequality   148

6.   Homer Gets a Tax Cut   162
         The Bush Tax Cuts   164
         Public Support for the Tax Cuts   170
         Unenlightened Self-Interest   176
         The Impact of Political Information   181
         Chump Change   186
         Into the Sunset   193

7.   The Strange Appeal of Estate Tax Repeal   197
         Public Support for Estate Tax Repeal   198
         Is Public Support for Repeal a Product of Misinformation? 205
         Did Interest Groups Manufacture Public Antipathy
             to the Estate Tax?   214
         Elite Ideology and the Politics of Estate Tax Repeal   217

8.   The Eroding Minimum Wage   223
         The Economic Effects of the Minimum Wage   227
         Public Support for the Minimum Wage   229
         The Politics of Inaction   232
         Democrats, Unions, and the Eroding Minimum Wage   239
         The Earned Income Tax Credit   246
         Reversing the Tide   247

9.   Economic Inequality and Political Representation   252
         Ideological Representation   254
         Unequal Responsiveness   257
         Unequal Responsiveness on Social Issues:
             The Case of Abortion   265
         Partisan Differences in Representation   267
         Why Are the Poor Unrepresented?   275

10. Unequal Democracy   283
         Who Governs?   285
         Partisan Politics and the "Have-Nots"   288
         Political Obstacles to Economic Equality   294
         The City of Utmost Necessity   298

Selected References   305

Index   317

Preface

THIS BOOK REPORTS the results of a six-year exploration of the political causes and consequences of economic inequality in America. It is inspired, in significant part, by a major change in American society over the past three decades—the substantial escalation of economic inequality that I refer to as the "New Gilded Age." That economic transformation has attracted considerable attention from economists but much less attention from political scientists. It seemed to me, as a student of American politics, that careful attention to public opinion, partisan politics, and public policy might shed valuable new light on how and why the economic fortunes of affluent, middle-class, and poor people have diverged so dramatically in the contemporary United States.

As a student of democracy, it also seemed important to me to explore the ramifications of escalating economic inequality for the American political system. Probably most sentient observers of American politics suspect that the concentration of vast additional wealth in the hands of affluent people has augmented their influence in the political arena, while the stagnating economic fortunes of middle-class and poor people have diminished their influence. However, systematic measurement of political influence is at a very rudimentary stage, leaving political scientists remarkably ill-equipped to confirm, refute, or qualify that suspicion. I have attempted here, through a combination of systematic statistical analysis and case studies, to assess the extent to which economic inequality in contemporary America gets translated into political inequality.

Some readers are likely to see the product of my efforts as a rather partisan book, at least by academic standards. For what it is worth, I can report that it did not start out that way. I began the project as an unusually apolitical political scientist. (The last time I voted was in 1984, and that was for Ronald Reagan.) While I was prepared to find that parties and partisanship play an important role in the politics of economic inequality, as they do in many domains of American politics, I was quite surprised to discover how often and how profoundly partisan differences in ideologies and values have shaped key policy decisions and economic outcomes. I have done my best to follow my evidence where it led me.

In telling this story I have attempted to balance the demands of scholarship and accessibility. My aim has been to make the text and figures comprehensible to general readers—at least to general readers who have some patience for the twists and turns of serious arguments and systematic evidence. Tables and notes provide additional scholarly detail, some of which will only be intelligible or interesting to people with some background in social science or statistics or both. I recognize that any compromise of this sort is bound to leave readers in both camps less than fully satisfied; however, I view it as a necessary accommodation to the prevalence of social-scientific illiteracy among Americans who read (and write) about politics and public affairs.

I suspect that the prevalence of social-scientific illiteracy in American public discourse is both a cause and an effect of the fact that social-scientific research is woefully undersupported in American society. However, I have been unusually fortunate in finding generous financial, institutional, and personal support for my work, and it is a great pleasure to acknowledge that support here.

Princeton University and its Woodrow Wilson School have provided time and facilities for research, as well as regular access to stimulating students and colleagues. I am grateful to the past and present deans of the Woodrow Wilson School, Michael Rothschild and Anne-Marie Slaughter, for building and maintaining a vibrant intellectual community in which to pursue serious analysis of significant public issues. I am also grateful to students in my Wilson School seminar on Inequality and American Democracy for serving as an invaluable test-audience for the first complete draft of the book, and to my colleagues Roland Bénabou, Angus Deaton, Alan Krueger, Jonathan Parker, and Mark Watson for providing generous advice about economic issues and literature.

Within the Woodrow Wilson School, my primary home for the past eight years has been the Center for the Study of Democratic Politics. The faculty, visitors, students, and staff there have provided abundant intellectual and moral support, including appropriate mixtures of criticism and encouragement in response to half-baked arguments presented in lunch seminars, conferences, and common room chats. I am especially grateful to Doug Arnold, Brandice Canes-Wrone, Michele Epstein, Marty Gilens, Dave Lewis, Nolan McCarty, and Markus Prior for helpful reactions and suggestions. As I have come to expect over the years, Chris Achen provided especially cogent advice and especially generous encouragement. He also graciously tolerated the constraints imposed by this project on the progress of our long-running collaborative work on democratic accountability. Next!

I have also benefited greatly, and repeatedly, from the generous support of the Russell Sage Foundation and its president, Eric Wanner. The first stages of my research were conducted as part of the Princeton Working Group on Inequality, one of several interdisciplinary research teams supported by the Russell Sage Foundation through its Social Dimensions of Inequality project. I thank Bruce Western, the ringleader of the Princeton Working Group, for involving me in the project, and Bruce, Paul DiMaggio,

Leslie McCall, Nolan McCarty, and Howard Rosenthal for providing a supportive collaborative setting in which to tackle issues well outside the range of my previous scholarly expertise. Annual meetings of the various Russell Sage Foundation working groups at Harvard (2001), Wisconsin (2002), Maryland (2003), Princeton (2004), Berkeley (2005), and UCLA (2007) served as a floating boot camp introducing me to many of the toughest issues and much of the best current research in the field.

The Russell Sage Foundation provided a separate grant to support the collection of new survey data on inequality and public policy as part of the 2002 National Election Study (NES). Those data figure prominently in chapters 5, 6, and 7 of this book—and in related work by many other scholars. It was a pleasure to collaborate with Nancy Burns and Don Kinder, the principal investigators of the 2002 NES, in designing the inequality module. I am grateful to them and to their colleagues at NES for implementing the survey and sharing the data. More generally, I am indebted to the long succession of principal investigators, staff, and overseers who have contributed to the invaluable accumulation and dissemination of NES data over more than half a century. Much of the analysis presented here would not have been possible without their efforts.

A third (and, so far, final) grant from the Russell Sage Foundation provided the concentrated time required to pull the various strands of my research together, fill in some important missing pieces, and turn it all into a book. Significant additional support for this phase of my work came from the Carnegie Corporation of New York in the form of a Carnegie Scholars Grant and from Princeton University in the form of a quota leave.

Along the way, Theda Skocpol invited me to participate in the American Political Science Association's Task Force on Inequality and American Democracy. I learned a great deal about inequality and how to study it from the distinguished group assembled by Theda, and especially from our able task force chair, Larry Jacobs. The Task Force's report and the volume of supporting material edited by Jacobs and Skocpol, *Inequality and American Democracy: What We Know and What We Need to Learn*, provide an authoritative introduction to many aspects of the politics of inequality that I have ignored or underemphasized here.

Over the past five years I have presented various versions of various portions of the book in lectures, colloquia, and conferences at UCLA, the University of Chicago, Columbia, Duke, Fordham, Harvard, Illinois, Michigan, Minnesota, Notre Dame, Oxford, the University of Pennsylvania, Penn State, Princeton, Syracuse, Wisconsin, Yale, the Brookings Institution, the Public Policy Institute of California, and the Juan March Institute in Madrid, and at annual meetings of the American Political Science Association (2002, 2003, 2005, and 2006), the American Economic Association (2003), the Midwest

Political Science Association (2005), the European Consortium for Political Research (2005), and the National Tax Association (2006). Each of these presentations generated stimulating questions and comments, helping me to hone my analyses and arguments.

Through these avenues and others I have been fortunate to benefit from helpful reactions and suggestions from Kathy Bawn, Robert Bernstein, Benjamin Bishin, Phil Converse, David Ellwood, John Griffin, Jennifer Hochschild, Sandy Jencks, Jacob Hacker, Douglas Hibbs, Skip Lupia, Paul Pierson, John Roemer, Thomas Schwartz, Jeff Stonecash, Rick Valelly, Lynn Vavreck, Ronald Weber, and Robert Weissberg, among others. As always, John Zaller has been an especially perceptive and supportive critic.

Jonathan Ladd, Gabriel Lenz, and Jeff Tessin provided able research assistance, producing very helpful literature reviews and carefully collecting and organizing data for my analyses. Helene Wood solved myriad logistical problems with skill and good cheer. Karen Pulliam and Shirley Smith of the U.S. Census Bureau provided assistance in interpreting the bureau's historical income data.

A much-abbreviated version of chapter 2 appeared in "Economic Behavior in Political Context" (*American Economic Review*, 2003, with Henry E. Brady). A rather different version of chapter 3 was published as "What's the Matter with *What's the Matter with Kansas?*" (*Quarterly Journal of Political Science*, 2006). Portions of chapters 5, 6, and 7 are based on "Homer Gets a Tax Cut" (*Perspectives on Politics*, 2005) and "Unenlightened Self-Interest: The Strange Appeal of Estate Tax Repeal" (*The American Prospect*, 2004). Portions of chapters 6, 7, and 8 were published in "A Tale of Two Tax Cuts, a Wage Squeeze, and a Tax Credit" (*National Tax Journal*, 2006). Portions of chapter 10 are based on "Is the Water Rising? Reflections on Inequality and American Democracy" (*PS: Political Science & Politics*, 2006). I am grateful to the publishers of these pieces for permission to draw upon them here.

Suzanne Nichols at the Russell Sage Foundation and Chuck Myers and his colleagues at Princeton University Press have ably shepherded the manuscript to publication. Suzanne commissioned anonymous reviews that provided very helpful feedback on an earlier draft of the book; I am especially grateful to one grumpy reviewer who went far beyond the call of duty in providing impetus and guidance for my efforts to clarify and tighten my argument. Chuck's own reading helped me excise much, though alas not all, of the jargon and academic indirection.

My daughters, Elizabeth and Meghan, somehow grew into unusually charming young adults during the years in which this book took shape. They have been a source of great pleasure, pride, and inspiration. Moreover, unlike most children in prefaces, they provided invaluable critical feedback, including detailed comments on the text.

Finally, my greatest and most heartfelt debt is to my wife, Denise, who has contributed so much to the rest of my life while I have been working. This book would not have been nearly as good, or nearly as much fun to write, without her.

Princeton, New Jersey
September 2007

UNEQUAL DEMOCRACY

CHAPTER 1

The New Gilded Age

IN THE FIRST sentence of one of the greatest works of modern political science, Robert Dahl posed a question of profound importance for democratic theory and practice: "In a political system where nearly every adult may vote but where knowledge, wealth, social position, access to officials, and other resources are unequally distributed, who actually governs?"[1]

Dahl's answer to this question, for one American city in the late 1950s, was that political power was surprisingly widely dispersed. Examining politics and policy making in New Haven, Connecticut, he concluded that shifting, largely distinct coalitions of elected and unelected leaders influenced key decisions in different issue areas. This pluralistic pattern was facilitated by the fact that many individuals and groups with substantial resources at their disposal chose not to devote those resources to political activity. Even "economic notables"—the wealthy property owners, businessmen, and bank directors constituting the top tier of New Haven's economic elite—were "simply one of the many groups out of which individuals sporadically emerge to influence the policies and acts of city officials."[2]

The significance of Dahl's question has been magnified, and the pertinence of his answer has been cast in doubt, by dramatic economic and political changes in the United States over the past half-century. Economically, America has become vastly richer and vastly more unequal. Perhaps most strikingly, the share of total income going to people at the level of Dahl's "economic notables"—the top 0.1% of income-earners—has more than tripled, from 3.2% in the late 1950s to 10.9% in 2005. The share going to the top 1% of income-earners—a much broader but still very affluent group—more than doubled over the same period, from 10.2% to 21.8%.[3] It seems natural to wonder whether the pluralistic democracy Dahl found in the 1950s has survived

---

[1] Dahl (1961), 1.

[2] Of the 238 people in this group, only three were among the 23 most influential participants in the city's politics and policy making. Nine more were "minor leaders"—all in the field of urban redevelopment, a policy area of distinctive relevance for their economic interests (Dahl 1961, 72 and chapter 6).

[3] These figures are from tabulations by Piketty and Saez (2003), updated at http://elsa .berkeley.edu/~saez/, table A3.

this rapid concentration of vast additional resources in the hands of America's wealthiest citizens.[4]

Meanwhile, the political process has evolved in ways that seem likely to reinforce the advantages of wealth. Political campaigns have become dramatically more expensive since the 1950s, increasing the reliance of elected officials on people who can afford to help finance their bids for reelection. Lobbying activities by corporations and business and professional organizations have accelerated greatly, outpacing the growth of public interest groups. Membership in labor unions has declined substantially, eroding the primary mechanism for organized representation of working people in the governmental process.

How have these economic and political developments affected "who actually governs?" In 2004, the Task Force on Inequality and American Democracy, convened by the American Political Science Association, concluded that political scientists know "astonishingly little" about the "cumulative effects on American democracy" of these economic and political changes. However, based on what we *do* know, the task force members worried "that rising economic inequality will solidify longstanding disparities in political voice and influence, and perhaps exacerbate such disparities."[5]

This book provides a multifaceted examination of the political causes and consequences of economic inequality in contemporary America. Political scientists since Aristotle have wrestled with the question of whether substantial economic inequality is compatible with democracy. My evidence on that score is not encouraging. I find that elected officials are utterly unresponsive to the policy preferences of millions of low-income citizens, leaving their political interests to be served or ignored as the ideological whims of incumbent elites may dictate. Dahl suggested that democracy entails "continued responsiveness of the government to the preferences of its citizens, considered as political equals."[6] The contemporary United States is a very long way from meeting that standard.

Economic inequality clearly has profound ramifications for democratic politics. However, that is only half the story of this book. The other half of the story is that politics also profoundly shapes economics. While technological change, globalization, demographic shifts, and other economic and social forces have produced powerful pressures toward greater inequality in recent

---

[4] Dahl himself has continued to revise and elaborate his account of the workings of American democracy. His *Dilemmas of Pluralist Democracy* (1982) is especially pertinent in this respect; chapter 8 addresses the ramifications of economic inequality for the American political system and the potential significance of economic inequality as a political issue. His most recent book, *On Political Equality* (2006), examines whether the ideal of political equality is compatible with fundamental aspects of human nature.

[5] Task Force on Inequality and American Democracy (2004), 662.

[6] Dahl (1971), 1.

decades, politics and public policy can and do significantly reinforce or mitigate those pressures, depending on the political aims and priorities of elected officials. I trace the impact of public policies on changes in the U.S. income distribution over the past half-century, from the tripled income share of Dahl's "economic notables" at the top to the plight of minimum wage workers at the bottom. I find that partisan politics and the ideological convictions of political elites have had a substantial impact on the American economy, especially on the economic fortunes of middle-class and poor people. Economic inequality is, in substantial part, a *political* phenomenon.

In theory, public opinion constrains the ideological convictions of political elites in democratic political systems. In practice, however, elected officials have a great deal of political leeway. This fact is strikingly illustrated by the behavior of Democratic and Republican senators from the same state, who routinely pursue vastly different policies while "representing" precisely the same constituents. On a broader historical scale, political latitude is also demonstrated by consistent, marked shifts in economic priorities and performance when Democrats replace Republicans, or when Republicans replace Democrats, in the White House. In these respects, among others, conventional democratic theory misses much of what is most interesting and important about the actual workings of the American political system.

My examination of the partisan politics of economic inequality, in chapter 2, reveals that Democratic and Republican presidents over the past half-century have presided over dramatically different patterns of income growth. On average, the real incomes of middle-class families have grown twice as fast under Democrats as they have under Republicans, while the real incomes of working poor families have grown *six times* as fast under Democrats as they have under Republicans. These substantial partisan differences persist even after allowing for differences in economic circumstances and historical trends beyond the control of individual presidents. They suggest that escalating inequality is *not* simply an inevitable economic trend— and that a great deal of economic inequality in the contemporary United States is specifically attributable to the policies and priorities of Republican presidents.

Any satisfactory account of the American political economy must therefore explain how and why Republicans have had so much success in the American electoral arena despite their startling negative impact on the economic fortunes of middle-class and poor people. Thus, in chapter 3, I examine contemporary class politics and partisan change, testing the popular belief that the white working class has been lured into the Republican ranks by hot-button social issues such as abortion and gay marriage. Contrary to this familiar story, I find that low-income whites have actually become more *Democratic* in their presidential voting behavior over the past half-century, partially counterbalancing Republican gains among more affluent white voters.

Moreover, low-income white voters continue to attach less weight to social issues than to economic issues—and they attach less weight to social issues than more affluent white voters do. The familiar image of a party system transformed by Republican gains among working-class cultural conservatives turns out to be largely mythical.

Then why *have* Republican presidential candidates fared so well over the past half-century? My analysis in chapter 4 identifies three distinct biases in political accountability that explain much of their success. One is a myopic focus of voters on very recent economic performance, which rewards Republicans' surprising success in concentrating income growth in election years. Another is the peculiar sensitivity of voters at all income levels to high-income growth rates, which rewards Republicans' success in generating election-year income growth among affluent families specifically. Finally, the responsiveness of voters to campaign spending rewards Republicans' consistent advantage in fundraising. Together, these biases account three times over for the Republican Party's net advantage in presidential elections in the post-war era. Voters' seemingly straightforward tendency to reward or punish the incumbent government at the polls for good or bad economic performance turns out to be warped in ways that are both fascinating and politically crucial.

In chapter 5, I turn to citizens' views about equality; their attitudes toward salient economic groups such as rich people, poor people, big business, and labor unions; and their perceptions of the extent, causes, and consequences of economic inequality in contemporary America. My analysis reveals considerable concern about inequality among ordinary Americans and considerable sympathy for working-class and poor people. However, it also reveals a good deal of ignorance and misconnection between values, beliefs, and policy preferences among people who pay relatively little attention to politics and public affairs, and a good deal of politically motivated misperception among better-informed people. As a result, political elites retain considerable latitude to pursue their own policy ends.

Chapters 6, 7, and 8 provide a series of case studies of politics and policy making in issue areas with important ramifications for economic inequality. Chapter 6 focuses on the Bush tax cuts of 2001 and 2003, which dramatically reduced the federal tax burdens of wealthy Americans. I find that public opinion regarding the Bush tax cuts was remarkably shallow and confused, considering the multi*trillion*-dollar stakes. More than three years after the 2001 tax cut took effect, 40% of the public said they had not thought about whether they favored or opposed it, and those who did take a position did so largely on the basis of how they felt about their own tax burden. Views about the tax burden of the rich had no apparent impact on public opinion, despite the fact that most of the benefits went to the top 5% of taxpayers; egalitarian values reduced support for the tax cut, but only among strong egalitarians who were also politically well informed.

Chapter 7 focuses on the campaign to repeal the federal estate tax. As with the Bush tax cuts more generally, I find that repeal of the estate tax is remarkably popular among ordinary Americans, regardless of their political views and economic circumstances, and despite the fact that the vast majority of them never have been or would be subject to estate taxation. Moreover, the strange appeal of estate tax repeal long predates the efforts of conservative interest groups in the 1990s to manufacture public opposition to the estate tax. Thus, the real political mystery is not why the estate tax was phased out in 2001, but why it survived for more than 80 years—and will likely return when the phaseout expires in 2011. The simple answer is that the views of liberal elites determined to prevent repeal have been more consequential than the views of ordinary citizens.

In chapter 8, I turn from wealthy heirs to working poor people and the eroding minimum wage. Here, too, the views of ordinary citizens seem to have had very little impact on public policy. The real value of the minimum wage has declined by more than 40% since the late 1960s, despite remarkably strong and consistent public support for minimum wage increases. My analysis attributes this erosion to the declining political clout of labor unions and to shifts in partisan control of Congress and the White House. As with the estate tax, the politics of the minimum wage underscores the ability of determined elites in the American political system to postpone or prevent policy shifts. However, in this case the determined elites have not been liberal Democrats intent on taxing the bequests of millionaires, but conservative Republicans intent on protecting the free market (and low-wage employers) from the predations of people earning $5.15 per hour.

My case studies of the Bush tax cuts, estate tax repeal, and the eroding minimum wage shed light on both the political causes and the political consequences of escalating economic inequality in contemporary America. In chapter 9, I attempt to provide a more general answer to Dahl's fundamental question: Who governs? I examine broad patterns of policy making across a wide range of issues, focusing on disparities in the responsiveness of elected officials to the views of their constituents. I find that the roll call votes cast by U.S. senators are much better accounted for by their own partisanship than by the preferences of their constituents. Moreover, insofar as constituents' views do matter, political influence seems to be limited entirely to affluent and middle-class people. The opinions of millions of ordinary citizens in the bottom third of the income distribution have *no* discernible impact on the behavior of their elected representatives. These disparities in representation persist even after allowing for differences between high- and low-income citizens in turnout, political knowledge, and contact with public officials.

Writing in the 1980s, at an early stage in the most recent wave of escalating inequality, political scientists Sidney Verba and Gary Orren depicted an ongoing back-and-forth between the powerful forces of economic inequality and political equality: "Political equality . . . poses a constant challenge to economic inequality as disadvantaged groups petition the state for redress. Egalitarian demands lead to equalizing legislation, such as the progressive income tax. But the continuing disparities in the economic sphere work to limit the effectiveness of such laws, as the economically advantaged groups unleash their greater resources in the political sphere. These groups lobby for tax loopholes, hire lawyers and accountants to maximize their benefit from tax laws, and then deduct the costs."[7]

In the long run of American political history, Verba and Orren's depiction seems apt. However, in the current economic and political environment it is easy to wonder whether the "constant challenge to economic inequality" posed by the ideal of political equality is really so constant or, in the end, so effective. This book provides strong evidence that economic inequality impinges powerfully on the political process, frustrating the egalitarian ideals of American democracy. The countervailing impact of egalitarian ideals in constraining disparities in the economic sphere seems considerably more tenuous.

ESCALATING ECONOMIC INEQUALITY

Most Americans have only a vague sense of the contours of the nation's income distribution—especially for parts of the income distribution that extend beyond their personal experience. Annual tabulations published by the U.S. Census Bureau provide a useful summary of the incomes of families at different points in the distribution. For example, in 2005 (the most recent year for which such tabulations are available), the typical American family had a total pre-tax income of $56,200. More than 15 million families—one out of every five—earned less than $25,600. A similar number earned more than $103,100. Even higher in the distribution, the richest 5% of American families had incomes of more than $184,500.[8]

The Census Bureau provides parallel annual family income tabulations going back to 1947 for families at the 20th, 40th, 60th, 80th, and 95th percentiles of the income distribution. These tabulations constitute the longest consistent data series included in the Census Bureau's Historical Income Tables.[9]

[7] Verba and Orren (1985), 19.

[8] "Table F-1: Income Limits for Each Fifth and Top 5 Percent of Families (All Races): 1947 to 2005." These data are derived from the Census Bureau's March Current Population Surveys and are intended to reflect total pre-tax income for families consisting of two or more people. The data and additional information are available from the Census Bureau Web site, http://www.census.gov/hhes/www/income/histinc/f01ar.html.

[9] The Census Bureau's definition of families excludes a growing proportion of households consisting of single or unrelated people. (In 2005, almost one-third of households were not families by the Census Bureau's definition, up from 18% in 1967. The median income of households was $46,300, about 18% less than the median income of families.) However, a parallel

Although they do not reflect the economic fortunes of very poor families at one extreme or very wealthy families at the other extreme, they do represent a broad range of economic circumstances, encompassing working poor families at the 20th percentile, middle-class families at the 40th and 60th percentiles, affluent families at the 80th percentile, and even more affluent families at the 95th percentile. Thus, they provide an invaluable record of the changing economic fortunes of American families over a period of almost six decades.[10]

The distribution of income in American society has shifted markedly in that time. The broad outlines of this transformation are evident in figure 1.1, which shows how the real pre-tax incomes (in thousands of 2006 dollars) of families at various points in the income distribution have changed since 1947. It is clear from figure 1.1 that the period since World War II has seen substantial gains in real income for families throughout the income distribution, but especially for those who were already well off. The average rate of real income growth over the entire period covered by the figure increased uniformly with each step up the income distribution, from about 1.4% per year for families at the 20th percentile to 2% per year for families at the 95th percentile.

The difference between 1.4% and 2% may sound small, but it has compounded into a dramatic difference in *cumulative* real income growth over the past half-century: 118% for families at the 20th percentile versus 199% for families at the 95th percentile. Of course, the contrast in economic gains between poor families and rich families is much starker in absolute terms than it is in percentage terms. Measured in 2006 dollars, the real incomes of families at the 20th percentile increased by less than $15,000 over this period, while the real incomes of families at the 95th percentile increased by almost $130,000.

These figures convey a striking disparity in the economic fortunes of rich and poor American families over the past half-century. However, they fail to capture another important difference in the experience of families near the bottom of the income distribution and those near the top: poor families have been subject to considerably larger fluctuations in income growth rates. For example, families at the 20th percentile experienced declining real incomes in 20 of the 58 years represented in figure 1.1, including seven declines of 3% or more; by comparison, families at the 95th percentile have experienced only one decline of 3% or more in their real incomes since 1951.

---

series of income tabulations for the larger universe of households displays generally similar income trends over the period for which the two series overlap, 1967–2005.

[10] Obviously, specific families do not remain at exactly the same point in the income distribution from year to year. Indeed, the specific families included in the Current Population Survey, from which these tabulations are derived, change from year to year. Nevertheless, the data reflect the general economic fortunes of poor, middle-class, and rich families and how they have changed.

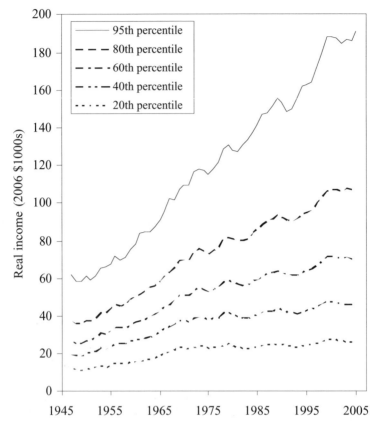

Figure 1.1 Family Incomes by Income Percentile, 1947–2005

Although it may not be immediately apparent in figure 1.1, the pattern of income growth in the past three decades has differed sharply from the pattern in the first half of the post-war era. In the 1950s and 1960s families in every part of the income distribution experienced robust income growth. Since the mid-1970s income growth has been a good deal slower and a good deal less evenly distributed. These differences are evident in figure 1.2, which compares cumulative rates of real income growth for families in various parts of the income distribution from 1947 to 1974 and from 1974 to 2005.[11]

From the late 1940s through the early 1970s American income growth was rapid and remarkably egalitarian, at least in percentage terms. Indeed, the real incomes of working poor families (at the 20th percentile of the income distri-

---

[11] This figure is modeled on a similar presentation of the same data by Mishel, Bernstein, and Boushey (2003), 57.

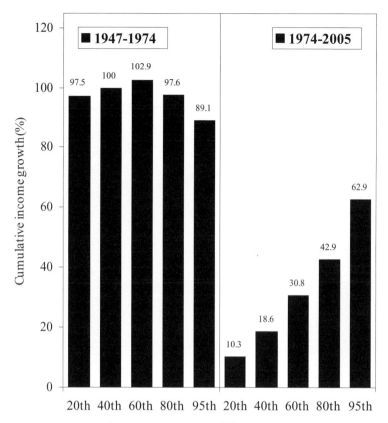

Figure 1.2 Cumulative Income Growth by Income Percentile, 1947–1974 and 1974–2005

bution) and affluent families (at the 80th percentile) both grew by the same 98% over this period. Income growth was slightly higher for middle-class families and slightly lower for families at the 95th percentile, but every income group experienced real income growth between 2.4% and 2.7% per year.

Over the past three decades, income growth has been much slower and much less evenly distributed. Even for families near the top of the income distribution, the average rate of real income growth slowed substantially (from 2.4% per year to 1.6% per year for families at the 95th percentile). For less affluent families, real income growth slowed to a crawl. Families at the 60th percentile experienced real income growth of less than 1% per year—down from 2.7% in the earlier period. The real incomes of families at the 20th percentile grew by only 0.4% per year—down from 2.6% in the earlier period. Much of the income growth that did occur was attributable to increases in working hours, especially from the increasing participation of women in the workforce.

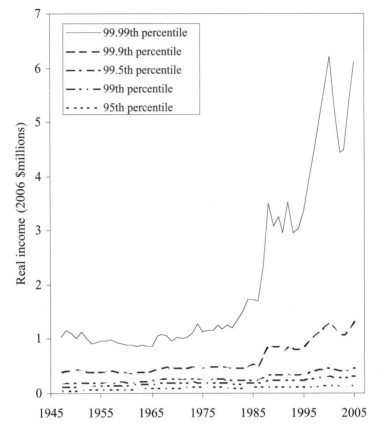

Figure 1.3 Top Incomes by Income Percentile, 1947–2005

Even the disparities in income growth for affluent, middle-class, and poor American families charted in figures 1.1 and 1.2 understate the extent of escalating inequality over the past 30 years, since much of the real action has been concentrated at the very top of the income distribution. While the Census Bureau figures document the experience of families affluent enough to have reached the 95th percentile of the national income distribution, they shed no light on what has happened to people with much higher incomes. As it turns out, income gains among the ultra-rich have vastly outpaced those among the merely affluent.

Economists Thomas Piketty and Emmanuel Saez have used information collected by the Internal Revenue Service to track the economic fortunes of people much higher up the economic ladder than the Census Bureau tabulations reach. Figure 1.3 presents their tabulations of the real incomes (in millions of 2006 dollars) of taxpayers at the 95th, 99th, 99.5th, 99.9th, and 99.99th percentiles of the income distribution since 1947.[12]

What is most striking in figure 1.3 is that, even at this elevated income level, income growth over the past 25 years has accelerated with every additional step up the economic ladder. For example, while the real income of taxpayers at the 99th percentile doubled between 1981 and 2005, the real income of taxpayers at the 99.9th percentile nearly tripled, and the real income of taxpayers at the 99.99th percentile—a hyper-rich stratum comprising about 13,000 taxpayers—increased *fivefold*. The real income cutoff for this hyper-rich stratum (not the *average* income but the *lowest* income of taxpayers in this group) was virtually constant for three decades following the end of World War II; but around 1980 it began to escalate rapidly, from about $1.2 million to $6.2 million by 2000. Although the real incomes of people in this group declined significantly in the stock market slump of 2000–2002, by 2005 they were once again in excess of $6 million.

In 2005, the *New York Times* published a 20-year retrospective on the list of the 400 wealthiest Americans produced annually by *Forbes* magazine. The *Times* noted that the *average* net worth of these 400 economic luminaries increased more than fourfold over that period (from $600 million in 1985 to $2.81 billion in 2005) and that their combined net wealth in 2005 exceeded the gross domestic product of Canada. "The median household income of Americans has been stuck at around $44,000 for five years now. The poverty rate is up. Members of the Forbes 400, meanwhile, are richer than Croesus, and every hour they are getting richer."[13]

Another illuminating way to look at Piketty and Saez's tabulations is in terms of the shares of total income going to people in different economic strata. Figure 1.4 shows these income shares for the top 5% of taxpayers (the solid line) and the top 1% (the dotted line) over a period of almost 90 years. For the period since World War II the picture here is quite consistent with the picture presented in figures 1.1 and 1.3. The share of income going to the rich remained remarkably constant from the mid-1940s through the 1970s and then began to escalate rapidly. For example, the top 5% of taxpayers

---

[12] Piketty and Saez (2003), table A4. The updated data reported in figure 1.2 are taken from Emmanuel Saez's Web site, http://elsa.berkeley.edu/~saez/. These figures derived from IRS data are not directly comparable with the Census Bureau figures charted in figure 1.1. For example, the Census Bureau's income figure for families at the 95th percentile in 2005 is $184,500; the corresponding IRS figure for the 95th percentile of tax filers is $130,400. The latter figure represents annual gross income reported on individual tax returns, excluding capital gains and government transfers such as Social Security and unemployment benefits. Comparisons are complicated by the fact that some families do not file tax returns, while others file more than one return. For recent years, Piketty and Saez assumed that nonfilers had incomes equal to 20% of the average income of filers.

[13] Nina Munk, "Don't Blink. You'll Miss the 258th-Richest American," *New York Times*, September 25, 2005, BU 3.

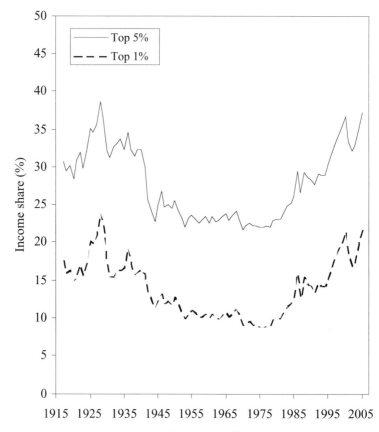

Figure 1.4 Income Shares of Top 5% and Top 1%, 1917–2005

accounted for 23.0% of total income in 1981 but 37.2% in 2005. The top 1% accounted for 10.0% of total income in 1981 but 21.8% in 2005; after declining gradually over most of the twentieth century, their share of the pie more than doubled in the course of a single generation.[14]

Two other features of the historical trends in income shares stand out in figure 1.4. One is that the increasing share of income going to people in the

[14] Piketty and Saez (2003), table A3, updated through 2005 at http://elsa.berkeley.edu/~saez/. Unlike the absolute income levels reported in figure 1.3, the income shares reported in figure 1.4 include capital gains as well as other sources of income. Piketty and Saez noted that capital gains are "a volatile component" of income and "tend to be realized in a lumpy way." However, the historical trends in income shares are generally similar whether capital gains are included or excluded (Piketty and Saez 2003, figure A2). Meanwhile, ignoring capital gains understates the income share of the richest taxpayers. For example, the average income share of the top 1% of taxpayers in 2001–2005 was 17.2% excluding capital gains but 18.8% including capital gains.

top 5% of the distribution is entirely accounted for by the increasing share going to the top 1%; the distance between the solid and dotted lines, which represents the share going to people between the 95th and 99th percentiles, remained virtually constant. As in figure 1.3, it is clear here that the really dramatic economic gains over the past 30 years have been concentrated among the extremely rich, largely bypassing even the vast majority of ordinary rich people in the top 5% of the income distribution. Indeed, economists Frank Levy and Peter Temin have used Piketty and Saez's data to show that more than four-fifths of the total increase in Americans' real pre-tax income between 1980 and 2005 went to the top 1% of taxpayers. As a front-page story in the *New York Times* put it, "The hyper-rich have emerged in the last three decades as the biggest winners in a remarkable transformation of the American economy."[15]

Because Piketty and Saez's tabulations go back to the advent of the federal income tax system, they also provide important historical perspective on the absolute magnitude of inequality in the contemporary American income distribution. Although it is impossible to compare current levels of inequality with those prevailing in the original Gilded Age in the late nineteenth century, it *is* possible to compare the position of today's economic elite with their counterparts in what most economic historians consider the other notable highpoint of economic inequality in American history, the 1920s. Whether we focus on the share of income going to the top 5% of taxpayers or the share going to the even richer top 1%, figure 1.4 suggests that current levels of inequality rival those of the Roaring Twenties, before the Great Depression wiped out much of the financial wealth of the nation's reigning upper class. By this metric, America's New Gilded Age is a retrogression of historic scope.[16]

INTERPRETING INEQUALITY

What are we to make of these economic trends? For some people, they reflect an era of economic dynamism and expanding opportunity. Others are

[15] Levy and Temin (2007), 49–50; David Cay Johnston, "Richest Are Leaving Even the Rich Far Behind," *New York Times*, June 5, 2005, 1.

[16] I do not know who first referred to the contemporary era as a "New Gilded Age." The term served as the title of a collection of pieces from the *New Yorker* magazine on "the culture of affluence" (Remnick 2000). It subsequently appeared in an influential essay by Paul Krugman in the *New York Times Magazine* in 2002 and in the headline of a front-page article by Louis Uchitelle in the *New York Times* in 2007: Paul Krugman, "For Richer: How the Permissive Capitalism of the Boom Destroyed American Equality," *New York Times Magazine*, October 20, 2002, 62–142; Louis Uchitelle, "Age of Riches: The Richest of the Rich, Proud of a New Gilded Age," *New York Times*, July 15, 2007, A1.

made uneasy by the sheer magnitude of the gulf between the rich and the poor in contemporary America, even if they cannot quite pinpoint why. Still others are less concerned about inequality per se than about the absolute living standards of the poor or about the extent of their opportunity to work their way up the economic ladder.

For the most part, discussions of escalating inequality have focused on four related issues: economic growth, economic mobility, fairness, and inevitability. One crucial—and highly contentious—question is whether dramatic income gains among the hyper-rich "trickle down" to middle-class and poor people, increasing the size of everyone's piece of the pie. After all, even the influential liberal political theorist John Rawls argued that inequality is just insofar as it contributes to the well-being of the least well-off members of society.[17]

Many ordinary Americans believe that "large differences in income are necessary for America's prosperity," as one standard survey question puts it.[18] However, economists who have studied the relationship between inequality and economic growth have found little evidence that large disparities in income and wealth promote growth.[19] There is not even much hard evidence in support of the commonsense notion that progressive tax rates retard growth by discouraging economic effort. Indeed, one liberal economist, Robert Frank, has written that "the lessons of experience are downright brutal" to the notion that higher taxes would stifle economic growth by causing wealthy people to work less or take fewer risks.[20]

Much of the economic argument for inequality hinges on the assumption that large fortunes will be invested in productive economic activities. In fact, however, there is some reason to worry that the new hyper-rich are less likely to invest their wealth than to fritter it away on jewelry, yachts, and caviar. According to one press report, the after-tax savings rate of households in the top 5% of the income distribution fell by more than half from 1990 through 2006 (from 13.6% to 6.2%), while real sales growth in the luxury retail industry averaged more than 10% per year.[21]

---

[17] Rawls (1971), chapter 2.

[18] This question has been included in several General Social Surveys conducted as part of the International Social Survey Program (ISSP). In four surveys conducted between 1987 and 2000, the proportion of the U.S. public agreeing that large differences in income are necessary for prosperity has ranged from 26% to 32%, while the proportion disagreeing has ranged from 38% to 58% (McCall 2005, appendix table 1).

[19] Alesina and Rodrik (1994); Persson and Tabellini (1994); Bénabou (1996); Perotti (1996).

[20] Robert H. Frank, "In the Real World of Work and Wages, Trickle-Down Theories Don't Hold Up," *New York Times*, April 12, 2007, C3.

[21] Anna Bernasek, "The Rich Spend Just Like You and Me," *New York Times*, August 6, 2006, BU 4. Bernasek drew upon detailed data on growth in the luxury retail sector through 2001, compiled by Parker, Ait-Sahalia, and Yogo (2004), supplemented with bits of more recent data from individual high-end retailers such as Tiffany.

Even if inequality does promote overall economic growth, that does not necessarily imply that it contributes to the well-being of the least well-off members of society. The benefits of economic growth may or may not "trickle down" to the poor. Although it is common for Americans to suppose that the nation's collective wealth makes even poor people better off than they otherwise would be, the reality is that poor people in America seem to be distinctly *less* well off than poor people in countries that are less wealthy but less unequal. A careful comparison of the living standards of poor children in 13 rich democracies in the 1990s found the United States ranking next to last, 20% below Canada and France and 35% below Norway, despite its greater overall wealth.[22] Moreover, even holding constant the absolute economic status of the least well-off, there is some reason to worry that inequality itself may have deleterious social implications in the realms of family and community life, health, and education.[23]

Another important strand of debate focuses on the extent of economic mobility and the relationship between inequality and mobility. As one journalistic account put it, "Mobility is the promise that lies at the heart of the American dream. It is supposed to take the sting out of the widening gulf between the have-mores and the have-nots. There are poor and rich in the United States, of course, the argument goes; but as long as one can become the other, as long as there is something close to equality of opportunity, the differences between them do not add up to class barriers."[24]

The dynamism of the modern economy is certainly reflected in the extent of turnover at the pinnacle of the income distribution. For example, the *New York Times*' 20-year retrospective on the *Forbes* list of the 400 richest Americans counted 255 "self-made fortunes" in 2005, up from 165 in 1985. The number of people on the list with undergraduate degrees from Harvard or Yale declined (from 37 to 25), while the number from California nearly doubled (from 49 to 96).[25]

Of course, the composition of the Forbes 400 may or may not reflect patterns of economic mobility in American society as a whole. Leaving aside this handful of billionaires, to what extent are the economic fortunes of

[22] The comparison is for children at the 10th percentile of the income distribution in each country, based on data from the Luxembourg Income Study. The authors suggest that this difference would be reduced (though not eliminated) by counting noncash benefits such as schooling—but only by assuming, rather implausibly, that American children regardless of family income levels benefit equally from public spending on education. See Osberg, Smeeding, and Schwabish (2004), 826–834.

[23] For a comprehensive review of scholarly research in these domains, see Neckerman (2004).

[24] Janny Scott and David Leonhardt, "Class in America: Shadowy Lines That Still Divide," *New York Times*, May 15, 2005, 1.

[25] Munk, "Don't Blink. You'll Miss the 258th-Richest American," BU 3.

ordinary Americans determined by their starting points in the economic hierarchy? One commentator, Michael Kinsley, warned that "immobility over generations is what congeals financial differences into old-fashioned, European-style social class."[26] However, recent evidence suggests that the United States already has "significantly less economic mobility than Canada, Finland, Sweden, Norway, and possibly Germany; and the United States may be a less economically mobile society than Britain."[27] These comparisons suggest—contrary to the fervent beliefs of many Americans— that the contemporary United States outclasses Europe in the rigidity of its hidebound European-style class structure.

Comparisons of intergenerational mobility over time within the United States also provide some evidence that mobility has declined over the past three decades, at least for men. One study measuring the impact of a wide range of family background factors (including family structure, race and ethnicity, parental education and income, and region) found that "the economic gap between advantaged and disadvantaged men increased because economic inequality increased" during the 1970s, 1980s, and 1990s, while "the gaps in women's outcomes remained constant." Another study found that the effect of parental income on men's economic fortunes "declined between 1940 and 1980 but increased during the 1980s and 1990s."[28]

A detailed analysis of income mobility across decades rather than generations also suggests that there has been at least a modest decline in mobility since the 1970s. The probability of any given family rising from the bottom quintile of the income distribution into the top quintile over the course of a decade increased slightly (from 3.3% in the 1970s to 4.3% in the 1990s). However, the proportion of families in the top quintile of the income distribution who remained there a decade later also increased, while the proportion of families falling from the top quintile into the bottom quintile, or from the top two quintiles into the bottom two quintiles, declined.[29]

Another key point of contention is the extent to which escalating inequality reflects the just rewards accruing to education and skills in the modern economy. According to one conservative observer, *New York Times* columnist David Brooks,

> the market isn't broken; the meritocracy is working almost too well. It's rewarding people based on individual talents. Higher education pays off because it provides technical knowledge and because it screens out people who are not organized, self-motivated and socially adept. But even among people with

[26] Michael Kinsley, "Mobility vs. Nobility," *Washington Post*, June 5, 2005, B07.

[27] Beller and Hout (2006), 30; Solon (2002).

[28] Beller and Hout (2006), 30, summarizing studies by Harding et al. (2005) and Aaronson and Mazumder (2005). See also Solon (2002); Hout (2004).

[29] Bradbury and Katz (2002), 66.

identical education levels, inequality is widening as the economy favors certain abilities. . . . What's needed is not a populist revolt, which would make everything worse, but a second generation of human capital policies, designed for people as they actually are, to help them get the intangible skills the economy rewards.[30]

On the other hand, Brooks's liberal counterpart on the *Times* op-ed page, Paul Krugman, attacked "the notion that the winners in our increasingly unequal society are a fairly large group—that the 20 percent or so of American workers who have the skills to take advantage of new technology and globalization are pulling away from the 80 percent who don't have these skills." Noting that the real incomes of college graduates have risen by less than 1% per year over the past three decades, Krugman argued that "the big gains have gone to a much smaller, much richer group than that." Nevertheless, the "80-20 fallacy," as he called it, "tends to dominate polite discussion about income trends, not because it's true, but because it's comforting. The notion that it's all about returns to education suggests that nobody is to blame for rising inequality, that it's just a case of supply and demand at work. . . . The idea that we have a rising oligarchy is much more disturbing. It suggests that the growth of inequality may have as much to do with power relations as it does with market forces."[31]

Krugman cited economists Ian Dew-Becker and Robert J. Gordon's detailed analysis of productivity and income growth over the past four decades. According to Dew-Becker and Gordon, "most of the shift in the income distribution has been from the bottom 90 percent to the top 5 percent. This is much too narrow a group to be consistent with a widespread benefit from SBTC [skill-biased technical change]." They found that some of the occupations that should have flourished if the dynamic economy of the 1990s was simply rewarding technical skills actually saw very modest income growth. For example, the earnings of mathematicians and computer scientists increased by only 4.8% between 1989 and 1997, while the earnings of engineers actually declined by 1.4%. In contrast, the earnings of CEOs increased by 100%.[32]

Evidence of a serious mismatch between skills and economic rewards seems likely to fan concerns about the "fairness" of recent changes in the U.S. income distribution. So, too, does the juxtaposition of rapid productivity growth with stagnant middle-class wages. Dew-Becker and Gordon found that economic productivity had increased substantially over the period covered by their analysis, but that "the broad middle of working America has

[30] David Brooks, "The Populist Myths on Income Inequality," *New York Times*, September 7, 2006, A29.

[31] Paul Krugman, "Graduates versus Oligarchs," *New York Times*, February 27, 2006, A19.

[32] Dew-Becker and Gordon (2005), 73, 74.

reaped little of the gains in productivity over the past 35 years. . . . The micro data tell a shocking story of gains accruing disproportionately to the top one percent and 0.1 percent of the income distribution." They characterized the first five years of the twenty-first century as "an unprecedented dichotomy of macroeconomic glow and gloom." On one hand, labor productivity and output growth exploded; on the other hand, median family income fell by 3.8 percent from 1999 to 2004.[33]

The "unprecedented dichotomy" noted by Dew-Becker and Gordon between booming output and stagnant or declining incomes for ordinary workers has been a recurrent political problem for the Bush administration. On the eve of the 2004 presidential campaign, the *New York Times* announced "A Recovery for Profits, But Not for Workers." A similar headline in the midst of the 2006 midterm campaign asked, "After Years of Growth, What about Workers' Share?" Press reports noted that the president was making little headway in convincing the American public that the economy was prospering, despite robust output growth and increasing average wages. The "strange and unlikely combination" of "strong and healthy aggregate macroeconomic indicators and a grumpy populace," one report said, was "a source of befuddlement to the administration and its allies."[34]

Faced with this "grumpy populace" and an imminent election, Treasury Secretary Henry Paulson acknowledged that "amid this country's strong economic expansion, many Americans simply aren't feeling the benefits." Paulson blamed that fact on "market forces" that "work to provide the greatest rewards to those with the needed skills in the growth areas." Paulson's predecessor as treasury secretary, John Snow, spoke in similar terms about the "long-term trend to differentiate compensation."

According to one observer, "'Long-term,' when used this way by this sort of official, tends to mean 'fundamentally unstoppable.' And, in this case, inexplicable, like a sort of financial global-warming process that may be manmade or (who knows?) a natural cycle that we would welcome if only we knew its function. Snow, a trained economist and former corporate C.E.O., doesn't pretend to be able to explain what's causing this whole compensation differential. Nor does he seem tortured by his ignorance. 'We've moved into a star system for some reason,' he said, 'which is not fully understood.'"[35]

[33] Ibid., 60, 3, 1.

[34] Louis Uchitelle, "A Recovery for Profits, But Not for Workers," *New York Times*, December 21, 2003, BU 4; Eduardo Porter, "After Years of Growth, What about Workers' Share?" *New York Times*, October 15, 2006, BU 3; Daniel Gross, "When Sweet Statistics Clash with a Sour Mood," *New York Times*, June 4, 2006, BU 3.

[35] Remarks Prepared for Delivery by Treasury Secretary Henry H. Paulson at Columbia University, August 1, 2006, http://www.treas.gov/press/releases/hp41.htm; Walter Kim, "Way Upstairs, Downstairs," *New York Times Magazine*, April 16, 2006, 11.

The notion that economic inequality is an inevitable, purely natural phenomenon has been given a pseudo-scientific patina by a self-proclaimed "econophysicist" at the University of Maryland, Victor Yakovenko. Yakovenko noted that, aside from a long upper tail, the dispersion of U.S. incomes closely approximates an exponential distribution—the same kind of distribution characteristic of many natural phenomena. According to an account of Yakovenko's work published in the *New York Times Magazine*'s 2005 survey of "The Year in Ideas," "To an econophysicist, the exponential distribution of incomes is no coincidence: it suggests that the wealth of most Americans is itself in a kind of thermal equilibrium. . . . Yakovenko told *New Scientist* that 'short of getting Stalin,' efforts to make more than superficial dents in inequality would fail."[36]

ECONOMIC INEQUALITY AS A POLITICAL ISSUE

Interpretations of economic inequality are politically consequential because they shape responses to inequality. If the differences between rich and poor in contemporary America "do not add up to class barriers," if "the market isn't broken" and "meritocracy is working," or if "efforts to make more than superficial dents in inequality" are doomed to failure, then inequality is unlikely to rise to the top of the political agenda. Many observers have been perplexed by the modest salience of inequality as a political issue in America. For example, Dahl wrote that, "For all the emphasis on equality in the American public ideology, the United States lags well behind a number of other democratic countries in reducing economic inequality. It is a striking fact that the presence of vast disparities in wealth and income, and so in political resources, has never become a highly salient issue in American politics or, certainly, a persistent one."[37] Is that because Americans assume that "efforts to make more than superficial dents in inequality" would fail?

The fact that most other rich democracies are considerably less unequal than the United States provides some reason to think that political arrangements short of Stalinism might not be entirely futile in mitigating economic inequality. For that matter, even the limited range of policies implemented in the United States over the past half-century has had substantial effects on prevailing levels of economic inequality. In short, politics matters.

If this claim seems controversial, that is probably because so much public discussion of economic inequality in the New Gilded Age ignores its political dimension. Journalists and commentators may not dwell on the "econophysics"

---

[36] Christopher Shea, "Econophysics," *New York Times Magazine*, December 11, 2005, 67.
[37] Dahl (1982), 175.

of thermal equilibrium as reflected in the exponential distribution, but they often frame discussions of inequality in a curiously passive, technical, and distinctly apolitical way. The standard perspective is typified by a 2006 cover story in *The Economist* on "Inequality in America." The report summarized trends in the American economy over the preceding decade:

> Thanks to a jump in productivity growth after 1995, America's economy has out-paced other rich countries' for a decade. Its workers now produce over 30% more each hour they work than ten years ago. In the late 1990s everybody shared in this boom. Though incomes were rising fastest at the top, all workers' wages far outpaced inflation.
>
> But after 2000 something changed. The pace of productivity growth has been rising again, but now it seems to be lifting fewer boats. . . . The fruits of produc-tivity gains have been skewed towards the highest earners, and towards compa-nies, whose profits have reached record levels as a share of GDP.[38]

The report provided no hint of what "something" might have changed after 2000. Nor did it offer any explanation for why "America's income disparities suddenly widened after 1980," nor why "during the 1990s, particularly to-wards the end of the decade, that gap stabilized and, by some measures, even narrowed."

Hello? George W. Bush? Ronald Reagan? Bill Clinton? In 3,000 words, the report offered no suggestion that any policy choice by these or other elected officials might have contributed to the economic trends it summa-rized. Rather, "the main cause was technology, which increased the demand for skilled workers relative to their supply, with freer trade reinforcing the effect." The report also suggested that "institutional changes, particularly the weakening of unions," might have "made the going harder for people at the bottom" and that "greedy businessmen" might be "sanction[ing] huge salaries for each other at the expense of shareholders."

Reports of this sort obviously do little to make "the presence of vast dis-parities in wealth and income" noted by Dahl "a highly salient issue in Amer-ican politics." Indeed, the authors of the *Economist*'s cover story began by assuring their readers that "Americans do not go in for envy. The gap be-tween rich and poor is bigger than in any other advanced country, but most people are unconcerned. Whereas Europeans fret about the way the eco-nomic pie is divided, Americans want to join the rich, not soak them. Eight out of ten, more than anywhere else, believe that though you may start out poor, if you work hard, you can make pots of money. It is a central part of the American Dream."[39]

[38] "The Rich, the Poor and the Growing Gap between Them," *The Economist*, June 17, 2006, 28.
[39] Ibid.

The political economy of inequality might be very different if, contrary to Dahl's observation, the presence of vast disparities in wealth and income *was* a highly salient issue in American politics. How likely is that, and how might it happen?

One admittedly unsystematic barometer of the popular zeitgeist is the annual "What People Earn" issue of *Parade Magazine*, a popular Sunday newspaper supplement claiming 71 million readers. For several years, *Parade* has published annual "Special Reports" including dozens of Americans' names, photos, occupations, and salaries. Most are ordinary people with five-figure incomes; some are immensely wealthy celebrities like Michael Jordan, Donald Trump, and SpongeBob Squarepants. (Interestingly, more conventional affluent professionals and businesspeople seem to be distinctly underrepresented.[40]) The stories accompanying these "salary surveys" have attempted to summarize the current economic climate and job prospects. In doing so, they have also provided some insight into the shifting resonance of economic inequality in contemporary American culture.

In early 2002, *Parade* depicted "the mood of the nation" as "resolutely confident despite wage freezes, benefit reductions and shrinking job security." An accompanying essay by financial writer Andrew Tobias put the gulf between the incomes of the rich and famous on one hand and ordinary people on the other in reassuring perspective, noting that in "Uganda or Peru . . . plumbers and librarians earn a whole lot less" than in the United States. "Yes. Life *is* unfair," Tobias wrote. "But for most of us, it could be a lot worse. And in America there's at least a fighting chance that, if you work at it, you—or your kids anyway—can close the gap."[41]

The following year, Tobias's essay "How Much Is Fair?" revisited the issue of economic inequality, but in a rather different tone. Tobias remained sanguine about the millions earned by Ben Affleck, Madonna, and Stephen King. ("I don't mind a bit. This is America! More power to them.") However, he was more skeptical about the earnings of CEOs, acknowledging that "most would agree it is best left to the free market to decide" how much they should be paid, but adding that in some cases "the market isn't really free and the CEO largely sets his own pay." Noting that one modestly paid CEO earned more than "the Joint Chiefs of Staff and the presidents of Harvard, Yale and Princeton—combined!" Tobias concluded, somewhat defensively,

[40] The 2007 survey included 97 people with incomes below $100,000, 16 with incomes between $100,000 and $750,000, and 29 multimillionaires (mostly entertainers and professional athletes). The modestly wealthy group included three political celebrities (Nancy Pelosi, John McCain, and Karl Rove), a professional golfer, and a "bronc rider," as well as a university president, a judge, two photographers, a railroad conductor, an architect, three real estate brokers, a mortgage broker, and a physician's assistant.

[41] Lynn Brenner, "How Did *You* Do?" *Parade Magazine*, March 3, 2002, 4–5; Andrew Tobias, "Are They Worth It?" *Parade Magazine*, March 3, 2002, 8.

that "it is not class warfare to face these facts, observe these trends and raise these questions. Many will conclude that all is as it should be. Others will say things have gotten out of whack. The ability to confront, debate and occasionally course-correct is one of our nation's greatest strengths."[42]

By 2004, *Parade* headlined that "The economy's growing again, and we're spending more—but jobs and wages aren't keeping pace." Some 30 paragraphs later, the report mentioned that "The gap between America's highest- and lowest-paid workers . . . got wider last year" and that the latter "lost ground to inflation." In 2005, the *Parade* report noted that productivity "has risen steadily; but economists say that, so far, the resulting benefits have gone into corporate profits."[43]

By 2007, the disparity between "government statistics" and the "daily experience" of workers had become a major theme of *Parade*'s annual report on the state of the U.S. economy. One prominent subhead announced that "most Americans didn't see the long economic boom reflected in their paychecks"; another reported that "the salary gains of the last five years have gone to the highest-paid workers." The body of the story reported that "many Americans are troubled by the income gap between the nation's highest earners and everyone else—a gap that has grown dramatically in recent decades."[44]

Meanwhile, in a very different segment of the Sunday magazine market, the *New York Times Magazine* in 2007 published a special "Money Issue" titled "Inside the Income Gap." Lengthy articles focused on class disparities in schooling, John Edwards's "poverty platform" in the 2008 presidential race, and the implications of an increasingly global labor market. However, the impact of these weighty examinations of the sociology and politics of economic inequality was diminished by the distracting interspersion of colorful advertisements for investment companies, exotic consumer goods, and high-end real estate. One three-page article on "The Inequality Conundrum" ("How can you promote equality without killing off the genie of American prosperity?") was woven around advertisements for a private bank and financial planning company ("an entire team of wealth experts"), high definition flat-screen televisions ("the ultimate TV experience"), the national airline of the Cayman Islands ("Endless beauty. Non-stop flights"), and luxury apartments on New York's Fifth Avenue ("From $10.25 million").[45]

The lifestyles of *New York Times Magazine* readers are emblematic of a striking social gulf between the people who are most likely to read lengthy

---

[42] Andrew Tobias, "How Much Is Fair?" *Parade Magazine*, March 2, 2003, 10–11.

[43] Lynn Brenner, "How Did *You* Do?" *Parade Magazine*, March 14, 2004, 4–12; Brenner, "How Did *You* Do?" *Parade Magazine*, March 13, 2005, 4–10.

[44] Lynn Brenner, "How Did *You* Do?" *Parade Magazine*, April 15, 2007, 4–8.

[45] "Inside the Income Gap," *New York Times Magazine*, June 10, 2007.

articles (or books!) on the subject of inequality and the people who have themselves been on the losing end of escalating inequality in the past 30 years. That social gulf has been exacerbated by the economic trends of the New Gilded Age; and it constitutes a significant obstacle to political progress in responding to those trends. One can only wonder how many affluent readers will get around to pondering "The Inequality Conundrum" as soon as they return from the Cayman Islands.

If the juxtaposition of social concern and conspicuous consumption in the *New York Times Magazine* symbolizes the ambivalent resonance of the New Gilded Age among its winners, the various conflicting themes in the *Parade* reports on "What People Earn" underscore the complexity of cultural norms and values shaping thinking about economic inequality among the people whose economic fortunes have stagnated. American workers are suffering from wage freezes, benefit reductions, and shrinking job security; but they are better off than their counterparts in Uganda or Peru. Celebrities are entitled to their millions; but perhaps there *is* something troubling about CEOs earning more than the combined salaries of the Joint Chiefs of Staff and the presidents of Harvard, Yale, and Princeton. The income gap between the rich and the rest has grown dramatically; but in America, you—or your kids anyway—can close the gap. Or maybe not.

INEQUALITY AND AMERICAN DEMOCRACY

To a famously perceptive foreign observer of nineteenth-century America, Alexis de Tocqueville, the spirit of equality was the hallmark of American culture: "Any man and any power which would contest the irresistible force of equality will be overturned and destroyed by it." However, Tocqueville recognized that equality in the social and political realms could coexist with a great deal of economic inequality. "There are just as many wealthy people in the United States as elsewhere," he observed. "I am not even aware of a country where the love of money has a larger place in men's hearts or where they express a deeper scorn for the theory of a permanent equality of possessions."[46]

Tocqueville's juxtaposition of social equality and economic inequality has been a recurrent theme in commentary on the place of equality in American political culture. According to Verba and Orren, for example, ordinary Americans have complex views about the value of equality:

> Their sentiments are far more egalitarian in some areas than in others. They assign different goods to different spheres of justice. There are spheres for

[46] Tocqueville (2003), 587, 64.

money, political power, welfare, leisure time, and love. . . . The aim of egalitarianism is not the elimination of all differences, which would be impossible, nor
even the elimination of differences within any one of these spheres, which
might also be impossible unless the state continually intervened. Rather, the
goal is to keep the spheres autonomous and their boundaries intact. Success in
one sphere should not be convertible into success in another sphere. Political
power, which is the most dangerous social good because it is the easiest to con-
vert, must be constrained against transmutation into economic power, and vice
versa.[47]

One of the most important questions explored in this book is whether
political equality can be achieved, or even approximated, in a society marked
by glaring economic inequalities. When push comes to shove, how imperme-
able are the boundaries separating the economic and political spheres of
American life?

At some points in American history, at least, those boundaries have been
remarkably permeable. The original Gilded Age in the late nineteenth century is a dramatic case in point. Rapid economic expansion and transformation coexisted with intense partisan conflict and political corruption. Social
Darwinism provided a powerful ideological rationale for letting the devil take
the hindmost. The mordant novel by Mark Twain and Charles Warner that
gave the era its name portrayed a political process in which the greedy and
cynical preyed on the greedy and gullible.[48]

In *Wealth and Democracy: A Political History of the American Rich*, political
analyst Kevin Phillips called attention to a variety of striking economic and political parallels between the "capitalist heydays" of the Gilded Age, the Roaring
Twenties, and the contemporary era. Economically, he argued, all three periods
were marked by "major economic and corporate restructuring," "bull markets
and rising, increasingly precarious levels of speculation, leverage, and debt,"
"exaltation of business, entrepreneurialism, and the achievements of free
enterprise," and "concentration of wealth, economic polarization, and rising
levels of inequality." Politically, all three periods featured "conservative politics
and ideology," "skepticism of government," "reduction or elimination of taxes,
especially on corporations, personal income, or inheritance," and "high levels of
corruption," among other factors.[49]

Having surveyed the rise and fall of great economic fortunes through more
than two centuries of American history, Phillips emphasized the regularity
with which concentrations of wealth in new industries, regions, and families
have been spurred, subsidized, and supported by government policies: "From
the nursery years of the Republic, U.S. government economic decisions in

[47] Verba and Orren (1985), 7–8.
[48] Twain and Warner (1873).
[49] Phillips (2002), 297. For an earlier exploration of similar themes, see Phillips (1990).

matters of taxation, central bank operations, debt management, banking, trade and tariffs, and financial rescues or bailouts have been keys to expanding, shrinking, or realigning the nation's privately held assets. . . . Occasionally public policy tilted toward the lower and middle classes, as under Jefferson, Jackson, and Franklin D. Roosevelt. Most often, in the United States and elsewhere, these avenues and alleyways have been explored, every nook and cranny, for the benefit of the financial and business classes."[50]

In the same vein, Paul Krugman has emphasized the importance of social and political forces in shaping the economic trends of the past 75 years:

> Middle-class America didn't emerge by accident. It was created by what has been called the Great Compression of incomes that took place during World War II, and sustained for a generation by social norms that favored equality, strong labor unions and progressive taxation. Since the 1970's, all of those sustaining forces have lost their power.
>
> Since 1980 in particular, U.S. government policies have consistently favored the wealthy at the expense of working families—and under the current [George W. Bush] administration, that favoritism has become extreme and relentless. From tax cuts that favor the rich to bankruptcy "reform" that punishes the unlucky, almost every domestic policy seems intended to accelerate our march back to the robber baron era.[51]

While economists have spent a good deal of scholarly energy describing and attempting to explain the striking escalation of economic inequality in the United States over the past 30 years, they have paid remarkably little attention to social and political factors of the sort cited by Krugman. For example, one comprehensive summary of the complex literature on earnings inequality attempted to ascertain "What shifts in demand, shifts in supply, and/or changes in wage setting institutions are responsible for the observed trend?" The authors pointed to "the entry into the labor market of the well educated baby boom generation" and "a long-term trend toward increasing relative demand for highly skilled workers" as important causal factors. Their closest approach to a political explanation was a passing reference to a finding that "the 25 percent decline in the value of the minimum wage between 1980 and 1988 accounts for a small part of the drop in the relative wages of dropouts during the 1980s."[52]

---

[50] Ibid., 214.

[51] Paul Krugman, "Losing Our Country," *New York Times*, June 10, 2005, A21.

[52] Levy and Murnane (1992), 1335, 1336, 1363–1364. Other prominent examples of economic analyses of wage inequality include Blank and Blinder (1986); Cutler and Katz (1991); and Hines, Hoynes, and Krueger (2001). A recent unpublished paper by Levy and Temin provides a richer institutional account, concluding that "only a reorientation of government policy can restore the general prosperity of the postwar boom, can recreate a more equitable distribution of productivity gains where a rising tide lifts all boats" (2007, 41).

It probably should not be surprising, in light of their scholarly expertise and interests, that economists have tended to focus much less attention on potential *political* explanations for escalating economic inequality than on potential *economic* explanations. In a presidential address to the Royal Economic Society, British economist A. B. Atkinson criticized his colleagues' tendency to ignore or downplay the impact on the income distribution of social and political factors, arguing that "we need to go beyond purely economic explanations and to look for an explanation in the theory of public choice, or 'political economy'. We have to study the behaviour of the government, or its agencies, in determining the level and coverage of state benefits."

Atkinson went on to criticize economists who *have* considered political factors for their uncritical reliance on the rather mechanical assumption that government policy responds directly to the economic interests of the so-called median voter—the ideological centrist whose vote should be pivotal in any collective decision arrived at, directly or indirectly, by majority rule. He urged them to go beyond this simple framework, to gauge the extent to which redistributive policies are shaped "by the ideology or preferences of political parties, or by political pressure from different interest groups, or by bureaucratic control of civil servants or agencies."[53]

Atkinson's criticism seems apt, since political economists wedded to the familiar majoritarian model have remarkable difficulty even in explaining why the numerous poor in democratic political systems do not expropriate the unnumerous wealthy. If taxes are proportional to income and government benefits are distributed equally, for example, everyone with below-average income—a clear majority of the electorate in any democratic political system with enough capitalism to generate a wealthy class—has an economic incentive to favor a tax rate of 100%.[54] Even if redistribution entails some waste, most people should favor some redistribution, and poorer people should prefer more. Furthermore, increases in economic inequality should result in higher taxes and more redistribution.[55]

Of course, the reality is that very few people—even very few poor people—favor aggressive redistribution of the sort implied by these simple economic models. Nor is aggressive redistribution anywhere in sight. Writing 25 years ago, before most of the substantial increase in economic inequality documented

[53] Atkinson (1997), 315, 316. On the importance of the "median voter" for electoral competition see Downs (1957).

[54] McCarty, Poole, and Rosenthal (2006, 124) calculated that the *average* income of American families in 2000 exceeded the *median* income (excluding noncitizens) by about 40%. Even if nonvoters are excluded from the calculation of the median, the average income of all families exceeded the median income *of voters* by more than 20%.

[55] Meltzer and Richard (1981) provided an influential formalization of the political economy of redistribution. Recent applications and extensions include Roemer (1999) and McCarty, Poole, and Rosenthal (2006, chapters 3–4).

in figures 1.1 and 1.3, Dahl noted that, "After half a century of the American welfare state . . . the after-tax distribution of wealth and income remains highly unequal."[56] Now, after three-quarters of a century of the American welfare state, the distributions of wealth and income are even more unequal than they were when Dahl wrote. Moreover, systematic analyses suggest that the extent of economic inequality has little impact on the extent of redistribution, either across nations or within the United States.[57] Certainly, recent American experience amply demonstrates that escalating economic inequality need not prevent the adoption of major policy initiatives further advantaging the wealthy over the middle class and poor. The massive tax cuts of the Bush era, whose gains went mostly to people near the top of the income distribution, are a dramatic case in point.[58]

In the following pages, I explore these glaring disjunctions between the predictions of simple majoritarian models and actual patterns of policy making in the United States over the past half-century. As Atkinson surmised, the disjunctions turn out to have a great deal to do with "the ideology or preferences of political parties" and with "political pressure from different interest groups." For example, I find in chapter 8 that although Americans have strongly and consistently favored raising the federal minimum wage, their elected representatives have allowed the real value of the minimum wage to decline by more than 40% since the late 1960s. Moreover, my analysis in chapter 9 shows that elected officials voting on a minimum wage increase paid no attention at all to the views of people poor enough to be directly affected by that policy change. My broader analysis indicates that this sort of unresponsiveness is no anomaly, but a very common pattern in American policy making.

The gap between the predictions of conventional political-economic models and the actual workings of American democracy also reflects the profound difficulties faced by ordinary citizens in connecting specific policy proposals to their own values and interests. Economic analyses often take such connections for granted; but for many people on many issues they are misconstrued or simply missing. Egalitarian impulses often fail to get translated into policy because ordinary citizens do not grasp the policy implications of their egalitarian values. For example, in chapter 7, I show that almost two-thirds of the people who say the rich pay less than they should in taxes nevertheless favor repealing the federal estate tax—a tax that only affects the richest 1–2% of taxpayers. Any serious attempt to understand the political economy of the New Gilded Age requires grappling with the political psychology of

---

[56] Dahl (1982), 172.

[57] Bénabou (1996); Perotti (1996); Rodriguez (1999, 2004).

[58] On the Bush tax cuts as a test of the responsiveness of the American political system to the policy preferences of the median voter, see Hacker and Pierson (2005).

American voters and with the real limitations of public opinion as a basis for democratic policy making.

Escalating economic inequality poses a crucial challenge to America's democratic ideals. The nature of that challenge has been nicely captured by Michael Kinsley: "According to our founding document and our national myth, we are all created equal and then it's up to us. Inequality in material things is mitigated in two ways: first, by equal opportunity at the start, and, second, by full civic equality despite material differences. We don't claim to have achieved all this, but these are our national goals and we are always moving toward them."[59]

It is a nice sentiment—but is it true? For partisans of American democracy the evidence is far from reassuring.

[59] Kinsley, "Mobility vs. Nobility," B07.

CHAPTER 2

The Partisan Political Economy

> . . . as our economy grows, market forces work to
> provide the greatest rewards to those with the
> needed skills in the growth areas. . . . This trend . . .
> is simply an economic reality, and it is neither fair
> nor useful to blame any political party.
> —Treasury Secretary Henry Paulson, 2006[1]

SECRETARY PAULSON'S ATTRIBUTION of increasing economic inequality to
impersonal "market forces" is politically convenient, given his prominent
position in an administration that has presided over booming corporate profits but stagnant wages for most working people. Nonetheless, his perspective
is symptomatic of a much more general tendency to think of the economy
as a natural system existing prior to, and largely separate from, the political
sphere.

In the run-up to the 2004 presidential election, for example, the Associated
Press (AP) reported that, "Over two decades, the income gap has steadily increased between the richest Americans, who own homes and stocks and got
big tax breaks, and those at the middle and bottom of the pay scale, whose
paychecks buy less." While the AP story noted that Democratic presidential
candidate John Kerry was attempting to make the economy a campaign issue,
the last word went to the chief economist for Wells Fargo: "This really has
nothing to do with Bush or Kerry, but more to do with the longer-term shift

in the structure of the economy." Similarly, in the run-up to the 2006
midterm election business columnist Ben Stein noted that "there is extreme
income inequality in this country. It is hard to say whether it's the fault of
President Bush, since there was also extreme income inequality under former
President Bill Clinton, and in fact there has always been extreme income inequality."[2]

The tendency to think of economic outcomes as natural and inevitable is
politically significant because it discourages systematic critical scrutiny of

---

[1] Remarks Prepared for Delivery by Treasury Secretary Henry H. Paulson at Columbia University, August 1, 2006, http://www.treas.gov/press/releases/hp41.htm.

[2] Associated Press, "Gap Between the Rich, Others Grows," *Trenton Times*, August 17, 2004,
A6; Ben Stein, "You Can Complain, or You Can Make Money," *New York Times*, October 15,
2006, BU 3.

their causes and consequences. If escalating inequality is "simply an economic reality," it seems pointless to spend too much energy worrying about
how and why it arises. Moreover, if "there has always been extreme income
inequality" under Republicans and Democrats alike, it seems pointless to
hope that public policies might mitigate that inequality. As prominent policy
analyst Lawrence Mead rather breezily put it, in a response to the report of
the American Political Science Association's Task Force on Inequality and
American Democracy cited in chapter 1, "The causes [of growing economic
inequality] are not well understood and have little tie to government."[3]

My aim in this chapter is to refute the notion that the causes of economic
inequality in contemporary America "have little tie to government." Indeed, I suggest that the narrowly economic focus of most previous studies
of inequality has caused them to miss what may be the most important single influence on the changing U.S. income distribution over the past half-
century—the contrasting policy choices of Democratic and Republican
presidents. Under Republican administrations, real income growth for the
lower- and middle-income classes has consistently lagged well behind the
income growth rate for the rich—and well behind the income growth rate
for the lower and middle classes themselves under Democratic administrations.

In addition to documenting these substantial partisan disparities in income
growth, the analyses presented in this chapter address a variety of potential
explanations for them. I show that the dramatic differences in patterns of
income growth under Democratic and Republican presidents are quite unlikely to have occurred by chance; nor can they be attributed to oil price
shocks or changes in the structure of the labor force or other purely economic factors, or to cyclical corrections by each party of the other party's policy excesses. Rather, they reflect consistent differences in policies and
priorities between Democratic and Republican administrations. In the first
half of the post-war era, these differences were expressed primarily in
macroeconomic policies and performance, with Democrats presiding over
significantly less unemployment and significantly more overall economic
growth than Republicans. Since the 1970s some of these macroeconomic
differences have been muted, but significant partisan differences in tax and
transfer policies have continued to produce significant partisan disparities in
patterns of post-tax income growth, with the middle class and, especially, the
working poor experiencing significantly more income growth under Democratic presidents than under Republican presidents.

The cumulative effect of these partisan differences has been enormous.
My projections based on the historical performance of Democratic and
Republican presidents suggest that income inequality would actually have

---

[3] Mead (2004), 671.

declined slightly over the past 50 years—completely erasing the substantial increase in inequality documented in chapter 1—had the patterns of income growth characteristic of Democratic administrations been in effect throughout that period. Conversely, continuous application of the patterns of income growth observed during periods of Republican control would have produced a much greater divergence in the economic fortunes of rich and poor people than we have actually experienced—a Platinum-Gilded Age.

PARTISAN PATTERNS OF INCOME GROWTH

As suggested in chapter 1, economists have generally paid only perfunctory attention to potential *political* explanations for increasing economic inequality in contemporary America. They have paid even less attention to *partisan* political explanations—perhaps because marked partisan differences in economic outcomes are difficult to account for within the framework of standard economic models.[4] While political economists have documented consistent partisan differences in economic policy, they have seldom focused on the implications of those differences for income inequality or for the specific economic fortunes of people in different parts of the income distribution.[5]

The most notable exception to this pattern of neglect is the work of Douglas Hibbs, who produced pioneering studies of the impact of partisan politics on a variety of macroeconomic outcomes, including the money supply, unemployment, real output, and income inequality. Using data from 1948 through 1978 (that is, before most of the substantial increase in income inequality documented in chapter 1), Hibbs found that the ratio of the share of post-tax income received by the top 20% of the income distribution to the share received by the bottom 40% declined during periods of Democratic control but increased during periods of Republican control. Applying these estimates to his entire period, Hibbs concluded that inequality declined markedly (by a total of about 25%) during the 14 years of Democratic control covered by his analysis, while remaining essentially unchanged during the 17 years of Republican control. Hibbs and Christopher Dennis extended this

---

[4] A rudimentary search of *JSTOR*, an online archive including articles from more than 50 economics journals, turned up 228 articles published since 1987 with the phrase "economic inequality" in the text; but only 19 of these made any mention of "political parties," "political party," "partisan," "Democrat," or "Republican," and only one brief piece (Bartels and Brady 2003) focused significantly on the role of partisan politics in exacerbating or mitigating economic inequality. In addition, Atkinson (1997) and Putterman, Roemer, and Silvestre (1998) argued for the general significance of political factors (and more specifically for the potential utility of models in which political parties may generate nonmedian policy outcomes) in the course of surveying economic research on income distribution and egalitarianism, respectively.

[5] Hibbs (1977, 1987); Keech (1980); Beck (1982); Alesina and Sachs (1988).

TABLE 2.1
Real Income Growth Rates by Income Level and
Presidential Partisanship, 1948–2005

Average annual real pre-tax income growth (%) for families at various points in the income distribution (with standard errors in parentheses). Partisan control measured from one year following inauguration to one year following subsequent inauguration.

	All Presidents	Democratic Presidents	Republican Presidents	Partisan Difference
20th percentile	1.42 (.50)	2.64 (.77)	.43 (.61)	2.21 (.97)
40th percentile	1.54 (.39)	2.46 (.58)	.80 (.49)	1.67 (.75)
60th percentile	1.73 (.34)	2.47 (.52)	1.13 (.43)	1.33 (.67)
80th percentile	1.84 (.33)	2.38 (.50)	1.39 (.42)	.99 (.65)
95th percentile	2.00 (.38)	2.12 (.65)	1.90 (.46)	.22 (.77)
N	58	26	32	58

Source: Calculations based on data from Census Bureau Historical Income Tables.

analysis through the early 1980s and embedded it in a somewhat broader analysis of partisan differences in macroeconomic policy.[6]

The analysis presented in this chapter extends Hibbs and Dennis's analyses in a variety of ways—most notably by incorporating 20 years of additional historical experience, including most of the period of escalating inequality described in chapter 1. My focus is on partisan patterns of real income growth for affluent, middle-class, and working poor families. I employ the tabulations from the U.S Census Bureau's Historical Income Tables introduced in chapter 1 to examine year-to-year changes in real pre-tax income for families at the 20th, 40th, 60th, 80th, and 95th percentiles of the income distribution from 1948 through 2005.

It will not be surprising, in light of the discussion in chapter 1, that the average rate of real income growth during this period was higher for affluent families than for those lower in the income distribution. These average growth rates, which appear in the first column of table 2.1, range from 2% for families at the 95th percentile down to 1.4% for families at the 20th percentile.

What may be surprising is that this pattern of differential growth is entirely limited to periods in which Republicans controlled the White House. The second and third columns of table 2.1 present separate tabulations of real income growth during Democratic and Republican administrations, respectively. Since it seems unreasonable to expect a new president to have an immediate impact on income growth in his first year in office, my measure of partisan

[6] Hibbs (1987), 232–243. The t-statistic for this partisan difference is 1.8, suggesting that it is very unlikely to be due to chance (Hibbs and Dennis 1988).

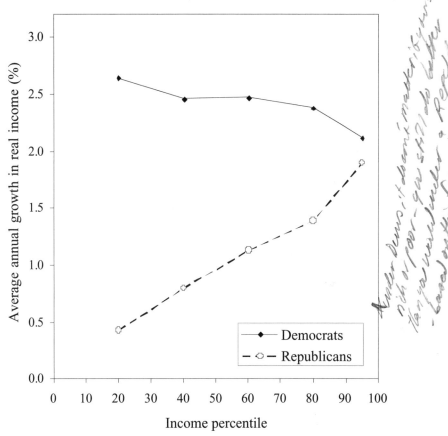

Figure 2.1 Income Growth by Income Level under Democratic and Republican Presidents, 1948–2005

control is lagged by one year; thus, income changes in 2001 are attributed to Democrat Bill Clinton, despite the fact that Republican George W. Bush took office in January of that year. The assumption of a one-year lag in partisan policy effects is consistent with macroeconomic evidence regarding the timing of economic responses to monetary and fiscal policy changes; it also fits the observed data better than a zero-, two-, three-, four-, or five-year lag.[7]

Figure 2.1 provides a graphical representation of the patterns documented in the second and third columns of table 2.1. The starkly different patterns of

[7] Christiano et al. (1999); Blanchard and Perotti (2002). I have investigated the statistical fit of alternative lags by replicating the analysis presented in table 2.3 using current (unlagged) presidential partisanship, as well as presidential partisanship lagged by two, three, four, or five years. In every case the resulting regression model fit the data 4 to 5% less well than the model with presidential partisanship lagged by one year.

income growth under Democratic and Republican administrations are very clear in the figure. Under Democratic presidents, poor families did slightly better than richer families (at least in proportional terms), producing a modest net decrease in income inequality; under Republican presidents, rich families did vastly better than poorer families, producing a considerable net increase in income inequality. In both cases, the patterns are essentially linear over the entire range of family incomes represented in the figure (that is, for incomes ranging from about $25,000 to $200,000 in 2005).

If patterns of income growth differ so dramatically under Democratic and Republican presidents, it seems natural to wonder whether similar differences are attributable to Democratic and Republican members of Congress. Unfortunately, the historical pattern of change in the partisan composition of Congress in the post-war era makes it very hard to tell. With Democrats holding an uninterrupted majority in the House of Representatives from 1955 through 1994 and Republicans in control from 1995 through 2006, any effect of variation in the partisan composition of Congress is likely to be confounded with the effects of broader economic trends. Thus, although simple tabulations of income growth levels suggest that they have generally been higher when Congress has been more Democratic, those differences cannot be considered dispositive.[8]

A PARTISAN COINCIDENCE?

The partisan differences in characteristic rates of income growth documented in figure 2.1 would seem to be of immense economic and political significance—if they are real. They suggest that middle-class and poor families in the post-war era have routinely fared much worse under Republican presidents than they have under Democratic presidents. By this accounting, economic inequality in contemporary America is profoundly shaped by partisan politics.

But to what extent are these patterns really attributable to partisan politics rather than to accidental historical factors? One way to address this question is to examine their consistency across a range of presidents and circumstances. To that end, figure 2.2 shows the level of income inequality in each year of the post-war period as reflected in one standard measure of

[8] Adding a measure of the average proportion of Democrats in the House and Senate to the regression equations reported in table 2.3 suggests that Democrats in Congress probably had positive effects on income growth, at least for low-income families; but the relevant parameter estimates are small (implying that even the largest observed shift in the partisan composition of Congress had much less effect on income growth than a shift in partisan control of the White House) and very imprecise (with an average t-statistic of .35).

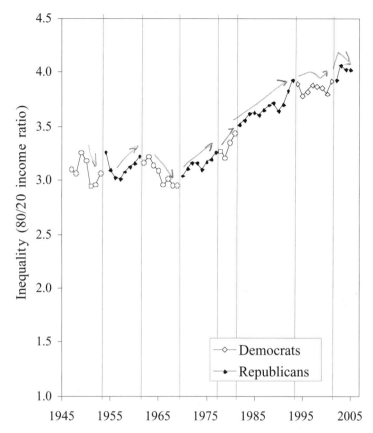

Figure 2.2 Income Inequality under Democratic and
Republican Presidents, 1947–2005

inequality, the ratio of incomes at the 80th percentile of the income distribution to those at the 20th percentile.

By this measure, income inequality was essentially constant from the late
1940s through the late 1960s, with families at the 80th percentile of the income distribution earning about three times as much as families at the 20th
percentile. Inequality increased fairly steadily through the 1970s and 1980s
before leveling off once again in the 1990s. These broad temporal trends
reinforce the impression that growing inequality is significantly related to
long-term technological and social changes.

Despite these long-term forces, distinguishing between Democratic and
Republican administrations (the white circles and black diamonds in the
figure, respectively) reveals the regularity with which Democratic presidents reduced and Republican presidents increased the prevailing level of

economic inequality, regardless of the long-term trend. Indeed, the effect of presidential partisanship on income inequality turns out to have been remarkably consistent since the end of World War II. The 80/20 income ratio increased under each of the six Republican presidents in this period—Eisenhower, Nixon, Ford, Reagan, George H. W. Bush, and George W. Bush. In contrast, four of five Democratic presidents—all except Jimmy Carter—presided over declines in income inequality. If this is a coincidence, it is a very powerful one.[9] Even in the highly inegalitarian economic climate of the 1990s, Bill Clinton managed to produce slightly stronger income growth for families at the 20th percentile than at the 80th percentile, though families at the very top of the income distribution did even better.

The strikingly consistent partisan pattern of changes in income inequality in figure 2.2 seems hard to attribute to a mere coincidence in the timing of Democratic and Republican administrations. That conclusion is reinforced by additional analyses focusing on various subsets of the 58-year period represented in figure 2.2. For example, families at the 20th percentile of the income distribution experienced much more robust income growth under Democratic presidents than under Republican presidents in both the first and second halves of the post-war era.[10] Substantial partisan differences appear even if any one or two administrations are omitted from the comparison,[11] if years with unusually high or low growth are ignored,[12] or if presidential election years or partisan transition years are excluded.[13] In each of these analyses, the overall pattern of partisan differences in income growth is qualitatively similar to the wedge-shaped pattern in figure 2.1.

It may be tempting to suppose that the very different patterns of income growth under Democratic and Republican presidents in figure 2.1 reflect a

[9] The probability of observing no more than one exception to the partisan pattern of increasing inequality under Republicans and decreasing inequality under Democrats in a random sequence of 11 increases and decreases would be $12 \div 2,048 = .006$.

[10] From 1947 to 1974, average income growth for families at the 20th percentile of the income distribution was 1.5% under Republican presidents and 3.8% under Democratic presidents; the partisan difference is 2.32 (with a t-statistic of 1.3). From 1974 to 2005, average income growth for families at the 20th percentile was −0.3% under Republicans and 1.3% under Democrats; the partisan difference is 1.59 (with a t-statistic of 1.7).

[11] Omitting each of the 11 post-war presidents in turn from the comparison reported in table 2.1 produces estimates of the partisan difference in income growth at the 20th percentile ranging from 1.49 (with a t-statistic of 1.5), omitting Lyndon Johnson, to 2.77 (with a t-statistic of 3.0), omitting Dwight Eisenhower.

[12] Excluding years in which real income growth at the 20th percentile was greater than 5% or less than −2% produces a partisan difference of 2.02 (with a t-statistic of 4.0).

[13] The partisan difference in income growth at the 20th percentile excluding presidential election years is 3.27. The corresponding estimate in a model excluding partisan transition years (1953, 1961, 1969, 1977, 1981, 1993, and 2001) is 2.47. The t-statistics for these estimates are 3.0 and 2.3, respectively.

TABLE 2.2

The Impact of Partisan Turnover on Partisan Differences in Real Income Growth
Rates, 1948–2005

Average annual real pre-tax income growth (%) for families at various points in the income
distribution (with standard errors in parentheses). Partisan control measured from one year following inauguration to one year following subsequent inauguration. "Partisan turnover" refers
to first-term Democrats who succeeded Republicans or first-term Republicans who succeeded
Democrats.

	All Presidents	Democratic Presidents	Republican Presidents	Partisan Difference
Partisan turnover				
20th percentile	1.38 (.75)	2.28 (1.00)	.71 (1.08)	1.57 (1.52)
40th percentile	1.52 (.54)	2.07 (.75)	1.11 (.76)	.96 (1.09)
60th percentile	1.60 (.47)	2.00 (.63)	1.30 (.67)	.71 (.95)
80th percentile	1.80 (.45)	2.19 (.62)	1.51 (.63)	.68 (.91)
95th percentile	1.89 (.45)	1.93 (.69)	1.86 (.61)	.07 (.92)
N	28	12	16	28
No partisan turnover				
20th percentile	1.46 (.68)	2.95 (1.19)	.16 (.61)	2.80 (1.29)
40th percentile	1.56 (.56)	2.80 (.88)	.48 (.63)	2.31 (1.06)
60th percentile	1.86 (.51)	2.86 (.82)	.97 (.57)	1.89 (.98)
80th percentile	1.87 (.48)	2.55 (.78)	1.27 (.57)	1.28 (.95)
95th percentile	2.10 (.62)	2.28 (1.07)	1.95 (.70)	.34 (1.25)
N	30	14	16	30

Source: Calculations based on data from Census Bureau Historical Income Tables.

cycle of partisan equilibration in which Democrats pursue expansionary policies in reaction to Republican contractions and Republicans produce contractions as an antidote to Democratic expansions. However, a detailed analysis
of the timing of partisan differences in income growth provides no support
for that notion. Table 2.2 provides tabulations of average income growth paralleling those in table 2.1, but separately for administrations in which the
president was of the opposite party as his predecessor (in the top panel of the
table) and those in which the president succeeded himself or a member of
his own party (in the bottom panel).

If slow growth for middle-class and poor families under Republican presidents represented an antidote to unsustainable expansion under Democratic
presidents, and vice versa, we would expect to see the greatest partisan differences in administrations where Republicans succeeded Democrats or Democrats succeeded Republicans. However, the actual pattern is exactly the
opposite: the partisan differences in average growth rates at every income
level were about twice as large in terms with no partisan turnover as they
were in the first terms of new partisan regimes. Democratic presidents

generally presided over similar income growth rates for families in every part of the income distribution, regardless of whether they were in their first or second terms; but average income growth was consistently higher (by a little more than half a percentage point) when Democrats succeeded Democrats than when Democrats succeeded Republicans. Conversely, most families (except the most affluent) did better under first-term Republican presidents than in subsequent Republican administrations; these differences, too, were on the order of half a percentage point.

Income growth was also considerably more unequal in Republican administrations with no partisan turnover than it was under first-term Republican presidents. In both cases there was a steady increase in average growth rates with each step up the income ladder; but the gap in economic fortunes between the rich and the poor was almost twice as large when Republican presidents were well-entrenched in the White House than when they succeeded Democrats. Clearly, these differences cannot be attributable to short-term corrections of misguided Democratic policies.

Another way to gauge the robustness of the partisan pattern of income growth in figure 2.1 is to consider a variety of potential nonpolitical explanations for the pattern. Perhaps Republican presidents have just been unlucky in occupying the White House at times when powerful external forces depressed income growth for middle-class and poor families. In order to explore this possibility, table 2.3 presents the results of a series of parallel statistical analyses relating each year's real income growth at each of the income levels tabulated by the Census Bureau to a variety of potentially relevant economic and social conditions. The estimated effects of partisan control in these analyses represent the difference in average income growth under Democratic and Republican presidents for families at each income level, net of any differences attributable to historical trends or current economic circumstances.[14]

One economic circumstance of particular significance for income growth rates is the real price of oil—perhaps the most volatile and economically important commodity in modern industrial economies. Since major oil price shocks are largely outside the control of presidents, it would be misleading to attribute income changes associated with those shocks to partisan politics. As it turns out, however, fluctuations in oil prices have had little impact on in-

---

[14] The Seemingly Unrelated Regression (SUR) estimator (Zellner 1962) exploits cross-equation correlations of the regression disturbances to produce more efficient parameter estimates than with ordinary least squares regression. Not surprisingly, the residuals from the parallel regression models considered here are strongly correlated, reflecting the extent to which economic shocks affect families at all income levels in similar ways. The 10 cross-equation correlations range from .27 to .90, with an average value of .68. As a result, some of the SUR parameter estimates reported in table 2.3 are a good deal more precise than the corresponding ordinary least squares parameter estimates.

TABLE 2.3

Statistical Analysis of Income Growth, 1949–2005

Annual real pre-tax income growth (%) for families at various points in the income distribution. Parameter estimates from Seemingly Unrelated Regression models (with standard errors in parentheses). Partisan control measured from one year following inauguration to one year following subsequent inauguration. "Linear trend" and "Quadratic trend" reflect cumulative change from 1949 through 2005.

	20th percentile	40th percentile	60th percentile	80th percentile	95th percentile
Democratic president	2.32 (.80)	1.60 (.56)	1.53 (.52)	1.23 (.51)	.50 (.64)
Oil prices (lagged %Δ)	−.032 (.016)	−.031 (.011)	−.035 (.011)	−.030 (.010)	−.032 (.013)
Labor force participation (Δ%)	4.66 (1.44)	4.46 (1.02)	2.95 (.95)	2.69 (.93)	3.58 (1.16)
Lagged growth	−.191 (.084)	−.249 (.074)	−.286 (.077)	−.296 (.090)	−.040 (.114)
Lagged 95th percentile	.395 (.151)	.244 (.111)	.201 (.104)	.187 (.109)	—
Linear trend	−12.84 (5.88)	−13.71 (4.17)	−8.76 (3.88)	−5.30 (3.75)	−4.18 (4.71)
Quadratic trend	9.68 (5.75)	10.18 (4.06)	5.33 (3.78)	2.54 (3.67)	2.83 (4.61)
Intercept	2.68 (1.26)	3.80 (.89)	3.60 (.83)	3.17 (.81)	2.80 (1.01)
Standard error of regression	2.89	2.02	1.89	1.84	2.31
R^2	.41	.52	.45	.37	.29
N	57	57	57	57	57

Source: Calculations based on data from Census Bureau Historical Income Tables.

Handwritten marginalia:

Left margin: particulates / take of product / an model of / w/oil → ? / Major +ve economic

Right margin: .50 (.64) → not reliable / 2.80 (1.01) reliable

Bottom: Rule of Thumb → Bartels doesn't use stars to show statistical significance ... instead, if you look at the parameter estimate (coefficient) / (standard error), if it's twice as half the estimate, it's reliable

come *inequality*; the statistical results presented in table 2.3 suggest that a 50% increase in the real price of oil would reduce the real incomes of families at every income level by a similar amount, about 1.5 percentage points.[15]

Income growth rates are also sensitive to changes in labor force participation, since adding another family member to the workforce is likely to produce a significant increase in family income. The proportion of adults in the labor force has increased from 59% in the late 1940s and 1950s to 67% at the turn of the twenty-first century, largely due to an increase in the number of working women. The statistical results presented in table 2.3 indicate that this increase significantly bolstered the incomes of American families, especially those in the bottom half of the income distribution.[16]

The price of oil and the increasing participation of women in the labor force are just two of a great many economic and social forces beyond the control of presidents that might be expected to affect the American economy and, perhaps, patterns of income inequality. For example, college education is much more common today than it was at the end of World War II, immigrants and the elderly make up larger shares of the population, the average size of families has become smaller, and imports constitute a larger share of the economy than they once did. Any or all of these changes may have contributed to changing patterns of income growth over the past half-century. However, because these long-term trends have been so glacial, and so intertwined, it is very difficult to discern their distinct effects on the shape of the income distribution.[17]

Fortunately, from the standpoint of *political* analysis, the very fact that these social and economic trends have been gradual and fairly steady implies that their effects are unlikely to be confounded with the effects of alterations in control of the White House, which occur episodically and have produced only a very slight increase over time in the frequency of Republican governance.[18] Thus, rather than attempting to pinpoint specifically how these and

[15] Annual percentage changes in the real price of oil are derived from monthly spot prices (for West Texas Intermediate) compiled by Dow Jones & Company and published by the Federal Reserve Bank of St. Louis, http://research.stlouisfed.org/fred2/series/OILPRICE/. By this measure, the real price of oil increased by 142% in 1974, by 52% in 2000, and by 48% in 1980. The largest decline was 47% in 1986.

[16] My measure is the annual change in the percentage of noninstitutionalized civilians over the age of 15 who are employed or seeking work, as tabulated by the Bureau of Labor Statistics, http://www.bls.gov/cps/cpsaat1.pdf.

[17] Correlations between annual levels of labor force participation, college education, immigration, elderly population, family size, and imports as a share of GDP range from .76 to .99 and average .89. Correlations between these measures and a simple linear trend range from .83 to .99 and average .93.

[18] The correlation between time and partisan control of the White House over the period covered by my analysis is .10. Correlations between partisan control and the social and economic indicators mentioned in the text range from .04 to .14 and average .10.

other long-term trends have affected patterns of income growth, I simply allow for the possibility that expected income growth rates have changed over time by including linear and quadratic trend terms in my analysis. Given the crudeness of this strategy for capturing long-term trends in income growth, it is important to note that the apparent effects of presidential partisanship are insensitive to a variety of alternative strategies for taking account of secular changes in the structure of the American economy and society. The statistical evidence for a partisan political effect turns out to be surprisingly robust in this respect.[19]

The estimated effects associated with the linear and quadratic trend terms in table 2.3 imply that average real income growth for families below the 95th percentile has declined by a little more than half a percentage point per decade over the post-war era. However, the negative trend in income growth was much milder for families near the top of the income distribution—only one quarter of a percentage point per decade.[20] In this respect, among others, there is a fairly striking disconnection between the pattern of income growth for families at the 95th percentile and the pattern for less affluent families. Income growth at the 95th percentile was also virtually unrelated to growth in the previous year and was relatively unaffected by presidential partisanship. Thus, the most affluent families represented in the Census Bureau's tabulations have been surprisingly insulated from the structural shifts in the U.S. economy that have eroded income growth among less affluent families over the past half-century; and they have fared very well regardless of which party controls the White House.

Income growth among these affluent families does seem to have spurred significant subsequent income growth among middle-class and, especially,

[19] For example, adding a cubic trend term to the regression models in table 2.3 increases the apparent impact of presidential partisanship by 11%, on average; the parameter estimates for Democratic presidents decline in roughly linear fashion from 2.54 (with a standard error of .77) at the 20th percentile to .66 (with a standard error of .61) at the 95th percentile. Replacing the linear and quadratic trend terms with an indicator variable for the period after 1973 decreases the apparent impact of presidential partisanship on income growth rates by an average of 8%; the parameter estimates for Democratic presidents decline in roughly linear fashion from 2.25 (with a standard error of .80) at the 20th percentile to .34 (with a standard error of .61) at the 95th percentile. Including social and economic trend variables, singly or in combination, also produces generally similar patterns of estimated partisan effects. For example, in the best-fitting model I have examined, which includes the value of imports as a share of GDP, the estimated partisan effects are all within 2% of the values reported in table 2.3.

[20] My time trend variable runs from 0 in 1949 to 1 in 2005. Thus, the total decline in annual income growth rates at each income level over the entire period covered by my analysis is captured by the sum of the "Linear trend" and "Quadratic trend" coefficients in the corresponding column of table 2.3. The implied declines per decade in average income growth rates are .55, .62, .60, .48, and .24, respectively, for families at the 20th, 40th, 60th, 80th, and 95th percentiles of the income distribution.

working poor families. This "trickle-down" phenomenon is reflected in the positive effects of the previous year's growth rate for families at the 95th percentile on current growth for families at lower income levels in table 2.3. Conversely, current growth for families at each income level was negatively related to the previous year's growth rate at the same income level, suggesting some tendency toward equilibration (with growth spurts in one year leading to slumps the following year, and vice versa), or perhaps some measurement error in the year-by-year growth rates derived from the Census Bureau's Current Population Surveys.

Despite the complicating effects of the constellation of explanatory factors represented in table 2.3, the impact of presidential partisanship emerges clearly in these analyses. Indeed, the partisan differences between Democratic and Republican presidents estimated in table 2.3 are remarkably similar in magnitude to those reported in table 2.1, declining in a roughly linear fashion from 2.3 percentage points at the 20th percentile to 0.5 percentage points at the 95th percentile of the family income distribution. These statistical results provide strong evidence that the striking differences in the economic fortunes of rich and poor families under Democratic and Republican administrations are not an artifact of the different conditions under which Democrats and Republicans have happened to hold the reins of government, but a reflection of the fundamental significance of partisan politics in the political economy of the post-war United States.[21]

PARTISAN DIFFERENCES IN MACROECONOMIC POLICY

Probing the remarkable partisan differences in patterns of income growth over the past half-century suggests that these differences are real, not a historical coincidence or a statistical illusion. But how do Democratic and Republican presidents actually *produce* such strikingly different patterns of income growth? That would constitute a fruitful research agenda for a small army of economists. Here, I merely attempt to sketch some consistent partisan differences in key policy areas in the post-war era, provide some examples of contrasting Democratic and Republican policy initiatives, and trace the connection between partisan differences in macroeconomic performance and partisan patterns of inequality. The case studies presented in chapters 6, 7, and 8, though still far from comprehensive, are intended to supplement this brief overview with more detailed examinations of partisan politics in two especially important areas, tax policy and minimum wage policy.

---

[21] The partisan differences for all but the 95th percentile are too large to be plausibly attributable to chance, with *t*-statistics ranging from 2.4 to 2.9.

One important source of partisan differences in income growth is that Democratic and Republican presidents have consistently pursued rather different macroeconomic policies, and those policies have had significant consequences for the changing shape of the U.S. income distribution. As Edward Tufte wrote, summarizing cross-national research through the mid-1970s, "Party platforms and political ideology set priorities and help decide policy. The consequence is that the governing political party is very much responsible for major macroeconomic outcomes—unemployment rates, inflation rates, income equalization, and the size and rate of expansion of the government budget."[22]

In the United States, as in many other industrial democracies, differences in the class composition of the parties' respective supporting coalitions have encouraged them to adopt distinctive macroeconomic priorities. Douglas Hibbs, writing in the mid-1980s, summarized these distinctive priorities simply and forcefully: "Democratic administrations are more likely than Republican ones to run the risk of higher inflation rates in order to pursue expansive policies designed to yield lower unemployment and extra growth." Hibbs added that "six of the seven recessions experienced since the Treasury–Federal Reserve Accord of 1951, which made possible activist monetary policies coordinated with fiscal policies, occurred during Republican administrations. Every one of these contractions was either intentionally created or passively accepted, at least for a while, in order to fight inflation."[23]

The testimony of policy makers, both contemporary and retrospective, provides ample evidence of important differences in economic philosophies and priorities between Republican and Democratic administrations. For example, Tufte noted that "the Eisenhower administration memoirs, fiscal histories, and diaries . . . bristle with determined statements on the need to avoid inflation and reduce the federal budget. Stimulative interventionist policies by the government were to be avoided because they ultimately stifled creative business initiative and because they served little purpose, since economic downturns and unemployment were seen as self-curing."

In stark contrast, within weeks of John Kennedy's inauguration, the new Democratic administration was being bombarded with pleas from a future Nobel laureate, Paul Samuelson, for stimulative interventionist policies: "WHAT THIS COUNTRY NEEDS IS AN ACROSS THE BOARD RISE IN DISPOSABLE INCOME TO LOWER THE LEVEL OF UNEMPLOYMENT, SPEED UP THE RECOVERY AND THE RETURN TO HEALTHY GROWTH, PROMOTE CAPITAL FORMATION AND THE GENERAL WELFARE, INSURE DOMESTIC TRANQUILITY AND THE TRIUMPH OF THE DEMOCRATIC PARTY AT THE POLLS."[24]

[22] Tufte (1978), 104.
[23] Hibbs (1987), 218.
[24] Tufte (1978), 17, 7.

Two more future Nobel laureates, James Tobin and Robert Solow, were among the key members of Kennedy's economic policy-making team who drafted the administration's blueprint for economic recovery, a report by the Council of Economic Advisers entitled "The American Economy in 1961: Problems and Policies." In their diagnosis, "the real challenge of economic policy in the months ahead" was to absorb some $50 billion in slack economic capacity. To that end, Kennedy had already "proposed programs in education, health, natural resources and highways, which, while fully justified on their own merits, promise additional benefit in the form of speedier recovery." If more stimulation proved necessary, "A further program for economic recovery might consider a speed-up in Government construction and related projects, an expansion of housing programs, and tax reduction."[25]

Income growth under Kennedy was substantially stronger than it had been under Eisenhower for middle-class and working poor families, although affluent families fared less well.[26] Kennedy's successor, Lyndon Johnson, presided over five years of extraordinarily rapid, broad-based income growth. From 1964 through 1969, the real incomes of families at the 95th percentile of the income distribution grew by 4.2% per year. The corresponding growth rates for families at the 80th, 60th, and 40th percentiles were 4.3%, 4.3%, and 4.5%, respectively. The only group that deviated from this remarkable pattern of proportional income growth was the working poor; their incomes grew even more rapidly than those of more affluent families, by 5.6% per year. That fact was at least partly attributable to a variety of new antipoverty policies and programs implemented as part of Johnson's "Great Society," including Medicare and Medicaid, Job Corps, Food Stamps, and the Community Action Program.

Johnson's successor, Richard Nixon, is sometimes viewed as a rather unconventional, nonideological Republican president, at least in the realm of domestic policy. However, the first few years of Nixon's presidency "fit the stylized pattern of Republican economic priorities well: An orthodox policy of fiscal and monetary restraint was pursued to raise the rate of unemployment and contain the inflationary pressures inherited from the Johnson administration." The result of these policies was also consistent with the typical Republican pattern: the robust egalitarian income growth that had persisted for five years under Johnson screeched to a halt in 1970, replaced by slow growth for the affluent and sharp declines in income for the working poor. Only in August 1971, with a reelection campaign on the

[25] Tobin and Weidenbaum (1988), 54, 46, 48–49.

[26] The average real income growth rate for families at the 20th percentile of the income distribution increased from 2.1% under Eisenhower to 3.8% under Kennedy. Middle-class incomes grew by 2.3% under Eisenhower and 3.3% under Kennedy, while the growth rate for families at the 95th percentile declined from 3.2% to 1.4%.

horizon, did Nixon launch a New Economic Policy including "fiscal stimulation, monetary expansion, a wage-price freeze, and a devaluation of the dollar."[27]

Nixon's New Economic Policy produced a booming economy in 1972, with real income growth ranging from 4.5% for working poor families to 6.6% for families at the 95th percentile of the income distribution. This robust growth contributed significantly to Nixon's landslide reelection. However, income growth slowed considerably in 1973 and disappeared in 1974. By the time Nixon resigned in disgrace in the wake of the Watergate scandal, in August 1974, the country was sliding into a severe recession.

The recession of 1974–1975 was triggered by a massive oil price shock engineered by the Organization of Petroleum Exporting Countries (OPEC). The real price of oil increased by 140% in 1974, throwing the industrial sector of the United States and other advanced economies into a tailspin. Accidental president Gerald Ford entered the White House in the midst of a major economic crisis not of his own making.

Although every president's economic performance is shaped by unpredictable and uncontrollable events, presidents' *responses* to those events are often strongly colored by their partisan priorities and predispositions. Given President Ford's conventional Main Street Republican background, it is perhaps unsurprising that he "initially refused to respond" to the OPEC price shock "with policies to restore aggregate demand," as most Democrats would have done. Instead, he "launched the 'Whip Inflation Now' program of fiscal and monetary restraint, which helped prolong the deep post-OPEC slump in employment and output through 1974 and into 1975. . . . Only after a long and sharp decline in real output did President Ford finally propose a one-year tax rebate in January 1975. The Democratic-dominated Congress passed the bill two and a half months later, after increasing the amount of the rebate substantially and redistributing it in favor of low-income and middle-income individuals."[28] Real incomes, which had declined significantly in 1975, rebounded in 1976—almost, but not quite, enough to get Ford reelected.

The economic recovery that had begun in President Ford's final year in office accelerated under his Democratic successor, Jimmy Carter. Real income growth in 1978 exceeded 5%, and the unemployment rate fell from 7% to 6%. From a distributional standpoint, the nature of the recovery shifted markedly. Under Ford, both the recession and the recovery were

---

[27] Hibbs (1987), 271. Real income growth rates in 1969 had ranged from 3.9% to 5.7%; in 1970 they declined monotonically from 1.9% for families at the 95th percentile of the income distribution to −2.7% for families at the 20th percentile.

[28] Hibbs (1987), 272.

marked by the class bias characteristic of Republican administrations: low-income families lost more real income than affluent families in 1975 and gained less in 1976 and 1977. In marked contrast, real income growth in 1978 was robust across the board, with families at the 20th and 40th percentiles gaining 5.6% and 5.9%, respectively.

President Carter's economic policies were surprisingly consistent with traditional Democratic tendencies and priorities, given his own ideological moderation, his often-rocky relations with the Democratic leadership in Congress, and the difficult economic times in which he governed—"An Age of Limits," as one scholarly account put it. Carter and Congress negotiated a stimulus package including tax cuts and increased government spending, as well as an increase in the minimum wage and an expansion of federal employment programs. The administration refused to tolerate higher unemployment in order to check inflation, reckoning that "the human and social costs of this approach are prohibitive," according to one White House policy memorandum.[29]

Within months of taking office, Carter obtained congressional support for almost $10 billion in new funding for employment programs, much of it through the Comprehensive Employment and Training Act (CETA). The new money, channeled through local governments, paid for training grants, full-time public service jobs for up to two years, and summer jobs for low-income high school students. Four years later, Carter's secretary of labor announced proudly that he had presided over "more than a two and a half fold increase" in funds for employment and training, and that "about 4 million economically disadvantaged persons received training and job opportunities" under CETA in each year of the Carter administration.[30]

The unemployment rate declined through most of Carter's term but spiked back up in the wake of a second major oil price shock in 1979–1980. Slow growth was coupled with double-digit price inflation—an unprecedented combination of economic ills dubbed "stagflation." Running for reelection in the midst of recession, as well as foreign crises in Iran and Afghanistan, Carter was defeated by a popular vote margin of almost 10 percentage points.

When Carter's Republican successor, Ronald Reagan, assumed office in 1981, the unemployment rate stood at 7.5%—exactly the same level as four years earlier. However, Reagan's response to the unemployment problem stemming from an oil price shock was dramatically different from Carter's.

---

[29] Bivin (2002), 198, 71, 128.

[30] Ray Marshall, "The Labor Department in the Carter Administration: A Summary Report—January 14, 1981," U.S. Department of Labor, http://www.dol.gov/oasam/programs/history/carter-eta.htm.

Reagan's first budget gutted the controversial public service employment component of CETA and significantly reduced funding for job training programs. When CETA expired in 1982, the Reagan administration reluctantly agreed to support a much smaller successor program, the Job Training and Partnership Act (JTPA), with no public service employment and primary reliance on the private sector rather than local governments. "At its peak," one summary of domestic policy in the Reagan years noted, "CETA had funded more than three-quarters of a million full-time public service jobs. JTPA funds training, but not wages, for a smaller number of participants, who are enrolled, on average, for less than half the year. Spending on employment and training programs fell from about $22 billion to about $8 billion (in 1992 dollars) between 1979 and 1982. . . . Spending was also reduced for Food Stamps, school lunches, legal services, and social services."[31]

President Reagan's broader macroeconomic policies reflected a decisive choice between the horns of the "stagflation" dilemma. As Hibbs put it, "Monetary policy during the Reagan years leaned harder and longer against inflation than at any time since the Eisenhower administrations. The monetary restraint succeeded in breaking the inflationary legacy of the 1970s, but at the cost of the highest unemployment rates since the last years of the Great Depression."[32]

MACROECONOMIC PERFORMANCE AND INCOME GROWTH

The contrasting responses of Jimmy Carter and Ronald Reagan to the economic ills of "stagflation" are emblematic of surprisingly consistent partisan differences in the macroeconomic policies and priorities of Democratic and Republican presidents in the post-war era. Rather than multiplying examples, I turn in this section to the question of how those contrasting policies have affected the economic fortunes of American families. As it turns out, they have resulted in striking differences in macroeconomic performance between Democratic and Republican presidents, and those differences account for much of the partisan difference in income growth patterns evident in figure 2.1.

Here, too, my analysis builds on pioneering work by Douglas Hibbs. His empirical analyses, based on data from 1953 through 1983, documented significant partisan differences in macroeconomic performance between Democratic and Republican administrations. In particular, Hibbs found that

[31] Danziger and Gottschalk (1995), 25.
[32] Hibbs (1987), 281.

Dems - unemployment → usually a negative relationship
GOP - inflation

GOP are more accepting of greater income inequality ⇒ inhow they tackle inflation.

TABLE 2.4
Macroeconomic Performance under Democratic and Republican
Presidents, 1948–2005

Average values of macroeconomic indicators (with standard errors in parentheses). Partisan control measured from one year following inauguration to one year following subsequent inauguration.

	All Presidents	Democratic Presidents	Republican Presidents	Partisan Difference
Unemployment (%)	5.63 (.19)	4.84 (.24)	6.26 (.24)	−1.42 (.34)
Inflation (%)	3.85 (.39)	3.97 (.71)	3.76 (.43)	.20 (.80)
Real per capita GNP growth (%)	2.15 (.31)	2.78 (.41)	1.64 (.43)	1.14 (.60)
N	58	26	32	58

Source: Calculations based on data from Bureau of Labor Statistics and Bureau of Economic Analysis.

"after adjustment lags the unemployment rate tends to be about 2 percentage points lower under the Democrats than under the Republicans" and that "real output tends to be about 6 percent higher."[33]

Table 2.4 and figure 2.3 present comparisons of overall macroeconomic performance between Democratic and Republican administrations over the longer (58-year) period covered by my analysis. Unlike Hibbs's nonlinear regression estimates, these are simple average values of unemployment, GNP growth, and inflation under each party's presidents, again assuming a one-year lag in presidential influence.[34] Despite these differences, the comparisons of unemployment and GNP growth rates are quite consistent with Hibbs's: the average level of unemployment over the entire post-war era has been almost 30% higher under Republican presidents than under Democrats, while the average rate of real per capita GNP growth has been more than 40% lower. However, despite Republicans' traditional emphasis on curbing inflation, the average inflation rate has been virtually identical under Republican and Democratic presidents over this period.[35] While dif-

[33] Ibid., 226. For an earlier version of these analyses, see Hibbs (1977).

[34] The annual unemployment rate for the civilian labor force is reported by the Bureau of Labor Statistics, http://www.bls.gov/cps/home.htm#empstat. The GNP growth rate is calculated from annual data on real GNP per capita (chained dollars) reported by the Bureau of Economic Analysis, http://www.bea.doc.gov, table 7.1. The inflation rate is calculated from the Census Bureau's consumer price index CPI-U-RS, http://www.census.gov/hhes/income/income03/cpiurs.html.

[35] The average annual *change* in the inflation rate, not shown in table 2.4, is also virtually identical under Republican and Democratic presidents (−0.18 versus +0.03; the *t*-statistic for the difference is 0.3).

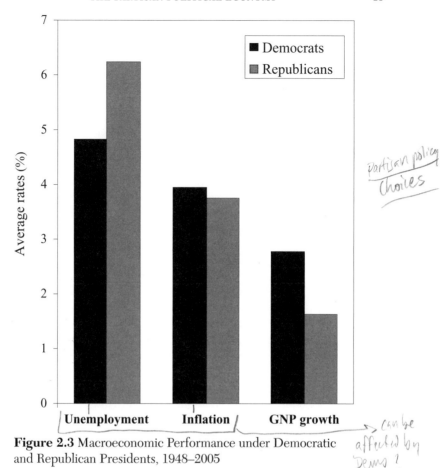

Partisan policy choices (handwritten)

Figure 2.3 Macroeconomic Performance under Democratic and Republican Presidents, 1948–2005

can be affected by Dems? (handwritten)

ferential sensitivity to inflation may have contributed to partisan differences in unemployment and GNP growth, as Hibbs suggested, it is less obvious that Republican presidents have actually been more successful than Democrats in containing inflation.[36]

[36] The simple averages reported in table 2.4 may obscure an important partisan difference in inflation performance by ignoring the possibility of secular trends in the "natural" rate of inflation. Adding linear, quadratic, and cubic trend variables to a regression of inflation on (lagged) presidential partisanship produces some statistical evidence of higher inflation rates under Democratic presidents: the relevant regression parameter estimate is .75. Unfortunately, the estimate is quite imprecise (with a standard error of .72), making it very hard to tell how much, if any, of the apparent Republican advantage in constraining inflation is real. Adding lagged inflation to the analysis implies a smaller but longer-lasting partisan effect, with a coefficient of .53 (.56) and a coefficient for lagged inflation of .54 (.11). Adding trend variables to a regression of unemployment on presidential partisanship reduces the estimated difference between

As with the partisan differences in income growth documented in figure 2.1, the partisan differences in macroeconomic outcomes documented in figure 2.3 cannot plausibly be attributed to differences in the circumstances in which Republican and Democratic presidents have occupied the White House. Embedding the partisan comparisons in a statistical analysis paralleling the analysis of income growth presented in table 2.3 provides strong evidence of significant partisan differences in unemployment and GNP growth between Republican and Democratic administrations, even after allowing for differences in specific economic circumstances and general historical trends.[37]

The partisan differences in macroeconomic performance documented in table 2.4 account for the lion's share of the partisan differences in income growth evident in table 2.3. Once differences in unemployment, inflation, and GNP growth are taken into account, the additional income growth attributable to Democratic presidents (in the first row of table 2.5) is only about half a percentage point—and that modest additional income growth is virtually constant across the income spectrum.

The rest of the statistical results presented in table 2.5 provide a clearer sense of how partisan differences in macroeconomic performance get translated into partisan patterns of income growth for middle-class and poor families. Unemployment and GNP growth have substantial effects on income growth rates for poor and middle-class families, but very little impact on the incomes of families near the top of the income distribution. Thus, the lower unemployment rates and higher GNP growth rates that have generally prevailed during Democratic administrations are much more beneficial to families near the bottom of the income distribution than to those near the top. Conversely, the impact of inflation is negligible near the bottom of the income distribution but much more significant at higher income levels.[38]

The statistical evidence presented in tables 2.4 and 2.5 provides a clear explanation for the partisan differences in pre-tax income growth for lower- and middle-class families documented in table 2.1. The policies of Democratic presidents have produced more employment and output growth, disproportionately

---

Democratic and Republican presidents by 16%, from −1.42 to −1.19 (with a standard error of .30). The apparent effect of Democratic presidents on GNP growth actually increases slightly, from 1.14 without trend variables to 1.21 (with a standard error of .64).

[37] In regression analyses paralleling those presented in table 2.3, the average unemployment rate is .76 percentage points lower under Democratic presidents (with a t-statistic of −4.0), and the average rate of GNP growth is 2.10 percentage points higher under Democratic presidents (with a t-statistic of 4.6). Allowing for delayed effects produced by lagged unemployment, inflation, and GNP growth in these models, the partisan differences implied by these statistical results are quite similar in magnitude to the raw partisan differences reported in the right-most column of table 2.4.

[38] Substituting the annual *change* in the inflation rate produces a similar but somewhat stronger pattern of differential effects on income growth. Indeed, the results suggest that efforts to rein in inflation may actually *reduce* real income growth among the working poor, other things being equal.

TABLE 2.5

Statistical Analysis of Income Growth Including Macroeconomic Conditions, 1949–2005

Annual real pre-tax income growth (%) for families at various points in the income distribution. Parameter estimates from Seemingly Unrelated Regression models (with standard errors in parentheses). Partisan control measured from one year following inauguration to one year following subsequent inauguration. "Linear trend" and "Quadratic trend" reflect cumulative change from 1949 through 2005.

	20th percentile	40th percentile	60th percentile	80th percentile	95th percentile
Democratic president	.51 (.64)	.45 (.41)	.52 (.37)	.61 (.42)	.51 (.62)
Unemployment (%)	−.849 (.307)	−.672 (.187)	−.577 (.167)	−.484 (.187)	−.115 (.267)
Inflation (%)	−.134 (.127)	−.269 (.082)	−.307 (.073)	−.376 (.084)	−.513 (.123)
GNP growth (%)	.798 (.144)	.523 (.091)	.481 (.079)	.293 (.089)	.126 (.129)
Oil prices (lagged %Δ)	−.005 (.013)	−.00 (.008)	−.008 (.007)	−.005 (.009)	−.007 (.013)
Labor force participation (Δ%)	2.72 (1.09)	3.34 (.71)	2.02 (.63)	2.35 (.72)	4.03 (1.05)
Lagged growth	−.110 (.089)	−.195 (.073)	−.213 (.074)	−.290 (.092)	−.044 (.108)
Lagged 95th percentile	.137 (.117)	.060 (.082)	.033 (.073)	.093 (.092)	—
Linear trend	.63 (5.69)	.29 (3.63)	4.85 (3.22)	8.01 (3.72)	7.73 (5.47)
Quadratic trend	−2.54 (5.43)	−2.59 (3.45)	−7.07 (3.06)	−9.69 (3.54)	−8.13 (5.20)
Intercept	4.99 (1.74)	5.61 (1.11)	5.01 (.98)	4.54 (1.08)	2.70 (1.51)
Standard error of regression	2.05	1.31	1.17	1.36	1.97
R^2	.70	.80	.79	.66	.48
N	57	57	57	57	57

Source: Calculations based on data from Census Bureau Historical Income Tables.

benefiting poor and middle-class families. Republican presidents have tended to focus more on containing inflation, which has negligible effects on real income growth near the bottom of the income distribution but substantial effects at the top.

The notion that these partisan differences in income growth reflect conscious policy choices on the part of Republican and Democratic presidents is reinforced by a more detailed analysis of their political timing. Alberto Alesina has noted that Democratic and Republican administrations are characterized by distinct cycles of economic growth, with expansion in the second year of a Democratic president's term followed by slower growth in the third and fourth years, and contraction in the second year of a Republican president's term followed by more robust growth in the third and fourth years.[39] These cycles are unsurprising in light of the fact that presidents have their greatest influence over policy in the first year of each new administration—the "honeymoon" period immediately following election or reelection; the effects of that influence are felt one year later, in the second year of each four-year term.

The political economic cycle identified by Alesina appears conspicuously in data on growth rates in real GNP per capita over the entire post-war era. In the second year of each four-year cycle Democrats presided over average GNP growth of 4.4%, while Republicans presided over average growth of −0.8%.[40] By contrast, in the first, third, and fourth years of each president's term average GNP growth rates were virtually identical: 2.3% for Democrats versus 2.5% for Republicans.

Alesina's political economic cycle also appears clearly in income growth rates for families in every part of the income distribution. Table 2.6 provides a comparison of average income growth rates under Democratic and Republican presidents in the second years of their terms (in the top panel of the table) and in the rest of each four-year term (in the bottom panel). The largest partisan differences by far appear in the second year of each administration—the first year in which the president's policies could be expected to have a significant economic effect. Democratic presidents in those years presided over average real income growth for the working poor of 5.7%, while the corresponding average growth rate under Republican presidents was −1.3%—a remarkable partisan difference of 7 percentage points. The corresponding partisan differences in income growth for middle-class and affluent families were also substantial, ranging from 5.4 percentage points at the 40th percentile down to 3.4 percentage points at the 95th percentile.

---

[39] Alesina (1988); Alesina and Rosenthal (1989); Alesina, Londregan, and Rosenthal (1993).
[40] The *t*-statistic for this difference is 5.5. The average partisan difference is virtually identical in "honeymoon" years with and without partisan turnover; thus, as with the partisan differences in income growth in table 2.2, there is no indication in the data that this effect reflects corrections of the opposition party's macroeconomic failings.

TABLE 2.6
Political Timing of Partisan Differences in Real Income Growth Rates, 1948–2005

Average annual real pre-tax income growth (%) for families at various points in the income distribution (with standard errors in parentheses). Partisan control measured from one year following inauguration to one year following subsequent inauguration. "Post-election ('honeymoon') years" are the second years of each four-year term (beginning one year following inauguration).

	All Presidents	Democratic Presidents	Republican Presidents	Partisan Difference
Post-election ("honeymoon") years				
20th percentile	1.72 (1.18)	5.74 (.89)	−1.29 (1.04)	7.03 (1.44)
40th percentile	1.48 (.90)	4.55 (.84)	−.82 (.68)	5.37 (1.07)
60th percentile	1.32 (.79)	3.96 (.61)	−.66 (.72)	4.62 (.99)
80th percentile	1.70 (.68)	4.08 (.47)	−.08 (.56)	4.16 (.76)
95th percentile	2.35 (.67)	4.28 (.71)	.90 (.69)	3.38 (1.01)
N	14	6	8	14
Other years				
20th percentile	1.33 (.55)	1.71 (.87)	1.01 (.71)	.71 (1.12)
40th percentile	1.56 (.43)	1.83 (.66)	1.33 (.57)	.50 (.87)
60th percentile	1.86 (.38)	2.02 (.63)	1.73 (.47)	.29 (.77)
80th percentile	1.88 (.38)	1.88 (.59)	1.88 (.49)	−.01 (.76)
95th percentile	1.89 (.46)	1.47 (.76)	2.23 (.56)	−.76 (.93)
N	44	20	24	44

Source: Calculations based on data from Census Bureau Historical Income Tables.

By comparison, partisan differences in income growth in other years were much more muted. Democratic presidents produced somewhat more income growth for middle-class and poor families in those years, while Republican presidents produced somewhat more income growth for affluent families; but neither of these partisan differences is large enough to be statistically reliable. Nor was the inequality in income growth between rich and poor families under Republican presidents nearly as stark in other years as in "honeymoon" years—the average growth rate was 1.2 percentage points higher for families at the 95th percentile than for families at the 20th percentile in other years, but 2.2 percentage points higher in the second year of each four-year term.

The dramatic differences in output and income growth associated with Democratic and Republican "honeymoon" periods are a testament to the ability of presidents in the post-Keynesian era to shape the economy to their partisan ends. Democratic presidents have routinely used these periods to produce vibrant economic growth for families in every part of the income distribution; in contrast, Republicans have routinely presided over economic contractions and declining incomes for middle-class and poor families. Partisan differences in macroeconomic priorities and performance have clearly had a very significant impact on the economic fortunes of American families over the past half-century, and that impact has been especially marked at the point in the electoral cycle when presidents are most politically influential.

PARTISAN POLICIES AND POST-TAX INCOME GROWTH

The partisan differences in income growth documented in table 2.1 are especially striking in light of the fact that the tabulations reported there focus entirely on pre-tax income figures. Those figures include cash benefits from the government such as Social Security and unemployment benefits; but they do not reflect any partisan differences in the distribution of noncash government benefits or in effective tax rates. Since taxes and transfers are the most obvious policy levers available to presidents with partisan distributional goals, the pre-tax income tabulations seem likely to miss much of what is distinctive about Democratic and Republican policies.

Partisan differences in economic philosophy and distributional priorities are especially striking in the realm of tax policy. The history of major postwar tax cuts is especially illuminating. Presidents of both parties have implemented significant tax cuts; but they have done so in very different ways and for very different reasons. For example, when President Kennedy's economic team argued for a tax cut in the early 1960s, they reasoned that "the beneficiaries of a personal income tax cut, especially in the lower brackets, would promptly spend a large part of the proceeds on goods and services, thereby stimulating production, employment, and income." In contrast, the supply-side theory adopted in the Reagan administration suggested that tax cuts "could not be given to the middle class or even the poor. In order to be successful, tax cuts had to be directed primarily toward the wealthy because of their larger role in saving and investing. . . . Tax cuts for everyone else might stimulate additional consumption, but that was not what supply-side economics was all about."[41]

President Reagan's tax policies reinforced preexisting trends contributing to increasing economic inequality. As Sheldon Danziger and Peter Gottschalk have pointed out, because of "technological changes, the globalization of markets, and other structural changes in the labor market . . . government tax and transfer policies would have had to become more redistributive than they had been in the 1970s just to keep poverty and inequality constant. Instead, because of the Reagan philosophy and legislative changes, income tax and antipoverty policies became less progressive." Similarly, Hibbs noted that Reagan

---

[41] Tobin and Weidenbaum (1988), 49; Karier (1997), 76.

"succeeded in reversing the trend of increasing federal commitments to the poor and near-poor," adding that, "most important of all, Reagan achieved a dramatic redistribution of the federal tax burden from corporations and high-income classes to moderate- and low-income groups.[42]

When Bill Clinton entered the White House in 1993, he apparently felt a good deal more constrained by the Federal Reserve Board and the bond markets than previous Democratic presidents had been. Rather than relying on macroeconomic stimulation or across-the-board tax cuts to complete the economy's recovery from the recession of 1991, Clinton focused on reducing the ballooning federal budget deficit. Nevertheless, in his first year in office he proposed, and Congress passed, a major expansion of the Earned Income Tax Credit for working poor people. Higher up the income ladder, tax brackets were revised to make them somewhat more progressive while increasing total revenue.[43]

Clinton succeeded so well at reining in the budget deficit that his successor, George W. Bush, inherited a substantial budget surplus. Bush took advantage of the opportunity to engineer a series of major tax cuts. However, in marked contrast to Clinton's strategy of targeting tax cuts to mitigate the effects on the income distribution of technological changes, globalization, and shifting labor markets, Bush exacerbated those effects by reverting to President Reagan's emphasis on reducing the tax burden of wealthy individuals and corporations.

I examine the politics and economic impact of the Bush tax cuts in much more detail in chapter 6. My aim here, however, is to provide a more general accounting of the impact of tax and transfer policies on the shape of the income distribution under Republican and Democratic presidents. Unfortunately, consistent Census Bureau tabulations of the distribution of post-tax income are only available from 1979 through 2003. Thus, the scope for systematic historical analysis of partisan effects on post-tax income growth is quite limited; rather than five Democratic and six Republican presidents over 58 years, the data encompass only 10 years of Democratic control (two under Carter and eight under Clinton) and 14 years of Republican control (eight under Reagan, four under George H. W. Bush, and two under George W. Bush). With that caveat, figure 2.4 shows the average rates of real after-tax income growth since 1980 under Democratic and Republican presidents for households at the 20th, 40th, 60th, and 80th percentiles of the income distribution.[44]

---

[42] Danziger and Gottschalk (1995), 29; Hibbs (1987), 281.

[43] As one sympathetic account had it, "Taxes were raised a bit and made more progressive (helping to balance the budget). What followed, contrary to alarmist predictions, was not an economic crash, but rather a sustained economic boom." Page and Simmons (2000), 158.

[44] "Table RDI-6: Income Limits for Each Fifth of Households, by Selected Definition of Income: 1979 to 2003," http://www.census.gov/hhes/income/histinc/rdi6.html. The table reports 15 different "Experimental Measures" of income. The one employed here is the most expansive,

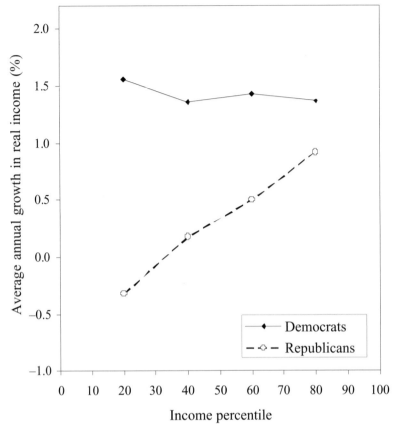

Figure 2.4 Post-Tax Income Growth under Democratic and
Republican Presidents, 1980–2003

In qualitative terms, the partisan pattern of post-tax income growth in figure 2.4 is strikingly similar to the partisan pattern of pre-tax family income
growth in figure 2.1. Households at every income level did about equally
well under Carter and Clinton, with average growth rates ranging from 1.4%
to 1.6%. On the other hand, Republican presidents presided over weaker income growth for households in the top half of the income distribution and

Definition 15, which subtracts federal and state taxes from the standard measure of pre-tax income and adds capital gains, health insurance supplements to wage or salary income, noncash
government transfers, and net imputed returns on home equity. Unlike the pre-tax income tabulations included in the Census Bureau's Historical Income Tables, these tabulations of "experimental measures" of income have not been updated to include more recent years, nor do they
include information on households at the 95th percentile of the income distribution.

TABLE 2.7

Partisan Differences in Real Pre- and Post-Tax Income Growth, 1980–2003

Average annual real income growth (%) for households at various points in the income distribution (with standard errors in parentheses). Partisan control measured from one year following inauguration to one year following subsequent inauguration.

	All Presidents	Democratic Presidents	Republican Presidents	Partisan Difference
Post-tax income growth				
20th percentile	.46 (.42)	1.56 (.59)	−.32 (.49)	1.89 (.76)
40th percentile	.67 (.32)	1.36 (.46)	.18 (.39)	1.17 (.60)
60th percentile	.89 (.30)	1.43 (.44)	.50 (.38)	.93 (.58)
80th percentile	1.11 (.31)	1.37 (.44)	.92 (.44)	.45 (.64)
N	24	10	14	24
Pre-tax income growth				
20th percentile	.39 (.47)	.93 (.89)	.00 (.50)	.93 (.95)
40th percentile	.47 (.40)	.67 (.75)	.33 (.46)	.33 (.83)
60th percentile	.63 (.39)	.74 (.72)	.55 (.45)	.19 (.81)
80th percentile	1.03 (.34)	1.10 (.60)	.98 (.42)	.12 (.71)
N	24	10	14	24

Source: Calculations based on data from Census Bureau Historical Income Tables.

little or no income growth for households in the bottom half of the income distribution. As with the partisan differences in pre-tax growth presented in figure 2.1, these partisan differences in post-tax growth are concentrated in the second year of each administration, when the policy initiatives adopted in the "honeymoon" period immediately following Inauguration Day are most likely to take effect.[45]

Despite the qualitative similarity, a comparison of the magnitude of partisan differences in figures 2.1 and 2.4 suggests that post-tax income growth was somewhat less subject to partisan effects than pre-tax income growth. That impression is confirmed by comparing the magnitudes of partisan differences in post-tax income growth, which are reported in the top panel of table 2.7, with the corresponding partisan differences in pre-tax income growth in table 2.1. For example, average pre-tax income growth for middle-income families was about 1.5 percentage points higher under Democratic presidents than under Republican presidents in table 2.1, but the corresponding difference in average post-tax income growth in table 2.7 is only about 1 percentage point.

[45] In "honeymoon" years, the differences in average post-tax income growth between Democratic and Republican presidents range from 5.0% for households at the 20th percentile of the income distribution to 3.0% for households at the 80th percentile. The corresponding differences in nonhoneymoon years range from 0.9% to −0.3%.

It seems odd to suppose that presidents have had less influence on the distribution of post-tax income than on the distribution of pre-tax income—especially in light of the dramatic differences in tax policies between Republican and Democratic presidents over the past quarter-century. This peculiarity is more apparent than real, however. A direct comparison of the magnitudes of partisan differences in figure 2.1 and figure 2.4 is quite misleading because the two figures refer to very different time periods—1947 through 2005 in figure 2.1 and 1980–2003 in figure 2.4.[46]

The tabulations presented in the lower panel of table 2.7 summarize pre-tax household income growth over the same 24-year period covered by the post-tax calculations in the upper panel of the table.[47] Here the partisan differences in average income growth rates are much smaller than in table 2.1, ranging from a bit less than one percentage point for households at the 20th percentile to only one-tenth of a percentage point at the 80th percentile.[48] These differences suggest that it has become much more difficult in the past quarter-century for presidents to influence the distribution of pre-tax income. The most plausible explanation for this difference is that the increasing impact on the American economy of global trade and credit flows, and the increasing domestic prestige and political independence of the Federal Reserve Board, have reduced the ability of presidents to pursue distinctive partisan macroeconomic policies.[49]

However, even as contemporary presidents have been increasingly constrained in their pursuit of partisan macroeconomic policies, they seem to have been quite successful in using taxes and transfers to shape the post-tax income distribution along familiar partisan lines. That impression is reinforced by the statistical analysis reported in table 2.8, which parallels the

[46] An additional difference is that the data summarized in figure 2.1 are for families of two or more people, while those summarized in figure 2.4 are for households. However, that distinction is inconsequential here; parallel calculations employing the pre-tax family and household data from 1980 through 2003 produce very similar results.

[47] The data employed in the lower panel of table 2.7 are based on the same definition of pre-tax income as in table 2.1 but for households rather than families to maximize comparability with the data in the upper panel.

[48] These partisan differences in pre-tax growth are nowhere close to being "statistically significant," even for households at the 20th percentile. However, the *declines* in partisan differences apparent in the post-1979 data by comparison with the earlier post-war period are not "statistically significant" either. Indeed, a variety of elaborations of the regression model in table 2.3 to allow for changes in the magnitude of partisan effects produced no statistically reliable evidence of either structural breaks or secular trends.

[49] The partisan difference in unemployment evident in table 2.4 persists even when the comparison is limited to the period from 1980 through 2003: the average unemployment rate was 6.9% under Republican presidents and 5.4% under Democratic presidents, for a difference of 1.49 (with a standard error of .54). However, the earlier partisan difference in average GNP growth entirely disappeared: real per capita growth averaged 1.8% under both Republicans and Democrats.

TABLE 2.8

Statistical Analysis of Post-Tax Income Growth, 1981–2003

Annual real post-tax income growth (%) for households at various points in the income distribution. Parameter estimates from Seemingly Unrelated Regression models (with standard errors in parentheses). Partisan control measured from one year following inauguration to one year following subsequent inauguration. "Linear trend" and "Quadratic trend" reflect cumulative change from 1949 through 2005.

	20th percentile	40th percentile	60th percentile	80th percentile
Democratic president	3.07 (.76)	2.34 (.52)	2.23 (.45)	1.51 (.64)
Oil prices (lagged %Δ)	-.039 (.014)	-.034 (.010)	-.037 (.009)	-.032 (.012)
Labor force participation (Δ%)	1.40 (1.59)	2.03 (1.10)	2.29 (.96)	2.49 (1.33)
Lagged growth	.004 (.131)	-.112 (.099)	-.196 (.089)	-.205 (.141)
Linear trend	19.01 (37.41)	-27.61 (26.23)	-62.70 (22.84)	-87.79 (31.55)
Quadratic trend	-14.31 (24.80)	17.28 (17.39)	39.90 (15.14)	56.78 (20.89)
Intercept	-6.87 (13.83)	10.42 (9.69)	24.04 (8.44)	33.62 (11.68)
Standard error of regression	1.34	.94	.81	1.12
R^2	.56	.62	.68	.46
N	23	23	23	23

Source: Calculations based on data from Census Bureau Historical Income Tables.

analysis of pre-tax income growth in table 2.3 using the available post-tax data. As in table 2.3, the statistical analysis shows that the partisan differences in income growth evident in simple tabulations persist even after taking systematic account of the differing economic circumstances in which Democrats and Republicans have held the White House. Indeed, in this case the estimated partisan effects are even larger than the corresponding raw differences in post-tax income growth in figure 2.4, ranging in roughly linear fashion from 3.1 percentage points for households at the 20th percentile of the income distribution to 1.5 percentage points for households at the 80th percentile.[50] These results provide surprisingly strong statistical evidence of characteristic partisan differences in post-tax income growth paralleling—and surpassing in magnitude—the differences in pre-tax income growth evident over the entire post-war period.

Unfortunately, the limitations of the post-tax income data make it impossible to distinguish between two possible interpretations of the changing partisan political economy of the United States over the past quarter-century. One possibility is that contemporary presidents, faced with the increasing difficulty of influencing the macroeconomy, have resorted to tax and transfer policies as alternative means to achieve their partisan ends. In this interpretation, redistribution through taxes and transfers (for example, Clinton's significant expansion of the Earned Income Tax Credit) is the modern Democrat's *substitute* for pre-tax redistribution through expansionary macroeconomic policies. The other, perhaps more likely, possibility is that earlier presidents relied on both macroeconomic policies and tax and transfer policies to pursue their partisan ends, producing larger partisan effects than appear in the pre-tax data—and larger partisan effects than contemporary presidents are able to achieve.

In any case, the partisan differences in post-tax income growth since 1980 are sufficiently large, and sufficiently familiar in their pattern, to reinforce the conclusion that partisan politics has a profound impact on the economic fortunes of poor and middle-class households in contemporary America. While Republican and Democratic presidents may have lost a considerable portion of their influence over the distribution of pre-tax income, they have managed to continue to produce marked partisan differences in the distribution of post-tax income, with Democrats presiding over higher average income growth across the board and substantially higher average growth for people of modest means. Here, too, the partisan political economy seems to be of fundamental importance for the economic fortunes of ordinary Americans.

---

[50] As with the parallel analysis of pre-tax income growth presented in table 2.3, the estimated partisan effects in table 2.8 are insensitive to plausible variations in model specification. For example, excluding the quadratic trend term does not change any of the estimated partisan effects by as much as 5%, while excluding both trend terms reduces the estimated partisan effects by only 8% to 11%.

DEMOCRATS, REPUBLICANS, AND THE RISE OF INEQUALITY

Economists associate the escalation of inequality over the past 30 years with important structural changes in the American economy, including demographic shifts, globalization, and technological change. I see no reason to doubt that these factors have played an important role in increasing the income gap between rich and poor people in the contemporary United States; but if this is "simply an economic reality," as Treasury Secretary Paulson asserted, it does not follow that nothing can be done to mitigate the economic and social consequences of that reality. Nor does the fact that "there has always been extreme income inequality," as Ben Stein observed, imply that presidents and their policy choices can have no significant effect on the extent of inequality at any given time.

The cumulative impact of these partisan policy choices is illustrated in figure 2.5. The dotted line in the center of the figure represents the actual course of inequality over the past half-century, as measured by the ratio of family incomes at the 80th and 20th percentiles of the income distribution. (This portion of the figure is simply repeated from figure 2.2.) The solid upper line represents the projected course of the 80/20 income ratio over the same period given the pattern of income growth that prevailed under Republican presidents during this period, while the lower line represents the projected course of the 80/20 income ratio under Democratic presidents. (These projections are constructed on the basis of the statistical analysis reported in table 2.3, the upper line assuming continuous Republican control and the lower line assuming continuous Democratic control throughout the period.)

The projections in figure 2.5 imply that continuous Democratic control would have produced an essentially constant level of economic inequality over the past three decades, despite all the technological, demographic, and global competitive forces emphasized in economists' accounts of escalating inequality. In contrast, continuous Republican control would have produced a much sharper polarization between rich and poor than has actually occurred over the past 30 years, with the 80/20 income ratio reaching a level about one-third higher than it actually did.[51]

The projections presented in figure 2.5 are based on an arguably unrealistic assumption: that if either party had uninterrupted control of the White House, it would do all the time what it in fact does only half the time. It is impossible to know whether either party would actually have the political will or the political power to produce economic redistribution of the cumulative

---

[51] The 80/20 income ratio increased by 27% between 1975 and 2005. The projections in figure 2.5 suggest that it would have increased by 45% under continuous Republican control but by only 3% under continuous Democratic control.

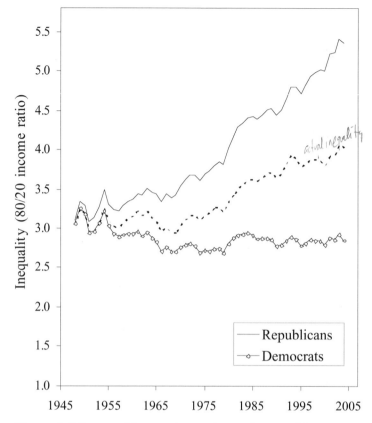

Figure 2.5 Projected Income Inequality under Republican and Democratic Presidents, 1947–2005

magnitude suggested by these projections. Nevertheless, the cumulative differences portrayed in figure 2.5 convey the fundamental significance of partisan politics in ameliorating or exacerbating economic inequality over the past half-century.

In the first 25 years of the post-war era, the partisan differences in income growth patterns documented in this chapter implied robust growth for middle-class and poor families under Democratic presidents and more modest growth under Republicans. In the less propitious economic circumstances prevailing in the early twenty-first century, not even a steady succession of Democratic presidents and policies would be likely to reproduce the robust broad-based income growth of the 1960s. However, that does not make the choice between Democrats and Republicans any less consequential.

The magnitude of what is at stake in partisan control of economic policy may be demonstrated by considering the ramifications of a few hundred votes in a single presidential election. In his first four years in office, President George W. Bush presided over a 2% cumulative increase in the real incomes of families at the 95th percentile of the income distribution, but a 1% *decline* in the real incomes of middle-class families and a 3% decline in the real incomes of working poor families. (Meanwhile, Piketty and Saez's tabulations of IRS data indicate that the real incomes of taxpayers at the 99th percentile increased by more than 7% over this period, while the real incomes of taxpayers at the 99.99th percentile increased by almost 18%.) However, the statistical analyses presented in table 2.3 imply that, had President Al Gore governed under the same economic circumstances, the real incomes of working poor families would probably have grown by about 6% (1.5% per year) over those four years, and the real incomes of middle-class families would probably have grown by about 4.5% (1.1% per year), while the real incomes of families at the 95th percentile would have remained unchanged.

As Edward Tufte insisted 30 years ago, "economic life vibrates with the rhythms of politics."[52] Thus, while it may be "neither fair nor useful to blame any political party" for the structural changes in the economy that make income growth and income inequality much more pressing issues now than they were in the post-war boom years of the 1950s and 1960s, it certainly seems fair—and perhaps even useful—to hold political parties accountable for the profound impact of their policies on the way those structural changes shape the economic fortunes of wealthy, middle-class, and poor American families.

Of course, whether voters *do* hold political parties accountable for the profound impact of their policies is another question. I address that question in chapters 3 and 4, which turn Tufte's maxim on its head by exploring the ways in which American political life vibrates with the rhythm of economics.

[52] Tufte (1978), 137.

Class Politics and Partisan Change

THE PARTISAN PATTERN of economic performance documented in chapter 2 raises a perplexing political question. Real income growth has historically been much stronger under Democratic presidents than under Republican presidents, especially for middle-class and poor people. So why do so many people—including middle-class and poor people—persist in voting for Republicans? After all, Republican candidates have won most of the presidential elections of the post-war era, including five of the last seven. If we imagine that voters want, or should want, to use their power at the ballot box to advance their own economic fortunes or those of their fellow citizens, something seems fundamentally amiss here.

The implications of this anomaly for economic inequality should be clear from figure 2.5, which suggests that the marked escalation of inequality over the second half of the post-war era would simply not have occurred under a steady diet of Democratic presidents and policies. Thus, the ability of Republicans to thrive in the electoral arena despite the negative impact of their policies on the economic fortunes of middle-class and poor people must loom large in any convincing account of the political economy of the New Gilded Age.

In chapter 4, I offer a novel explanation for the striking electoral success of Republican presidential candidates in the post-war era. However, in this chapter I first pause to consider a more straightforward explanation—that voters care about many other things besides income. Perhaps they prefer Republican positions on cultural issues, race, or foreign policy, and consciously accept lower income growth in order to get their preferred policies in these other domains. In that case, the apparent frustration of the economic interests of middle-class and poor people simply reflects the secondary status of economic issues on the contemporary political agenda—and the inevitable fact that voters in a two-party system must sometimes sacrifice secondary concerns in order to support candidates who share their views on the issues they care about most.[1]

---

[1] This formulation begs the second-order question of why Democratic candidates do not simply mimic popular Republican positions on these other issues and then coast to victory on the strength of superior economic management. One possibility is that they are politically incompetent or wrong-headed. A more systematic explanation, investigated by political economist John Roemer, is that intraparty conflict between ideologues and opportunists produces

Arguments of this sort figure prominently in both scholarly and popular accounts of contemporary American electoral politics. One especially lively example, which received a great deal of attention in the months before and after the 2004 election, is Thomas Frank's *What's the Matter with Kansas?* In Frank's telling, "conservatives won the heart of America" by convincing Kansans and other people of modest means to vote against their own economic interests in an effort to defend traditional cultural values against radical bicoastal elites. Their political successes have been facilitated by the fact that "Democrats no longer speak to the people on the losing end of a free-market system that is becoming more brutal and more arrogant by the day." The result is a new "dominant political coalition" uniting "business and blue-collar" in an increasingly conservative Republican Party. The political winners in this coalition are the "assortment of millionaires and lawyers and Harvard grads" pushing the Republican economic agenda of tax cuts, deregulation, free trade, and corporate welfare. As for the working-class cultural conservatives who provide the crucial political support for these policies, "All they have to show for their Republican loyalty are lower wages, more dangerous jobs, dirtier air, a new overlord class that comports itself like King Farouk—and, of course, a crap culture whose moral free fall continues, without significant interference from the grandstanding Christers whom they send triumphantly back to Washington every couple of years."[2]

The supposedly decisive role of "values voters" in the 2004 election seemed to reinforce both the empirical force and the political significance of Frank's analysis. While academics derided the exit poll finding that "moral values" were the most important issue in the campaign, journalists and pundits seized on the notion that Frank's working-class cultural conservatives swung the election to the Republicans. In the first four days following the election, the *New York Times* alone published half a dozen articles trumpeting this theme. The *Times'* in-depth exit poll analysis was headlined "Moral Values Cited as a Defining Issue of the Election." Maureen Dowd wrote that Bush "got re-elected by dividing the country along fault lines of fear, intolerance, ignorance, and religious rule." Garry Wills hailed Bush strategist Karl Rove's "brilliance" in calculating that "the religious conservatives, if they could be turned out, would be the deciding factor." Steven Waldman claimed that "opposition to gay marriage probably paid [*sic*] a significant role in Mr. Bush's victory, especially in drawing voters to the polls in Ohio, where a referendum against gay marriage passed easily."[3]

---

policy platforms that fail to reflect voters' preferences on an issue-by-issue basis. The result is a "policy bundle effect" in which voters are forced to choose between competing packages combining popular and unpopular policy positions. See Roemer (2001).

[2] Frank (2004), 245, 8, 196, 136.

[3] Katharine Q. Seelye, "The Voters: Moral Values Cited as a Defining Issue of the Election," *New York Times*, November 4, 2004, P4; Maureen Dowd, "The Red Zone," *New York Times*,

In a piece written even before the outcome of the election was clear, *Times* columnist Nicholas Kristof wrote that Kerry supporters "should be feeling wretched about the millions of farmers, factory workers, and waitresses who ended up voting—utterly against their own interests—for Republican candidates." Kristof praised *What's the Matter with Kansas?* as "the best political book of the year," citing approvingly Frank's assertion that "Democratic leaders have been so eager to win over suburban professionals that they have lost touch with blue-collar America." A few days later Kristof returned to that theme, arguing that "Democrats need to give a more prominent voice to Middle American, wheat-hugging, gun-shooting, Spanish-speaking, beer-guzzling, Bible-toting centrists."[4]

My aim in this chapter is to clarify the role of class, "moral values," and economic issues in contemporary American electoral politics by examining class-related patterns of issue preferences, partisanship, and voting behavior over the past half-century. I focus on four related questions inspired by recent accounts of working-class cultural conservatism and its political ramifications. First, has the white working class abandoned the Democratic Party? Second, has the white working class become more conservative? Third, do "moral values" trump economics as a basis of working-class voting behavior? And fourth, are religious voters distracted from economic issues?

My answer to each of these questions is "no." My analysis suggests that economic issues remain centrally important in contemporary American electoral politics, *especially* among "the people on the losing end" of the free-market system. Moreover, the political views of those people have changed rather little over the past few decades, while their support for Democratic presidential candidates has actually increased. If Republican electoral success is indeed a puzzle, the solution seems to have little to do with the cultural conservatism of the white working class.

IN SEARCH OF THE WORKING CLASS

The notion that American politics has been transformed by the defection of working-class social conservatives from the Democratic Party is not new. As far back as Richard Nixon's first year in the White House, Kevin Phillips published an attention-getting blueprint for constructing *The Emerging Republican Majority* along neopopulist conservative lines. In the mid-1970s, political scientists

---

November 4, 2004, A25; Garry Wills, "The Day the Enlightenment Went Out," *New York Times*, November 4, 2004, A25; Steven Waldman, "On a Word and a Prayer," *New York Times*, November 6, 2004, A19.

[4] Nicholas D. Kristof, "Living Poor, Voting Rich," *New York Times*, November 3, 2004, A19; Kristof, "Time to Get Religion," *New York Times*, November 6, 2004, A19.

Everett Ladd and Charles Hadley proclaimed "an inversion of the old class relationship in voting" due to "the transformations of conflict characteristic of
postindustrialism." At the end of the Reagan era, journalists Thomas and Mary
Edsall argued that "working-class whites and corporate CEOs, once adversaries at the bargaining table, found common ideological ground in their shared
hostility to expanding government intervention." At about the same time, political scientists Robert Huckfeldt and Carol Kohfeld emphasized the extent to
which "race served to splinter the Democratic coalition" when the policy commitments of the civil rights era provoked "racial hostility, particularly on the
part of lower-status whites." All of these works, and many others, suggested
that the class basis of New Deal voting patterns had given way to a new cleavage structure in which conservative ideology and cultural issues brought large
numbers of working-class whites into the Republican camp.[5]

However, systematic analyses of class divisions in partisanship and voting
have seemed to contradict important elements of this familiar story. Most
notably, Jeffrey Stonecash's 2000 book, *Class and Party in American Politics*,
provided a good deal of evidence that "less-affluent whites have not moved
away from the Democratic Party and that class divisions have not declined in
American politics." Stonecash showed that net Republican gains since the
1950s have come entirely among middle- and upper-income voters, widening rather than narrowing the traditional gap in partisanship and voting between predominantly Democratic lower income groups and predominantly
Republican upper income groups. In a more recent analysis along similar
lines, Nolan McCarty, Keith Poole, and Howard Rosenthal found that income has become an increasingly strong predictor of Republican partisanship and presidential voting since the 1950s.[6] But if *more affluent* voters are
the ones who have become more Republican, where are all those working-
class cultural conservatives?

Assessments of class voting and partisan change turn out to hinge importantly on how one chooses to define evocative but rather nebulous terms
like *working class*. The potential for confusion is vividly illustrated in a
piece written six months after the 2004 election by *New York Times* columnist David Brooks. In "Meet the Poor Republicans." Brooks wrote that
"we've seen poorer folks move over in astonishing numbers to the G.O.P.
George W. Bush won the white working class by 23 percentage points in
this past election."[7] On its face, this sounds like a glaring contradiction of
Stonecash's claim that "less-affluent whites have not moved away from the
Democratic Party." Who is right? Or did 2004 mark a sea change in American class politics?

[5] Phillips (1969); Ladd with Hadley (1975), 240, 232; Edsall and Edsall (1991), 154; Huckfeldt and Kohfeld (1989), 84.

[6] Stonecash (2000), 118; McCarty, Poole, and Rosenthal (2006), chapter 3.

[7] David Brooks, "Meet the Poor Republicans," *New York Times*, May 17, 2005, sect. 4, 14.

No sea change is necessary to reconcile these claims. The apparent discrepancy simply reflects very different notions of who counts as "working class." Stonecash compared low-, middle-, and high-income voters, while Brooks's definition of "the white working class" turns out to include all white voters without college degrees. In the latter group, Bush's plurality in a 2004 exit poll was indeed 23 percentage points.[8]

The problem with Brooks's account is that it is quite misleading to describe people without college degrees as "poorer folks." Even in 2004, after decades of increasingly widespread college education, two-thirds of white voters (and even larger proportions of white nonvoters and nonwhites) were in this group. In light of their numbers, it probably should not be surprising that their economic circumstances were fairly representative of American society. For example, 40% had family incomes in excess of $60,000; and when offered the choice, more than half actually called themselves "middle class" rather than "working class." Meanwhile, among the subset of Brooks's "poorer folks" who might plausibly be considered "poor" in concrete economic terms—white voters without college degrees whose incomes fell in the bottom third of the national income distribution—Bush's margin of victory in 2004 was not 23 percentage points but less than two percentage points.

Throughout this chapter I follow the leads of Stonecash, Brooks, and many other writers in this domain by limiting my analysis to whites. Doing so obviously produces a distorted picture of the contemporary party system, and those distortions are especially significant for an analysis of class-related cleavages, given the strong and persistent correlation between race and economic status in American society.[9] Nevertheless, the distinctiveness of white political behavior over the past half-century and the overwhelming focus on whites in the existing scholarly and popular literature make this limitation expedient for my purposes here.

Perhaps unfortunately, the literature reflects no comparable consensus regarding an appropriate definition of the term *working class*. Some analysts, like Brooks, focus on people without college degrees. By that definition, "working-class" white voters have indeed become more Republican since the 1950s, while whites with college degrees have not. That fact is evident from figure 3.1, which summarizes the voting behavior of white voters in presidential elections since 1952, using data from the authoritative National Election

[8] Brooks's figure is based on data from the Edison/Mitofsky 2004 exit poll. The comparable figure from the 2004 National Election Study survey is only slightly smaller, 19.7 percentage points.

[9] Averaging over the entire period since 1952, whites were slightly less likely to fall in the bottom third of the income distribution (28%) than in the top third (34%). In contrast, nonwhites (including Hispanics) were more than twice as likely to fall in the bottom third of the distribution (45%) as in the top third (20%).

Study (NES) surveys.[10] The figure includes separate trend lines showing the Democratic share of the two-party vote among white college graduates (the solid line) and white voters without college degrees (the dashed line). Over the entire half-century, the average Democratic presidential vote among whites without college degrees has declined by about six percentage points, while the average Democratic vote among white college graduates has *increased* by about 16 percentage points.[11] The consistent gap in voting behavior between these two groups evident in the 1950s and 1960s has disappeared since 1980, just as one might expect from the academic and journalistic literature on the declining significance of class in American electoral politics.

The changing pattern of voting behavior documented in figure 3.1 is both intriguing and important. However, for at least three reasons it should not be taken as evidence of a partisan realignment among white working-class cultural conservatives.

First, since the overall shift in voting behavior is both larger and more consistent among college graduates than among people without college degrees, it seems odd to portray the "working class" as the vanguard of whatever political development these changes are supposed to reflect. Second, it is important to bear in mind that the make-up of the two educational groups in figure 3.1 has changed markedly over the past half-century. For example, college graduates made up only 8% of the adult population in 1960 but 27% by 2003. (Meanwhile, the proportion of people without high school diplomas declined from 59% to 15%.)[12] Much of the change evident

[10] Data and documentation are publicly available from the NES Web site, http://www .electionstudies.org/. In presidential election years, the NES surveys have included pre-election interviews conducted between Labor Day and Election Day and post-election reinterviews with 85–90% of the pre-election respondents; in midterm years (except 2002) the surveys have included post-election interviews only. Most of the surveys have been conducted in respondents' homes by interviewers employed by the University of Michigan's Survey Research Center; however, some recent studies have also included interviews conducted by telephone. The survey samples are intended to be representative of citizens of voting age living in households in the continental United States (excluding Alaska and Hawaii). Since young people, racial and ethnic minorities, and males are underrepresented, my analyses throughout this book employ post-stratification weights constructed to reproduce the distribution of age, sex, and race/ethnicity reported by the Census Bureau for each election year. (Given the data available in the surveys and in Census Bureau tabulations, I am able to distinguish whites from nonwhites in 1952–1966, blacks from nonblacks in 1968–1978, and blacks, Hispanics, and others in 1980–2004.) My analyses of presidential voting behavior are additionally weighted to reproduce the actual two-party popular vote in each election, compensating for a slight exaggeration of support for the winning candidate in most years.

[11] Since comparing any two particular elections may be misleading due to election-specific idiosyncratic factors, these figures represent linear trends in the Democratic presidential vote for each group over the entire period from 1952 through 2004.

[12] U.S. Census Bureau, *Statistical Abstract of the United States: 2004–2005*, table no. 212, http://www.census.gov/prod/www/statistical-abstract-2001_2005.html.

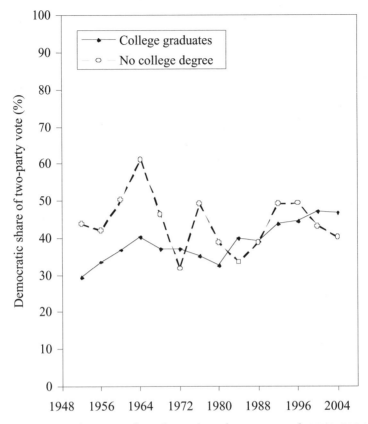

Figure 3.1 White Presidential Vote by Education Level, 1952–2004

in the figure may reflect these compositional changes in the electorate rather than actual partisan conversion.[13]

Finally, and most importantly, the lack of correspondence between formal education and concrete economic circumstances makes educational attainment

---

[13] Similar issues arise when people are categorized on the basis of their occupation (or a family member's occupation) as "working class" or "middle class." Textbook descriptions of a long-term decline in class voting (for example, Bibby 1996, 273–274; Hershey 2005, 123–125) frequently cite Abramson, Aldrich, and Rohde's quadrennial analyses of voting patterns among white manual workers and white-collar workers in support of the notion that "class differences are eroding" (Abramson, Aldrich, and Rohde 1994, 154; 2002, 115). However, these analyses are greatly complicated by major changes in the prevalence and social significance of "manual" and "white-collar" work, as well as by the proliferation of two-income households. To their credit, Abramson, Aldrich, and Rohde (2002, 115) have acknowledged that "our argument that class-based voting has declined depends on the way we have defined social class." They have also

problematic as a basis for identifying the "working class." Insisting on a definition that portrays a sizable majority of middle-income Americans (and many
who are even more affluent) as "working class" invites confusion and conflation
of exactly the sort reflected in Brooks's misleading depiction of the voting
behavior of "poorer folks" and Frank's references to the "puzzle" of growing
Republican allegiance among "the poor . . . the weak and the victimized."[14]

Ironically, Frank himself claimed to be interested in class differences "in
the material, economic sense, not in the tastes-and-values way our punditry defines class."[15] By that criterion, the most apt and straightforward
basis for measuring class status would seem to be family income. Of
course, absolute income, like educational attainment, has increased substantially since the 1950s. Moreover, it is easy to think of specific circumstances in which a person's current family income does not accurately
reflect her economic standing.[16] Nevertheless, as a general matter, it does
not seem implausible to suppose that people's *relative* positions in the *current* income distribution provide a meaningful, historically consistent indication of their class status.

In light of these considerations—and in keeping with my focus on the political causes and consequences of material *economic* inequality—my practice throughout this book is to categorize people's class status on the basis of
their family incomes relative to the overall distribution of incomes at any
given time. More specifically, the terms *low-income* and *working class* are
used interchangeably to refer to people with family incomes in the bottom
third of the income distribution in each election year. (In 2004, these families had incomes below $35,000.) Similarly, the terms *middle income* and

---

attempted, though sometimes only partially successfully, to document the complexities involved in
using crude and sometimes inconsistent occupational data to produce a consistent classification of
social class over a 50-year period. For example, in an explanatory note describing the data analysis
that led them to conclude that middle-class white voters were more Democratic than working-
class white voters in the 2000 presidential election, Abramson, Aldrich, and Rohde (2002, 292) explained that, "As the relatively small size of the working class in 2000 results largely from a
redefinition in the way our measure of class is constructed, in these estimates we will assume that
the sizes of the white working class and the white middle class were the same as in the 1996 NES."

[14] Frank (2004), 1.

[15] Ibid., 104. In a subsequent essay critiquing a preliminary version of the analysis reported
here, however, Frank (2005) advocated using educational status to define the "working class."
My published response (Bartels 2006b) presented statistical analyses paralleling those presented in this chapter, but with voters classified on the basis of educational status rather than
income. Although defining the white "working class" as people without college degrees does
produce a downward trend in Democratic support, Frank's interpretation of that trend as a
manifestation of cultural conservatism fares no better for people without college degrees than
for people with low incomes.

[16] The most obvious complexity is that current income may be an imperfect measure of economic status for retired people. I have replicated most of the analyses presented here excluding
NES respondents over the age of 65 and found no significant differences in the results.

middle class are used to refer to people with family incomes in the middle
third of the income distribution in each year (in 2004, $35,000 to $70,000)
and the term *high income* to refer to people with family incomes in the top
third of the income distribution in each year (in 2004, $70,000 or more).[17]

HAS THE WHITE WORKING CLASS ABANDONED
THE DEMOCRATIC PARTY?

The political significance of relying on income rather than education as the
basis for defining class is evident in figure 3.2, which summarizes the voting
behavior of low-income and high-income white voters in presidential elections since 1952. The solid line in this figure represents the Democratic share
of the two-party presidential vote among white voters in the bottom third of
the income distribution in each election year, while the dashed line shows the
corresponding vote share among white voters in the top third of the income
distribution.[18] A comparison of these two trend lines suggests a pattern precisely the opposite of the one in figure 3.1—a pattern not of convergence but
of marked divergence in the voting behavior of low- and high-income white
voters. In this light, the notion that working-class defections from the Democratic Party over the past 40 years have eroded the New Deal pattern of class
voting appears to be quite wrong on both counts—wrong about the old pattern and wrong about how it has evolved in recent decades.

With respect to the class cleavage of the New Deal era, figure 3.2 shows that
the gap in Democratic electoral strength between lower- and upper-income
groups was already quite modest by the 1950s. Averaging over the period from
1952 through 1972, Democratic presidential candidates garnered 46% of the
votes of whites in the bottom third of the income distribution, 47% of those in
the middle third, and 42% of those in the upper third. In only one of these six
elections (in 1964) did the gap in Democratic support between lower-income
whites and upper-income whites exceed six percentage points. In the two close
elections of 1960 and 1968, Democratic candidates actually did slightly better
among affluent white voters than among low-income white voters.

From 1976 through 2004, however, a strong and fairly consistent income
gradient was evident in the presidential voting behavior of white Americans.

[17] The exact proportions of the sample in each income group vary somewhat from year to
year due to the coarseness of the income categories employed in the NES surveys. In the 2004
survey, for example, 31.0% of the respondents reported family incomes of less than $35,000,
25.7% reported family incomes between $35,000 and $70,000, and 31.1% reported family incomes in excess of $70,000; the remaining 12.2% declined to report their income, and I have
not included them in any of the three income groups.
[18] The Democratic vote share for the middle third of the income distribution is omitted from
the figure for visual clarity, but it generally falls between those for the lower and upper thirds.

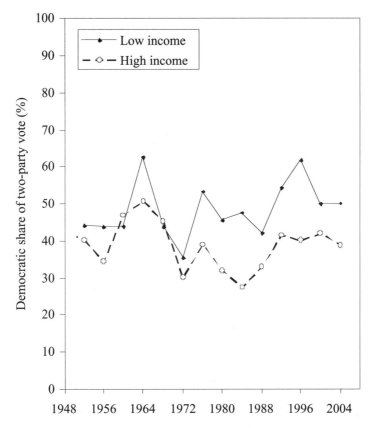

Figure 3.2 White Presidential Vote by Income Class, 1952–2004

Averaging over the eight presidential elections of that period, we find that whites in the bottom third of the income distribution cast 51% of their votes for Democrats, as compared with 44% of middle-income whites and 37% of upper-income whites. The gap in Democratic support between upper-income whites and lower-income whites thus increased from four percentage points in the earlier period to 14 percentage points after 1976. The 2004 election was, as it happens, quite consistent with the pattern since 1976: John Kerry received 50% of the two-party vote among whites in the lower third of the income distribution and 39% among those in the upper third of the income distribution—a difference of 11 percentage points.

It should be clear from these comparisons that over the past half-century economic status has become more important, not less important, in structuring the presidential voting behavior of white Americans. Moreover, the general trend in support for Democratic presidential candidates among whites in the bottom third of the income distribution has been upward, not downward. Nor is this merely an artifact of anemic working-class support for Adlai Stevenson running against Dwight Eisenhower in the first two elections of this sequence; Al Gore and John Kerry did better among low-income whites in the close elections of 2000 and 2004 than John Kennedy and Hubert Humphrey did in the close elections of 1960 and 1968. While Democratic presidential candidates have lost significant support among white voters over the past half-century, those losses have been entirely concentrated among relatively affluent white voters—and they have been partially offset by *increasing* support for Democratic candidates among poorer white voters.

A similar pattern of class divergence appears in survey data on partisan attachments. Figure 3.3 shows the trends in party identification for whites in the top and bottom thirds of the income distribution in NES surveys from 1952 through 2004.[19] Here, too, the income gap has increased, not decreased. In the early 1950s the Democratic margin in party identification was 11 percentage points greater among poor whites than among affluent whites. By the end of the period, that gap had doubled.

Of course, there is an important difference between the patterns in figures 3.2 and 3.3: while the gap in Democratic presidential votes between low-income and high-income whites has increased substantially over the past half-century, there is rather little evidence of any overall shift in the partisan division of the vote. Over the entire period, the decline in the Democratic share of the two-party presidential vote amounted to a little more than two percentage points. By comparison, the Republican trend in party identification has been much more pronounced. Through the 1950s and 1960s, the Democrats enjoyed a small but consistent plurality in partisan attachments among whites in the top third of the income distribution and an even larger plurality among those in the bottom third of the income distribution. However, by 2004 Democrats outnumbered Republicans by only four percentage points among low-income whites, while Republicans outnumbered Democrats by 18 percentage points among high-income whites.

Simply focusing on the decline in net Democratic identification among low-income whites—from 22% in 1952 to 4% in 2004—would seem to confirm Brooks's claim that "we've seen poorer folks move over in astonishing numbers to the G.O.P." However, it seems odd to attribute the Democrats' problems to the white working class when the corresponding declines among middle- and high-income whites are about twice as large—36% and 32%, respectively.[20]

---

[19] These data represent the entire adult population, not just the major-party presidential voters represented in figures 3.1 and 3.2.

[20] Imposing linear trends over the entire 52-year period implies declines of 17.7% (with a standard error of 2.6%) for low-income whites, 35.7% (with a standard error of 2.5%) for middle-income whites, and 31.5% (with a standard error of 2.4%) for high-income whites.

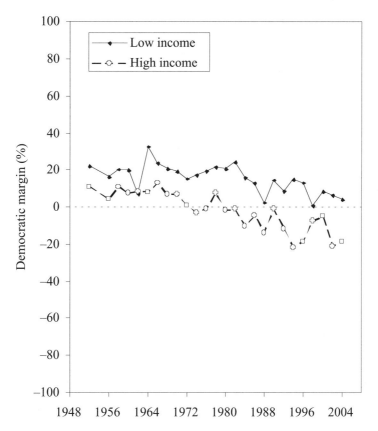

Figure 3.3 White Party Identification by Income Class, 1952–2004

In any case, the decline in Democratic identification among low-income whites in figure 3.3 is hardly the broad national phenomenon one might expect on the basis of Frank's book and similar accounts. Indeed, to a good approximation, the net decline in Democratic identification among poor whites over the past half-century is *entirely* attributable to the demise of the Solid South as a bastion of Democratic allegiance. That fact is evident from figure 3.4, which provides a comparison of trends in party identification for low-income whites in the South and in the rest of the country.[21]

---

[21] I employ the U.S. Census Bureau's regional classification, in which the South includes the 11 former Confederate states plus Delaware, Kentucky, Maryland, Oklahoma, West Virginia, and the District of Columbia. Focusing only on the former Confederate states would make the regional disparities described in the text look even larger.

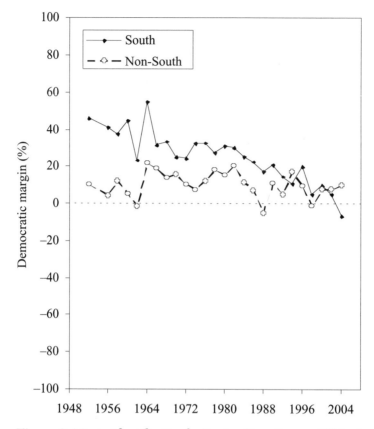

Figure 3.4 Party Identification by Region (Low-Income Whites), 1952–2004

The South has seen a massive, fairly steady decline in net Democratic identification over the entire half-century, from 46% (a 65–19 Democratic margin) in 1952 to −6% (a 38–32 Republican margin) in 2004. However, outside the South there is no evident trend in party identification among low-income whites. Indeed, a simple comparison of beginning and end points shows that Democrats outnumbered Republicans among low-income whites outside the South by exactly the same 10 percentage points in 2004 (a 31–21 Democratic margin) as in 1952 (a 41–31 Democratic margin).

While the erosion of Democratic identification among low-income whites is entirely concentrated in the South, the growing disparity in Democratic attachments between poor whites and more affluent whites appears clearly

TABLE 3.1

Trends in White Democratic Party Identification by Region and Income Class,
1952–2004

Cumulative changes in Democratic margin of party identification, measured by linear trends
(with standard errors in parentheses; data are clustered by election year).

	Total (N=38,163)	South (N=11,120)	Non-South (N=26,027)
Total (N=38,163)	−28.1 (2.3)	−65.7 (3.0)	−13.3 (2.9)
High income (N=13,085)	−31.5 (3.4)	−83.3 (4.5)	−15.1 (4.2)
Middle income (N=11,809)	−35.7 (4.4)	−75.7 (6.8)	−22.0 (4.7)
Low income (N=10,660)	−17.7 (3.2)	−42.8 (4.8)	−4.4 (3.9)

Source: Calculations based on data from 1952–2004 National Election Study surveys.

both in the South and in the rest of the country. The tabulations presented
in table 3.1 indicate that net Democratic identification declined almost
twice as fast among middle- and high-income white southerners as among
low-income white southerners between 1952 and 2004. Outside the South
the disparity was even greater, with net Democratic identification declining
three to five times as fast in the middle- and high-income groups as in the
low-income group.

These class disparities in Democratic fortunes are striking, and contrary to much conventional wisdom. The distinctive trends in Democratic allegiance between the South and the rest of the country are even
more striking: net Democratic identification declined by 13 percentage
points outside the South but by 66 percentage points within that region.
The sources of that regional transformation are not hard to identify. In
the 1950s the historical legacy of the Civil War and the contemporary
reality of Jim Crow racial politics still submerged class differences
among southern whites in a system of "unquestioning attachment, by
overwhelming majorities, to the Democratic party nationally," as V. O.
Key Jr. put it in his classic 1949 survey of southern politics.[22] As dramatic policy shifts by national Democratic Party leaders on civil rights
issues—and suburbanization, desegregation, and intensive electoral mobilization of both blacks and whites—eroded that system, the anomalous pattern of partisanship in the South gradually but relentlessly gave
way to a pattern not too dissimilar from the one prevailing in the rest of
the country.

Presidential voting patterns have also changed significantly over the past
half-century, though the magnitudes of the shifts in voting behavior are a good

[22] Key (1949), 11.

TABLE 3.2
Trends in White Democratic Presidential Vote by Region and Income Class,
1952–2004

Cumulative changes in Democratic percentage of major-party presidential votes, measured
by linear trends (with standard errors in parentheses; data are clustered by election year).

	Total (N = 13,658)	South (N = 3,488)	Non-South (N = 10,170)
Total (N = 13,658)	−2.4 (4.2)	−15.5 (4.6)	+2.5 (4.8)
High income (N = 5,359)	−5.3 (4.1)	−20.4 (6.4)	−0.4 (4.2)
Middle income (N = 4,196)	−6.1 (5.7)	−18.2 (6.7)	−1.8 (6.2)
Low income (N = 3,315)	+6.4 (4.6)	−6.3 (6.1)	+12.1 (5.5)

Source: Calculations based on data from 1952–2004 National Election Study surveys.

deal smaller than for partisan identification. The tabulation presented in table 3.2
shows that Democratic presidential candidates lost from 12 to 14 percentage
points more among middle- and high-income white voters than among low-
income white voters, with similar class disparities evident in the South and in
the rest of the country. Within each income group, Democratic presidential
candidates lost from 16 to 20 percentage points more in the South than outside the South. Indeed, the Democratic presidential vote declined by a total of
15 percentage points among white southerners but actually increased by two
percentage points among whites in the rest of the country.

Although tons of ink have been devoted to the demise of the Democratic
Party's New Deal coalition, remarkably few analysts seem to have noticed
that the net decline in support for Democratic presidential candidates
among white voters over the past half-century is *entirely* attributable to partisan change in the South. It is equally notable, in light of the alleged aban-
donment of the Democratic Party by working-class cultural conservatives,
that white voters in the bottom third of the income distribution have actually become *more loyal* in their support of Democratic presidential candidates over this period. Republican gains have come not among "poorer
folks" but among middle- and upper-income voters—and even those gains
have been concentrated almost entirely in the South.

HAVE WORKING-CLASS WHITES BECOME MORE CONSERVATIVE?

One common explanation for the electoral success of Republican candidates over the past four decades is that the white working class has become
increasingly conservative in its political outlook. Some observers credit this
shift to the ideological conviction and small-town charm of Ronald Reagan. Others see it as a reaction to the racial and cultural upheaval of the

1960s. According to Thomas and Mary Edsall, the conservative shift is due to "hostility to expanding government intervention." For Thomas Frank, much of the fault lies with "Democrats [who] no longer speak to the people on the losing end" of the free-market system, leaving themselves "vulnerable to cultural wedge issues like guns and abortion and the rest whose hallucinatory appeal would ordinarily be far overshadowed by material concerns."[23]

Unfortunately, characterizations of this sort are seldom based on systematic analysis of the political views of ordinary citizens. It is tempting to imagine that significant shifts in elite ideology and rhetoric must have their parallels in the public. However, the truth of the matter is that mass opinion often bears rather little connection to the tidy ideological landscape that political elites take for granted.[24] Thus, while ideological debate among elected officials and public intellectuals does seem to have shifted significantly to the right over the past 30 years, it is far from obvious that the political views of ordinary citizens have become noticeably more conservative.

Here I examine whether the policy preferences of low-income whites have indeed become more conservative, either in absolute terms or by comparison with more affluent white citizens. I begin by considering responses to two policy questions asked repeatedly in National Election Study surveys since 1972. The first of these questions focuses on the general issue of government activism stressed by Edsall and Edsall, asking whether "the government should see to it that every person has a job and a good standard of living."[25] The second question focuses on the preeminent cultural "wedge issue" of the past three decades: the circumstances, if any, under which abortion should be legal.[26] Figures 3.5 and 3.6, respectively, present opinion readings for these two issues in each year in which the questions were

[23] Edsall and Edsall (1991), 154; Frank (2004), 245.

[24] The most forceful and influential demonstration of this fact is an essay by Philip Converse, now more than 40 years old, on "The Nature of Belief Systems in Mass Publics" (Converse 1964).

[25] "Some people feel that the government in Washington should see to it that every person has a job and a good standard of living. Others think the government should just let each person get ahead on his own. Where would you place yourself on this scale, or haven't you thought much about this?" Responses on the seven-point scale are recoded to range from −1 for "just let each person get ahead on his own" to +1 for "see to it that every person has a job and a good standard of living."

[26] "There has been some discussion about abortion during recent years. Which one of the opinions on this page best agrees with your view? 1. By law, abortion should never be permitted. 2. The law should permit abortion only in case of rape, incest, or when the woman's life is in danger. 3. The law should permit abortion for reasons other than rape, incest, or danger to the woman's life, but only after the need for the abortion has been clearly established. 4. By law, a woman should always be able to obtain an abortion as a matter of personal choice." Responses are recoded to range from −1 for "abortion should never be permitted" to +1 for "a matter of personal choice." The question wording employed in NES surveys before 1980 was

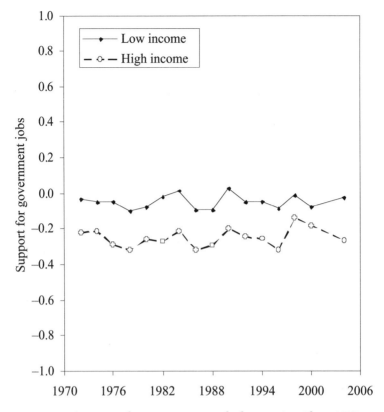

Figure 3.5 Support for Government Jobs by Income Class, 1972–2004 (Whites Only)

included in the NES survey.[27] Each figure shows average opinions for whites in the bottom third of the income distribution and, for purposes of comparison, average opinions for whites in the top third of the income distribution.[28]

There is no evidence of a significant conservative shift since the early 1970s, either among low-income whites or among high-income whites, on either of the issues for which the NES surveys provide consistent repeated

---

slightly different but produced a quite similar distribution of responses when both versions were used in 1980, so I have combined responses to both versions to produce the trend lines in figure 3.6.

[27] The abortion item was omitted from the 1974 and 2002 NES surveys. The government jobs question was also omitted in 2002.

[28] In each case, the average opinions of middle-income whites (not shown in the figures) consistently fall between those of the low- and high-income groups.

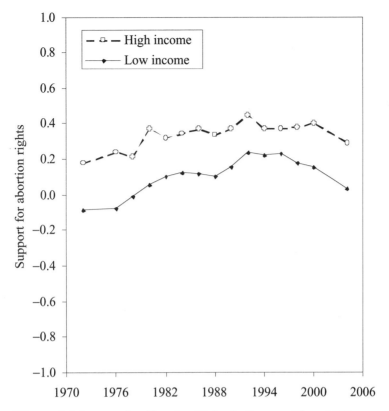

Figure 3.6 Support for Abortion Rights by Income Class, 1972–2004 (Whites Only)

readings. For the question about government jobs and income support, figure 3.5 shows a gap in views by income level, with poorer whites less conservative than affluent whites; but no trend is evident in the opinions of either group. For abortion, figure 3.6 does show discernible movement, with both income groups becoming more liberal (pro-choice) from the early 1970s through 1992 and more conservative (pro-life) thereafter. The net result of these shifts left both groups modestly more liberal in 2004 than they had been in the 1970s. However, the relative positions of the two income groups remained quite stable throughout this period, with low-income whites consistently less supportive of abortion rights than more affluent whites were.

What is most apparent in these figures is the consistent moderation of low-income whites by comparison with more affluent whites. On the issue of government jobs, where the balance of opinion among affluent whites has been conservative, low-income whites are less conservative. On the issue of abortion rights, where most affluent whites have been liberal, low-income whites are less liberal.[29] Given these consistent patterns, it strains credibility to cast the American working class in the vanguard of an ideological "backlash" of any sort. More generally, these figures contradict the notion that low-income whites have become more conservative over the past three decades. For that matter, it is hard to find much evidence of significant ideological movement in any income group on these two issues, aside from the gradual rise and (partial) fall of support for abortion rights evident in figure 3.6.

In addition to the questions on government jobs and abortion tracked in figures 3.5 and 3.6, four other issue questions have appeared consistently in NES surveys since 1984; these questions focus on government spending and services,[30] defense spending,[31] aid to blacks,[32] and the appropriate social role of women.[33] Table 3.3 summarizes movement on each of these issues from 1984 to 2004.[34] Over that period, the only issue on which there has been a substantial conservative shift in average opinion is defense spending; within

[29] In part, these patterns are an artifact of my coding of issue positions, which treats "don't know" and "haven't thought" responses as equivalent to middle-of-the-road positions. Since working-class whites are somewhat more likely than affluent whites to offer those responses, they are more likely to be placed at the middle of the issue scales. More importantly, however, they are also simply more likely to choose middle-of-the-road positions on these and other issues.

[30] "Some people think the government should provide fewer services, even in areas such as health and education, in order to reduce spending. Other people feel that it is important for the government to provide many more services even if it means an increase in spending. Where would you place yourself on this scale, or haven't you thought much about this?" Responses on the seven-point scale are recoded to range from −1 for "government should provide many fewer services; reduce spending a lot" to +1 for "government provide many more services; increase spending a lot."

[31] "Some people believe that we should spend much less money for defense. Others feel that defense spending should be greatly increased. Where would you place yourself on this scale, or haven't you thought much about this?" Responses on the seven-point scale are recoded to range from −1 for "greatly increase defense spending" to +1 for "greatly decrease defense spending."

[32] "Some people feel that the government in Washington should make every possible effort to improve the social and economic position of blacks. Others feel that the government should not make any special effort to help blacks because they should help themselves. Where would you place yourself on this scale, or haven't you thought much about it?" Responses on the seven-point scale are recoded to range from −1 for "blacks should help themselves" to +1 for "government should help blacks."

[33] "Recently, there has been a lot of talk about women's rights. Some people feel that women should have an equal role with men in running business, industry, and government. Others feel that women's place is in the home. Where would you place yourself on this scale, or haven't you thought much about this?" Responses on the seven-point scale are recoded to range from −1 for "women's place is in the home" to +1 for "women and men should have an equal role."

[34] As with the shifts in party identification and voting behavior summarized in tables 3.1 and 3.2, the shifts in issue positions reported in table 3.3 represent linear trends over the entire 20-year period rather than a comparison of the first and last elections alone.

TABLE 3.3
Shifts in Issue Preferences of White Voters by Income Class, 1984–2004

Cumulative changes in average issue positions (with standard errors in parentheses). Positive numbers indicate liberal trends; negative numbers indicate conservative trends. Data are clustered by election year; white major-party presidential voters only.

	High income	Middle income	Low income
Government services (−1 to +1)	+.10 (.04)	+.08 (.05)	+.08 (.06)
Defense spending (−1 to +1)	−.22 (.10)	−.24 (.10)	−.20 (.07)
Government jobs (−1 to +1)	+.01 (.05)	−.01 (.07)	+.00 (.05)
Abortion (−1 to +1)	−.02 (.03)	−.03 (.02)	−.09 (.07)
Aid to blacks (−1 to +1)	−.15 (.07)	−.08 (.09)	−.08 (.07)
Women's role (−1 to +1)	+.13 (.10)	+.15 (.11)	+.28 (.10)
N	2,015	1,688	1,176

Source: Calculations based on data from 1984–2004 National Election Study surveys.

each of the three income groups, that shift amounts to about one-tenth of the total length of the opinion scale. A smaller conservative shift occurred on the issue of aid to blacks, especially among the most affluent white voters. Meanwhile, *liberal* shifts in average opinion are evident on the issue of government services and, more dramatically, on the issue of gender roles. The largest single shift reported in the table—for low-income white voters on the issue of gender roles—left them considerably more liberal in 2004 than they had been in 1984.

As is true of the longer trends in issue preferences depicted in figures 3.5 and 3.6, it would be very difficult to interpret the shifts reported in table 3.3 as evidence of any broad ideological movement in the American electorate. White voters have developed a somewhat greater appetite for defense spending in recent years; but on the core economic and cultural issues at the center of contemporary elite debate—most notably, government spending and abortion—there is very little evidence of significant changes in mass opinion, whether we focus specifically on the white working class or on the views of the white electorate more generally.

DO "MORAL VALUES" TRUMP ECONOMICS?

Even if white working-class voters have not become more conservative in recent decades, they may *seem* more conservative—and vote more Republican—because Republicans have succeeded in shifting the focus of political debate from economic issues, where low-income voters are generally relatively liberal (as in figure 3.5), to cultural issues, where they are generally relatively conservative (as in figure 3.6). According to

Thomas Frank, "backlash leaders systematically downplay the politics of economics. The movement's basic premise is that culture outweighs economics as a matter of public concern—that *Values Matter Most*, as one backlash title has it. On those grounds it rallies citizens who would once have been reliable partisans of the New Deal to the standard of conservatism."[35]

This account suggests that white working-class voters have reluctantly accepted economic conservatism as part of a package deal because, given the current configuration of the American party system, that has been the only effective way for them to pursue cultural conservatism. But is that account consistent with observed patterns in voting behavior? Do working-class voters attach more weight to cultural issues than they used to? Do they attach more weight to cultural issues than to economic issues? For that matter, do they attach more weight to cultural issues than higher-income voters do?

Each of those questions can be explored by examining the relationship between issue preferences and presidential votes over the past two decades. The three columns of table 3.4 report the results of separate statistical analyses of presidential voting behavior for white voters in the top, middle, and bottom thirds of the income distribution.[36] Each column shows how voters in the corresponding income class weighed each of the six issues that have appeared consistently in NES surveys since 1984.[37]

These results provide no support for the notion that contemporary American politics is primarily driven by cultural issues. Among white voters in all three income groups, the two issues most strongly related to presidential vote choices are government spending and services and defense spending. The preeminent cultural issue, abortion, ranks fourth among upper- and middle-income white voters and fifth among those in the bottom third of the income distribution. The combined weight attached to the two purely economic issues in the table—government spending and services and government jobs and income maintenance—exceeds the weight attached to the cultural issues of abortion and women's role by almost 50% for voters in the bottom third of the income distribution and by more than 100% for those in

[35] Frank (2004), 6.

[36] It would be unrealistic to assume that the choices of the individual voters surveyed in any given election year were statistically independent. In order to avoid conveying a misleading impression of statistical precision, all of my analyses of survey data from multiple election years are clustered to allow for arbitrary correlations among the disturbances for voters surveyed in the same year.

[37] In addition to voters' views on the six policy issues, each analysis includes separate intercepts for each election year (not reported in the table) to capture election-specific considerations unrelated to these policy views, such as economic conditions, scandals, and the personal qualities of the competing candidates.

TABLE 3.4
Issue Preferences and Presidential Votes by Income Class, 1984–2004

Probit parameter estimates (with standard errors in parentheses) for probability of Democratic presidential vote. Data are clustered by election year; separate intercepts for each income class in each election year are not shown; white major-party voters only.

	High income	Middle income	Low income
Government services (−1 to +1)	1.08 (.10)	.86 (.06)	.52 (.17)
Defense spending (−1 to +1)	1.00 (.14)	.79 (.14)	.83 (.15)
Government jobs (−1 to +1)	.52 (.05)	.54 (.09)	.31 (.08)
Abortion (−1 to +1)	.47 (.10)	.43 (.07)	.23 (.10)
Aid to blacks (−1 to +1)	.35 (.11)	.18 (.06)	.18 (.08)
Women's role (−1 to +1)	.25 (.07)	.23 (.10)	.33 (.08)
Log likelihood	−915.4	−865.0	−684.2
Pseudo-R^2	.31	.25	.16
N	2,015	1,688	1,176

Source: Calculations based on data from 1984–2004 National Election Study surveys.

the upper- and middle-income groups. It would be very difficult to conclude from these results that "culture outweighs economics as a matter of public concern."[38]

The analyses presented in table 3.4 include voters in every presidential election since 1984. Thus, they shed light on the political importance of six salient issues over the half-dozen most recent presidential elections. However, they do not address the question of whether cultural issues have increased in absolute or relative importance over that period. The analyses presented in table 3.5 do address that question by allowing for changes in the apparent weights attached to each of the six issues in the voting decisions of each income group. The entries in the top half of the table show the estimated changes in the weights attached to each issue by high-, middle-, and low-income voters between 1984 and 2004.[39] The entries in the bottom half of the table show the resulting weights for each issue in each income group at the end of this period.

[38] Frank (2004), 6.

[39] The probit parameter estimates reported in the top half of table 3.5 are for interaction terms constructed by multiplying each issue position by a linear trend variable ranging from zero in 1984 to one in 2004. The parameter estimates in the bottom half of the table represent the main effects of issue positions in a probit analysis including interaction terms constructed by multiplying each issue position by a complementary linear trend variable ranging from one in 1984 to zero in 2004. (These two versions of the analysis are mathematically equivalent, except that the parameter estimates for the interaction terms have opposite signs, and the main effects represent 1984 issue weights in the first version and 2004 issue weights in the second version.)

TABLE 3.5
Change in Weight of Issue Preferences by Income Class, 1984–2004

Probit parameter estimates (with standard errors in parentheses) for probability of Democratic presidential vote. Data are clustered by election year; separate intercepts for each income class in each election year are not shown; white major-party voters only.

	High income	Middle income	Low income
Change in weight, 1984–2004			
Government services	+.09 (.31)	+.15 (.23)	+.19 (.31)
Defense spending	−.11 (.50)	+.55 (.35)	+.29 (.37)
Government jobs	−.02 (.10)	+.41 (.19)	+.11 (.14)
Abortion	+.64 (.06)	+.44 (.12)	+.03 (.35)
Aid to blacks	−.04 (.29)	+.02 (.26)	+.15 (.19)
Women's role	+.42 (.27)	+.11 (.23)	+.29 (.20)
Weight in 2004			
Government services	1.14 (.25)	.96 (.16)	.60 (.19)
Defense spending	.96 (.36)	1.13 (.29)	.99 (.27)
Government jobs	.51 (.08)	.75 (.14)	.37 (.12)
Abortion	.78 (.03)	.65 (.04)	.24 (.21)
Aid to blacks	.32 (.16)	.18 (.18)	.25 (.09)
Women's role	.50 (.21)	.32 (.18)	.49 (.15)
Log likelihood	−903.6	−855.2	−681.6
Pseudo-R²	.32	.26	.16
N	2,015	1,688	1,176

Source: Calculations based on data from 1984–2004 National Election Study surveys.

The estimated changes in issue weights in table 3.5 are mostly positive rather than negative, suggesting that the relationship between policy preferences and presidential votes has generally become stronger over the past 20 years, especially for middle- and low-income white voters. The increases are particularly notable for the cultural issues included in the analysis, abortion and women's role. In that sense, at least, the notion that "moral values" have become increasingly prominent in contemporary politics is nicely borne out by the survey evidence.

However, the general pattern of issue weights at the end of this period, in the bottom half of table 3.5, continues to suggest that economic issues are considerably more consequential than cultural issues. Even in 2004, the issue of government spending and services was the weightiest of the five domestic policy issues among each of the three income groups; and the combined weight of government services and government jobs exceeded the combined weight of abortion and women's role in every income group. Thus, while contemporary American politics is *increasingly* about cultural issues, it continues to be *primarily* about economic issues.

The other important pattern to note in table 3.5 is that the increase in issue weights for cultural issues over the past 20 years is largest among high-income voters, not among low-income voters. This disparity is especially apparent in the case of abortion, which became vastly more important among affluent white voters but showed little or no increase in importance among those in the bottom third of the income distribution. Contrary to much elite rhetoric regarding the partisan significance of "moral values," the rise of cultural issues has mostly affected relatively affluent (and culturally liberal) white voters, *not* culturally conservative low-income whites.

The analyses presented in tables 3.4 and 3.5 are obviously limited by the fact that only six issues have been included consistently in NES surveys over the past 20 years. Perhaps the real action in contemporary American politics is in "cultural wedge issues" that were not even salient in the 1980s. Fortunately, the 2004 NES survey covered a much broader range of issues, including several that have loomed large in recent discussions of class politics and voting behavior, such as gay marriage,[40] immigration,[41] gun control,[42] school vouchers,[43] and the death penalty.[44] Table 3.6 provides a list of all 15 issues included in the 2004 survey. The table also shows the results of a statistical procedure, factor analysis, which combines respondents' positions on these 15 distinct issues into three summary scales reflecting policy preferences in the general domains of economic policy, cultural policy, and security policy.[45]

Each of the three resulting issue scales is a weighted average of responses to all 15 issue questions; however, the scoring weights reported in the table show that each issue scale mostly reflects responses to a handful of substantively related issue questions. For example, the economic issue

[40] "Should same-sex couples be allowed to marry, or do you think they should not be allowed to marry?"

[41] "Do you think the number of immigrants from foreign countries who are permitted to come to the United States to live should be increased a lot, increased a little, left the same as it is now, decreased a little, or decreased a lot?"

[42] "Do you think the federal government should make it more difficult for people to buy a gun than it is now, make it easier for people to buy a gun, or keep these rules about the same as they are now? A lot [more difficult/easier] or somewhat [more difficult/easier]?"

[43] "Do you favor or oppose having the government give parents in low-income families money to help pay for their children to attend a private or religious school instead of their local public school? Do you [favor/oppose] it strongly or not strongly?"

[44] "Do you favor or oppose the death penalty for persons convicted of murder? Strongly or not strongly?"

[45] The factor analysis reported in table 3.6 includes a promax rotation, which allows for correlated issue preferences across the three domains. Not surprisingly, these correlations turn out to be substantial: .65 for economic and cultural issues, .58 for cultural and security issues, and .57 for economic and security issues.

TABLE 3.6

Structure of Issue Preferences, 2004

Scoring weights based on factor analysis of issue preferences; promax rotation. $N=609$ (white major-party presidential voters only).

	Economic issue scale	Cultural issue scale	Security issue scale
Government services	**.173**	.036	−.018
Health care	**.161**	.028	−.005
Government jobs	**.158**	−.003	.050
Social Security privatization	.077	.020	.000
Environmental protection	.067	**.100**	.042
Abortion	.015	**.177**	−.025
Women's role	.008	**.163**	.005
Gay marriage	.006	**.131**	.039
School vouchers	.052	.060	−.058
Military intervention	.046	**.139**	**.124**
Aid to blacks	.054	.012	**.162**
Immigration	−.060	.014	**.161**
Death penalty	.024	−.023	**.118**
Gun control	.047	.044	.050
Defense spending	.053	.049	**.143**

Economic issue scale: mean = .008; standard deviation = .322.
Cultural issue scale: mean = .157; standard deviation = .360.
Security issue scale: mean = −.185; standard deviation = .298.
Source: Calculations based on data from 2004 National Election Study survey.

scale predominantly reflects responses to the questions about government spending and services, health care,[46] government jobs, and Social Security privatization.[47] The cultural issue scale puts substantial weight on responses to questions about abortion, women's role, gay marriage, and the environment,[48]

[46] "There is much concern about the rapid rise in medical and hospital costs. Some people feel there should be a government insurance plan which would cover all medical and hospital expenses for everyone. Others feel that all medical expenses should be paid by individuals through private insurance plans like Blue Cross or other company paid plans. Where would you place yourself on this scale, or haven't you thought much about this?"

[47] "A proposal has been made that would allow people to put a portion of their Social Security payroll taxes into personal retirement accounts that would be invested in private stocks and bonds. Do you favor this idea, oppose it, or neither favor nor oppose it? Do you [favor/oppose] it strongly or not strongly?"

[48] "Some people think it is important to protect the environment even if it costs some jobs or otherwise reduces our standard of living. Other people think that protecting the environment is not as important as maintaining jobs and our standard of living. Where would you place yourself on this scale, or haven't you thought much about this?"

TABLE 3.7

Issue Preferences and Presidential Votes by Income Class, 2004

Probit parameter estimates (with standard errors in parentheses) for probability of Democratic presidential vote. White major-party voters only.

	High income	Middle income	Low income
Economic issue scale (−1 to +1)	2.37 (.66)	2.63 (.59)	2.74 (.62)
Cultural issue scale (−1 to +1)	2.66 (.56)	1.41 (.55)	1.17 (.45)
Security issue scale (−1 to +1)	1.39 (.65)	1.80 (.67)	1.19 (.53)
Intercept	−.60 (.25)	−.19 (.23)	−.26 (.18)
Log likelihood	−55.4	−61.8	−72.2
Pseudo-R²	.60	.51	.35
N	208	184	160

Source: Calculations based on data from 2004 National Election Study survey.

as well as a question about military intervention.[49] The question about military intervention also gets substantial weight in the security issues scale, along with questions on defense spending, immigration, aid to blacks, and the death penalty.

Summarizing each NES survey respondent's detailed issue preferences in these three more general issue scales facilitates the task of weighing which issues were most strongly related to voting behavior in the 2004 presidential election. Table 3.7 presents the results of statistical analyses paralleling those in table 3.4, but with presidential vote choices related to voters' positions on the three summary issue scales rather than specific issue questions. As in table 3.4, the analyses are presented separately for white voters in the top, middle, and bottom thirds of the income distribution.

Reading across the first row of table 3.7, the statistical results indicate that economic issues have had a substantial, and roughly similar, impact on the voting behavior of high-, middle-, and low-income white voters. However, cultural issues seem to have had a much more differentiated impact. White voters in the top third of the income distribution attached as much or more weight to cultural issues as to economic issues; in contrast, those in the bottom third of the income distribution attached less than half as much weight to cultural issues. (Middle-income voters fell between these two extremes but were much closer to low-income voters than to high-income voters.) Indeed, among working-class white voters the apparent weight of economic issues in the

[49]"Some people believe the United States should solve international problems by using diplomacy and other forms of international pressure and use military force only if absolutely necessary. Others believe diplomacy and pressure often fail and the U.S. must be ready to use military force. Where would you place yourself on this scale, or haven't you thought much about this?"

2004 election exceeded the *combined* weight of cultural and security issues. For these people—contrary to Frank's account—the "hallucinatory appeal" of "cultural wedge issues like guns and abortion and the rest" continues to be "far overshadowed by material concerns" of the sort reflected in responses to the NES questions about government spending and services, health care, and jobs.

ARE RELIGIOUS VOTERS DISTRACTED
FROM ECONOMIC ISSUES?

The statistical analyses reported in table 3.5 suggest that cultural issues have become more important factors in presidential voting behavior over the past 20 years—but primarily for affluent white voters rather than those in the middle and bottom of the income distribution. Similarly, in table 3.7 cultural issues appear to have received a good deal more weight in the 2004 presidential election from high-income white voters than from middle- or low-income white voters. These results suggest that the emphasis in recent political commentary on working-class cultural conservatism is largely misplaced.

The dramatic rise of the "religious right" in contemporary American politics suggests, however, that cultural conservatism may be crucial to recent Republican successes, even if *working-class* cultural conservatism is not.[50] After all, religious observance in America is by no means limited to the working class; in fact, church attendance is slightly more common among affluent people than among those with lower incomes. Perhaps Thomas Frank's account of deluded cultural conservatives is essentially correct, except that the people who are being distracted from economic issues by the "flamboyant public piety" of "grandstanding Christers" come more or less equally from all parts of the economic spectrum.[51]

The potential political significance of religious observance is underlined by the fact that a sizeable partisan gap has developed between people who frequently attend religious services and those who rarely or never do. That fact is evident from figure 3.7, which compares the presidential votes of white voters who attend religious services once a month or less and those who attend almost every week or more. (Over the entire half-century covered by the NES surveys, the latter group includes 41% of the total NES sample and 48% of white presidential voters; by 2004 the percentages had shrunk to 34% and 37%, respectively.)

---

[50] Leege et al. (2002) provided a rich account of contemporary cultural politics, with a particular focus on religious developments in chapter 10.

[51] Frank (2004), 71, 136.

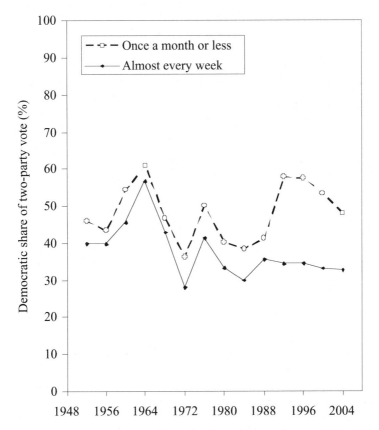

Figure 3.7 White Presidential Vote by Church Attendance, 1952–2004

From 1952 through 1988 there was a small and quite consistent gap in voting behavior between frequent and infrequent churchgoers, with the infrequent attendees being slightly more Democratic. That gap widened dramatically in 1992, and although it has narrowed somewhat in the two most recent presidential elections, it remains substantial. In 2004, President Bush enjoyed a two-to-one margin among white voters who attended religious services regularly but only a four-point (52–48) margin among those who attended infrequently.

Has the increasing political significance of cultural issues in recent elections contributed to the partisan cleavage between frequent and infrequent churchgoers? Conversely, have religious values and institutions contributed to the growing political relevance of cultural issues among American voters? In order to address those questions I compared the effects of specific political issues on the presidential vote choices of frequent

TABLE 3.8
Issue Preferences and Presidential Votes by Religiosity, 1984–2004

Probit parameter estimates (with standard errors in parentheses) for probability of Democratic presidential vote. Frequent churchgoers said they attended religious services every week or almost every week. Highly religious people said religion provides "a great deal" of guidance in their day-to-day living. Data are clustered by election year; separate intercepts for each group in each election year are not shown; white major-party voters only.

	Infrequent churchgoers	Frequent churchgoers	Highly religious
Government services (−1 to +1)	.82 (.06)	.97 (.06)	.82 (.11)
Defense spending (−1 to +1)	.92 (.10)	.78 (.13)	.64 (.11)
Government jobs (−1 to +1)	.53 (.05)	.38 (.04)	.35 (.05)
Abortion (−1 to +1)	.30 (.06)	.34 (.05)	.41 (.07)
Aid to blacks (−1 to +1)	.30 (.06)	.13 (.11)	.19 (.08)
Women's role (−1 to +1)	.17 (.06)	.20 (.05)	.18 (.03)
Log likelihood	−1,625.1	−1,166.1	−921.1
Pseudo-R^2	.25	.19	.18
N	3,118	2,272	1,798

Source: Calculations based on data from 1984–2004 National Election Study surveys.

and infrequent churchgoers. The analyses reported in table 3.8 focus on the relationship between policy views and voting behavior in all six presidential elections from 1984 through 2004. The results presented in the first column of the table are for white voters who attended religious services "once or twice a month" or less (59% of all white voters). The second column shows the corresponding relationship among those who attended religious services "every week" or "almost every week" (41% of all white voters). The third column focuses on a somewhat more selective group, the one-third of white voters who said religion provides "a great deal" of guidance in their day-to-day lives.

Comparing the estimated issue weights for infrequent churchgoers (in the first column of the table) with those for frequent churchgoers (in the second column) suggests that frequent churchgoers probably attached more weight to cultural issues. However, these differences are small, and they are dwarfed by the differences across issues within the group of frequent churchgoers. For example, even among white voters who said they attended religious services every week or almost every week, abortion received less weight than government spending and services, defense spending, and government jobs; and the two cultural issues (abortion and gender roles) received less than half as much combined weight as the two purely economic issues (government services and government jobs). Even white voters who said that religion provided a great deal of guidance in their daily lives attached only half as much weight to abortion as they did to government spending and services, and only half as much weight to gender roles as to government jobs. These differences underline the predominance of economic issues, not cultural issues, even among those white voters who were most likely to be influenced by religious communities and values.

One cultural issue—abortion—has become a much more important consideration in voting behavior over the past 20 years. That is hardly surprising, given the increasing consistency with which Democratic and Republican elites have adopted pro-choice and pro-life positions, respectively, over this period.[52] However, the statistical results reported in table 3.9, which allow for trends in the weights associated with each issue over the period from 1984 through 2004, suggest that the political significance of abortion has increased just as much among infrequent churchgoers as among those who attend church regularly. Thus, although religious convictions and religious institutions have played an important role in the rise of abortion as a political issue, the corresponding mobilization among secular voters—who are much more likely to be pro-choice than pro-life[53]—has been every bit as powerful.

The bottom panel of table 3.9 shows the estimated weights for each issue at the end of this 20-year evolution. The results indicate that abortion was about 10% more important among frequent churchgoers than among infrequent churchgoers, and almost 40% more important among highly religious white voters than among those who seldom or never went to church. However, even highly religious white voters were much less fixated on abortion than one might guess from recent commentary on the politics of the religious right. Whether we focus on people who attend religious services regularly or those who say that religion provides crucial guidance in their daily lives, the statistical results presented in the bottom half of table 3.9 show that the weight of abortion and gender roles combined continues to fall well short of the weight attached to the traditional economic issue of government services. Despite the rise of abortion as a prominent political issue over the past 20 years and its particular significance among highly religious voters, even highly religious voters continue to vote much more on the basis of economic issues than of cultural issues.

CLASS POLITICS, ALIVE AND WELL

Liberal political observers are inclined to think of the New Deal era as the natural starting point of modern American politics and to wonder how the

---

[52] Adams (1997); Carmines and Woods (1997).

[53] Average positions on the abortion rights scale ranged from −.19 among white voters who said they attended religious services every week to +.56 among those who said they never attended.

TABLE 3.9
Change in Weight of Issue Preferences by Religiosity, 1984–2004

Probit parameter estimates (with standard errors in parentheses) for probability of Democratic presidential vote. Frequent churchgoers said they attended religious services every week
or almost every week. Highly religious people said religion provides "a great deal" of guidance
in their day-to-day living. Data are clustered by election year; separate intercepts for each group
in each election year are not shown; white major-party voters only.

	Infrequent churchgoers	Frequent churchgoers	Highly religious
Change in weight, 1984–2004			
Government services	+.14 (.15)	−.02 (.16)	+.28 (.27)
Defense spending	+.22 (.24)	+.11 (.43)	−.36 (.28)
Government jobs	+.04 (.12)	+.14 (.08)	+.07 (.10)
Abortion	+.30 (.10)	+.30 (.04)	+.40 (.08)
Aid to blacks	+.01 (.11)	+.31 (.30)	+.33 (.14)
Women's role	+.19 (.14)	+.13 (.13)	+.04 (.09)
Weight in 2004			
Government services	.90 (.12)	.94 (.11)	.98 (.17)
Defense spending	1.05 (.19)	.84 (.33)	.44 (.21)
Government jobs	.55 (.07)	.45 (.06)	.38 (.08)
Abortion	.44 (.07)	.49 (.02)	.61 (.06)
Aid to blacks	.30 (.09)	.28 (.21)	.37 (.10)
Women's role	.29 (.11)	.28 (.09)	.20 (.07)
Log likelihood	−1,618.7	−1,161.0	−914.7
Pseudo-R^2	.25	.20	.19
N	3,118	2,272	1,798

Source: Calculations based on data from 1984–2004 National Election Study surveys.

Democratic Party has managed to squander the "natural" electoral advantage
it built under Franklin Roosevelt. The simple answer to that question is that
the Democratic Party's "natural" electoral advantage was based primarily on
its *un*natural political monopoly in the racially oppressive Solid South of the
Jim Crow era. As the party system of the contemporary South has gradually
come to resemble that of the country as a whole, the two parties nationally
have come to find themselves in exactly the sort of closely contested electoral
equilibrium one might expect in a competitive two-party system.

Nevertheless, having lost two successive presidential elections—albeit by
extremely close margins—some Democrats seem to have concluded that
their party must be reinvented for the new millennium. According to one
prominent political reporter, "The big conversation going on in Democratic
Washington at the moment, at dinner parties and luncheons and think-tank
symposia, revolves around how to save the party." The prescriptions focus on

ideology, infrastructure, rhetorical strategies, and more. However, a surprisingly large fraction seems to be predicated on the notion that "Democrats need to give a more prominent voice to Middle American, wheat-hugging, gun-shooting, Spanish-speaking, beer-guzzling, Bible-toting centrists" in an effort to inoculate the party against the "hallucinatory appeal" among working-class whites of "cultural wedge issues like guns and abortion."[54]

The analysis presented in this chapter implies no particular political strategy for Democrats—or, for that matter, for Republicans. For all I know, more gun shooting and beer guzzling would be all to the good (though presumably not at the same time). However, if the basis for that diagnosis is a belief that Democratic support has eroded more among working-class whites than among affluent whites, it seems pertinent to observe that that belief is simply false. And if the proffered political cure is grounded in a belief that working-class whites are especially sensitive to cultural issues, it seems pertinent to observe that that belief is also false. Economic issues continue to be of paramount importance in contemporary American politics, as they have been for most of the past 150 years; and they are especially paramount among people of modest means.[55]

A recent cross-national analysis by John Huber and Piero Stanig puts the current U.S. pattern of class voting in striking perspective. Comparing political attitudes and voting patterns in 20 democracies with varying social structures and political institutions, Huber and Stanig found that the gap in right-wing electoral support between rich and poor voters was considerably *larger* in the United States than in the supposedly class-based political systems of Europe.[56] The notion that America is exempt from the fractious class politics of the Old World seems to be no more tenable than the (possibly related) notion that American society is marked by unusually high levels of intergenerational economic mobility.

Huber and Stanig considered a variety of potential social and political explanations for cross-national variations in the extent of class polarization in voting behavior. The two factors that seem most pertinent for explaining the high level of class polarization in the United States are party polarization and

---

[54] Matt Bai, "The New Boss," *New York Times Magazine*, January 30, 2005, 38–71; Kristof, "Time to Get Religion," A19; Frank (2004), 245.

[55] At the elite level, Poole and Rosenthal (1997) provided a good deal of evidence suggesting that economic issues have defined the primary dimension of conflict in Congress since the Civil War. They also provided evidence of a second, racial dimension of conflict through the middle third of the twentieth century, when significant numbers of southern segregationists and northern liberals coexisted in the Democratic Party's congressional delegation. While there is no comparable evidence on the bases of mass partisanship and voting behavior before the era of systematic survey research, economic issues have probably been of primary importance at that level as well—with a similar exception for the South in the Jim Crow era.

[56] Huber and Stanig (2006).

religious fractionalization. Party polarization—the ideological distance between the most centrist right- and left-wing parties—tends to reduce right-
wing support among poor voters, presumably because it forces them to
support a more extreme right-wing party than in systems with more moderate conservative options. Since the United States has only two major parties
to choose from, with a good deal of ideological distance between them, the
"cost" of casting a conservative vote is greater in the United States than in systems with more moderate right-wing alternatives. The plausibility of this explanation is bolstered by the fact that class polarization in U.S. voting
behavior increased at more or less the same time as ideological polarization
between Republican and Democratic elites.[57]

According to Huber and Stanig, religious fractionalization—measured by
the probability that two randomly selected voters belong to different religious
groups—generally increases support for right-wing parties but does so more
strongly among more affluent voters than among poor voters. Thus, the fact
that the United States is highly fractionalized along denominational lines
should be expected to increase the gap in right-wing electoral support between poor voters and those at higher income levels. Here the internal evidence from the United States seems more mixed. On one hand, it is true that
church attendance has a somewhat stronger impact on voting behavior among
more affluent voters than among low-income voters.[58] On the other hand, the
political relevance of religiosity has increased in recent years for reasons that
seem to have little to do with religious fractionalization in Huber and Stanig's
sense. Indeed, white Protestants and Catholics who attend church regularly
have generally become more similar in their presidential voting behavior since
the early 1990s, while those who attend church infrequently have not.[59]

Regardless of how well Huber and Stanig's cross-national analysis succeeds
in pinpointing the specific causes of class polarization in the United States,
the fact remains that the extent of class polarization in the contemporary
American party system is substantial, not only by recent historical standards
but also by comparison with the pattern prevailing in the world's other
democracies. To a remarkable degree, and contrary to much speculation, traditional class politics is alive and well.

---

[57] McCarty, Poole, and Rosenthal (2006), chapters 1–3.

[58] Since 1991, high-income white voters who attend church every week have cast 74% of
their presidential votes for Republicans, while those who never attend have cast 45% of their
votes for Republicans—a 29-point disparity. The corresponding disparities for middle- and low-
income white voters were 30 points and 23 points, respectively.

[59] The average difference in Republican presidential vote shares between white Protestants
and white Catholics who attend church at least once a week declined from 27 percentage points
(70% versus 43%) before 1992 to 18 percentage points (73% versus 55%) thereafter. Among infrequent churchgoers the difference between Protestants and Catholics increased slightly, from
8 percentage points (60% versus 52%) to 10 percentage points (55% versus 45%).

What, then, of those perplexing Republican successes at the polls? If they are not attributable to "values" issues and working-class cultural conservatism, where *do* they come from? I turn to that question in chapter 4. The answers I offer are surprising and disheartening, suggesting that a great deal of economic inequality in America is attributable to false consciousness of rather different kinds than Thomas Frank had in mind.

Partisan Biases in Economic Accountability

> Of all races in an advanced stage of civilization, the
> American is the least accessible to long views. . . .
> Always and everywhere in a hurry to get rich, he does
> not give a thought to remote consequences; he sees
> only present advantages. . . . He does not remember,
> he does not feel, he lives in a materialist dream.
> —Moiseide Ostrogorski, 1902[1]

THE ANALYSIS OF party coalitions presented in chapter 3 identified the most
important explanation for why Republicans have been more successful in recent national elections than they were during the New Deal era—the shift
of the Solid South from Democratic to Republican control in the wake of the
civil rights movement. That shift has produced a remarkably even partisan
balance in the national electorate, with middle- and upper-income whites
leaning toward the Republicans and poorer whites and African Americans
being predominantly Democratic. Republican candidates won 51.7% of all
the votes cast for major-party candidates in the fourteen presidential elections from 1952 through 2004; Democratic candidates captured 48.3%.

However, this account leaves unresolved the puzzle raised by the partisan
pattern of income growth documented in chapter 2: how do Republicans win
even a bare plurality of votes when most of the electorate has been substantially worse off under Republican presidents than under Democrats? Even
allowing for some class bias in turnout, it is clear that most voters—including
most *Republican* voters—have experienced much more economic prosperity
under Democratic presidents than under Republican presidents. Why, then,
have Democrats not been rewarded and Republicans not been punished for
the striking partisan gap in income growth documented in figure 2.1?

My resolution of this puzzle hinges on three notable biases in the workings
of economic accountability in contemporary American electoral politics. First,
voters are myopic, responding strongly to income growth in presidential election years but ignoring or forgetting most of the rest of the incumbent administration's record of economic performance. As Ostrogorski surmised more
than a century ago, the American voter "sees only present advantages." Second,

[1] Ostrogorski (1902), 302–303.

election-year income growth for affluent families is much more consequential than income growth for middle-class and poor families—even among middle- and low-income voters. And third, voters are swayed by the balance of campaign spending between incumbents and challengers. As it happens, each of these biases produces a significant electoral advantage for Republican presidential candidates. Together, they are large enough to account for four of the nine Republican victories in presidential elections since 1952.

The partisan political ramifications of myopia are especially striking. It is by no means obvious that this quirk of voter psychology should have profound implications for the balance of power between Democrats and Republicans over the past half-century. That it does is the result of a remarkable disparity in the timing of income growth under Democratic and Republican presidents in the post-war era. The analyses presented in chapter 2 show that Democrats have generally presided over much more robust income growth, especially for families of modest means. However, that partisan pattern of income growth has been reversed in presidential election years, with families in every part of the income distribution experiencing considerably more growth under Republican presidents than they have under Democratic presidents. It is impossible to be certain whether this pattern reflects clever Republican strategizing, a predictable byproduct of partisan differences in economic policies in the "honeymoon" period at the beginning of each president's four-year term, or some odd cosmic joke. In any event, it has had a momentous impact on American electoral politics over the past half-century, and thus also on the politics of economic inequality.

MYOPIC VOTERS

The political puzzle of Republican electoral success is predicated on the notion that voters will assess which party has produced a better record of income growth, either for themselves or for the country as a whole, and vote accordingly. That notion seems to be supported by a great deal of evidence linking the state of the economy and the political fortunes of the incumbent party in both presidential and congressional elections.[2] It also seems eminently sensible, since competent governments in the post-Keynesian era are thought to exert real influence over the course of the national economy. Indeed, the strong tendency of voters to reward incumbents for good economic times and punish them for bad times is often viewed as a mark of the rationality of democratic

---

[2] This literature is too vast to cite in detail. Kramer (1971) and Tufte (1978) made important early contributions. Erikson (1989; 1990) provided concise and clear analyses of presidential and midterm results, respectively. For presidential elections, Bartels and Zaller (2001) compared a variety of alternative measures of economic performance and probed the robustness of the statistical results to variations in model specification.

electorates. One of the earliest academic analysts of economic voting, Gerald Kramer, characterized his results as demonstrating "that election outcomes are in substantial part responsive to objective changes occurring under the incumbent party; they are not 'irrational,' or random, or solely the product of past loyalties and habits, or of campaign rhetoric and merchandising." Another prominent political scientist, V. O. Key Jr., interpreted evidence of retrospective voting as support for his "perverse and unorthodox argument" that "voters are not fools."[3]

One of the primary attractions of this perspective on electoral accountability is that it does not seem to require too much from ordinary citizens. According to another influential theorist of retrospective voting, Morris Fiorina, voters "typically have one comparatively hard bit of data: they know what life has been like during the incumbent's administration. They need *not* know the precise economic or foreign policies of the incumbent administration in order to see or feel the *results* of those policies. . . . In order to ascertain whether the incumbents have performed poorly or well, citizens need only calculate the changes in their own welfare."[4]

Analysts have routinely treated this feature of the retrospective theory of political accountability as unproblematic. Individual voters' economic perceptions may reflect substantial partisan biases, rationalization, and sheer randomness, but the electorate as a whole is assumed to respond systematically and sensibly to actual economic experience under the incumbent administration.[5]

Here I examine one important respect in which the rationality of the American electorate falls short of this standard: the time-horizon over which voters assess changes in the state of the economy.[6] If voters want to reward incumbents for contributing to their own incomes or the economic fortunes of society as a whole—or to punish incumbents for failing to provide prosperity—they should be sensitive to economic conditions "over the incumbent's entire term of office, with little or no backward time discounting of performance outcomes," as Douglas Hibbs put it. However, the striking fact is that virtually all analyses of retrospective economic voting focus on economic conditions during the election year, or even some fraction of the election year, rather than over the longer haul of an entire term.[7] In effect,

[3] Kramer (1971), 140; Key (1966), 7.

[4] Fiorina (1981), 5.

[5] On idiosyncratic economic experience, rationalization, and partisan bias see Kramer (1983); Conover, Feldman, and Knight (1987); Bartels (2002); Erikson (2004).

[6] My analysis here builds upon joint work with Christopher Achen (Achen and Bartels 2004).

[7] Hibbs (2004), 7. Hibbs's own analysis is rare in focusing on the extent of temporal discounting in voters' reactions to economic conditions. He found relatively modest discounting of past economic performance; however, other analysts employing similar models have found that recent economic performance is much more relevant than previous performance (Bartels and Zaller 2001; Erikson, Bafumi, and Wilson 2002; Achen and Bartels 2004).

they assume that voters attempt "to ascertain whether the incumbents have performed poorly or well" on the basis of a very limited—and potentially misleading—assessment of "changes in their own welfare."

Is that assumption warranted? Figure 4.1 summarizes the relationship between cumulative income growth and the incumbent party's electoral fortunes in the fourteen presidential elections from 1952 through 2004. Election years are arrayed along the horizontal axis based on the total growth in real disposable personal income per capita in the second, third, and fourth years of each administration—the years in which the incumbent president's policies might plausibly have some impact on the state of the economy. The vertical axis shows the popular vote margin (in percentage points) for the incumbent party's presidential candidate.

Figure 4.1 displays a strong, though not overwhelming, connection between cumulative income growth and presidential election outcomes. On one hand, the incumbent party's vote margin was slightly negative in each of

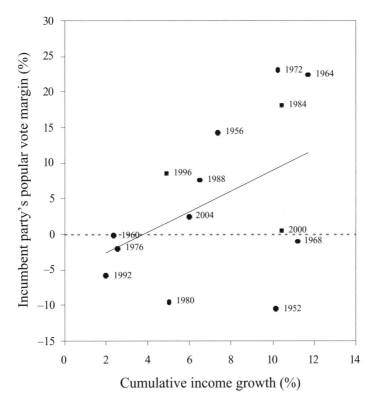

Figure 4.1 Cumulative Income Growth and Presidential Election Outcomes, 1952–2004

the three elections in which cumulative income growth was less than 3%. On the other hand, the incumbent party's average vote margin was about 10 percentage points in the six elections in which cumulative income growth exceeded 10%. However, the range of outcomes in those six elections reflects the imprecision of the overall relationship between cumulative income growth and election outcomes: incumbent presidents won reelection by landslides in three of those cases (1972, 1964, and 1984), but incumbent vice presidents were narrowly defeated in two others (1968 and 2000, albeit with a slim popular vote margin in the latter case), and in 1952 the incumbent party's candidate was trounced despite much-higher-than-average cumulative income growth.

By comparison, the relationship depicted in figure 4.2 is a good deal stronger and more consistent. The difference here is that elections are arrayed along the horizontal axis not on the basis of cumulative income growth over the president's second, third, and fourth years in office, but rather on

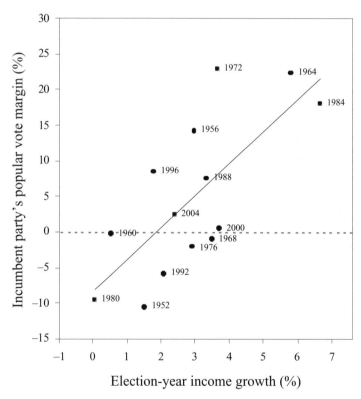

Figure 4.2 Election-Year Income Growth and Presidential Election Outcomes, 1952–2004

the basis of income growth in the presidential election year only. Knowing how the economy fared during the election year turns out to be much more helpful in accounting for the incumbent party's fortunes than knowing how it fared over the entire three years leading up to the election.

The relationships presented graphically in figures 4.1 and 4.2 are elaborated in the statistical analyses reported in table 4.1. In addition to economic conditions, these statistical analyses include the incumbent party's tenure in office as an additional explanatory factor. There is a fairly strong tendency for the incumbent party's electoral fortunes to decline with each additional year that it has held the White House. Presumably this pattern reflects the cumulative effect of exhausted policy agendas, personnel turnover, and accumulating scandals on voters' desire for a change in leadership. Over the course of a typical four-year term, these forces reduce the incumbent party's popular vote margin by three to six percentage points.

The statistical analysis reported in the first column of table 4.1 relates the incumbent party's popular vote margin to the rate of cumulative income growth over the president's second, third, and fourth years in office. The results parallel figure 4.1 in suggesting that each additional percentage point of cumulative income growth translated into a gain of about 1.4 percentage points in the incumbent party's expected vote margin. The second column of the table presents the results of a parallel statistical analysis based not on cumulative income growth but on election-year income growth. As one might expect from a comparison

TABLE 4.1

Myopic Economic Voting in Presidential Elections, 1952–2004

Ordinary least squares regression parameter estimates (with standard errors in parentheses) for incumbent party's popular vote margin (%).

	{1}	{2}	{3}
Cumulative income growth (%)	1.39 (.61)	—	—
Election-year (Year 4) income growth (%)	—	3.63 (1.05)	3.49 (1.09)
Year 3 income growth (%)	—	—	1.96 (1.54)
Year 2 income growth (%)	—	—	−.17 (.87)
Incumbent party tenure (years)	−1.53 (.48)	−1.12 (.42)	−.85 (.52)
Intercept	5.70 (6.04)	2.21 (5.20)	−2.69 (6.54)
Standard error of regression	7.75	6.49	6.61
Adjusted R^2	.51	.66	.65
N	14	14	14

Source: Calculations based on data from Bureau of Economic Analysis.

of figures 4.1 and 4.2, this version of the analysis does a significantly better job of accounting for the actual election outcomes.[8] The relationship between income growth and the incumbent party's vote margin is also substantially stronger, with each percentage point of election-year income growth increasing the incumbent party's expected margin by 3.6 percentage points.

Taking separate account of income growth in the second and third years of the president's term, in the third column of table 4.1, does nothing to improve upon the simpler analysis employing election-year income growth alone. Income growth in the third year of each president's term may have had some effect on the next election outcome, but that effect is probably only about half as large as the effect of election-year income growth. Income growth in the second year of each president's term seems to have been utterly forgotten—which is to say, politically irrelevant—by the time of the next election.

These results suggest that presidential elections are important occasions for economic accountability, but with significant limitations due to the systematic cognitive limitations of voters. In particular, election outcomes are sensitive to real changes in the nation's economic fortunes under the incumbent party—but only if those changes occur in close proximity to Election Day. Voters reward their elected leaders for *some* good times and punish them for *some* bad times. Does this myopic focus on "present advantages" have significant political consequences?

THE POLITICAL TIMING OF INCOME GROWTH

More than a quarter-century ago, political scientist Edward Tufte noted that the electorate's short time horizon with respect to economic evaluations could produce "a bias toward policies with immediate, highly visible benefits and deferred, hidden costs—myopic policies for myopic voters." Tufte worried that political manipulation of economic policy could generate significant social costs due to wasteful government spending and other forms of "economic instability and inefficiency" aimed at making the economy flourish around election time. He provided statistical evidence of electoral cycles in transfer payments, income growth, unemployment, and inflation, as well as considerable qualitative evidence of specific efforts by incumbents to produce those cycles. Richard Nixon in 1972 was a particularly

---

[8] The standard error of the regression, which measures the average deviation between actual election margins and the margins implied by the statistical analysis, is 6.5 percentage points. As one reader has noted, this level of accuracy would not win many office betting pools. Nevertheless, it represents an improvement of more than 15% over the analysis based on cumulative income growth.

energetic manipulator of everything from the money supply (through his erstwhile political ally Arthur Burns, the chairman of the Federal Reserve Board) to effective dates of increases in Social Security benefits and payroll taxes; as Tufte delicately put it, "The extremes of 1972 were special because Richard Nixon was special."[9]

Subsequent research on political business cycles has produced less clear results. According to one observer, "while the general logic behind the theory is quite persuasive, the empirical evidence for electoral-economic cycles is spotty at best."[10] Figure 4.3 redeploys the Census Bureau's figures on income growth from chapters 1 and 2 to explore whether presidents have produced unusual income growth in election years. Separately for families at the 20th and 95th percentiles of the income distribution, the figure shows average levels of real income growth in each year of the election cycle, beginning with the year in which a new (or reelected) president is inaugurated and continuing through the subsequent presidential election year.

The pattern of income growth under Republican presidents (represented by the black bars in the figure) is generally consistent with Tufte's account of a political business cycle. Whether we focus on the working poor (in the left panel) or wealthy families (in the right panel)—or, for that matter, on families at intermediate income levels—the average rate of real income growth clearly peaked in presidential election years.[11] In stark contrast, the second year of each Republican term—the first year plausibly affected by the current president's economic policies—was generally marked by slow growth; in fact, working poor families experienced *negative* average income growth in the second years of Republican administrations.

If Tufte's concerns about the possibility of a political business cycle seem to be confirmed by the economic record of Republican administrations, Democratic presidents have quite remarkably turned Tufte on his head. Tracing the gray bars in figure 4.3 over the course of the election cycle suggests that Democratic presidents have produced substantially *less* income growth in presidential election years than at other times. (As with Republican presidents, similar patterns hold for families at intermediate income levels.) Under Democrats, average income growth reached its peak during the second year of each four-year

---

[9] Tufte (1978), 143, 63. Tufte argued that Nixon's enthusiasm for political manipulation of the economy arose in significant part from his unhappy experience with an *un*manipulated economy in his first presidential campaign in 1960. According to Nixon (quoted by Tufte 1978, 6): "In October, usually a month of rising employment, the jobless rolls increased by 452,000. All the speeches, television broadcasts, and precinct work in the world could not counteract that one hard fact." Nixon lost the election by fewer than 120,000 votes.

[10] Schultz (1995), 79.

[11] The election-year bonuses in average income growth by comparison with nonelection years range from 1.6 percentage points for families at the 80th percentile to 2.5 percentage points for families at the 40th percentile.

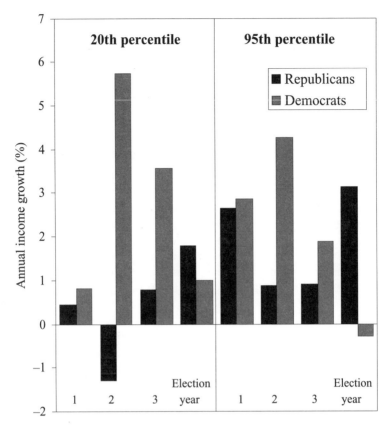

Figure 4.3 Electoral Cycle in Income Growth under Republican and Democratic Presidents, 1948–2005

term, then declined markedly in the third and fourth years. Thus, the "spotty" evidence of an electoral cycle in income growth reflects two very different partisan regimes—one highly cyclical and the other countercyclical.

The reason for this remarkable pattern is by no means obvious. However, the most plausible explanation is that the characteristic economic strategies of Democratic and Republican presidents in the "honeymoon" periods at the *beginning* of each four-year term have predictable spillover effects at the time of the next election. The analysis presented in table 2.2 showed that the largest partisan differences in income growth, by far, were concentrated in the second year of each four-year presidential term—the first year in which new post-election policies could actually influence income growth. Democratic presidents have routinely produced extremely strong income growth for families in every part of the income distribution in these "honeymoon"

TABLE 4.2

Presidential Elections and Partisan Income Growth, 1948–2005

Annual real pre-tax income growth (%) for families at various points in the income distribution (with standard errors in parentheses). Partisan control measured from one year following
inauguration to one year following subsequent inauguration.

	All Presidents	Democratic Presidents	Republican Presidents	Partisan Difference
Presidential election years				
20th percentile	1.42 (.94)	1.00 (1.51)	1.79 (1.26)	−.79 (1.95)
40th percentile	1.96 (.68)	1.11 (1.02)	2.69 (.89)	−1.58 (1.34)
60th percentile	1.96 (.76)	1.44 (1.33)	2.41 (.88)	−.97 (1.56)
80th percentile	1.72 (.74)	.69 (1.10)	2.62 (.94)	−1.93 (1.44)
95th percentile	1.54 (.82)	−.28 (1.11)	3.14 (.89)	−3.42 (1.41)
N	15	7	8	15
Nonelection years				
20th percentile	1.42 (.60)	3.25 (.89)	−.02 (.69)	3.27 (1.11)
40th percentile	1.40 (.47)	2.96 (.68)	.16 (.52)	2.79 (.85)
60th percentile	1.65 (.39)	2.84 (.52)	.71 (.48)	2.14 (.71)
80th percentile	1.88 (.36)	3.01 (.50)	.98 (.44)	2.03 (.67)
95th percentile	2.16 (.43)	3.00 (.70)	1.49 (.52)	1.51 (.85)
N	43	19	24	43

Source: Calculations based on data from Census Bureau Historical Income Tables.

years. However, these expansionary bursts cannot be sustained indefinitely;
by the time of the next presidential election, income growth under Democratic presidents has typically slowed to a crawl, especially for families near
the top of the income distribution.

The usual pattern under Republican presidents is exactly the opposite. The
second years of Republican administrations have consistently seen significant
economic contractions. Indeed, only one of the last eight Republican "honeymoon" periods resulted in positive income growth for middle-class and poor
families.[12] But contractions, like expansions, have a finite duration, and by the
time of the next presidential election income growth has typically rebounded
significantly.

Table 4.2 provides a detailed comparison of income growth rates under
each party in presidential election years and nonelection years. Under

---

[12] The exception is 1986, the second year of Ronald Reagan's second term. Two other cases,
1982 and 2002, represented continuations of recessions that were already underway when new
Republican presidents took office. However, Dwight Eisenhower in 1954 and Richard Nixon in
1970 presided over sharp recessions despite having inherited booming economies from their
Democratic predecessors; in both cases, middle-class and working poor families were hardest
hit, while upper-income families fared significantly better.

Republican presidents, average growth at every income level has been about two percentage points higher in presidential election years than in nonelection years. In stark contrast, Democratic presidents have produced much less income growth in presidential election years than in nonelection years. These differences, too, are on the order of two percentage points, with real incomes at all levels growing by about 3% in nonelection years but only about 1% in presidential election years. The real incomes of affluent families (at the 95th percentile of the income distribution) actually *declined* slightly in election years in which Democrats held the White House.

The partisan pattern of election-year income growth documented in the top panel of table 4.2 is presented graphically in figure 4.4. As with the overall pattern of income growth presented in figure 2.1, it is clear here that affluent families experienced more growth than poor families under Republican presidents,

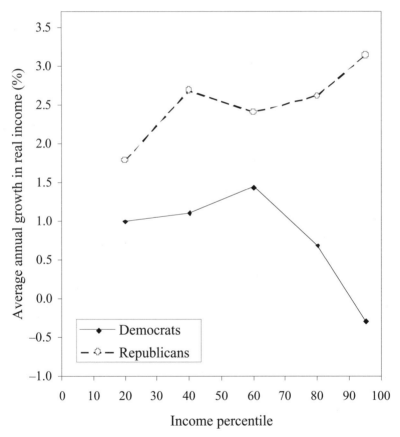

Figure 4.4 Income Growth in Presidential Election Years, by Party, 1948–2004

while middle-class and poor families experienced more growth than affluent families under Democratic presidents. Thus, the two parties' traditional distributional priorities are evident even in presidential election years.

The striking difference between figure 4.4 and figure 2.1 is in the relative performance of the two parties' presidents in election and nonelection years. When the partisan comparison of income growth patterns is limited to presidential election years, families at every income level turn out to have fared much better under *Republican* presidents than under Democrats. In election years, even working poor families saw almost twice as much income growth under Republican presidents (1.8%) as under Democratic presidents (1.0%). Whether through political skill or pure good luck, Republican presidents have been remarkably successful in targeting income growth to coincide with presidential elections. Democrats, however, have been remarkably *unsuccessful* in producing election-year prosperity.

If voters judiciously weighed the entire record of income growth over each incumbent's term, this striking disparity between Democratic and Republican administrations in the timing of income growth would be politically inconsequential. Good and bad times would be factored into voters' assessments of incumbent performance regardless of when they occurred. Conversely, if partisan patterns of income growth were identical in election years and nonelection years, economic myopia would be a mere psychological curiosity and of little political relevance—simply one more entry in an extensive catalog of heuristics and biases that shape human decision making. In tandem, however, the myopia of voters and the success of post-war Republican presidents in producing robust income growth in the run-up to presidential elections have significantly bolstered electoral support for Republican candidates.

Democratic presidents, in contrast, have routinely been punished by myopic voters for slow election-year growth but given little credit for robust income growth in nonelection years. The analysis presented in the third column of table 4.1 suggests that voters gave Democratic presidents *no* electoral credit for consistently producing stupendous income growth in the second years of their four-year terms (ranging from 4.0% for upper-middle-class families to 5.7% for the working poor), while Republican presidents have paid *no* electoral cost for consistently presiding over declines in real income for middle-class and working poor families in the second years of their four-year terms.

The political consequences of these biases in economic accountability are highlighted in table 4.3, which compares the actual Republican popular vote margin in each of the past 14 elections with the projected margin subtracting the effect of economic myopia.[13] The projections suggest that economic

---

[13] The projected vote margins without myopia are based on the assumption that voters in each election year would have weighed income growth in the second, third, and fourth years of the incumbent president's term equally, using the average of the estimated weights for these

TABLE 4.3

The Effect of Economic Myopia on Presidential Election Outcomes, 1952–2004

Boldface entries represent years in which actual and projected election winners differ.

Election year	Actual Republican vote margin	Projected margin without myopia	Difference
1952	+10.5%	−0.6%	**+11.1%**
1956	+14.3%	+7.2%	+7.1%
1960	−0.2%	−3.1%	+3.0%
1964	−22.4%	−18.2%	−4.1%
1968	+1.0%	−0.1%	**+1.1%**
1972	+23.0%	+21.9%	+1.1%
1976	−2.1%	−10.5%	+8.5%
1980	+9.4%	+2.9%	+6.5%
1984	+18.0%	+8.4%	+9.7%
1988	+7.6%	+5.9%	+1.7%
1992	−5.8%	−7.8%	+2.0%
1996	−8.5%	−8.0%	−0.5%
2000	−0.5%	−2.6%	**+2.1%**
2004	+2.4%	+2.0%	+0.4%
Average	+3.3%	−0.2%	+3.5%

Source: Calculations based on parameter estimates in table 4.1, column {3}.

myopia added 3.5 percentage points to the average Republican vote margin in these 14 elections—no small difference, given that the average Republican vote margin was only 3.3 percentage points. Myopia seems to have benefited Republican candidates in 12 of the 14 elections, and it was probably decisive in three of the nine Republican victories in the post-war era: Dwight Eisenhower in 1952, Richard Nixon in 1968, and George W. Bush in 2000 probably all owed their accessions to the White House to the fact that voters forgot (or simply ignored) strong periods of income growth early in the terms of their Democratic predecessors.

CLASS BIASES IN ECONOMIC VOTING

Since partisan differences in average income growth are greatest for middle-class and working poor families, those families are the most obvious economic losers from the partisan bias in accountability produced by voters'

three years in the third column of table 4.1. This assumption implies that each additional percentage point of income growth would have increased the incumbent party's popular vote margin by 1.76 percentage points, regardless of whether that growth occurred in the election year or in either of the two preceding years.

short time-horizons. The result, obviously, is to exacerbate economic inequality. As if that were not enough, middle-class and poor families are also distinctly disadvantaged by a different kind of bias in economic voting—a significant class bias in sensitivity to income growth. American voters, regardless of their own place in the income distribution, seem to be quite sensitive to the economic fortunes of high-income families but much less sensitive to income growth among middle-class and poor families. Here, too, the political result is to bolster the Republican Party, and the economic result is to further exacerbate income inequality.

In exploring the possibility of class bias in economic voting, it may be helpful to begin by assessing the contributions of voters at different income levels to the overall relationship between economic conditions and presidential election outcomes documented in figure 4.2 and table 4.1. Because the National Election Study (NES) surveys introduced in chapter 3 include almost 16,000 people who reported voting for one or the other of the major-party candidates in the 14 presidential elections from 1952 through 2004, they make it possible to examine the distinctive responsiveness of various subgroups of the electorate, including high-, middle-, and low-income voters, to national economic conditions. The survey data also make it possible to take account of other potentially relevant characteristics of individual voters—most importantly, the long-standing psychological attachment to a political party that powerfully influences the political attitudes and behavior of most American voters.[14]

The statistical analyses of presidential election outcomes reported in table 4.1 showed that the incumbent party's electoral fortunes are strongly affected by election-year income growth and by how long the incumbent party has held office. The first column of table 4.4 presents the results of a parallel analysis employing NES survey data from the same 14 elections, relating individual voters' presidential votes to these same factors, plus the voters' own partisan attachments. These results are quite consistent with those presented in table 4.1. They imply that each additional percentage point of real income growth increased an otherwise undecided voter's probability of supporting the incumbent party by about 3.1 percentage points, while each additional year in office reduced her probability of supporting the incumbent party by about 1.4 percentage points.[15]

[14] The classic scholarly explication of party identification and its effects is by Campbell et al. (1960). Bartels (2000) measured changes over the past half-century in the relationship between party identification and voting behavior.

[15] The statistical results presented in table 4.4 are not directly comparable with those presented in table 4.1, since they are based on probit analyses of the *probability* of voting for the incumbent party's presidential candidate rather than ordinary regression analyses of the incumbent party's aggregate vote *margin*. One implication of the probit model is that the implied effects of the explanatory factors are nonlinear, reaching their maximum levels among voters who are otherwise equally likely to support either party. (For example, the impact of economic

TABLE 4.4
Economic Voting by Income Group, 1952–2004

Probit parameter estimates (with standard errors in parentheses) for probability of incumbent party vote. Data clustered by election year; major-party voters only.

	Full sample	High income	Middle income	Low income
Election-year income growth (%)	.077 (.046)	.082 (.059)	.110 (.037)	.017 (.052)
Incumbent party tenure (years)	−.034 (.014)	−.039 (.015)	−.025 (.014)	−.043 (.016)
Incumbent party identification (−1 to +1)	1.542 (.079)	1.639 (.099)	1.509 (.075)	1.468 (.082)
Intercept	.088 (.257)	.159 (.277)	−.082 (.215)	.311 (.303)
Log likelihood	−6,596.1	−2,356.4	−2,057.6	−1,759.1
Pseudo-R²	.40	.42	.39	.40
N	15,976	5,911	4,848	4,242

Source: Calculations based on data from 1952–2004 National Election Study surveys and Bureau of Economic Analysis.

Repeating the same analysis separately for high-, middle-, and low-income voters produces generally similar results (presented in the second, third, and fourth columns of table 4.4), with one very notable exception: voters in the bottom third of the income distribution appear to have been much less sensitive than more affluent voters were to election-year income growth. Insofar as presidential elections have served as referenda on the economic stewardship of the incumbent party, systematic rewards and punishments seem to have been provided primarily by voters in the middle and upper portions of the income distribution.

Why would low-income voters be so insensitive to national economic conditions? One possible explanation for this class difference is that the measure of income growth employed in table 4.4—the percentage change in real disposable income per capita—does not really reflect the economic experiences

---

conditions is assumed to be greater among political independents than among strong partisans, since the latter are likely to vote for their party's candidate regardless of whether the economy is booming or slumping.) The estimated effects reported in the text, for an otherwise undecided voter, are about twice as large as the *average* effects for the electorate as a whole, which imply that an additional percentage point of election-year income growth would increase the incumbent party's vote *margin* by 3.5 points and that an additional year in office would decrease the incumbent party's vote margin by 1.5 points. The corresponding estimates in the second column of table 4.1 are 3.6 points and 1.1 points, respectively.

of low-income families, even over the limited time horizon of the election year. Perhaps employing a more specific measure of low-income growth would produce more robust evidence of economic voting. With that possibility in mind, the first column of table 4.5 repeats the statistical analysis reported in the fourth column of table 4.4, but with the election-year growth rate for families at the 20th percentile of the income distribution included as an additional explanatory factor. (Since low-income voters in the NES surveys reported family incomes in the bottom third of the income distribution in each election year, the growth rate for families at the 20th percentile should provide a fair indication of their average economic fortunes.)

Taking separate account of low-income growth produces some evidence of economic voting among low-income voters; but the apparent effect is quite modest. Even more remarkably, the remaining columns of table 4.5 provide considerably stronger statistical evidence of low-income voters' responsiveness to growth rates at higher income levels. Low-income voters seem to be more sensitive to election-year growth rates for more affluent families than they are for families at their own income level. Most remarkably of all, the income-specific growth rate that does the best job of accounting for the vote choices of low-income voters is the growth rate for families at the 95th percentile of the income distribution—the most affluent families represented in the Census Bureau data. Low-income voters appear to be highly responsive to income growth among the rich, even while they attach no apparent weight to overall income growth.

If even low-income voters are sensitive to economic growth among the most affluent families, what about middle- and high-income voters? The statistical analyses reported in table 4.6 indicate that they, too, are much more likely to support the incumbent party when families near the top of the income distribution experience robust election-year income growth. (These analyses add the specific income growth rate for families at the 95th percentile to each of the class-specific analyses of economic voting presented in table 4.4; thus, the fourth column of table 4.6 simply repeats the fifth column of table 4.5, which reported the sensitivity of low-income voters to income growth at the 95th percentile.) The results rather remarkably suggest that in every income group, high-income growth had a much more powerful effect than overall income growth on electoral support for the incumbent party. For the electorate as a whole, each percentage point of income growth for affluent families seems to have produced as much additional support for the incumbent party as *four* points of growth in overall real disposable income per capita.

Although the statistical results presented in table 4.6 are based on thousands of individual vote choices, they represent only 14 distinct configurations of election-year contexts. Thus, it is not impossible that the apparent electoral significance of high-income growth is merely a statistical fluke.

TABLE 4.5

The Electoral Impact of Income-Specific Growth among Low-Income Voters, 1952–2004

Probit parameter estimates (with standard errors in parentheses) for probability of incumbent party vote. Data clustered by election year; major-party voters only.

	20th percentile	40th percentile	60th percentile	80th percentile	95th percentile
Election-year income growth (%)	−.015 (.036)	−.031 (.031)	−.027 (.039)	−.011 (.042)	−.031 (.027)
Income-specific growth (indicated percentile)	.036 (.026)	.072 (.025)	.059 (.032)	.066 (.023)	.097 (.014)
Incumbent party tenure (years)	−.045 (.014)	−.043 (.013)	−.054 (.013)	−.047 (.014)	−.048 (.012)
Incumbent party identification (−1 to +1)	1.476 (.077)	1.498 (.075)	1.485 (.078)	1.495 (.075)	1.545 (.066)
Intercept	.361 (.223)	.309 (.190)	.394 (.212)	.290 (.232)	.311 (.165)
Log likelihood	−1,749.0	−1,738.8	−1,743.1	−1,741.1	−1,715.3
Pseudo-R²	.40	.41	.41	.41	.42
N	4,242	4,242	4,242	4,242	4,242

Source: Calculations based on data from 1952–2004 National Election Study surveys, Bureau of Economic Analysis, and Census Bureau Historical Income Tables.

TABLE 4.6
The Electoral Impact of High-Income Growth by Income Group, 1952–2004

Probit parameter estimates (with standard errors in parentheses) for probability of incumbent party vote. Data clustered by election year; major-party voters only.

	Full sample	High income	Middle income	Low income
Election-year income growth (%)	.023 (.020)	.032 (.038)	.052 (.012)	−.031 (.027)
High-income growth (95th percentile)	.102 (.010)	.104 (.012)	.102 (.010)	.097 (.014)
Incumbent party tenure (years)	−.040 (.013)	−.045 (.014)	−.029 (.011)	−.048 (.012)
Incumbent party identification (−1 to +1)	1.607 (.071)	1.692 (.101)	1.580 (.069)	1.545 (.066)
Intercept	.100 (.121)	.152 (.149)	−.082 (.076)	.311 (.165)
Log likelihood	−6,424.4	−2,293.9	−2,002.0	−1,715.3
Pseudo-R^2	.42	.44	.40	.42
N	15,976	5,911	4,848	4,242

Source: Calculations based on data from 1952–2004 National Election Study surveys, Bureau of Economic Analysis, and Census Bureau Historical Income Tables.

However, if it *is* a fluke, it is a very persistent one. It certainly is not attributable to any one anomalous election, since the effect holds up strongly when each election is dropped from the analysis in turn.[16] Nor is it limited to years in which Republicans, or Democrats, held the White House, or to the first half or the last half of the post-war era.[17] Nor is there comparable evidence of sensitivity to income growth among less affluent families.[18]

[16] The estimated effects of high-income growth for the full sample range from .090 (omitting the 1980 election) to .110 (omitting the 1952 election).

[17] In the eight elections with Republican incumbents the estimated effect of high-income growth was .090; in the six elections with Democratic incumbents the estimated effect was .101. In the seven elections from 1952 through 1976, the estimated effect was .096; in the seven elections from 1980 through 2004, the estimated effect was .159.

[18] Substituting real income growth at the 80th, 60th, 40th, or 20th percentile of the income distribution for income growth at the 95th percentile significantly reduces the statistical fit of the probit model. The estimated effects of the specific growth rates range from .072 for income growth at the 80th percentile to .030 for income growth at the 20th percentile. Including all five income growth measures simultaneously (with or without the overall measure of election-year income growth) leaves the estimated effect of high-income growth virtually unchanged, and none of the other income-specific growth rates has an estimated effect larger than .01 or an associated t-statistic larger than .33.

THE WEALTHY GIVE SOMETHING BACK: PARTISAN
BIASES IN CAMPAIGN SPENDING

Why do affluent, middle-class, and poor voters all seem so exquisitely sensitive to election-year income growth for the wealthiest families? One likely possibility is that their subjective impressions of how the national economy is faring are subject to a class bias—perhaps because the mass media pay more attention to the economic fortunes of affluent people than to the economic fortunes of middle-class and poor people. This does appear to be part of the explanation; perceptions of national economic conditions appear to be disproportionately sensitive to income growth for families at the top of the income distribution. However, this class bias in voters' perceptions of national economic conditions is not strong enough to account for most of the apparent class bias in economic voting in table 4.6.[19]

If biased perceptions of economic conditions are not the answer, what else might account for the odd sensitivity of voters at every income level to election-year income gains among affluent families? Perhaps income gains for affluent families get translated into campaign contributions to the incumbent party, which in turn influence the behavior of other voters in ways that are not directly captured in the statistical analyses presented here. Certainly, most campaign contributions come from relatively wealthy people.[20] If they are inspired to show their gratitude to the incumbent party by giving a bit more generously when the election-year economy is flush, that would produce an indirect but nonetheless potent connection between high-income growth and presidential voting behavior.

The statistical analysis reported in the first column of table 4.7 relates the incumbent party's spending advantage in each election to real income growth

[19] NES surveys since 1980 have regularly included a question asking whether "over the past year the nation's economy has gotten better, stayed the same, or gotten worse." A statistical analysis of responses to that question indicates that they are sensitive to overall election-year income growth, as one might expect, but also to the specific income growth rate for families at the 95th percentile of the income distribution. The latter effect is about half as large as the former effect, suggesting that the specific economic fortunes of affluent families had a significant impact on perceptions of the state of the national economy, over and above the impact of general income growth, even among people who were themselves far from affluent. However, much of the statistical impact of high-income growth rates on electoral support for the incumbent party documented in table 4.6 persists even when voters' perceptions of the national economy are included in the analyses as a separate explanatory factor. Thus, the electoral significance of high-income growth does not appear to be entirely, or even primarily, mediated by biased perceptions of national economic conditions.

[20] For example, Verba, Schlozman, and Brady (1995, 194, 565) found that people in the top quartile of the income distribution accounted for almost three-quarters of the total campaign contributions in their 1989 Citizen Participation Study. The broad middle class accounted for almost all the rest; people in the bottom quintile of the income distribution accounted for only 2% of total contributions.

TABLE 4.7

Sources of Incumbent Party's Campaign Spending Advantage, 1952–2004

Ordinary least squares regression parameter estimates (with standard errors in parentheses) for incumbent party's spending advantage (in 2006 dollars per voter).

	{1}	{2}	{3}	{4}
High-income growth (95th percentile)	.295 (.102)	.135 (.078)	—	.082 (.067)
Election-year income growth (%)	—	—	.248 (.081)	.216 (.084)
Republican incumbent	—	1.59 (.40)	1.86 (.28)	1.66 (.32)
Intercept	−.55 (.33)	−1.13 (.26)	−1.73 (.31)	−1.69 (.30)
Standard error of regression	.95	.63	.53	.51
Adjusted R²	.36	.72	.81	.81
N	14	14	14	14

Source: Calculations based on data from Alexander (1980), Federal Election Commission, Bureau of Economic Analysis, and Census Bureau Historical Income Tables.

for families at the 95th percentile of the income distribution—the sorts of people who are most likely to be contributors to political campaigns. My measure of each presidential candidate's campaign spending is scaled in dollars per voter (in inflation-adjusted 2006 dollars). By that measure, spending has increased substantially over the past half-century, from 60 to 80 cents per voter in the 1950s to $3.00 to $5.00 per voter in recent elections.[21] The spending differential between the two candidates in each election ranges from a few cents (in 1960) to about $2.00 (in 1980).

There is indeed a significant relationship between the incumbent party's spending advantage and income growth at the top of the income distribution, as the results presented in the first column of table 4.7 show. However,

[21] The system of financing presidential election campaigns has also changed markedly over the past half-century, most notably with the institution of public funding following the Watergate scandal in the early 1970s. In principle, public funding equalized spending by the two-major party candidates in every campaign from 1976 through 1996. (George W. Bush in 2000 was the first candidate to decline public funding in order to avoid associated spending limits.) However, a rising tide of spending by parties, congressional candidates, and other groups during this period undoubtedly had important spillover effects on voters in presidential elections. I attempt to allow for these changes by measuring campaign spending somewhat differently in the pre- and post-Watergate eras. From 1952 through 1972, I use estimates of presidential campaign spending compiled by Alexander (1980). For subsequent elections, I count the public funds allocated to the presidential candidates (or their own spending if they declined public funding), plus half the additional spending by parties and allied interest groups in each presidential election year.

this analysis makes no allowance for the fact that election-year income growth rates, especially at the top of the income distribution, have generally been much higher under Republican presidents than under Democratic presidents. And since campaign contributors are likely to have other, ideological reasons to prefer Republican candidates to Democrats, the relationship between incumbent partisanship and high-income growth may produce a spurious statistical connection between high-income growth and the incumbent candidate's campaign spending advantage.

In order to allow for this possibility, the analysis presented in the second column of table 4.7 includes the party of the incumbent president as an additional explanatory factor. As expected, Republican incumbents have generally enjoyed much larger spending advantages than Democratic incumbents have. Taking account of this difference reduces the apparent effect of high-income growth on campaign contributions by more than half, although the effect is still clearly positive.

The apparent effect of high-income growth on campaign contributions is further reduced by allowing for the possibility that campaign contributors may also be sensitive to *overall* economic conditions. Relating the incumbent party's spending advantage to overall election-year growth rather than high-income growth, in the third column of table 4.7, produces an even stronger relationship. And when both high-income growth and overall election-year income growth are included in the analysis, in the fourth column of table 4.7, the apparent effect of the former is even further reduced, while the latter has a much stronger effect. Thus, although income growth among affluent families probably does have a distinct positive effect on the incumbent party's spending advantage, that effect seems to be modest by comparison with the effects of partisanship and overall election-year income growth.

Figure 4.5 provides a graphical summary of the historical relationship between partisanship, election-year income growth, and presidential campaign spending. The substantial difference in spending advantages between Republican incumbents (represented by black dots) and Democratic incumbents (the white diamonds) is very clear in the figure. Every Republican incumbent (or successor) spent at least slightly more than his Democratic challenger, while every Democratic incumbent (or successor) spent at least slightly *less* than his Republican challenger. However, within each party there was also a marked tendency for incumbent candidates to spend more, relative to their opponents, in years with robust election-year income growth. The difference in the incumbent candidate's expected spending advantage between the best and worst election-year economies ($1.63 per voter) is almost as large as the expected difference between Republican and Democratic incumbents ($1.86 per voter).

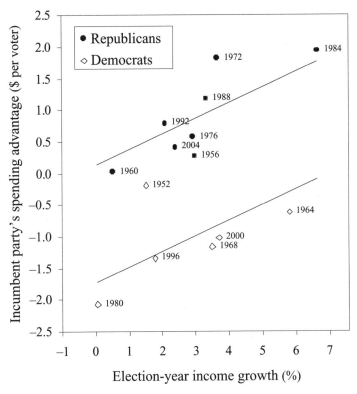

Figure 4.5 Election-Year Income Growth and Incumbent Spending Advantage, 1952–2004

The 1952 election represents a notable anomaly in the overall relationship between campaign spending and election-year income growth. Democratic candidate Adlai Stevenson spent almost as much as his Republican challenger, Dwight Eisenhower, despite the fact that income growth was slower than usual that year. Perhaps Stevenson was advantaged by the fact that the Democratic Party had occupied the White House for the 20 preceding years; in any event, ignoring the 1952 election would only strengthen both the relationship between campaign spending and election-year income growth and the apparent partisan advantage of Republicans over Democrats.[22]

---

[22] Omitting the 1952 election from the analysis reported in the second column of table 4.7 increases the estimated Republican spending advantage by 12% and the estimated effect of election-year growth by 17%.

Table 4.8 elaborates the statistical analyses of presidential voting behavior presented in table 4.6 to allow for the impact of differential campaign spending. The results for the entire electorate suggest that campaign spending did have a substantial effect on voters' choices. For a voter who was otherwise equally well-disposed toward both candidates, they imply that each additional dollar of campaign spending increased the probability of supporting the candidate who spent the money by almost four percentage points. The implied effect is smaller for voters who were predisposed on other grounds to favor one candidate or the other. Nevertheless, this effect is large enough (and sufficiently precisely estimated) to provide strong evidence that campaign spending has had a significant electoral impact in presidential elections over the past half-century.[23]

Surprisingly, campaign spending seems to have had a considerably stronger effect among affluent voters than among voters of modest means. The separate analyses for high-, middle-, and low-income voters suggest that campaign spending was twice as effective among high-income voters as among middle-income voters—and that campaign spending had no perceptible effect among voters in the bottom third of the income distribution.

POLITICAL CONSEQUENCES OF BIASED ACCOUNTABILITY

The statistical analyses presented in table 4.8 demonstrate that presidential campaign spending has had a significant impact on voting behavior over the past half-century. However, they do not speak directly to the political *consequences* of that fact. Those consequences are spelled out more clearly in the first column of table 4.9, which reports the estimated impact of differential campaign spending on the outcome of each of the past 14 presidential elections.[24] Since Republican candidates spent at least slightly more money than

[23] There is some reason to worry that the estimated effects of campaign spending in table 4.8 might be biased by unobserved features of the election context that influence both the incumbent party's spending advantage and the incumbent party's electoral success. However, replacing the observed spending advantage in each election year with predicted values derived from the regression analyses in table 4.7 has very little effect on the parameter estimates in table 4.8. For the full sample, the estimated effects of campaign spending based on these predicted values are slightly larger than the corresponding estimate in table 4.8 (6% and 19% larger, respectively, for predicted values derived from the regression models reported in the second and fourth columns of table 4.7). The estimates for separate income subgroups are also generally similar to those reported in table 4.8.

[24] My projections are based on the separate results for high-, middle-, and low-income voters presented in the second, third, and fourth columns of table 4.8. Thus, they allow for greater sensitivity to campaign spending on the part of high-income voters. They also allow for greater sensitivity on the part of voters who were otherwise equally likely to support either candidate (most notably, those who claimed that they did not identify with, or "lean" toward, either party). Having estimated the impact of equal campaign spending on each major-party

TABLE 4.8

The Electoral Impact of Campaign Spending by Income Group, 1952–2004

Probit parameter estimates (with standard errors in parentheses) for probability of incumbent party vote. Data clustered by election year; major-party voters only.

	Full sample	High income	Middle income	Low income
Incumbent spending advantage ($/voter)	.097 (.033)	.181 (.039)	.086 (.034)	-.015 (.047)
Election-year income growth (%)	-.001 (.018)	-.009 (.024)	.027 (.015)	-.028 (.028)
High-income growth (95th percentile)	.084 (.011)	.071 (.014)	.088 (.009)	.100 (.014)
Incumbent party tenure (years)	-.044 (.009)	-.053 (.008)	-.034 (.007)	-.048 (.012)
Incumbent party identification (-1 to +1)	1.619 (.068)	1.697 (.096)	1.594 (.069)	1.541 (.063)
Intercept	.232 (.105)	.379 (.114)	.046 (.068)	.292 (.155)
Log likelihood	-6,404.9	-2,269.4	-1,997.5	-1,715.2
Pseudo-R^2	.42	.44	.41	.42
N	15,976	5,911	4,848	4,242

Source: Calculations based on data from 1952–2004 National Election Study surveys, Alexander (1980), Federal Election Commission, Bureau of Economic Analysis, and Census Bureau Historical Income Tables.

TABLE 4.9

The Effects of Unequal Campaign Spending, High-Income Growth, and Economic Myopia on Presidential Election Outcomes, 1952–2004

Projected impact on Republican popular vote margin. **Boldface** entries represent years in which actual and projected election winners differ.

Election year	Estimated effect of unequal campaign spending	Estimated effect of differential sensitivity to high-income growth	Combined effect of myopia, high-income growth, and unequal spending
1952	+0.8%	−5.1%	+2.2%
1956	+1.1%	+12.7%	**+15.8%**
1960	+0.1%	+11.9%	+11.1%
1964	+2.2%	+9.3%	+5.6%
1968	**+4.1%**	**+13.3%**	**+17.6%**
1972	+3.6%	+11.9%	+16.9%
1976	+2.7%	−0.2%	+10.4%
1980	+7.7%	+8.7%	**+22.0%**
1984	+8.0%	−11.9%	+8.0%
1988	+5.2%	−4.5%	+5.1%
1992	+2.7%	−4.4%	+2.3%
1996	+4.8%	+3.0%	+7.3%
2000	**+3.6%**	**+13.9%**	**+16.5%**
2004	+1.7%	−11.0%	−7.7%
Average	+3.5%	+3.4%	+9.5%

Source: Calculations based on parameter estimates in table 4.8.

their Democratic opponents did in each of those elections, it is not surprising to find that they did at least slightly better in every election than they would have if spending had been equal.[25] In five cases, their popular vote margin was at least four points larger than it would have been, and in two cases— 1968 and 2000—Republican candidates won close elections that they very

voter in the NES surveys, I aggregated these estimated effects (multiplied by the proportion of major-party voters in each year's electorate) to produce the differences reported in the first column of table 4.9. Computing projected popular vote margins directly from the survey data for each election year would produce less accurate estimates, since the probit analyses reported in table 4.8 do not include election-specific intercepts (and thus the sum of predicted probabilities implied by the probit results does not necessarily match the actual election result for each year).

[25] It has always been something of a puzzle why shifts in the partisan loyalties of American voters have not figured in most aggregate-level analyses of presidential election outcomes, since party identification is easily the strongest predictor of individual voting behavior. The fact that Republican presidential candidates have routinely outspent their Democratic opponents

probably would have lost had they been unable to outspend incumbent Democratic vice presidents.

The estimated impact of differential campaign spending on the average Republican vote margin over all 14 elections amounts to 3.5 percentage points—virtually the same average effect as for economic myopia in table 4.3. As with the estimated effect of economic myopia, the estimated effect of differential campaign spending in table 4.9 is large enough to account for the entire net popular vote margin for Republican presidential candidates in the period covered by my analysis. Thus, we have two distinct and equally powerful explanations for Republicans' electoral success over the past half-century.

Neither of those explanations, however, takes account of the peculiar sensitivity of voters to election-year income growth among high-income families. Even after allowing for the effect of differential campaign spending, the statistical analyses reported in table 4.8 indicate that incumbent party candidates did markedly better in election years when high-income growth was especially robust. The effect is substantial, and too precisely estimated to be plausibly attributable to chance.[26] It is also quite consistent across income groups; indeed, the results suggest that low-income voters were probably more sensitive to high-income growth than high-income voters were.

This persistent sensitivity of voters across the income spectrum to high-income growth provides a third distinct, powerful explanation for Republican successes in presidential elections. As the tabulation of election-year income growth rates in figure 4.4 makes very clear, Republicans have presided over even more election-year growth for rich families than for middle-class and poor families, while Democrats have presided over even more dismal election-year growth for affluent families than for middle-class and poor families. (The partisan difference in election-year income growth

---

suggests a possible resolution to that puzzle: analyses taking account of the Democrats' advantage in party identification but not the Republicans' advantage in campaign spending would be strongly biased toward producing null results, since the two advantages are largely offsetting.

[26] As with the high-income growth effects reported in table 4.6, the effects reported in table 4.8 persist even when any one election is omitted from the analysis (the estimates for the full sample range from .075 to .095), or when the analysis is limited to the seven elections from 1952 through 1976 (.070) or to the seven elections from 1980 through 2004 (.153). The high-income growth effect also appears in the eight elections with Republican incumbents (.092) but not in the six elections with Democratic incumbents. (In that subset of cases, the estimated effect of campaign spending is about 60 times as large as in table 4.8, and the estimated effects of election-year income growth, high-income growth, and incumbent party tenure are equally implausible; clearly it is asking too much of these data to estimate five distinct aggregate-level effects on the basis of six elections.)

for families at the 95th percentile is 3.4 percentage points; the corresponding differences for less affluent families range from 0.8 to 1.9 percentage points.)

The electoral implications of voters' distinctive sensitivity to these partisan differences in high-income growth are summarized in the second column of table 4.9.[27] As with the effects of economic myopia and differential campaign spending, the effect of voters' sensitivity to high-income growth has been to bolster the Republicans' average vote margin by about 3.5 percentage points. However, the variability of this effect from one election to the next is much greater than for economic myopia or differential campaign spending. For example, in 1956 and 1972, Republican incumbents were greatly advantaged by the sensitivity of voters to robust high-income growth, since the incomes of affluent families grew about twice as fast as overall incomes did in those years (6.2% and 6.6%, respectively; versus 3.0% and 3.6%). In contrast, Republican incumbents in 1984 and 2004 won much narrower victories on the basis of relatively slow growth among affluent families (3.4% and –0.6%) than they would have on the basis of stronger overall income growth (6.6% and 2.4%).

Finally, the third column of table 4.9 summarizes the combined effects of the three separate partisan biases examined in this chapter—economic myopia, differential campaign spending, and voters' sensitivity to high-income growth.[28] The results suggest that the combined effect of these three distinct partisan biases was only slightly smaller than the sum of the three separate effects reported in tables 4.4 and 4.9. Absent these biases, the average Republican vote margin in presidential elections over the past half-century would have been more than nine percentage points less than it actually was.

---

[27] The projections are constructed along the same lines as those reported in the first column of table 4.9. Voters are allowed to be myopic (responding only to election-year income growth), and they are allowed to be responsive to campaign spending to the extent implied by the statistical results reported in table 4.8. Differences between actual and projected voting behavior are computed by comparing each voter's probability of casting a Republican vote based on the parameter estimates and data in table 4.8 with the corresponding probability calculated by substituting the overall income growth rate in each election year for the observed growth rate among families at the 95th percentile of the income distribution.

[28] The relevant counterfactual for these calculations is how each election would have turned out if the two major-party candidates had spent the same amount of money on their campaigns and if economic voting had been based entirely on the cumulative growth in real disposable income per capita for the entire population over the second, third, and fourth years of the incumbent president's term. The projections are based on the income-specific probit parameter estimates reported in table 4.8, with differential campaign spending in each election year set to zero and the cumulative income growth rates shown in figure 4.1 substituted for both election-year income growth and high-income growth rates.

Since the actual Republican vote margin over this period was only 3.3%, the magnitude of the shift in support attributable to partisan biases in economic accountability is obviously profoundly consequential. In four instances—1956, 1968, 1980, and 2000—the estimated effects of partisan biases are large enough to have been essential to Republican presidential victories. These elections include three of the four cases in the past 70 years in which Republican challengers have managed to oust Democratic incumbents or their successors from the White House. Dwight Eisenhower in 1952 was probably the only Republican in this era who would have won the job in his own right, without the benefit of incumbency or superior campaign spending or myopic voters.

The analyses presented in this chapter have only begun to unravel the ways in which contemporary American electoral politics is shaped by partisan biases in economic accountability. More data and more detailed analysis will be necessary to confirm the patterns established here and to clear up significant remaining uncertainties—perhaps most importantly, providing a clearer account of the peculiar sensitivity of voters to the economic fortunes of families at the top of the income distribution. In the meantime, however, it seems clear that voters' inaccessibility to long views, their tendency to see only present advantages, and their "materialist dream" of economic solidarity with the upper class all create important failures of economic accountability in the American electoral process.

From a political standpoint, the most important consequence of those failures of accountability has been to greatly bolster the electoral fortunes of the Republican Party. Absent the partisan biases documented here, my analysis suggests that Republican presidential candidates would probably have won only about half as many elections as they actually did win over the past half-century. In light of the substantial cumulative impact of Republican policies on the economic fortunes of middle-class and poor families demonstrated in chapter 2, that counterfactual point implies that a great deal of economic inequality in contemporary America is a curious byproduct of peculiarities in voting behavior utterly unrelated to voters' taste or tolerance for inequality.

This account provides plenty of grist for political observers disposed to attribute Republican electoral successes to false consciousness. However, this is not the familiar, largely mythical story of white working-class voters seduced by abortion and gay marriage. The false consciousness seems to be much more widespread than that story suggests—and it focuses squarely on the mechanisms of retrospective evaluation that contemporary political scientists have placed at the heart of democratic accountability. If "voters are not fools," as V. O. Key Jr. insisted, neither are they the "rational god of vengeance and of reward" that he and many other sophisticated scholars have counted upon to ensure the responsiveness of elected officials to the interests of their constituents.[29] The resulting failures of accountability have had crucial consequences for the course of American electoral politics, and thus for the workings of the American political economy—including the production of economic inequality.

[29] Key (1966), 7; (1964), 568. Although the colorful phrase "rational god of vengeance and reward" is frequently (mis)quoted in connection with the optimistic view of retrospective accountability Key set out in *The Responsible Electorate*, its actual use in his earlier textbook, *Politics, Parties, & Pressure Groups*, is more specific and negatory: "The Founding Fathers, by the provision for midterm elections, built into the constitutional system a procedure whose strange consequences lack explanation in any theory that personifies the electorate as a rational god of vengeance and of reward."

Do Americans Care about Inequality?

THE ANALYSIS PRESENTED in chapter 4 suggests that much of the Republican Party's electoral success in the post-war era—and thus, much of the escalation in economic inequality associated with Republican administrations and policies—is a by-product of partisan biases in economic accountability. From the standpoint of democratic theory, that is a peculiarly unsatisfying conclusion. As good democrats, we like to think that government policy stems, directly or indirectly, from the Will of the People. If it stems instead from such irrelevant quirks of voter psychology as myopia, misperceptions, and responsiveness to campaign spending, the warm glow seems distinctly diminished.

Democratic optimists, however, will note that elections are by no means the only possible avenue by which the Will of the People may shape public policy. Political science provides many examples of analyses demonstrating significant direct effects of public opinion on public policy, regardless of whether Republicans or Democrats happen to be in charge.[1] Thus, my accounts of policy making in chapters 6, 7, 8, and 9 will involve careful weighing of the apparent influence of public sentiment on one hand and partisan elite ideology on the other.

Assessing and interpreting the role of public opinion in the policy-making process require, first, some clear understanding of what that public opinion *is*. Citizens may have crystallized views regarding specific matters of public policy—or they may not. Insofar as citizens do have meaningful policy preferences, those preferences may be internally consistent and sensibly related to their broader political values—or they may not. Public opinion touching on issues related to inequality is likely to be especially complex, given the deep and multifaceted resonance of the value of equality in American political culture.

Much popular commentary suggests that ordinary Americans find inequality both natural and unobjectionable—that the ideal of equality, despite its prominence in our official ideology, has little real resonance in American

---

[1] Perhaps the most ambitious work along these lines is by Erikson, MacKuen, and Stimson (2002)—though, as I note in chapter 10, their statistical analyses seem to imply smaller direct effects of public opinion on policy and larger electoral effects than one might gather from their prose. For my own contribution to this literature, a case study of the Reagan defense buildup in the early 1980s, see Bartels (1991).

political culture. According to sociologist Nathan Glazer, for example, "Americans, unlike the citizens of other prosperous democracies, not to mention those of poor countries, do not seem to care much about inequality. . . . [E]ven after the Enron and other scandals, most Americans remain apathetic about inequality: What we have today is outrage against those who do not play fair—not outrage over inequality as such." In a similar vein, business writer Robert Samuelson argued that, "on the whole, Americans care less about inequality—the precise gap between the rich and the poor—than about opportunity and achievement: are people getting ahead?"[2]

Analysts of American ideology have often emphasized the potential for conflict and contradiction between the core values of economic opportunity and political equality. For example, Jennifer Hochschild reported that, in the economic domain, her rich and poor respondents "agree on a principle of differentiation, not of equality. . . . They define political freedom as strict equality, but economic freedom as an equal chance to become unequal." Similarly, Herbert McClosky and John Zaller wrote that vast differences in wealth and life chances result "partly from the play of economic interests and the desire of those who have prospered to retain their advantages, and partly from the widespread acceptance of a powerful set of values associated with the private enterprise system that conflicts with egalitarianism." Stanley Feldman provided evidence that people use distinct, often-conflicting principles to assess "micro-justice" (individual rewards) and "macro-justice" (the social distribution of rewards).[3]

In light of these conflicts and complexities, it should not be surprising that analysts have also noted important exceptions to the general pattern of acceptance of economic inequality. For example, Hochschild found that "almost everyone, rich and poor, is incensed that the very wealthy do not pay their fair share of taxes. They argue that loopholes are too large and that the tax structure itself is insufficiently progressive." McClosky and Zaller noted "signs of resentment toward the advantages enjoyed by corporations and the wealthy. A sizable majority of the mass public believes that corporations and the rich 'really run the country,' that they do not pay their fair shares of taxes, and that they receive better treatment in the courts than poor people do. A fair number of respondents (though not a majority) also believe that the laws mostly favor the rich."[4]

In this chapter I explore four important facets of Americans' views about equality. First, I examine public support for broad egalitarian values, and the social bases and political consequences of that support. Second, I examine

[2] Glazer (2003), 111; Robert J. Samuelson, "Indifferent to Inequality?" *Newsweek*, May 7, 2001, 45.

[3] Hochschild (1981), 111, 278; McClosky and Zaller (1984), 63; Feldman (2003).

[4] Hochschild (1981), 280; McClosky and Zaller (1984), 177–178.

public attitudes toward salient economic groups, including rich people, poor people, big business, and labor unions, among others. As with more abstract support for egalitarian values, I investigate variation in attitudes toward these groups and the political implications of that variation. Third, I examine public perceptions of inequality and opportunity, including perceptions of growing economic inequality, normative assessments of that trend, and explanations for disparities in economic status. Finally, I examine how public perceptions of inequality, its causes and consequences, and its normative implications are shaped by the interaction of political information and political ideology.

The first half of the chapter provides strong evidence of the importance of egalitarian values in American political culture. Most people express support for equality in the abstract; and, perhaps more surprisingly, those egalitarian values are translated into support for a variety of concrete social welfare policies, including government services, employment programs, health insurance, and aid to blacks. At a more visceral level, survey respondents say they feel much warmer toward "working class people" and "poor people" than toward "business people" and "rich people." Most also believe that rich people pay less than they should in taxes.

All of this sounds like fertile ground for a populist backlash against the escalating inequality of the New Gilded Age. Perhaps it is. However, the second half of this chapter provides some significant grounds for doubt. Three-fourths of Americans say that "the difference in incomes between rich people and poor people in the United States today" is larger than it was 20 years ago; but those responses appear to reflect cynical folk wisdom more than close attention to actual economic trends. The proportion of the public agreeing with the sardonic adage that "the rich get richer and the poor get poorer" increased markedly in the 1960s and early 1970s—a period in which the poor became rather *less* poor, though poverty became more salient. However, the substantial increase in economic inequality over the following three decades had virtually no effect on perceptions of inequality. Meanwhile, among people who did recognize that income differences have increased, more than one-third said they had not thought about whether that is a good thing or a bad thing.

Public ignorance and inattention have important implications for the politics of inequality—implications I shall explore in more detail in chapter 6. However, my consideration of public opinion in the realm of inequality also highlights a very different limitation on the translation of egalitarian values into populist politics. Whereas uninformed people are often unlikely to grasp the political relevance of their beliefs and values, well-informed people may often deny or distort inconvenient facts, preserving a false consistency between their beliefs about the causes, extent, and meaning of inequality in contemporary American society on one hand and their ideological or partisan predilections on the other. In this way, too, genuine allegiance to the ideal of

equality may comfortably coexist with fervent support for policies that exacerbate inequality.

EGALITARIAN VALUES

Sure, we hold this truth to be self-evident, that all men are created equal; but
it is far from self-evident what that means. Is it inconsistent with American
ideals for corporate CEOs to earn 400 times as much as their workers? Are
ordinary Americans offended by the fact that the top 1% of income-earners
have hauled in 80% of the total gains in taxable income over the past quarter-
century? Is it wrong for millions of children to grow up without access to
decent schools and routine health care? If not, then escalating economic inequality may, after all, be a perfectly understandable and unobjectionable outcome of (small "d") democratic politics.

One useful starting point in examining public thinking about economic inequality in the New Gilded Age is to assess people's allegiance to equality as a
general value, sidestepping for the moment the complexities that may arise in
applying that value to specific cases. While it would be foolhardy to confuse
pronouncements of support for equality in the abstract with support for specific policies promoting specific kinds of equality in specific circumstances, it
would be equally foolhardy to deny that people's allegiance to abstract values
may have important practical consequences.

As it happens, National Election Study surveys over the past 20 years have
regularly asked random samples of Americans a detailed battery of questions
about egalitarian values, as well as questions about a wide variety of concrete
political issues in which equality might figure as an important consideration.
Responses to these questions make it possible to gauge the extent and bases
of public support for equality in the abstract—and to assess the impact of
egalitarian values on specific policy preferences. Table 5.1 provides a basic
summary of the responses.[5]

The distributions of responses show that the first question in table 5.1
elicited much more egalitarian opinion than the other questions did. More
than 85% of the respondents agreed that "Our society should do whatever is
necessary to make sure that everyone has an equal opportunity to succeed,"
and 60% agreed strongly with that statement. Interpreted literally, these responses imply an astounding level of public support for what would have to
be a very radical program of social transformation. Local funding of public
schools would have to cease; inherited wealth would have to be outlawed;

---

[5] Feldman (1988) provided a detailed discussion of the theoretical pedigree and measurement properties of these items.

TABLE 5.1

Public Support for Egalitarian Values

	Agree strongly	Agree somewhat	Neither; Don't know	Disagree somewhat	Disagree strongly
Our society should do whatever is necessary to make sure that everyone has an equal opportunity to succeed	60.2%	27.5%	5.3%	5.0%	2.0%
If people were treated more equally in this country we would have many fewer problems	30.5%	34.0%	13.7%	15.5%	5.6%
One of the big problems in this country is that we don't give everyone an equal chance	21.6%	29.7%	14.1%	23.8%	10.9%
It is not really that big a problem if some people have more of a chance in life than others	7.7%	24.4%	18.9%	28.8%	20.3%
We have gone too far in pushing equal rights in this country	16.3%	29.1%	15.1%	20.8%	18.2%
The country would be better off if we worried less about how equal people are	18.3%	29.3%	15.6%	21.3%	15.6%

$N = 15,313$.

Source: 1984–2004 National Election Study surveys.

every child would have to be assigned competent and loving parents; prejudices based on race, ethnicity, religion, and sex would have to be eradicated, along with social and economic advantages derived from intelligence, physical attractiveness, and freakish athletic skills. Of course, this is not really what people mean when they agree that we "should do whatever is necessary to make sure that everyone has an equal opportunity to succeed." Nevertheless, their willingness to endorse such a statement, even as a matter of verbal ritual, provides a striking testament to the force of "equal opportunity" in American culture.

More generally, the questions in table 5.1 referring to "an equal chance" or equal treatment generated favorable responses from half to two-thirds of the respondents, while those referring to "how equal people are" and "pushing equal rights" were rather less popular.[6] These differences suggest a consequential distinction in public thinking between equality of opportunity and equality of results. Nevertheless, more detailed analysis of individual response patterns suggests that there is a fair degree of consistency in people's responses to all six questions, regardless of their precise wording. Thus, it is convenient to combine responses to all six questions in a summary scale measuring general support for egalitarian values.[7] The summary scale values range from −1 to +1, with an average value of +.21. Twenty percent of the NES respondents had very egalitarian scale scores (in excess of +.5), while only 3% had very inegalitarian scores (below −.5).

As might be expected, people with higher family incomes were generally less supportive of egalitarian values than those with lower incomes. However, the statistical analysis presented in the first column of table 5.2 indicates that the magnitude of that relationship is quite modest, with the average difference between people at the very top of the income distribution and those at the very bottom amounting to only .11 on the −1 to +1 egalitarianism scale. These results suggest that people's own economic circumstances have surprisingly little impact on their views about the value of equality.

The analysis reported in the second column of table 5.2 documents the relationship between egalitarian values and a much broader range of social characteristics. Again, most of the differences evident here are quite modest. African Americans (and, to a lesser extent, Hispanics) are markedly more egalitarian than non-Hispanic whites. People in younger birth cohorts and those who have been to college are also somewhat more egalitarian. Frequent churchgoers, however, are somewhat less egalitarian than those who attend religious services less regularly or not at all.

[6] The battery of questions in table 5.1 is carefully balanced, with the first three inviting respondents to *agree* with egalitarian sentiments and the last three inviting them to *disagree* with egalitarian sentiments. The fact that the first three all elicit more egalitarian responses than the last three raises a concern that some respondents may simply be prone to agree rather than disagree with such statements regardless of their content. A comparison of responses to the third and fourth questions, which seem closest to being mirror images of each other, is reassuring on this score: the two questions generated very similar distributions of responses, with pluralities of 51–35 and 49–32, respectively, for the egalitarian position.

[7] A factor analysis of responses to all six questions produces a fairly strong first factor (with an eigenvalue of 1.5) and a much weaker second factor (with an eigenvalue of 0.5). The factor loadings suggest that the first factor represents general support for egalitarian values (with factor loadings ranging from .42 for the popular "equal opportunity to succeed" question to .56 for the "better off if we worried less" question), while the second factor distinguishes between "agree" and "disagree" items (the first three items and last three items in table 5.1, respectively). Since all six items load fairly similarly on the first (substantive) factor, I combine them into a summary scale by simply averaging each respondent's answers to the six questions, counting "strongly" inegalitarian responses to each question as −1, "somewhat" inegalitarian responses as −.5, "neither" or "don't know" responses as 0, "somewhat" egalitarian responses as +.5, and "strongly" egalitarian responses as +1.

TABLE 5.2
Social Bases of Support for Egalitarian Values

Ordinary least squares regression parameter estimates (with standard errors in parentheses). Egalitarian scale ranges from −1 to +1. Data are clustered by year; year-specific intercepts not shown.

	{1}	{2}	{3}
Family income (0 to 1)	−.110 (.016)	−.101 (.013)	−.055 (.012)
No high school diploma	—	.001 (.007)	−.006 (.009)
Some college	—	.036 (.011)	.039 (.011)
College graduate	—	.099 (.010)	.091 (.012)
Black	—	.314 (.017)	.246 (.017)
Hispanic	—	.091 (.013)	.056 (.013)
Female	—	.059 (.007)	.034 (.005)
South	—	−.041 (.008)	−.040 (.010)
West	—	−.001 (.009)	.002 (.010)
Northeast	—	.019 (.008)	.004 (.009)
Urban	—	.043 (.008)	.018 (.007)
Rural	—	−.012 (.007)	−.008 (.006)
Church attendance (0 to 1)	—	−.091 (.007)	−.032 (.010)
Year of birth (1889 to 1986)	—	.00235 (.00014)	.00220 (.00020)
Democratic Party identification (−1 to +1)	—	—	.102 (.006)
Liberal ideology (−1 to +1)	—	—	.210 (.010)
Standard error of regression	.382	.360	.338
R^2	.02	.12	.23
N	15,313	15,313	14,458

Source: Calculations based on data from 1984–2004 National Election Study surveys.

The analysis reported in the third column of table 5.2 adds party identification and ideology as additional explanatory factors. As might be expected, these political dispositions are fairly strongly related to egalitarian values. Even after statistically controlling for the effects of demographic characteristics, the average difference in support for egalitarian values between strong Republicans and strong Democrats amounts to one-tenth of the overall scale, while the average difference between extreme conservatives and extreme liberals amounts to an additional one-fifth of the overall scale. Clearly, allegiance to the ideal of equality is a good deal stronger on the political left than it is on the political right.[8]

[8] Of course, egalitarian values may contribute to the development of left-wing political views as well as being *affected by* those views. However, a detailed analysis by Goren (2005) suggests that egalitarianism and other "core values" are more strongly affected by partisan attachments than vice versa. In the case of egalitarianism, the estimated effect of party identification on egalitarian values is about twice as large as the reciprocal effect of egalitarian values on party identification.

TABLE 5.3
The Impact of Egalitarian Values on Policy Preferences

Ordinary least squares regression parameter estimates (with standard errors in parentheses). Policy preferences range from −1 (for the most conservative position) to +1 (for the most liberal position). Data are clustered by year; year-specific intercepts not shown.

	Government jobs	Government services	Aid to blacks	Health insurance
Egalitarianism (−1 to +1)	.557 (.032)	.543 (.021)	.557 (.010)	.454 (.044)
Standard error of regression	.559	.496	.524	.619
R^2	.14	.14	.16	.09
N	12,035	12,460	13,138	9,029
Egalitarianism (−1 to +1)	.426 (.031)	.307 (.025)	.465 (.016)	.264 (.035)
Democratic Party identification (−1 to +1)	.112 (.008)	.108 (.007)	.062 (.017)	.138 (.015)
Liberal ideology (−1 to +1)	.189 (.026)	.208 (.027)	.155 (.005)	.272 (.033)
Standard error of regression	.543	.477	.517	.595
R^2	.19	.20	.18	.16
N	11,596	12,055	12,700	8,580

Source: Calculations based on data from 1984–2004 National Election Study surveys.

Of course, given the high level of generality of the survey items comprising the egalitarian values scale, it is possible that the responses to these items represent little more than lip service to the ideal of equality. Do they have any real, concrete political impact? The analyses presented in table 5.3 strongly suggest that they do. These analyses show that people who were more egalitarian took much more liberal positions on each of the major social welfare policy issues that have appeared consistently in NES surveys over the past 20 years—support for government jobs and income maintenance, for government spending and services, for government aid to blacks, and for government health insurance.[9]

The analyses reported in the top panel of the table show how positions on each of these issues varied with attachment to egalitarian values. For government jobs, government spending, and aid to blacks, the average policy positions of the most egalitarian people were a full point to the left of the average

[9] The wording of these survey questions appears in chapter 3.

policy positions of the most inegalitarian people—a difference between moderately liberal positions on one hand and solidly conservative positions on the other. For views about health insurance, the corresponding difference was a little smaller but still substantial.

In light of the relationship between egalitarian values on one hand and ideology and partisanship on the other, one may wonder whether the apparent effects of egalitarian values in the top panel of table 5.3 are simply indirect effects of these more concrete political allegiances. However, that does not turn out to be the case. Not surprisingly, Democrats and liberals were significantly more supportive of government action in each of these issue areas than Republicans and conservatives were. Nevertheless, even after accounting for differences in policy preferences due to party identification and ideology, the analyses presented in the bottom panel of table 5.3 show that egalitarian values had a substantial independent impact. For three of the four issues (government jobs, aid to blacks, and government services), the estimated effect of egalitarian values on policy preferences is equal to or greater than the *combined* effects of party identification and ideology.

These surprisingly strong effects of egalitarian values on policy preferences are especially striking in light of the overall level of support for egalitarian values in the American public. If opponents of equality were just as numerous as proponents of equality, even the strong effects on policy preferences in table 5.3 would not alter the average level of public support for government action in these policy areas. However, the combination of net support for egalitarian values in table 5.1 and strong effects of egalitarian values on policy preferences in table 5.3 translates into significant additional public support for liberal policies. For the issues of government jobs and aid to blacks, the overall distributions of public opinion are a good deal less conservative than they would otherwise be; for the issues of government services and health insurance, distributions of opinion that would otherwise be precisely balanced between liberal and conservative extremes instead lean in a liberal direction.[10] In this respect, at least, Americans' support for egalitarian values is much more than just lip service—it has significant political consequences. As Sidney Verba and Gary Orren put it, "values are instrumental in shaping the public policies that give practical effect to political belief."[11]

---

[10] For the NES respondents included in the analyses reported in the bottom panel of table 5.3, the average values on the −1 (conservative) to +1 (liberal) policy scales are −.19 for aid to blacks, −.12 for government jobs, +.04 for government services, and +.07 for health insurance. The corresponding averages setting the effects of egalitarian values in the bottom panel of table 5.3 to zero would be −.29 for aid to blacks, −.21 for government jobs, −.02 for government services, and +.01 for health insurance.

[11] Verba and Orren (1985), 2.

RICH AND POOR

Ordinary people's responses to such abstract questions as whether we should "make sure that everyone has an equal opportunity to succeed" or whether we have "gone too far in pushing equal rights in this country" turn out to be strongly related to their views about important issues of public policy. However, it seems unlikely that most public thinking about inequality occurs at such a high level of abstraction. Indeed, political scientists have amassed a good deal of evidence suggesting that ordinary citizens engage in rather little abstract reasoning in most realms of politics, relying instead on positive or negative attitudes toward salient social groups to shape their reactions to specific public policies, political candidates, and social conditions.[12]

In the realm of economic inequality, such salient groups might include rich people, poor people, big business, and the working class, among others. NES surveys over the years have measured public attitudes toward these and a variety of other relevant groups using a "feeling thermometer." Survey respondents are invited to rate each group on a scale ranging from 0 to 100, with 50 meaning "you don't feel particularly warm or cold" toward the group, ratings above 50 representing "favorable and warm" feelings, and ratings below 50 representing "unfavorable and cool" feelings. Table 5.4 summarizes the distribution of feeling thermometer ratings for various groups in the 2004 NES survey, showing both the average rating for each group and the proportion of respondents who gave each group a rating higher than the neutral value of 50. The groups are listed in order of popularity: at one extreme, "working class people" received favorable ratings from more than 90% of the NES respondents, with an average rating of 82 out of 100; at the other extreme, "illegal immigrants" received favorable ratings from only a quarter of the respondents, with an average rating of 41.

What, if anything, do these "feeling thermometer" ratings suggest about the politics of inequality? To the extent that people's political views are colored by their sympathy for economic classes they are, perhaps surprisingly, quite likely to side with "poor people" (with an average rating of 73) over "rich people" (with an average rating of 60). A comparison of the individual ratings for these two groups indicates that 57% of the NES respondents rated poor people at least 10 points higher, while only 13% rated rich people at least 10 points higher. Thus, while ordinary Americans may hope, and perhaps even expect, to become rich someday, in the meantime they express rather little warmth for those who have already made it.

"Big business" fared even worse than rich people, with an average rating of 56—higher than gays, Muslims, and liberals, but lower than feminists, labor

---

[12] The classic statement of this point is by Converse (1964). Kinder (1983) provided a detailed survey of related research.

TABLE 5.4
"Feeling Thermometer" Ratings for Social Groups, 2004

Ratings on 0 (least favorable) to 100 (most favorable) "feeling thermometer."

	Average rating	Percentage over 50	N
Working class people	82.3	92.7%	1,056
Women	82.2	89.0%	1,052
Older people	81.9	90.4%	1,059
The military	79.5	86.0%	1,054
Middle class people	76.7	86.3%	1,051
Young people	73.6	80.8%	1,055
Whites	73.3	74.3%	1,041
Poor people	73.2	79.4%	1,049
Men	72.6	76.2%	1,052
Blacks	71.4	73.6%	1,042
Southerners	70.1	68.9%	1,038
Business people	69.2	74.7%	1,047
Catholics	69.0	69.1%	1,037
Hispanic Americans	67.7	67.5%	1,037
Asian Americans	67.2	65.0%	1,025
Jews	66.7	63.0%	1,027
Environmentalists	65.3	70.6%	1,043
Conservatives	61.0	59.7%	1,019
The Catholic Church	60.3	57.1%	1,036
Rich people	59.9	54.9%	1,043
Christian fundamentalists	58.5	51.6%	1,003
The Democratic Party	57.7	55.2%	1,178
Labor unions	57.7	54.9%	1,048
People on welfare	55.9	47.4%	1,045
Feminists	55.8	47.8%	1,028
Big business	55.7	51.9%	1,045
Liberals	54.6	46.1%	1,014
Republican Party	54.2	50.8%	1,176
Muslims	53.4	38.6%	999
Gay men and lesbians	47.7	32.0%	1,044
Illegal immigrants	40.6	24.9%	1,039

Source: 2004 National Election Study survey.

unions, and people on welfare. The less pejorative phrase "business people" elicited much warmer feelings (with an average rating of 69); however, even "business people" were rated less favorably than poor people (with 26% of the respondents rating business people at least 10 points higher while 40% rated poor people at least 10 points higher).

Meanwhile, "labor unions" (with an average rating of 58) fared only slightly better than "big business" and much worse than (presumably unorganized) "working class people." "Working class people" (with an average rating of 82) were held in even higher esteem than "middle class people" (with an average rating of 77). The difference in average ratings between the two groups is less than six points on the 100-point thermometer scale; but 36% of the respondents rated working-class people at least 10 points higher, while only 10% rated middle-class people at least 10 points higher. Given the frequent characterization of America as a society that exalts the middle class, it seems remarkable that most Americans express even more positive feelings about working-class people than about middle-class people.

The statistical analyses reported in table 5.5 relate the attitudes toward rich people and poor people tapped by the NES feeling thermometer ratings to the same social characteristics considered as bases of egalitarian values in table 5.2. As in table 5.2, the first column shows the impact of family income considered in isolation. It should not be surprising that rich people felt significantly warmer toward "rich people" than poor people did. What may be more surprising is that even people at the very top of the income distribution felt less warm toward "rich people" than toward "poor people," on average.[13]

Including a variety of additional characteristics in the analysis, as shown in the second column of table 5.5, reduces the apparent impact of income only slightly. Differences in educational attainment appear to rival differences in economic status in shaping attitudes toward rich and poor people, with college graduates more than 10 points warmer toward rich people than those without high school diplomas. Older people, Hispanics, and churchgoers were also somewhat warmer toward rich people, but those effects were smaller in magnitude.[14]

The analysis presented in the third column of table 5.5 includes partisanship and ideology as additional explanatory factors. As might be expected,

[13] The intercept reported in the first column of table 5.5, −22.2, represents the expected difference in thermometer ratings between "rich people" and "poor people" for respondents at the very bottom of the income scale. The sum of the intercept and the family income coefficient, −22.2 + 17.5 = −4.7, represents the expected difference between "rich" and "poor" thermometer ratings for respondents at the very top of the income scale.

[14] The parameter estimates for age and age squared imply that respondents in their late thirties were least sympathetic toward rich people relative to poor people. Younger respondents were only slightly more sympathetic toward rich people, but older respondents were significantly more sympathetic toward rich people. The expected difference in relative ratings between a respondent in her late thirties and one in her mid-seventies is 6.2 points on the thermometer scale, exceeding all but the income and education differences. Allowing for the effects of partisanship and ideology, in the last column of table 5.5, produces qualitatively similar but even stronger age differences.

TABLE 5.5

Social Bases of Attitudes toward Rich People and Poor People

Ordinary least squares regression parameter estimates (with standard errors in parentheses) for differences in feeling thermometer ratings of "rich people" and "poor people." Positive numbers imply warmer feelings toward the rich; negative numbers imply warmer feelings toward the poor.

	{1}	{2}	{3}
Family income (0 to 1)	17.5 (2.8)	13.1 (3.3)	11.2 (3.3)
No high school diploma	—	−6.4 (2.5)	−6.1 (2.5)
Some college	—	0.8 (2.0)	0.5 (2.0)
College graduate	—	4.2 (2.2)	5.0 (2.2)
Black	—	0.2 (2.5)	3.5 (2.6)
Hispanic	—	5.7 (2.5)	7.0 (2.4)
Female	—	−2.4 (1.6)	−1.5 (1.5)
South	—	−1.8 (2.0)	−2.6 (2.0)
West	—	3.2 (2.3)	3.4 (2.3)
Northeast	—	−1.3 (2.3)	−0.8 (2.3)
Rural	—	0.3 (2.0)	−0.5 (1.9)
Church attendance (0 to 1)	—	3.5 (2.0)	1.2 (2.0)
Age	—	−.33 (.25)	−.47 (.24)
Age squared	—	.0044 (.0025)	.0059 (.0025)
Republican Party identification (−1 to +1)	—	—	4.5 (1.3)
Conservative ideology (−1 to +1)	—	—	5.4 (2.0)
Intercept	−22.2 (1.6)	−17.0 (6.0)	−13.2 (5.9)
Standard error of regression	24.6	24.4	24.0
Adjusted R²	.03	.05	.10
N	1,034	1,034	1,034

Source: Calculations based on data from 2004 National Election Study survey.

conservatives and Republicans tended to rate rich people more favorably than liberals and Democrats did. However, the apparent effects of both these factors combined did not equal the differences attributable to income or to education. Moreover, even people who were both conservatives and Republican identifiers expressed considerably warmer views, on average, toward poor people than toward rich people.

The 2002 and 2004 NES surveys included another set of questions tapping attitudes toward rich people and poor people in the context of a more concrete policy issue. These questions asked whether rich people, poor people, and the respondents themselves are asked to pay too much, too little, or about

TABLE 5.6

Perceived Tax Burdens, 2002 and 2004

"Do you feel you are asked to pay more than you should in federal income taxes, about the right amount, or less than you should? What about rich people? What about poor people?"

	2002	2004	Combined
Own tax burden			
Pay more than they should	47.3%	38.8%	43.0%
Pay about the right amount	45.6%	51.9%	48.8%
Pay less than they should	4.0%	5.1%	4.5%
Rich people			
Pay more than they should	15.3%	10.8%	13.0%
Pay about the right amount	30.4%	25.3%	27.8%
Pay less than they should	52.6%	59.2%	55.9%
Poor people			
Pay more than they should	44.2%	45.6%	44.9%
Pay about the right amount	44.1%	42.9%	43.5%
Pay less than they should	9.0%	6.9%	7.9%
N	1,511	1,212	2,723

Source: 2002 and 2004 National Election Study surveys.

the right amount in federal income taxes. The distributions of responses to these questions are presented in table 5.6.[15]

As with the feeling thermometer ratings of rich people and poor people, these responses demonstrate a rather striking skew in favor of the poor over the rich. For example, 45% of the NES respondents said that poor people are asked to pay more than they should in federal income taxes, while only 13% said that rich people are asked to pay more than they should. However, more than half the respondents said that rich people are asked to pay *less* than they should, while only 8% said that poor people are asked to pay less than they should. Of course, these responses may be based on very inaccurate perceptions of how much rich people and poor people are actually asked to pay in federal income taxes. Still, if taken at face value, they seem to demonstrate substantial public support for increasing, rather than decreasing, the progressivity of the tax system.

[15] The tax burden questions were each asked twice in the 2002 NES survey, before and after the election. The pre-election responses are reported in table 5.6 and analyzed in table 5.7, since they seem less likely to be affected by sensitization stemming from the extensive battery of questions focusing on inequality and tax policy in the 2002 NES survey.

Respondents' perceptions regarding their own tax burdens were not too different from their perceptions regarding the tax burdens borne by poor people. Fewer than 5% said they are asked to pay *less* than they should, but almost half said they are asked to pay "about the right amount." The proportion who said they are asked to pay too much was almost identical to the proportion who said poor people are asked to pay too much (43% versus 45%). Insofar as these results imply any sort of class solidarity on the part of ordinary Americans, it is class solidarity with the poor rather than with the rich.

Table 5.7 summarizes how these perceived tax burdens varied with people's social and political characteristics.[16] Responses to the tax burden questions are coded to range from −1 (for those who think they, or rich people, or poor people are asked to pay too little) to +1 (for those who think they, or rich people, or poor people are asked to pay too much). Thus, positive entries imply more sympathetic perceptions of a group's (or one's own) tax burdens, while negative entries indicate less sympathetic perceptions.

It should probably not be surprising that more affluent people and conservatives were more likely than poorer people and liberals to say that they are asked to pay too much in federal income taxes. Middle-aged people were also substantially more likely than younger or older people to say that they are asked to pay too much—a pattern that presumably reflects changes over the course of the life cycle in work status, tax liability, and, perhaps, reliance on government benefits.[17] However, the apparent differences in perceived tax burdens associated with race, ethnicity, and educational attainment are somewhat more puzzling. On one hand, other things being equal, Hispanics were significantly less likely than non-Hispanic whites to say that they are asked to pay too much, but African Americans were considerably *more* likely to say that. On the other hand, other things being equal, people without high school diplomas and people with college degrees were *both* significantly *less* likely than high school graduates to say that they are asked to pay too much.

Perhaps unsurprisingly, Republicans and conservatives were generally more sympathetic regarding the tax burdens of rich people, while Democrats

[16] This analysis combines respondents from the 2002 and 2004 NES surveys. The differences in average responses between the two surveys evident in table 5.6 are captured by the "2004 survey" variable included in table 5.7. Analyzing the two surveys separately produces generally similar patterns of statistical estimates in 2002 and 2004.

[17] The statistical results reported in table 5.7 imply that, other things being equal, respondents' perceptions of their own tax burdens increased gradually (by a total of .10 on the −1 to +1 scale) between the ages of 18 and 41, then declined at an accelerating rate (by .11 between the ages of 41 and 65, and by a further .18 between the ages of 65 and 80). This pattern presumably reflects the fact that most people's earnings—and, thus, their tax payments—increase through their twenties and thirties and decline following retirement.

TABLE 5.7
Social Characteristics and Perceived Tax Burdens

Ordinary least squares regression parameter estimates (with standard errors in parentheses). Tax burden scales range from −1 (pay less than they should) to +1 (pay more than they should).

	Own tax burden	Rich tax burden	Poor tax burden
Family income			
(0 to 1)	.153 (.045)	.043 (.056)	−.095 (.051)
No high school			
diploma	−.225 (.035)	.072 (.043)	−.124 (.039)
Some college	−.066 (.027)	−.032 (.034)	.001 (.031)
College graduate	−.157 (.030)	.077 (.038)	−.035 (.034)
Black	.097 (.037)	.141 (.045)	.055 (.041)
Hispanic	−.144 (.034)	.060 (.042)	−.080 (.037)
Female	.007 (.021)	−.057 (.027)	.045 (.024)
South	.003 (.029)	.070 (.035)	−.026 (.032)
West	.019 (.033)	.013 (.041)	−.008 (.037)
Northeast	−.050 (.033)	.054 (.040)	.035 (.037)
Rural	−.034 (.028)	.034 (.035)	.020(.032)
Church attendance			
(0 to 1)	−.003 (.029)	.067 (.036)	.032 (.032)
Age	.0151 (.0034)	−.0164 (.0042)	.0055 (.0038)
Age squared	−.000185 (.000034)	.000157 (.000042)	−.000089 (.000038)
Republican Party			
identification			
(−1 to +1)	.039 (.018)	.227 (.023)	−.062 (.021)
Conservative			
ideology (−1 to +1)	.127 (.027)	.140 (.034)	−.058 (.031)
2004 survey	−.093 (.021)	−.120 (.026)	.041 (.024)
Intercept	.203 (.083)	−.111 (.102)	.355 (.093)
Standard error			
of regression	.547	.679	.617
Adjusted R²	.09	.09	.03
N	2,723	2,723	2,723

Source: Calculations based on data from 2002 and 2004 National Election Study surveys.

and liberals were more sympathetic toward poor people. However, the latter effects are modest in magnitude. For that matter, most of the social and political characteristics included in table 5.7 seem to have been less important in shaping perceptions of poor people's tax burdens than in shaping perceptions of rich people's tax burdens. A rare exception is family income, which had a very modest positive effect on sympathy for rich people and a somewhat larger (but still fairly modest) negative effect on sympathy for poor people. Another exception is not having a high school diploma. Surprisingly, people in this lowest educational stratum were noticeably more respectful of the tax burden borne by rich people and even more noticeably *un*sympathetic regarding the tax burden of poor people.

Notwithstanding exceptions of this sort, what is most noteworthy in people's attitudes about the tax burdens of the rich and the poor—as in attitudes about these groups more generally—is that the rich are viewed much less sympathetically, and the poor are viewed much more sympathetically, than one might expect. While it may be true that "Americans do not go in for envy," as a report in *The Economist* put it, neither do they seem especially solicitous of rich people or their problems.[18] Nor do they seem to be punitive in their attitudes toward poor people—except when the focus is shifted to "people on welfare," and even *they* are viewed more favorably than big business, liberals, or the Republican Party. Insofar as the policy preferences of ordinary citizens are colored by their class sympathies, those sympathies are more likely to reinforce broadly egalitarian values than to negate them.

PERCEPTIONS OF INEQUALITY

The political activation of ordinary citizens' values and sympathies is far from automatic. Values and sympathies are likely to be politically significant only when they are connected to consequential political actors or issues. Given the enormous complexity of politics and public affairs, connections of that sort may require a good deal of political information and attention among citizens. For example, egalitarian impulses are likely to gain real political traction only when citizens perceive contradictions between egalitarian ideals and social realities. As the acute political observer Walter Lippmann noted more than 80 years ago, much everyday political thinking occurs in a "pseudo-environment" only loosely connected to social reality, postponing or preventing "the murder of a Beautiful Theory by a Gang of Brutal Facts."[19]

In the present context, it seems well worth exploring how much ordinary Americans know about the Brutal Facts of escalating inequality sketched in chapter 1. Fortunately, the 2002 and 2004 NES surveys included a variety of questions probing respondents' perceptions of economic inequality, its causes, and its consequences. Table 5.8 presents the distribution of responses to questions in the surveys assessing people's recognition of and reaction to the marked increase in income inequality over the past two decades. The first question in this sequence asked whether "the difference in incomes between rich people and poor people in the United States today is larger, smaller, or

---

[18] "The Rich, the Poor and the Growing Gap between Them," *The Economist*, June 17, 2006, 28.

[19] Lippmann (1922), 10.

TABLE 5.8

Perceptions of Economic Inequality

"Do you think the difference in incomes between rich people and poor people in the United States today is larger, smaller, or about the same as it was 20 years ago? (Would you say the difference in incomes is) much larger [smaller] or somewhat larger [smaller]? [If larger or smaller,] Do you think this is a good thing, a bad thing, or haven't you thought about it?"

	A good thing	A bad thing	Haven't thought; DK	Total
Much larger	2.5%	31.3%	10.5%	44.3%
Somewhat larger	2.2%	12.5%	16.6%	31.4%
About the same	—	—	—	16.4%
Somewhat smaller	1.6%	0.5%	2.4%	4.4%
Much smaller	0.3%	0.6%	0.2%	1.2%
Don't Know; Not Asked	—	—	—	2.2%
Total	6.6%	45.0%	29.8%	100%

$N = 2,577$.

Source: 2002 and 2004 National Election Study surveys.

about the same as it was 20 years ago." Those who said "larger" or "smaller" were asked whether the difference is *much* larger or smaller or only *somewhat* larger or smaller; they were also asked whether the change is "a good thing" or "a bad thing."

The distribution of responses in table 5.8 seems to demonstrate widespread public recognition of the sheer fact of growing economic inequality in contemporary America. Three-fourths of the NES respondents said the difference in incomes between rich people and poor people was larger than it was 20 years ago, and 44% said it was *much* larger. Only about 6% said it was smaller.

However, the reality of this apparent recognition is called into question by the stability of Americans' perceptions of inequality over the past 30 years. As it turns out, survey respondents have consistently been quite likely to endorse the notion that inequality is increasing, regardless of actual economic trends. In a detailed survey of Americans' awareness of rising inequality, Leslie McCall presented a time series, dating back to the mid-1970s, of responses to a Harris Poll question asking, "Do you tend to feel or not feel that . . . the rich get richer and the poor get poorer?" As McCall summarized her results, "this question does not appear to be tapping perceptions of high *levels* of inequality, or at least not perceptions that are accurate. Nor is it necessarily tapping a more general sense that inequality is rising in one period (the 1990s) as compared to an earlier period (the 1970s). Moreover, the vast majority of Americans agree throughout the 1970s, 1980s, and 1990s, that American society is

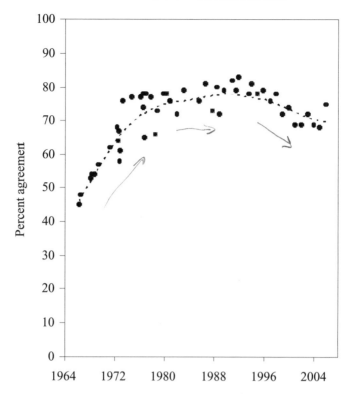

Figure 5.1 "The Rich Get Richer and the Poor Get Poorer"

structured in a way that benefits the rich and penalizes the poor, or more loosely that rising inequality is a natural state of affairs."[20]

Figure 5.1 presents an even longer tracking of responses to the Harris question, derived from 51 surveys conducted between April 1966 and November 2005. The responses to the Harris question over this longer period do show a significant increase in public perceptions of economic inequality. However, that increase was concentrated in the late 1960s and early 1970s—a period in which actual economic inequality was modest by today's standards and probably not yet increasing.

By 1973, about three-quarters of the Harris respondents agreed that "the rich get richer and the poor get poorer." That percentage fluctuated in a relatively narrow band (from a low of 65% to a high of 83%) for the next 30 years. There is some evidence of an increase in the late 1980s and early

[20] McCall (2005), 8.

1990s, with a corresponding decline in the mid- to late 1990s; but these shifts are quite modest. The remarkable fact is that, by this measure, perceptions of economic inequality were no more prevalent at the end of George W. Bush's first term than during Gerald Ford's administration.

The fact that public perceptions of economic inequality bear so little relationship to actual trends in inequality must temper any overly optimistic assessment of the extent to which ordinary people are aware of changes in the relative fortunes of the rich and the poor. However, it does not follow that perceptions of economic inequality are meaningless or politically inconsequential. Even a ritualistic endorsement of the folk wisdom that "the rich get richer and the poor get poorer" may signal unhappiness with this apparently self-reinforcing reality. In the NES surveys, most of the people who said that the difference in incomes between rich people and poor people had increased added that that was "a bad thing." Only about 6% of those who said that inequality had increased said that was a good thing; the rest said they "haven't thought about" whether increasing inequality is good or bad.

If we ask where there is potential political support for egalitarian redistribution in these responses, the obvious place to begin is with the 31% of the public who said that the difference in incomes between rich and poor is much larger than it was *and* that that is a bad thing. These people are at the core of a somewhat larger group—almost 45% of the public—who both recognized and regretted the fact that economic inequality has increased. In contrast, outright supporters of economic inequality—those who applauded the fact that inequality has increased or believed with regret that inequality has declined—constituted only about 6% of the public.

The remainder of the public can be thought of as divided into two broad groups. The first of these, consisting of almost 25% of the total population, did not recognize that economic inequality had increased. (Most of these people said that the difference in incomes between rich people and poor people was "about the same" as 20 years ago, but about 5% thought it had decreased.) People in this group lacked, but could conceivably acquire, a *factual* basis for seeing growing economic inequality as a public policy problem. The second group, consisting of 27% of the public, recognized that inequality had increased, but they had not thought about whether that was good or bad. What these people seem to have lacked is a *moral* basis for seeing growing economic inequality as a public policy problem.

Perhaps, like a few of the people in Jennifer Hochschild's much more detailed conversations about distributive justice, people in this second group "do not seek redistribution because they do not care one way or the other about it." But if her respondents are indicative, it is more likely that they "are not forced to face the question of redistribution" in their day-to-day lives and thus "fail to support any system of distributive justice very fully. They sometimes seek equality; at other times, they seek differentiation; too often, they do not know what they want or even how to decide what the possibilities are."[21]

In addition to asking respondents about their perceptions and evaluations of economic inequality, the 2002 NES survey included a battery of questions inviting respondents to *explain* why, "in America today, some people have better jobs and higher incomes than others do."[22] The fixed-choice questions offered a variety of potential explanations ranging from "some people just don't work as hard" to "discrimination holds some people back" to "God made people different from one another." Respondents were asked to indicate whether each potential explanation is "very important," "somewhat important," or "not important." Their answers are summarized in table 5.9, which lists the seven potential explanations in order of popularity.

The quintessential American belief that economic success is a matter of hard work fares well in table 5.9, with about 45% of the public saying that unequal effort is a "very important" cause of economic inequality. However, there is even more support (about 55%) for the notion that unequal access to a good education is very important. Two other social factors, discrimination and government policies, also loom fairly large as explanations for economic inequality. And while one-third of the respondents said that differences in "inborn ability to learn" are very important, almost half rejected the idea that income differences exist because "God made people different from one another." These responses certainly do not suggest that most Americans view economic inequality as a merely natural phenomenon, even if they do think it is attributable in part to differences in character and ability.

Some evidence also suggests that Americans' attitudes about economic inequality may have shifted in recent years. For example, in a 1987 survey conducted as part of the International Social Survey Program, Americans were evenly split on the question of whether "large income differences are necessary for a country's prosperity." But support for that proposition had declined noticeably in a follow-up survey conducted in 1992 and declined still further by 1999, to a level almost identical to those prevailing in the United Kingdom, Germany, Spain, Sweden, and Norway. Over the same 12-year period, the differences in salaries respondents considered appropriate for people in a variety of specific jobs declined by almost 25%. These

[21] Hochschild (1981), 279, 278, 283.

[22] Half of the respondents got the open-ended questions in the pre-election survey and the fixed-choice questions in the post-election survey; the other half got the fixed-choice questions in the pre-election survey and the open-ended questions in the post-election survey. My analysis here is limited to the fixed-choice questions, regardless of whether they were asked before or after the election. The responses from the two random half-samples were generally similar, except that those who responded in the pre-election survey attached somewhat more importance to "government policies"—despite the fact that subsequent portions of the pre- and post-election interviews called attention to a variety of relevant government tax and spending policies.

TABLE 5.9
Explanations for Economic Inequality

"Next, we'd like to know why you think it is, that in America today, some people have better [worse] jobs and higher [lower] incomes than others do. I'm going to read you some possible explanations, and I want you to tell me how important you think each is—very important, somewhat important, or not important at all."

	Very important	Somewhat important	Not important
Some people don't get a chance to get a good education	54.5%	35.1%	9.1%
Some people just don't work as hard	44.7%	41.4%	12.9%
Some people have more in-born ability to learn	33.8%	42.1%	23.4%
Discrimination holds some people back	26.4%	50.2%	22.5%
Government policies have helped high-income workers more	26.0%	38.2%	33.6%
Some people just choose low-paying jobs	19.4%	38.8%	39.6%
God made people different from one another	22.2%	26.5%	48.5%

$N = 1,427$.
Source: 2002 National Election Study survey.

results suggest that Americans probably have less tolerance for economic inequality than they used to, and even that their views about its necessity are not much different from those prevailing in other, more egalitarian democracies.[23]

FACTS AND VALUES IN THE REALM OF INEQUALITY

So, do Americans care about inequality? Here, as so often, it is easy to disagree about whether the glass is half full or half empty. Almost 45% of Americans say that the difference in incomes between rich people and poor people has increased over the past 20 years and that that is a bad thing—but an even larger proportion either do not acknowledge the fact or have not thought

[23] Calculated from data provided by Osberg and Smeeding (2003), tables 2.1 and 4.2-1.

about whether it is good or bad. More than 60% agree that government policies have exacerbated economic inequality by helping high-income workers more—but more than a third disagree—and more than 85% say that "some people just don't work as hard." Half the public thinks that rich people are asked to pay less than they should in federal income taxes—but almost half does not think so.

What accounts for these differences in perceptions of inequality and its causes and implications? In particular, why is there so much apparent resistance to acknowledging the extent of inequality in a society where almost 90% of the public agrees that we "should do whatever is necessary to make sure that everyone has an equal opportunity to succeed"?

Psychologists have spent considerable scholarly energy elaborating "just world" or "system justification" theories. Their basic idea is that "living in an unpredictable, uncontrollable, and capriciously unjust world would be unbearably threatening, and so we cling defensively to the illusion that the world is a just place." In the economic realm, one result is a widespread belief in the basic fairness of capitalism, even among people who seem to be on the losing end of the free-market system. At the individual level, similar psychological pressures produce unrealistic optimism about one's own economic prospects and an illusion of control over uncontrollable events, both "adaptive forms of self-deception that facilitate coping with environmental stress and uncertainty."[24]

Although the psychological urge to deny injustice and economic vulnerability is presumably universal, some scholars have maintained that political conservatives are, as a matter of personality, especially sensitive to the stresses of an unpredictable, uncontrollable environment—and thus especially strongly motivated to deny its threatening features. On the other hand, conservatives may be especially likely to downplay the potentially troubling features of the prevailing economic system, not because they have fundamentally different personalities but simply because they are psychologically committed to a belief in the justice and efficiency of that system. As one study put it, "conservatism is a prototypical system-justifying ideology, in that it preserves the status quo and provides intellectual and moral justification for maintaining inequality in society." Either way, we might expect ideological rationalization to produce considerable consistency between perceptions of fact and assessments of value in the realm of inequality.[25]

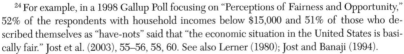

[24] For example, in a 1998 Gallup Poll focusing on "Perceptions of Fairness and Opportunity," 52% of the respondents with household incomes below $15,000 and 51% of those who described themselves as "have-nots" said that "the economic situation in the United States is basically fair." Jost et al. (2003), 55–56, 58, 60. See also Lerner (1980); Jost and Banaji (1994).

[25] Jost et al. (2003), 63. On personality and political ideology more generally, see McClosky (1958) and Stenner (2005).

TABLE 5.10

Perceived Opportunity to Succeed

"Do you think everyone in American society has an opportunity
to succeed, most do, or do only some have this opportunity?"

	Everyone	Most	Only some
Total sample	28.8%	47.9%	22.3%
Family income			
Under $50,000	26.4%	44.3%	27.9%
$50,000–$99,999	28.8%	50.5%	20.2%
$100,000 plus	23.1%	58.5%	15.4%
Party identification			
Democrat	17.9%	49.0%	33.2%
Independent	18.3%	56.5%	23.5%
Republican	42.8%	47.3%	8.5%

Source: 2004 Maxwell Poll on Civic Engagement and Inequality.

Some evidence of politically motivated perceptions regarding the extent of economic opportunity appears in a 2004 survey on Civic Engagement and Inequality sponsored by Syracuse University's Maxwell School of Citizenship and Public Affairs. Table 5.10 summarizes responses to a question asking whether "everyone in American society has an opportunity to succeed," "most do," or "only some have this opportunity." Overall, almost 30% of the respondents said that "everyone" has an opportunity to succeed, and more than three-quarters said that all or most people do. Even among people with below-average incomes, almost 30% said that "everyone" has an opportunity to succeed and fewer than 30% said that "only some have this opportunity."[26]

Comparing the views of Democrats, Independents, and Republicans reveals substantial disparities in perceptions of opportunity. Republicans were more than twice as likely as Independents or Democrats to say that everyone has an opportunity to succeed. However, Independents and Democrats were three or four times as likely as Republicans to say that only some people have that opportunity. Thus, while faith in the reality of equal opportunity is fairly robust in every partisan group, the extent of that faith seems to be strongly influenced by partisan attachments.

Significant partisan disparities also appear in responses to a pair of questions in the 2002 NES survey tapping public perceptions of how the interests of rich people and poor people are reflected in the contemporary American

[26] Stonecash (2005).

party system. One questions asked, "Which political party do you think is generally better for poor people—the Democrats, the Republicans, or is there not much difference between them?" A parallel question asked which party is better for "rich people." The responses of Republican and Democratic partisans to this pair of questions were very different, but not in the way one might expect. Only 8% of Republican identifiers and only 2% of Democratic identifiers said that their own party was generally better for both rich people and poor people. However, Republicans were almost twice as likely to say that neither party is generally better for either group (39%) than to endorse the conventional view that the Republican Party is better for the rich and the Democratic Party is better for the poor (20%). In sharp contrast, 67% of Democrats endorsed the conventional view, and only 10% claimed that neither party was generally better for either group. In short, Democrats were much more likely to see the contemporary partisan landscape in terms of class interests, whereas Republicans were much less likely to do so.

The statistical analyses reported in table 5.11 shed further light on the ideological bases of differences in perceptions of the extent and implications of economic inequality in American society. The questions on which these analyses are based range from purely factual—whether "the difference in incomes between rich people and poor people in the United States today is

TABLE 5.11
Political Ideology and Perceptions of Inequality

Ordered probit parameter estimates (with standard errors in parentheses). Additional response thresholds not shown.

	Income gap has increased	Larger gap is a bad thing[a]	Poor don't get a fair trial	Hard work is very important
Conservative ideology (−1 to +1)	−.298 (.049)	−.560 (.062)	−.418 (.077)	.408 (.066)
Family income (0 to 1)	.091 (.081)	.509 (.101)	.240 (.128)	−.201 (.110)
2004 survey	.229 (.044)	.121 (.054)	—	—
Intercept	.639 (.053)	−.066 (.063)	.670 (.072)	−.058 (.064)
Log likelihood	−3,040.4	−1,644.5	−1,010.6	−1,378.8
Pseudo-R²	.01	.03	.02	.01
N	2,525	1,976	1,499	1,414

[a] Includes only those respondents who said the difference in incomes between rich people and poor people has increased.

Source: Calculations based on data from 2002 and 2004 National Election Study surveys.

larger, smaller, or about the same as it was 20 years ago"—to purely normative—whether increasing income differences are "a good thing" or "a bad thing." The analyses also include two questions from the 2002 NES survey that are factual in nature but less straightforward than the question about the difference in incomes between rich people and poor people. One of these questions asked whether "a poor person has the same chance of getting a fair trial as a wealthy person does"; the other asked whether the fact that "some people just don't work as hard" is a "very important" explanation for economic inequality. For each of these questions, the table shows how responses varied with political ideology. (The analyses also allow for differences due to family income levels, as well as for differences in responses between 2002 and 2004 for questions asked in both years.)

Perhaps not surprisingly, the largest effect of political ideology is for the purely normative question—whether the increasing difference in incomes between rich people and poor people is a good thing or a bad thing. (People who said the difference in incomes had not increased, or did not know—about 24% of the NES respondents—are excluded from this analysis.) Extreme conservatives were only half as likely as extreme liberals to say that growing inequality is a bad thing (38% versus 79%) and almost three times as likely to say that it is a good thing, or (more commonly) that they had not thought about whether it was good or bad (62% versus 21%).[27] This difference underlines the extent to which "conservatism . . . provides intellectual and moral justification for maintaining inequality in society."[28]

It should not be surprising that conservatism provides moral justification for inequality. However, it *should* be surprising that ideological commitments also had substantial effects on responses to the factual questions included in the table. Extreme conservatives were twice as likely as extreme liberals to say that hard work is a very important explanation for income differences (60% versus 28%). They were also more than three times as likely as extreme liberals to insist that poor people have the same access to justice that rich people do (36% versus 11%)—though even most extreme conservatives disagreed with this proposition. Given the complexity of these questions and the paucity of hard evidence available to adjudicate them, liberals and conservatives managed to construct very different, ideologically congenial pictures of the social reality of inequality.

Even in the case of the most straightforwardly factual question included in the table—whether the income gap between rich and poor had increased—the responses of conservatives and liberals were strongly colored by their

---

[27] These probabilities represent response tendencies for extreme conservatives and extreme liberals with median incomes, and they split the difference in responses between people interviewed in 2002 and 2004.

[28] Jost et al. (2003), 63.

ideological perspectives. Almost 90% of extreme liberals, but only 73% of extreme conservatives, thought that income differences had increased. Put the other way, conservatives were more than twice as likely as liberals to deny that the difference in incomes between rich people and poor people had grown larger. In light of the magnitude of the economic trends described in chapter 1, it is striking that more than one in four extreme conservatives persisted in believing that income differences between rich people and poor people have not, in fact, increased over the past two decades.

The statistical results presented in table 5.11 are derived from the responses of a representative national sample of the adult population. Such a sample includes many people who pay little attention to news and have only the vaguest grasp of public affairs. Perhaps these relatively uninformed people account for the ideological disparities in perceptions evident in the table. Are inattentive citizens simply substituting ideological biases for solid information about trends in economic inequality?

In order to address that possibility, the statistical analyses presented in table 5.11 must be elaborated to allow for differences between well-informed and uninformed respondents within each ideological group. I do that using general measures of political information in the NES surveys. The 2004 NES survey included questions asking: (1) which party had more members in the House of Representatives prior to the election; (2) which party had more members in the Senate prior to the election; (3) which party was more conservative at the national level; (4) what job or political office Dennis Hastert held; (5) what job or office Dick Cheney held; (6) what job or office Tony Blair held; and (7) what job or office William Rehnquist held. I constructed a political information scale based on correct answers to these seven questions. (Two of the 1,066 respondents answered all seven questions correctly; 22% gave five or more correct answers, while 42% gave two or fewer correct answers.) Unfortunately, the 2002 NES survey did not include an analogous battery of factual questions about politics. Instead, I employed a subjective rating of respondents' "general level of information about politics and public affairs" (on a five-point scale ranging from "very low" to "very high") provided by the interviewer at the end of each interview.[29]

When the NES survey respondents are differentiated on the basis of political information, it appears that general political awareness makes people

[29] For evidence regarding the validity of the interviewers' assessments of respondents' political information, see Zaller (1985). For respondents interviewed both before and after the 2002 election, I averaged the ratings provided (almost always by different interviewers) at the end of the pre-election and post-election interviews. For respondents who were not reinterviewed after the election (11% of the sample in 2002 and 12% in 2004), I used the pre-election interviewers' ratings only. In every case, I calibrated the resulting information scale to reflect each respondent's position in the overall distribution of political information, from 0 (for the least-informed) to 1 (for the most informed). The actual range is from .014 to .999.

markedly more pessimistic on a variety of scores about the extent and implications of inequality in contemporary America. The statistical results presented in table 5.12 imply that people at the top of the information scale were
significantly more likely than those at the bottom to say that income differences had increased (84% versus 74%) and much more likely to see that as a
bad thing (73% versus 46%). They were also significantly more likely to deny
that "a poor person has the same chance of getting a fair trial as a wealthy
person does" (85% versus 71%).[30] These differences and others suggest that
better-informed people had distinctive views about the nature, sources, and
consequences of economic inequality.[31]

Most of the differences between better-informed and less-informed people in table 5.12 parallel those between liberals and conservatives in table
5.11. Better-informed people were more likely to say that income inequality
has increased and more likely to say that is a bad thing. They were also more
likely to say that poor people are disadvantaged in the legal system and
(slightly) less likely to say that differences in hard work are a very important
cause of inequality. In each of these respects, political information shifted
people's views in the same direction as liberal political ideology.

Although the primary effects of political information and liberal ideology
were generally reinforcing, table 5.12 also presents strong evidence of
interactions between information and ideology: increasing political awareness seems to have had very different effects on liberals and conservatives.
Indeed, for each of the four questions included in the table, greater political
awareness shifted the views of liberals and conservatives in opposite
directions.

This pattern is evident even for the most straightforwardly objective question analyzed in the table—whether differences in income between rich people and poor people had increased or decreased. The solid and dotted lines in

[30] These percentage differences are calculated for ideological moderates with average incomes. Since the statistical results presented in table 5.12 provide strong evidence of *interactions* between political information and ideology, the effects of information among liberals and
conservatives are quite different from those reported here. These differences are highlighted in
figures 5.2, 5.3, and 5.4.

[31] Better-informed people also provided systematically different *explanations* for economic
inequality, stressing social causes (inequality in educational opportunities, discrimination, and
government policies) more heavily than less-informed people did. They were also somewhat
less likely to say that rich people are asked to pay too much in taxes—but no more or less likely
to say that poor people are asked to pay too much or that *they* are asked to pay too much. Nor
were they more or less likely to think that corporate accounting scandals are widespread. As for
perceptions of the partisan politics of inequality, they were much more likely to recognize the
differences in positions of the Democratic and Republican parties on specific tax policies and
much more likely to say that the Republicans are "generally better for rich people" and that the
Democrats are "generally better for poor people."

TABLE 5.12

Political Information, Ideology, and Perceptions of Inequality

Ordered probit parameter estimates (with standard errors in parentheses). Additional response thresholds not shown.

	Income gap has increased	Larger gap is a bad thing[a]	Poor don't get a fair trial	Hard work is very important
Political information (0 to 1)	.365 (.093)	.728 (.117)	.470 (.165)	−.150 (.138)
Conservative ideology (−1 to +1)	.210 (.113)	.094 (.141)	−.111 (.191)	−.037 (.170)
Political information ×ideology	−.971 (.193)	−1.294 (.251)	−.618 (.348)	.843 (.298)
Family income (0 to 1)	.015 (.086)	.347 (.106)	.144 (.135)	−.194 (.116)
2004 survey	.240 (.045)	.142 (.055)	—	—
Intercept	.502 (.062)	−.352 (.077)	.491 (.094)	.014 (.083)
Log likelihood	−3,024.0	−1,618.0	−1,005.8	−1,374.5
Pseudo-R²	.02	.05	.02	.02
N	2,525	1,976	1,499	1,414

[a] Includes only those respondents who said the difference in incomes between rich people and poor people has increased.

Source: Calculations based on data from 2002 and 2004 National Election Study surveys.

figure 5.2 reflect the response tendencies of extreme liberals and extreme conservatives, respectively, based on the statistical results presented in table 5.12. At low levels of political information, the figure shows that conservatives and liberals were about equally likely to recognize that income differences had increased over the past 20 years. However, the perceptions of better-informed conservatives and liberals diverged significantly. Among liberals, recognition of increasing income inequality rose markedly with general political awareness, to 86% for people of average political awareness (corresponding to the open circle halfway along the solid line) and a near-unanimous 96% at the highest information level.[32] However, the proportion of extreme conservatives who were willing to admit that economic inequality had increased actually decreased with political information, from 80% among those who were generally least informed about politics to 70% for people of average political awareness

---

[32] Among ideological moderates, recognition of the growing income gap increased less dramatically than among liberals, but still significantly: from 74% at the lowest information level to 84% at the highest information level.

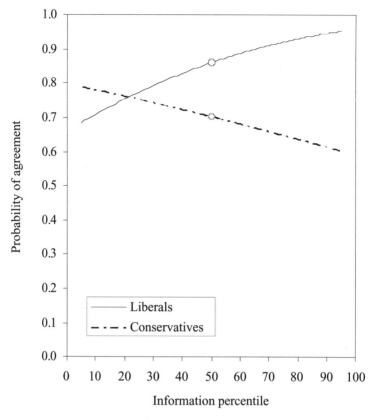

Figure 5.2 Perceptions of Increasing Income Differences by
Ideology and Information Level

to a little less than 60% among those at the top of the distribution of political
information.[33]

The pattern of ideological polarization in figure 5.2 will appear familiar
to readers of John Zaller's influential book, *The Nature and Origins of Mass
Opinion*. Zaller's model of opinion formation encompasses situations in
which a "mainstream message" produces uniform shifts in opinion among politically aware conservatives and liberals. However, in situations where political elites are ideologically polarized, Zaller's model implies a very different
pattern, with politically aware conservatives and liberals pulled in opposite directions by the contrasting arguments of their respective elites. The result is

---

[33] For extreme conservatives, the information effect implied by the probit analysis is −.606
(with a standard error of .192); for extreme liberals the effect is +1.336 (with a standard error
of .235).

a characteristic diverging pattern, with undifferentiated (and generally moderate) policy preferences among less aware conservatives and liberals, but increasing ideological disparity among those who are more attentive to elite rhetoric.[34]

The significance of political awareness in Zaller's model stems from the fact that logical (or merely conventional) connections between broad ideologies and specific policies are not likely to be automatically and identically evident to all conservatives and liberals. Rather, their apprehension requires careful thought—or, more likely, second-hand exposure to careful thought—about specific facts and values in the light of broad ideological commitments. People who are unusually attentive to political discourse and sophisticated in their political thinking are especially likely to grasp those connections.

The difference here is that political awareness produced sharp ideological polarization not just in policy preferences, but also in perceptions of a seemingly straightforward, objective fact. Rather than contributing to accurate apprehension of that fact by conservative and liberal observers alike, political awareness seems mostly to have taught people how the political elites who share their ideological commitments would *like* them to see the world. In particular, what is most significant in figure 5.2 is the effect of political information among conservatives. Rather than being more likely to recognize the reality of growing inequality, those conservatives who were most politically aware were most likely to *deny* that income differences had increased. In this instance, political awareness did more to facilitate ideological consistency than it did to promote an accurate perception of real social conditions.[35]

While perceptions of increasing income differences provide a striking example of ideological disparity in the effect of political information, the example is by no means an isolated one. The statistical analysis presented in table 5.12 reveal an even larger ideological disparity for the impact of political information on people's *moral assessments* of increasing inequality than on their *factual perceptions* of increasing inequality. Among ideological moderates, the probability of saying that increasing inequality is a bad thing (among those who recognized that inequality has, in fact, increased) ranged from 46% among the least-informed to 73% among the best-informed. The impact

[34] Zaller (1992), chapters 6 and 9.

[35] Christopher Achen and I have developed a mathematical model of political inference in which political awareness increases the weight attached to both partisan predispositions and reality in the construction of political judgments (Achen and Bartels 2006). Insofar as the former effect dominates the latter effect, this model implies not only that partisan disparities in political judgment will be concentrated among people who are high in political awareness, as in Zaller's model, but also that people who are generally better-informed about politics may be most inaccurate in their political perceptions. Shani (2006) has presented a good deal of empirical evidence suggesting that partisan biases in perceptions of political conditions are exacerbated by political information. On partisan biases in perceptions more generally, see Bartels (2002a).

of information among liberals was even greater, with the best-informed virtually unanimous in saying that increasing inequality is a bad thing. Among conservatives, however, the impact of political awareness was reversed: the
best-informed conservatives were significantly *less* likely than those who were
relatively uninformed to say that an increasing income gap between rich people and poor people is a bad thing.[36] Thus, for moral assessments as well as
factual perceptions of inequality, the impact of information is strongly condi-
tioned by ideological predispositions.

   Figure 5.3 shows how ideology and political information combined to influence the probability that respondents in the NES surveys would both recognize *and* regret the growth of economic inequality. Among extreme liberals
(represented by the solid line in the figure) that probability increased dramatically with increases in general political awareness. At the bottom of the
distribution of information, only about two-thirds of extreme liberals recognized that inequality had increased, and fewer than half of those who recognized an increase said that was a bad thing. (Most of the rest said they had not
thought about whether increasing inequality was good or bad.) However,
among the best-informed liberals, more than 95% recognized that inequality
had increased, and more than 95% of that 95% said that was a bad thing. In
contrast, among extreme conservatives (represented by the dotted line in figure 5.3) the effect of political information was to depress both recognition of
growing inequality and opposition to growing inequality. Thus, while the
least-informed conservatives were about as likely as the least-informed liberals to recognize and regret growing inequality, only about one in six of the
best-informed conservatives did so.

   Qualitatively similar interactions between political information and ideology also appear in responses to the other questions included in table 5.12.
For example, highly informed liberals were much more likely than uninformed liberals to deny that a poor person has the same chance as a wealthy
person of getting a fair trial (96% versus 75%); but highly informed conservatives were slightly *less* likely than uninformed conservatives to perceive
economic bias in the legal system (62% versus 67%).[37] An even starker ideological gap appears in assessments of the importance of hard work as an
explanation for income differences, which are presented graphically in figure 5.4. At the bottom of the information scale, conservatives and liberals
were equally likely to see differences in hard work as a very important
source of economic inequality. However, conservatives and liberals at the

---

[36] For extreme conservatives, the information effect implied by the probit analysis is −.566
(with a standard error of .245); for extreme liberals the effect is +2.022 (with a standard error
of 0.306).

[37] The implied information effects in the probit analysis are +1.088 (with a standard error of
.421) for extreme liberals and −.149 (with a standard error of .344) for extreme conservatives.

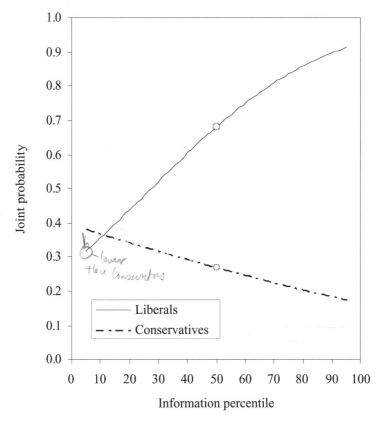

Figure 5.3 Probability of Recognizing *and* Regretting Increasing Income Differences

top of the information scale had vastly different views on this issue: more than 70% of highly informed conservatives, but only 15% of highly informed liberals, considered it very important that "some people just don't work as hard."[38]

The patterns of ideological polarization evident in figures 5.2, 5.3, and 5.4 suggest that American beliefs about inequality are profoundly political in their origins and implications. Well-informed conservatives and liberals differ markedly, not only in their normative assessments of increasing inequality, as one might expect, but also in their perceptions of the causes, extent, and consequences of inequality. This is not simply a matter of people with different values drawing different conclusions from a set of agreed-upon facts. Analysts

[38] The implied information effects in the probit analysis are +.693 (with a standard error of .309) for extreme conservatives and −.993 (with a standard error of .347) for extreme liberals.

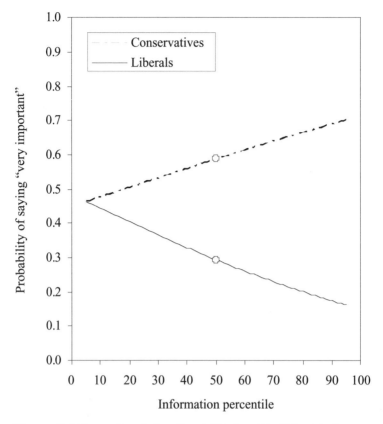

Figure 5.4 "Some People Just Don't Work as Hard" by Ideology and Information Level

of public opinion in the realm of inequality—as in many other realms—would do well to recognize that the facts themselves are very much subject to ideological dispute. For their part, political actors in the realm of inequality—as in many other realms—would do well to recognize that careful logical arguments running from factual premises to policy conclusions are unlikely to persuade people who are ideologically motivated to distort or deny the facts. While it is certainly true, as Jennifer Hochschild has argued, that "Where You Stand Depends on What You See," it is equally true that what you are willing to see depends in significant part on where you stand.[39]

At the same time, it is important to bear in mind that cleavages in beliefs and values are much more muted among relatively uninformed people than

[39] Hochschild (2001).

among those who pay close attention to politics. In fact, liberals and conservatives in the least-informed stratum of the public are virtually indistinguishable in the analyses reported in table 5.12.[40] In the context of factual questions, this apparent consensus across ideological lines may seem reassuring. When it comes to policy preferences, however, agreement between uninformed liberals and conservatives may suggest that people on one side or the other—or both—are failing to recognize the implications of their own values for their views about crucial public issues.

The analysis in the next four chapters turns from facts and values to public policies. My aim is to account for how policies are formulated in the American political system of unequal democracy. Chapters 6, 7, and 8 provide detailed case studies of key policies with major ramifications for the economic fortunes of rich, middle-class, and working poor Americans: the Bush tax cuts of 2001 and 2003, the campaign to repeal the estate tax, and the long-term erosion of the federal minimum wage. Chapter 9 provides a much more general analysis of policy-making across a broad range of issues.

In examining the role of public opinion in the policy-making process, it will be crucial to consider the ways in which citizens' policy preferences reflect political values and sympathies of the sort examined in this chapter. However, it will be equally important to bear in mind the extent to which many ordinary citizens fail to translate their broad values and ideological impulses into consistent views about specific policy issues. The analyses presented in chapters 6 and 7 will suggest that the *political* significance of economic inequality is mostly lost on many Americans. Although they may express genuine allegiance to egalitarian values, they are not sufficiently attuned to the political debate to see how those values are implicated in major policy choices.

---

[40] The one instance in table 5.12 in which the main effect of ideology (that is, the effect of ideology among people at the bottom of the distribution of political information) is large enough to be reliably distinguishable from zero is for the factual question about increasing differences in incomes—and that effect suggests, quite implausibly, that uninformed conservatives were more likely than uninformed liberals to recognize that incomes had become more unequal. I suspect that this anomalous result reflects some nonlinearity in the effect of political information that is not adequately captured by the simple statistical specification reported in the table.

Homer Gets a Tax Cut

THE PORTRAIT OF public opinion presented in chapter 5 provides several impressive-looking grounds for optimism regarding the politics of inequality. Most Americans express strong support for egalitarian values; they feel warmer toward middle-class and poor people than toward rich people and business people; and they think the rich should bear a larger share of the tax burden. In light of these views, a naïve observer might expect the growing economic inequality documented in chapter 1 to provoke a substantial popular backlash, impelling elected officials to engage in aggressive redistribution, raising taxes on the wealthy and investing heavily in programs enhancing human capital and bolstering economic opportunity for the middle and lower classes.

Far from it. Indeed, quite to the contrary, the most significant domestic policy initiative of the past decade has been a massive government-engineered transfer of additional wealth from the lower and middle classes to the rich in the form of substantial reductions in federal income taxes. Congress passed, and President Bush signed, two of the largest tax cuts in history in 2001 and 2003. One accounting put the total cost to the federal Treasury of those cuts from 2001 through 2013 at $4.6 trillion—more than twice the federal government's total annual budget at the time the measures were adopted.[1] Many of the specific provisions of the Bush tax cuts disproportionately benefited wealthy taxpayers, including cuts in the top rate, reductions in taxes on dividends and capital gains, and a gradual elimination of the estate tax. As a result, according to projections by the Institute on Taxation and Economic Policy, the total federal tax burden in 2010 will decline by 25% for the richest 1% of taxpayers and by 21% for the next richest 4%, but by only 10% for taxpayers in the bottom 95% of the income distribution.[2]

What is most remarkable is that this massive upward transfer of wealth attracted a good deal of support and surprisingly little opposition from ordinary Americans, despite their egalitarian-sounding views. My primary aim in this chapter is to explore and explain these public reactions. My analysis suggests, first, that public opinion about the Bush tax cuts was remarkably tenuous. Notwithstanding the multi*trillion*-dollar stakes, surveys conducted in 2002 and 2004 found 40% of the public saying they had not thought about whether they favored or opposed the 2001 tax cut. Among those who had, supporters outnumbered opponents by a substantial margin.

My analysis suggests that most of these people supported tax cuts not because they were indifferent to economic inequality, but because they failed to bring relevant values to bear in formulating their policy preferences. Most of the people who recognized and regretted the fact that economic inequality has been increasing nevertheless supported President Bush's tax cuts. People who wanted to spend more money on a variety of government programs were *more* likely to support tax cuts than those who did not, other things being equal. And people's opinions about tax cuts were strongly shaped by their attitudes about their *own* tax burdens, but virtually unaffected by their attitudes about the tax burden of the rich—even in the case of the estate tax, which only affects the wealthiest 1 or 2% of taxpayers.

---

[1] The $4.6 trillion figure is for both tax cuts combined and includes additional interest payments stemming from the resulting increase in the federal budget deficit; in addition, it assumes that a variety of nominally temporary rate reductions and credits will subsequently be made permanent. See John Springer, "Administration Tax Cut Proposals Would Cost $2.7 Trillion through 2013," Center on Budget and Policy Priorities, March 10, 2003, www.cbpp.org.

[2] This calculation is based on the assumption that major provisions scheduled to expire by 2010 would, in fact, be extended. Absent that assumption, the total tax cut for the richest 1% is reduced by about one-third and the total tax cut for the bottom 95% is reduced by about one-half, making the disparity in benefits even greater. See "Effects of First Three Bush Tax Cuts Charted," Citizens for Tax Justice, June 4, 2003, www.ctj.org.

The response of the American public to the Bush tax cuts provides a dramatic case study of apparent misconnection between egalitarian sentiments and concrete policy preferences. More broadly, the success of President Bush and his allies in crafting and implementing such an ambitious policy shift with so little political fallout provides a dramatic case study of the considerable latitude provided by the American political system to policy makers pursuing their own ideological goals.

THE BUSH TAX CUTS

Tax cutting was a centerpiece of George W. Bush's 2000 presidential campaign platform. Less than five months after President Bush took office, and at his urging, Congress passed the Economic Growth and Tax Relief Reconciliation Act (EGTRRA), a major package of tax cuts including phased reductions in federal income tax rates, increased child credits, higher limits on contributions to tax-free retirement and educational savings accounts, and a gradual elimination of the federal estate tax. According to the Joint Committee on Taxation, the total EGTRRA package will cost the federal Treasury more than \$1.3 trillion through 2011.[3]

The key legislative vehicle for the 2001 tax cut was the annual congressional budget resolution. Although the budget reconciliation process was constructed in the 1970s to facilitate budget-balancing, two decades of parliamentary maneuvering provided a precedent for extending its application from deficit-cutting to tax-cutting. As a report in the legislative newsmagazine *CQ Weekly* explained in the midst of the process, "Such bills are given special procedural protections: a shield from a filibuster, a 20-hour limit on debate and restrictions on amendments. In the evenly split senate, these advantages will be essential to enact anything like the tax package that Bush ceremonially presented to Congress on Feb. 8. Without an adopted budget resolution, the chances for the broadest and deepest tax cut in 20 years all but disappear."[4]

The budget resolution provided crucial procedural leverage for President Bush and the Republican congressional leadership. However, that leverage came with a substantial cost: because the congressional budget process operates within a 10-year time frame, only policy changes within that time frame would be considered germane for consideration within the context of

---

[3] Joint Committee on Taxation, "Estimated Budget Effects of the Conference Agreement for H.R. 1836," May 26, 2001.

[4] Andrew Taylor, "Law Designed for Curbing Deficits Becomes GOP Tool for Cutting Taxes," *CQ Weekly*, April 7, 2001, 770; Daniel J. Parks with Andrew Taylor, "The Republican Challenge: Roping the Fiscal Strays," *CQ Weekly*, February 10, 2001, 314.

the annual budget resolution. Thus, implementing tax cuts through the budget reconciliation process necessitated "sun-setting" provisions causing them to expire at the end of a decade, returning the whole tax system to the status quo ante. The president and his allies could hope and expect that future Congresses would feel compelled to make the cuts permanent—at an additional cost to the Treasury of more than $200 billion per year—but that outcome was by no means guaranteed.

For that matter, during President Bush's first 100 days in office some political observers thought it was politically unrealistic to suppose that his ambitious tax-cutting agenda could achieve even a bare majority in the evenly divided Senate. In early February, a congressional journalist questioned "whether the final product will look anything like the proposal Bush transmitted to Capitol Hill." With the shadow of recession lengthening, a bipartisan group of Senate moderates began to lobby for a "trigger mechanism" conditioning the implementation of tax cuts on the realization of projected budget surpluses. Polling data signaled a public preference for bolstering Social Security and Medicare over tax cuts, suggesting "that the American people believe the Democrats are right," according to Senate Minority Leader Tom Daschle. Charles Grassley, the chairman of the Senate Finance Committee and a Bush ally, acknowledged that "We have some nervous Nellies in both parties."[5]

By early May, Grassley and his Democratic counterpart, Max Baucus, were "tweaking" Bush's proposal in the Senate Finance Committee. Grassley and Baucus "followed the outlines of Bush's plan," but "rewrote the pieces, often in ways designed to keep the package's scope and cost within the confines of the budget. In addition, they crammed in several more provisions, principally to secure the support of four pivotal fiscal moderates on the panel"—Republicans James Jeffords and Olympia Snowe and Democrats Robert Torricelli and Blanche Lincoln. Grassley and Baucus fended off dozens of amendments and motions to recommit, eventually crafting a bill that cleared their committee with the support of all ten Republicans and four of ten Democrats.[6]

A week later, when the bill reached the Senate floor, it survived another cavalcade of amendments. A bid by Republican John McCain to trim the top rate reduction and expand the 15% tax bracket failed on a tie vote, with five

[5] Lori Nitschke, "Tax Plan Destined for Revision," *CQ Weekly*, February 10, 2001, 318; Lori Nitschke, "Proposals to Alter Bush's Tax Plan Multiply Despite White House Appeals for Unity," *CQ Weekly*, February 17, 2001, 377; Andrew Taylor, "Tax Fight Energizes Democrats," *CQ Weekly*, March 3, 2001, 465; Lori Nitschke, "Tax-Cut Bipartisanship Down to One Chamber," *CQ Weekly*, March 10, 2001, 529.

[6] Lori Nitschke, "Scaled-Down Version of Bush Tax Plan Taking Bipartisan Form at Senate Finance," *CQ Weekly*, May 5, 2001, 1003; Lori Nitschke, "Senate Tax Bill Trade-Offs Leave a Fragile Coalition," *CQ Weekly*, May 19, 2001, 1145.

Republicans (McCain, Lincoln Chafee, Susan Collins, Jeffords, and Arlen Specter) joining 45 Democrats in favor and five Democrats (Baucus, John Breaux, Max Cleland, Zell Miller, and Ben Nelson) joining 45 Republicans in opposition. A miscellaneous collection of minor amendments cobbled together by Grassley and Baucus was adopted by voice vote, and the bill was passed by a 62–38 margin.[7]

A dozen Democrats voted in favor of the bill on the Senate floor. According to one account, that was "a sign that it had captured the middle ground." Perhaps; however, it is striking that 11 of those 12 Democrats had helped to craft the Finance Committee's bill (Baucus, Breaux, Lincoln, and Torricelli) or faced very tough reelection fights in 2002 (Jean Carnahan, Cleland, Tim Johnson, and Mary Landrieu) or were themselves multimillionaires (Diane Feinstein, Herbert Kohl, and Nelson).[8]

For their part, Republicans faced the imminent defection of pivotal senator James Jeffords from their ranks and the shadow of new, more pessimistic budget surplus projections. "White House officials abandoned the administration's previous resistance to compromise and urged their Republican allies to quickly embrace any version of a tax cut deal that could become law." Just two days later "the weary Republican leadership in the House and Senate agreed to a deal with the ever-more-powerful centrist Senate Democrats," and both chambers adopted a conference report representing a "slightly altered version" of the Senate bill.[9]

The final product was widely criticized for providing too much tax relief to the wealthy and too little to the middle class and the working poor. McCain, one of two Senate Republicans who voted against the conference report, announced, "I cannot in good conscience support a tax cut in which so many of the benefits go to the most fortunate among us at the expense of middle-class Americans who most need tax relief." A study released by the research and advocacy group Citizens for Tax Justice estimated that the top 1% of households would receive a total of $477 billion in tax breaks over the 10-year period covered by the bill (an average of $34,247 per household per year), while the bottom 60% would receive a total of $268 billion (an average of $325 per

[7] Lori Nitschke, "Tax Cut Deal Reached Quickly As Appetite for Battle Fades," *CQ Weekly*, May 26, 2001, 1251.

[8] Nitschke, "Tax Cut Deal Reached Quickly As Appetite for Battle Fades." As it turned out, Carnahan and Cleland were defeated in 2002, Johnson was reelected by a 50–49 margin, and Landrieu won by a 52–48 margin in a runoff election. Kohl, Feinstein, and Nelson reported net worth in excess of $5 million in 2002, according to a CNN tally: Sean Loughlin and Robert Yoon, "Millionaires Populate U.S. Senate," CNN.com, June 13, 2003, http://www.cnn.com/2003/ALLPOLITICS/06/13/senators.finances/. The twelfth Democratic vote in favor of the tax cut was cast by Zell Miller of Georgia, who famously endorsed President Bush at the 2004 Republican National Convention.

[9] Nitschke, "Senate Tax Bill Trade-Offs Leave a Fragile Coalition"; Nitschke, "Tax Cut Deal Reached Quickly As Appetite for Battle Fades."

household per year). Moreover, because most of the broad-based tax cuts in the law took effect immediately while most of the benefits for very wealthy taxpayers were back-loaded, "the distribution of the tax cuts changes remarkably over time," with the estimated share of benefits going to the top 1% of households increasing gradually from 7.3% in 2001 to 51.8% in 2010.[10]

Even aside from its distributional implications, the back-loading of benefits raised alarms on fiscal grounds. Facing the necessity of keeping the putative 10-year cost of the tax cut within the cap imposed by the congressional budget resolution, "in crafting the final compromise, conferees followed the Senate model of postponing some effective dates and lengthening some phase-ins to make room for some priorities of both conservatives and moderates." Kent Conrad, the ranking Democrat on the Senate Budget Committee, called the result " 'a monument to fiscal irresponsibility' because so many of its provisions would take effect in the second part of the decade, when the Baby Boomers neared retirement and the surplus projections on which the tax cut depends are the least reliable." Robert Greenstein, the executive director of the Center on Budget and Policy Priorities, a liberal think tank, claimed that the "budget gimmickry" in the bill "exceeds anything we can recall." Charles Rangel, the ranking Democrat on the House Ways and Means Committee, warned that "the Republicans have lit the fuse on a time bomb. . . . Our kids and grandkids are the real losers today, because they will have to dig out of the hole that this tax bill causes."[11]

Meanwhile, Republicans and their conservative allies began to prepare the ground for additional rounds of tax-cutting. Rangel's Republican counterpart, House Ways and Means chairman Bill Thomas, complained that "$1.35 trillion stretched out over 10 years just doesn't get you what it used to." A representative of the U.S. Chamber of Commerce acknowledged that "we have a long list" of proposals for business tax breaks omitted from the EGTRRA package. Charles Schwab proposed a dividend tax cut to bolster the stock market, and, "Conveniently, the White House's top economist, R. Glenn Hubbard, had an elegant proposal on just that subject for the president."[12]

Sure enough, in January 2003 President Bush proposed a further "economic growth" package including more than $700 billion in additional tax cuts—and, in a modest concession to the lingering effects of the 2001 recession, $4 billion

---

[10] Daniel J. Parks with Bill Swindell, "Tax Debate Assured a Long Life As Bush, GOP Press for New Cuts," *CQ Weekly*, June 2, 2001, 1304; "Year-by-Year Analysis of the Bush Tax Cuts Shows Growing Tilt to the Very Rich," Citizens for Tax Justice, June 12, 2002, www.ctj.org.

[11] Nitschke, "Tax Cut Deal Reached Quickly As Appetite for Battle Fades"; Nitschke, "Senate Tax Bill Trade-Offs Leave a Fragile Coalition"; Parks with Swindell, "Tax Debate Assured a Long Life As Bush, GOP Press for New Cuts."

[12] Parks with Swindell, "Tax Debate Assured a Long Life As Bush, GOP Press for New Cuts"; Jill Barshay, "White House Bonds with Moderates for Victory on Dividend Cuts," *CQ Weekly*, May 17, 2003, 1173.

for personal reemployment accounts.[13] The centerpiece of the new package was a proposal to exempt corporate dividends from taxation as personal income and reduce capital gains taxes on sales of corporate stock. Bush also proposed accelerating major elements of the 2001 tax cut scheduled to take effect between 2006 and 2010, including reductions in the top four tax rates, making them effective immediately.

Bush's plan "drew a cautious response from many in his own party. . . . Grassley called Bush's proposal 'good policy,' but said it will not win Senate passage without changes to draw the votes of GOP moderates and some Democrats."[14] Critics called attention to the apparent mismatch between the putative goal of short-term economic stimulus and the upper-class tilt of the new round of proposed tax cuts.[15] (Almost half of all capital gains income goes to households with incomes over $1 million.) They also raised alarms about the budgetary consequences of major additional tax cuts in the altered climate of economic stagnation, increasingly pessimistic deficit forecasts, and an expanding global war on terror. As one business reporter observed, Bush "proposed massive tax cuts during the 2000 campaign, when things were booming, and proposed the same cuts when things tanked. Now he wants more cuts." The *New York Times* claimed that "Bush's Multitude of Tax-Cut Ideas Leaves Even Supply-Siders Dizzy."[16]

In March, three pivotal moderate Republican senators (Chafee, Snowe, and George Voinovich) concerned about the budget deficit and the cost of the war in Iraq sided with Democrats in moving to limit the new tax cut to $350 billion—less than half of what President Bush had proposed. Grassley acceded to their demand, precipitating a feud with the more hard-line House leadership. Republicans in the House and Senate bargained, postured, and traded accusations of "arrogance and broken promises" for two more months before settling on a compromise bill brokered by Vice President Richard Cheney, the Jobs and Growth Tax Relief Reconciliation Act (JGTRRA).[17]

---

[13] The Joint Committee on Taxation put the 11-year price tag at $726 billion, including $396 billion for the dividend tax repeal. Joint Committee on Taxation, "Estimated Budget Effects of the Revenue Provisions Contained in the President's Fiscal Year 2004 Budget Proposal," March 4, 2003.

[14] Jill Barshay and Alan K. Ota, "White House Tax Cut Package Gets a Wary Hill Reception," *CQ Weekly*, January 11, 2003, 68.

[15] Critics were not alone in noting this apparent mismatch. According to one political columnist sympathetic to the proposal, "When critics say the plan the president proposed Tuesday will have negligible short-term stimulative effects, the right responses are: Of course. And: good." George F. Will, "The Long and Short of the 'Stimulus Package'," *Washington Post*, January 8, 2003, A19.

[16] Allan Sloan, "The Tax Cut: Whose Is Bigger?" *Newsweek*, May 5, 2003, 53; Edmund L. Andrews, "Too Many Pennies from Heaven?" *New York Times*, February 16, 2003, BU 15.

[17] David E. Rosenbaum and David Firestone, "$318 Billion Deal is Set in Congress for Cutting Taxes," *New York Times*, May 22, 2003, A1; John Cochran, "GOP Turns to Cheney to Get the Job Done," *CQ Weekly*, May 31, 2003, 1306.

Despite adhering to the moderates' $350 billion ceiling, JGTRRA succeeded in accommodating much of what Bush had asked for by making the most popular elements—tax breaks for married couples and an increased child credit—expire in two years, and the more expensive cuts in taxes on dividends and capital gains expire in five years. The revised package was passed by the House (231–200) and by the Senate (51–50, with Cheney casting the tie-breaking vote). Of 532 votes cast, only 13 (eight in the House and five in the Senate) crossed party lines.

This new round of tax cuts was subjected to even more scathing criticism than the 2001 law, not only from the political left but also from the center. According to political columnist David Broder, "The Republicans in Congress cobbled together one of the strangest, least plausible tax bills in history and sent it off to President Bush, who discovered hidden virtues in a measure whose provisions he had repeatedly called woefully inadequate for the task of stimulating a sickly economy."[18] A former Republican cabinet official complained in equally strong terms about "Republicans' irresponsible obsession with tax cutting."[19]

Criticism of JGTRRA was heightened when it became clear that a "last-minute revision by House and Senate leaders" would prevent millions of families with incomes between $10,500 and $26,625 from receiving $400 checks reflecting the increased child credit in the new bill. In the face of that criticism, the Senate Republican leadership and the Bush White House signaled their willingness to extend the child credit, at a cost of $3.5 billion. An amendment to that effect passed the Senate by a margin of 94–2. (One supporter, Republican Trent Lott, "voted for it while mimicking a person gagging by poking a finger toward his open mouth.") The House, however, was less amenable. "At a House GOP Conference meeting . . . members were urged to seek to reframe the debate as being about a 'welfare' provision, not a 'child tax credit,' because the proposed tax break would go to those who pay no federal income taxes." House leaders refused to consider the measure except as part of a broader package including $78 billion in additional tax cuts for middle- and upper-income taxpayers. Democrats called that "an indirect attempt by the House to kill the tax credits." Charles Rangel "said it was 'one of the most cynical and hypocritical moves' he had ever seen." A few weeks later, child credit checks began to go out to more than 25 million middle-class families; the "firestorm" of criticism regarding the exclusion of working poor families quickly burned itself out, and their checks never arrived.[20]

[18] David Broder, "The Tax-Cut Skeptics Back Home," *Washington Post*, May 28, 2003, A19.

[19] Peter G. Peterson, "Deficits and Dysfunction," *New York Times Magazine*, June 8, 2003, 18.

[20] David Firestone, "Tax Law Omits $400 Child Credit for Millions," *New York Times*, May 29, 2003, A1; Jill Barshay and Alan K. Ota, "GOP Scrambles to Limit Damage of Child Tax Credit Controversy," *CQ Weekly*, June 7, 2003, 1371; David Firestone, "House Expands Child Credit As Part of a Larger Tax Cut," *New York Times*, June 13, 2003, A28.

Meanwhile, despite having seen President Bush's 2003 proposal cut in half, conservatives expressed optimism regarding prospects for further tax cuts. As one observer put it, "to conservative groups, who have every intention of pushing for an annual tax cut, arguments over the size of each one are hardly worth worrying about in the long run. 'We're going to be negotiating over the size of the tax cut every year for 10 years,' said Grover Norquist, president of Americans for Tax Reform. 'At the end of 10 years, you're going to see how much progress 'not getting everything you want' gets you.'" House Majority Leader Tom DeLay called the shrunken JGTRRA cuts "awesome," adding, "And it's only the beginning." Senate Majority Whip Mitch McConnell echoed DeLay's assessment: "All I can tell you is, we keep on winning, and we expect to win again."[21]

PUBLIC SUPPORT FOR THE TAX CUTS

The policy priorities reflected in the 2001 and 2003 tax cuts—reductions in the top marginal tax rates, more favorable treatment of business and investment income, and a phase-out of the estate tax—were all long-standing priorities of conservative Republicans. To varying degrees, each provided much more substantial benefits to wealthy taxpayers than to people of modest means. Anyone looking at the evidence presented in table 5.6 on public attitudes about the tax burden borne by rich people would have good grounds for imagining that tax cuts aimed so disproportionately at the very wealthy would have generated substantial public opposition. In fact, however, the public was generally quite supportive of the Bush tax cuts. The same National Election Study (NES) surveys that showed majority support for the proposition that rich people pay less than they should in federal income taxes also demonstrated a remarkable degree of public support for the "big tax cut" passed in 2001—a policy designed in large part to ensure that rich people would pay much less in federal income taxes in the coming decade.

Respondents in the 2002 NES survey were asked two different versions of the "big tax cut" question: half the respondents were asked whether they favored or opposed the tax cut "Congress passed," while the other half were asked about the tax cut "President Bush signed."[22] The distributions of opinion for both versions of the question are shown in figure 6.1. A comparison of the results suggests that associating the tax cut explicitly with President Bush

---

[21] Alan K. Ota, "Tax Cut Package Clears Amid Bicameral Rancor," *CQ Weekly*, May 24, 2003, 1245; David Nather, "GOP Infighting: Not Fatal," *CQ Weekly*, May 31, 2003, 1309.

[22] "As you may recall, [Congress passed/President Bush signed] a big tax cut last year. Did you FAVOR or OPPOSE the tax cut, or is this something you haven't thought about? Did you [favor/oppose] the tax cut STRONGLY or NOT STRONGLY?"

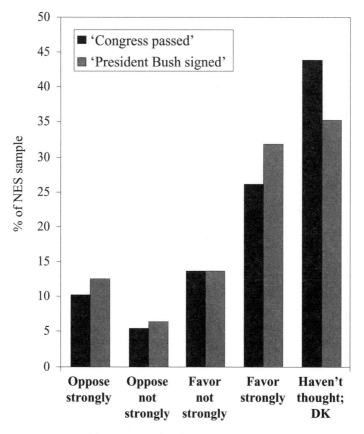

Figure 6.1 Public Support for the 2001 Tax Cut

had a slightly polarizing effect, increasing strong support by almost six percentage points but also increasing opposition by a few percentage points. However, the more surprising fact is that, regardless of how the question was posed, supporters of the tax cut outnumbered opponents by more than two to one, with most of those supporters saying they favored the tax cut "strongly." These results parallel the results of an earlier NES survey, conducted during the 2000 presidential campaign, in which almost two-thirds of the respondents agreed "that most of the expected federal budget surplus should be used to cut taxes."[23]

[23] "Recently, there has been a lot of talk about how to spend the extra money the federal government is likely to have in the near future. Some people have proposed that most of the expected federal budget surplus should be used to cut taxes. Do you approve or disapprove of this proposal? Do you approve [disapprove] of this proposal strongly or not strongly?" Approve strongly, 47%—Approve not strongly, 18%—Disapprove not strongly, 12%—Disapprove

TABLE 6.1

Public Expectations for the 2001 Tax Cut

"As you may know, George W. Bush has proposed a $1.6 trillion tax cut over ten years. . . . I am going to read you a list of things that might happen if a tax cut were passed. For each item that I read, please tell me whether you think it is something that you expect to happen or whether it is something that you do not expect to happen."

	Expect	Do not expect	Depends; Not sure
The wealthy will benefit more from the tax cut than the middle class	74%	21%	5%
The tax cut won't give enough help to those with lower incomes	57%	38%	5%
It will help prevent an economic recession	50%	40%	10%
Special-interest groups will benefit the most from a tax cut	50%	40%	10%
The tax cut will leave too little money for social programs	42%	50%	8%
The average taxpayer will get substantial tax relief	38%	57%	5%
You personally will get substantial tax relief	28%	67%	5%

$N = 2,024$.

Source: NBC News/*Wall Street Journal* Poll, March 2001.

The extent of public support for the Bush tax cuts is especially impressive in light of widespread public suspicion, even before they were passed, that the benefits would go mostly to the rich. For example, an NBC News/*Wall Street Journal* Poll in March 2001 asked respondents about "things that might happen if a tax cut were passed." The results are presented in table 6.1. These results document significant public concerns about the likely distribution of benefits from the Bush plan. Almost three-fourths of the respondents said they expected the wealthy to benefit more than the middle class. Two-thirds doubted that they, personally, would get "substantial tax relief." A smaller majority doubted that the "average taxpayer" would get substantial relief, and most people also said they expected that the tax cut "won't give enough help to those with lower incomes."

Similar concerns appeared in a variety of other surveys. A CBS News Poll the following month found 55% of the respondents saying that "rich peo-

---

strongly, 20%. On the other hand, an even larger proportion of the 2000 NES respondents agreed that "most of the expected federal budget surplus should go to protecting social security and Medicare." Approve strongly, 64%—Approve not strongly, 17%—Disapprove not strongly, 8%—Disapprove strongly, 8%.

ple" would "benefit most" from Bush's 2001 tax cut plan; only 26% said that "middle-income people" would benefit most.[24] A Harris Poll in June 2003 found 42% saying the 2003 tax cut would help "the rich" a lot and only 11% said it would help "the middle class" a lot.[25] What is striking, though, is that in each of these cases a clear plurality of the respondents said they favored the tax cuts despite their skepticism regarding the likely distribution of benefits.[26]

Political scientists Jacob Hacker and Paul Pierson provided a more comprehensive compilation of results from 25 separate opinion surveys conducted in the early months of 2001 on the topic of President Bush's proposed tax cut. On average, they found 56% of the respondents supporting the president's plan and only 33% opposing it. However, Hacker and Pierson argued that "for determining voter preferences, these results are close to meaningless" because they "say almost nothing about what kind of tax cuts the public wanted and how much priority they gave them."[27]

In an effort to shed light on the latter question, Hacker and Pierson compiled ten surveys from 1999, 2000, and early 2001 in which respondents were offered choices between tax cuts and other potential uses of the federal budget surplus. Depending upon the menu of alternatives offered, support for tax cuts ranged from 14% to 36% in these surveys. When tax cuts were pitted against Social Security, Medicare, or both, sizable majorities preferred the latter option. With debt reduction added to the mix, no single option commanded majority support. When "domestic programs" and Social Security (or Social Security and Medicare) were included as separate choices, debt reduction and tax cuts together commanded support from only about one-third of the public. Hacker and Pierson concluded from this evidence that "voters consistently saw tax cuts as a lower priority than plausible alternative uses of the forecasted surpluses."[28] However, these results may mostly reflect the

---

[24] "From what you've heard so far, who do you think would benefit most from George W. Bush's tax cut plan: rich people, poor people, or middle-income people?" Rich people, 55%—Poor people, 4%—Middle-income people, 26%—Other, Don't know, 13%.

[25] "Do you think that the tax cut will help the rich a lot, some, only a little, or not at all?" A lot, 42%—Some, 30%—Only a little, 12%—Not at all, 6%—Not sure, 10%. "Do you think that the tax cut will help the middle class a lot, some, only a little, or not at all?" A lot, 11%—Some, 39%—Only a little, 31%—Not at all, 11%—Not sure, 8%.

[26] March 2001 NBC News/*Wall Street Journal* Poll: "As you may know, George W. Bush has proposed a $1.6 trillion tax cut over ten years. Do you favor or oppose this proposal?" Favor, 57%—Oppose, 32%—Not sure, 11%. April 2001 CBS News Poll: "Do you favor or oppose George W. Bush's $1.6 trillion tax cut for the country over the next 10 years?" Favor, 51%—Oppose, 37%—Don't know, 12%. June 2003 Harris Poll: "The Congress passed and the President has signed a new tax cut. Overall do you think this tax cut was a good or bad thing?" Good thing, 50%—Bad thing, 35%—Not sure, 15%.

[27] Hacker and Pierson (2005a), 37.

[28] Ibid., 38–39.

remarkably high levels of public support for Social Security and Medicare. When tax cuts and debt reduction were pitted against "improving funding for needed government programs," with no specific mention of Social Security or Medicare, only 16% to 22% of the survey respondents chose government programs while 32% to 41% chose debt reduction and 34% to 42% chose "an across-the-board tax cut."[29]

Hacker and Pierson might have added that when survey respondents were offered a choice between President Bush's plan and alternative tax-cutting proposals actually circulating in Washington in the spring of 2001, they mostly preferred the alternatives. In the March NBC News/*Wall Street Journal* poll, respondents agreed by a margin of 52% to 41% that "we should only allow cuts in the income tax rates for middle- and low-income taxpayers, so the government has enough money for debt reduction and specific spending increases in priority areas such as education."[30] In a *Los Angeles Times* Poll conducted a few days later, respondents favored a Democratic proposal for a tax cut "about half as big with more money devoted to spending on domestic programs such as Medicare and education and reducing the debt" by a margin of 55% to 30%.[31] In contrast, a CBS News/*New York Times* Poll con-

---

[29] "The federal government will have a surplus of funds in the next few years. For which one of the following would you like to see the surplus funds used—reducing the national debt, improving funding for needed government programs, or providing an across-the-board tax cut?" NBC News/*Wall Street Journal* Poll, June 2000: Reducing the national debt, 32%—Improving funding for needed government programs, 22%—Providing across-the-board tax cut, 38%—All/None/Other (volunteered), 7%—Not sure, 4%. NBC News/*Wall Street Journal* Poll, July 2000: Reducing the national debt, 32%—Improving funding for needed government programs, 20%—Providing across-the-board tax cut, 42%—All/None/Other (volunteered), 4%—Not sure, 2%. NBC News/*Wall Street Journal* Poll, September 2000: Reducing the national debt, 41%—Improving funding for needed government programs, 16%—Providing across-the-board tax cut, 34%—All/None/Other (volunteered), 7%—Not sure, 2%. None of these figures, from the Roper Center's *iPOLL* archive, match those reported by Hacker and Pierson for the only NBC News/*Wall Street Journal* Poll in their table; I have been unable to determine the source of this discrepancy.

[30] "I am going to read you two positions on taxes and spending and then ask which comes closer to your view. Statement A: President Bush says that the budget surplus is large enough to cut income-tax rates for all taxpayers, while still leaving room for debt reduction and some spending increases in priority areas such as education. Statement B: Democrats say that the budget surplus is not that large and we should only allow cuts in the income tax rates for middle- and low-income taxpayers, so the government has enough money for debt reduction and specific spending increases in priority areas such as education." Statement A (Agree with President Bush), 41%—Statement B (Agree with Democrats), 52%—Neither/depends (volunteered), 4%—Not sure, 3%.

[31] "George W. Bush has proposed a tax cut of $1.6 trillion and eliminating about two-thirds of the national debt over the next 10 years, which is about $2 trillion. Democrats say the tax cut should be about half as big with more money devoted to spending on domestic programs such as Medicare and education and reducing the debt. Which comes closer to your view?" Bush's proposal, 30%—Democrats' proposal, 55%—Neither (volunteered), 4%—Don't know, 11%. *Los Angeles Times* Poll, March 2001.

ducted only a week later found respondents favoring President Bush's plan to divide the surplus equally between tax cuts, debt reduction, and "other purposes including government spending" over a Democratic proposal to "use more than half of the budget surplus to reduce the debt" by a margin of 49% to 41%.[32] But another NBC News/*Wall Street Journal* Poll the following month found respondents favoring "the Senate's $1.2 trillion tax cut" to "the President's $1.6-trillion tax cut" by a margin of 57% to 32%.[33]

Based on their detailed examination of public opinion data like these, Hacker and Pierson concluded that, "Far from representing popular wishes, the size, structure, and distribution of the tax cuts passed in 2001 were directly at odds with majority views. . . . The most striking characteristic of the tax cuts . . . is how far a policy produced by elected officials diverged from the preferences of most voters." While I do not doubt that most voters would have preferred alternative packages of tax cuts, spending increases, and deficit reduction to the package that actually emerged from the legislative process in 2001, I believe it is a mistake to suppose that *any* specific package could be said to represent "popular wishes" or "majority views" regarding such a complex matter of public policy. For one thing, detailed probing would almost certainly reveal a good deal of ambivalence, uncertainty, and outright contradiction in the views of individual citizens regarding the various provisions of any specific plan.[34] What is more, even if individual citizens were splendidly clear and consistent, "majority views" would not be; political theorists have demonstrated that for policy issues of any real complexity, there is generally *no* specific policy outcome that could not be defeated by some other proposal in a majority vote.[35] Thus, the appealing-seeming notion of popular sovereignty is both psychologically unrealistic and logically incoherent.

---

[32] "Which approach for using the budget surplus do you prefer—George W. Bush's (use about a third of the budget surplus to cut taxes, about a third to reduce the debt, and about a third for other purposes including government spending and a reserve fund), or the Democrats' in Congress (use more than half of the budget surplus to reduce the debt and divide the rest equally among a tax cut, other government spending, and a reserve fund)?" Bush's, 49%—Democrats' in Congress, 41%—Neither (volunteered), 3%—Both (volunteered), 1%—Don't know, 6%. CBS News/*New York Times* Poll, March 2001.

[33] "As you may know, President Bush proposed a $1.6-trillion tax cut to return more of the surplus to the taxpayers and to encourage long-term economic growth. The Senate proposed reducing the President's tax cut to $1.2 trillion to leave more money for domestic policy priorities and for reducing the national debt. Which proposal do you favor—the President's $1.6-trillion tax cut or the Senate's $1.2-trillion tax cut?" President Bush's $1.6-trillion tax cut, 32%—Senate's $1.2-trillion tax cut, 57%—Neither/Depends (volunteered), 5%—Not sure, 6%. NBC News/*Wall Street Journal* Poll, April 2001.

[34] On these aspects of public opinion, see, for example, Hochschild (1981), chapter 8; Zaller (1992), chapters 4–5; Bartels (2003).

[35] The classic formal treatment of the logical limitations of collective choice procedures is Arrow (1951). Riker (1982) provided a less technical explication of these limitations and a discussion of their implications for democratic theory.

In any case, democracies do not make public policy on the basis of "popular wishes," at least not in any straightforward sense. Democratic policy agendas are set by elected leaders, not by voters. As political scientist E. E. Schattschneider aptly put it more than 60 years ago, "The people are a sovereign whose vocabulary is limited to two words, 'Yes' and 'No.' "[36] In the case of the tax cuts, President Bush posed the question and the people's response, insofar as they responded at all, was a vigorous "Yes."

UNENLIGHTENED SELF-INTEREST

Taken at face value, the results of opinion surveys provide considerable evidence of strong public support for tax cuts along the lines pursued by President Bush—at least if the alternative was no tax cut. However, there are good reasons to suspect that public opinion in this domain should *not* be taken entirely at face value. Notwithstanding the vastness of the stakes, public thinking about the Bush tax cuts seems to have been remarkably superficial. Perhaps the strongest evidence of this fact appears in figure 6.1. Unlike most commercial opinion surveys, the 2002 NES survey invited respondents to say that they "haven't thought about" whether they favored or opposed the 2001 tax cut. Remarkably, in view of the fiscal and political significance of the tax cut, 40% of the respondents availed themselves of that opportunity.[37] Even associating the tax cut with President Bush only reduced the proportion who said they "haven't thought about it" to about 35%, while asking about the tax cut "Congress passed" left almost 45% of the respondents unable to say whether they favored or opposed it.

A good deal of additional evidence of public inattention and uncertainty in the general domain of tax policy appeared in an extensive 2003 survey of Americans' views on taxes sponsored by National Public Radio, the Kaiser Foundation, and Harvard University's Kennedy School of Government. Asked whether they pay more in federal income tax or Social Security and Medicare tax, 34% of respondents said they didn't know (and most of the rest were probably wrong).[38] Asked whether they were eligible for the Earned

[36] Schattschneider (1942), 52.

[37] Figure 6.1 does not differentiate between people who said they "haven't thought about" whether they favored or opposed the tax cut and those who volunteered that they didn't know whether they favored or opposed it. Since the former group outnumbered the latter group by 504 to 11, I simply refer to both groups as not having thought about whether they favored or opposed the tax cut.

[38] "Over the course of a year, do you pay more federal income tax, or more Social Security and Medicare Tax, or don't you know?" More federal income tax, 52%—More Social Security and Medicare, 14%—Don't know, 34%—Refused, 1%. (In fact, a substantial majority of taxpayers pay more in payroll taxes than in federal income tax.)

Income Tax Credit, 28% said they did not know.[39] Asked whether Americans pay more or less of their income in taxes than Western Europeans, 42% said they did not know.[40] Asked whether they had heard about a proposal in Washington to do away with taxes on corporate dividends—the centerpiece of President Bush's new tax proposal and a prominent feature of political debate in the month before the survey—61% said no.[41] Asked whether the 2001 tax cuts should be speeded up, 48% said they did not know.[42] Asked whether the cuts should be made permanent rather than being allowed to expire in 2011, 60% said they did not know.[43] Asked whether speeding up the cuts and making them permanent would mainly help high-income, middle-income, or lower-income people, 41% said they did not know.[44]

In short, while public opinion was generally supportive of the Bush tax cuts, there is also plenty of evidence of ignorance and uncertainty about the workings of the tax system and the policy options under consideration—or actually adopted—in Washington. Much of the public was unclear about basic facts in the realm of tax policy; some of what the public did know was patently false; and a remarkable number of people, when offered the chance, said that they had not thought about a policy innovation whose consequences are reckoned by experts in *trillions* of dollars.

How did ordinary people, ignorant and uncertain as they were in this omain, formulate any views at all about such a complex matter of public policy? If they happened to know that the tax cut was proposed and pushed by President Bush, they may have relied on partisan sentiment to favor or

[39] "The last time you filed your taxes, were you eligible for the Earned Income Tax Credit, or not, or don't you know?" Yes, 21%—No, 50%—Don't know, 28%.

[40] "Compared with the citizens of Western European countries, do you think Americans pay a higher percentage of their income in taxes, a smaller percentage of their income in taxes, about the same percentage of their income in taxes, or don't you know enough to say?" A higher percentage, 21%—a smaller percentage, 30%—About the same percentage, 6%—Don't know enough, 42%.

[41] "There is a proposal in Washington now to do away with personal income taxes on corporate dividends. Dividends are what many companies pay to owners of their stock. Have you heard about this proposal, or not?" Yes, 38%—No, 61%—Don't know, 1%.

[42] "As you may know, in 2001 Congress passed President Bush's proposals for tax cuts that are to be phased in over the next few years. Do you favor or oppose speeding up those tax cuts so they go into effect sooner, or don't you know enough to say?" Favor, 31%—Oppose, 21%—Don't know enough to say, 48%.

[43] "As you may know, the 2001 tax cuts are set to expire in 2011. Do you support or oppose making those tax cuts permanent, or don't you know enough to say?" Support, 23%—Oppose, 17%—Don't know enough to say, 60%.

[44] "In his State of the Union address President Bush proposed speeding up the tax cuts and making them permanent. Do you think this mainly would help high-income people, middle-income people, or lower-income people, or would it treat everyone equally, or don't you know enough to say?" High income people, 29%—Middle income people, 7%—Lower income people, 6%—Treat everyone equally, 18%—Don't know enough to say, 41%.

TABLE 6.2

Self-Interest, Political Values, and Support for the 2001 Tax Cut

Parameter estimates from instrumental variables regression analyses (with standard errors in parentheses). Support for the tax cut ranges from −1 (oppose strongly) to +1 (favor strongly). Respondents who said they "haven't thought about" the tax cut are excluded from the analysis.

	{1}	{2}	{3}
Own tax burden			
(−1 to +1)	.370 (.094)	.251 (.092)	.477 (.107)
Rich tax burden			
(−1 to +1)	.354 (.070)	−.067 (.081)	−.058 (.082)
Poor tax burden			
(−1 to +1)	.049 (.119)	.137 (.113)	−.046 (.126)
Republican Party			
identification (−1 to +1)	—	.607 (.134)	.495 (.138)
Conservative ideology			
(−1 to +1)	—	.248 (.209)	.479 (.216)
Government spending			
preferences (−1 to +1)	—	—	.282 (.194)
Perceived government			
waste (0 to 1)	—	—	−.901 (.271)
Family income (0 to 1)	−.001 (.094)	−.242 (.096)	−.266 (.100)
"President Bush" wording	−.030 (.051)	−.140 (.049)	−.082 (.052)
Intercept	.305 (.074)	.341 (.080)	.809 (.229)
Standard error of regression	.745	.711	.710
Adjusted R^2	.11	.19	.20
N	889	889	889

Source: Calculations based on data from 2002 National Election Study survey.

oppose it. If they associated tax-cutting with small government, they may have been swayed by opinions about government programs or general ideological predispositions. The statistical analyses reported in table 6.2 indicate that party identification and political ideology did have significant effects on people's views about the tax cut: as expected, Republicans and conservatives were much more likely to support the tax cut than Democrats and liberals were.[45] However, the apparent effects of government spending preferences, perceptions of government waste, and people's own income levels are less readily explicable. People with higher incomes and those who thought the

[45] The statistical results presented in table 6.2 are derived from an instrumental variables estimator, which produces less efficient parameter estimates than ordinary regression analysis but avoids substantial biases due to measurement error in the survey responses employed as explanatory variables. I use the difference in feeling thermometer ratings assigned to conservatives and liberals as an instrument for *Conservative ideology*, respondents' 2000 presidential votes as an instrument for *Republican party identification*, an index derived from eight government

government wastes a lot of money were generally *less* supportive of the tax cut, other things being equal, while those who said they supported more spending on a variety of government programs were *more* likely to favor the tax cut. These results suggest a good deal of confusion in the connections between people's political values and their policy preferences—even when the 40% of NES respondents who said they had not thought about whether they favored or opposed the tax cut are excluded from the analysis.[46]

The impression of confusion is reinforced when we turn to the apparent impact of people's views about tax burdens on their support for the 2001 tax cut. The most salient feature of the tax cut was, obviously, that taxes would be cut. Thus, it is hardly surprising that ordinary people reasoning about the tax cut drew heavily upon their views about taxes. What may be surprising, however, is that they seem to have done so in ways that mostly reflect rather simple-minded—and sometimes misguided—considerations of self-interest stemming from their views about their own tax burdens.

Respondents in the NES surveys were not asked directly whether they thought they would benefit personally from the Bush tax cut. However, the question about respondents' own tax burdens sheds significant indirect light on the impact of perceived self-interest among other potential influences on their views about tax policy. To the extent that people who thought they paid more than they should in taxes were more likely to support the tax cut, even after allowing for the effects of partisanship, political ideology, and other characteristics, it seems plausible to infer that the additional support had something to do with their subjective sense of their own tax burden. The parallel questions in the NES survey about the tax burdens of rich people and poor people provide a valuable check on reasoning of this sort, since more general antipathy to taxes would presumably be reflected in one or both of those questions as well as in the question about respondents' *own* tax burdens.

Since the 2001 tax cut included some direct benefits for most taxpayers, there was some reason for respondents who thought they are asked to pay too much to support it. However, since most of the benefits were targeted to wealthy taxpayers—according to one estimate, 63% to the top one-fifth of households and 36% to the top one-hundredth, but only 20% to the bottom three-fifths—most respondents had even better reason to oppose the tax

---

spending items in the post-election wave of the 2002 NES survey as an instrument for the corresponding index of *Government spending preferences* in the pre-election wave of the survey, and perceptions of trust in government (whether government can be trusted to do what is right, whether government is run for the benefit of all, and whether government officials are crooked) as instruments for *Perceived government waste*. More detailed discussion of the statistical analyses appears in Bartels (2005).

[46] A more complex estimation strategy designed to guard against potential selection bias due to this censoring of the sample (Heckman 1979) produced generally similar parameter estimates.

cuts if they felt that rich people are asked to pay too little, and perhaps some additional reason to oppose the cuts if they felt that they are asked to pay too much—since tax cuts for the rich would be likely, one way or another, to increase their own future taxes through burden-shifting.

Considering the apparent effects of tax burdens alone, in the first column of table 6.2, the statistical results suggest that respondents who wanted rich people to bear a larger share of the tax burden *were* significantly more likely to oppose the tax cut than those who said the rich pay too much or about the right amount.[47] However, the additional analyses reported in the second and third columns of the table suggest that this apparent effect mostly reflects the correlation of perceptions of rich people's tax burdens with respondents' more general political values. Once differences in partisanship and ideology are taken into account, views about whether rich people should pay more or less in taxes—a consideration that seems on its face to be of considerable relevance in evaluating a policy whose benefits were targeted mostly to people in the upper reaches of the income distribution—had no apparent effect on views about the tax cut.

In marked contrast, respondents' views about their *own* tax burdens had a strong independent impact on support for the tax cut, even after allowing for the effects of broader partisan and ideological predispositions. Indeed, in the analysis presented in the third column of table 6.2, respondents' perceptions of their own tax burdens rivaled partisanship and ideology as predictors of support for the tax cut. Moreover, because the distribution of responses to the question about respondents' own tax burdens was highly skewed (with 51% of the respondents saying they are asked to pay too much and only 4% saying they are asked to pay too little), this effect turns out to account for most of the net support for the tax cut in the NES sample.[48]

Additional analysis suggests that this impact was even greater for respondents who were asked about the tax cut "Congress passed" rather than the tax

---

[47] The parameter estimates are from instrumental variables regression analyses with perceived tax burdens in the 2002 post-election NES survey used as instruments for the corresponding perceived tax burdens in the pre-election survey. (Since the tax cut questions appeared in the pre-election wave of the survey, using perceived tax burdens in the post-election wave as instruments for perceived tax burdens in the pre-election wave guards against the possibility that survey context or question ordering effects inflate the relationship between perceived tax burdens and views about the tax cut.) The correlations between perceived tax burdens in the pre-election and post-election surveys are .55 for respondents' own taxes, .55 for the rich, and .44 for the poor. Even with some allowance for genuine change in respondents' views between the two surveys, correlations of this magnitude suggest that the responses are subject to substantial measurement error.

[48] The sample mean value for the (−1 to +1) tax cut variable (excluding respondents who said they "haven't thought about" whether they favored or opposed it) was .354. Multiplying the sample mean perceived *Own Tax Burden* among these same respondents, .478, by the corresponding parameter estimate in the third column of table 6.2, .477, accounts for 64% of this net support for the tax cut.

cut "President Bush signed." In the absence of any clear cues about where the tax cut came from or whose interests it served, people seem mostly to have fallen back on simple-minded self-interest in deciding what (if anything) they thought about it.[49]

THE IMPACT OF POLITICAL INFORMATION

I have argued that public support for the Bush tax cuts derived in considerable part from unenlightened considerations of self-interest among people who did not recognize the implications of President Bush's policies for their own economic well-being or their broader political values. Millions of citizens believed that the federal government should spend more money on a wide variety of programs, that the rich are asked to pay too little in taxes, and that growing economic inequality is a bad thing—but they simultaneously supported policies whose main effects have been to reduce the tax burden of the rich, constrain funding for government programs, and exacerbate growing economic inequality. One is left to wonder how these people might resolve the contradictions implied by their simultaneous antipathies toward inequality and taxation—if they recognized those contradictions.

Elsewhere, I have proposed a way to explore admittedly hypothetical questions of this sort by observing how the political preferences of well-informed citizens differ from those of less-informed citizens who are similar in politically relevant ways.[50] If well-informed citizens have systematically different perceptions and preferences, the logic goes, might not additional information move less-informed citizens in the same directions? In the present context, if well-informed citizens seem to reason differently, draw on different premises, and reach different conclusions about tax policy, might not additional information move less-informed citizens to do likewise?

Obviously, empirical analyses along these lines require some reliable way to distinguish well-informed citizens from less-informed citizens. To that end, I rely here on the same general measures of political information employed in

---

[49] The results reported in table 6.2 are from analyses combining responses to both versions of the question. Results for the two half-samples considered separately (not shown) suggest that the impact of respondents' own perceived tax burdens was substantially greater for the tax cut "Congress passed" than for the tax cut "President Bush signed." For example, in analyses paralleling those reported in the third column of table 6.2, the estimated effects of respondents' own perceived tax burdens was .670 (with a standard error of .153) on views about the tax cut "Congress passed," but .299 (with a standard error of .151) on views about the tax cut "President Bush signed."

[50] Bartels (1990). Empirical analyses along similar lines include Bartels (1996); Delli Carpini and Keeter (1996); Fishkin (1997); Althaus (1998); and Gilens (2001).

TABLE 6.3

Political Information, Ideology, and Attention to the 2001 Tax Cut

Ordered probit parameter estimates (with standard errors in parentheses). Additional response thresholds are included in the analyses but not shown here.

	Have "thought about" tax cut	Say tax cut is "very important"	Republicans support tax cut	Democrats oppose tax cut
Political information (0 to 1)	1.686 (.109)	.712 (.133)	1.716 (.143)	1.133 (.136)
Conservative ideology (−1 to +1)	.232 (.129)	.782 (.165)	.696 (.168)	.100 (.162)
Political information ×ideology	−.021 (.232)	−1.061 (.287)	−.682 (.311)	.290 (.292)
Family income (0 to 1)	.584 (.099)	−.141 (.111)	.587 (.118)	.273 (.113)
"President Bush" wording	.223 (.072)	.019 (.059)	.146 (.062)	.258 (.060)
2004 survey	.016 (.064)	—	—	—
Intercept	−.953 (.080)	−.898 (.088)	−1.157 (.091)	−1.052 (.087)
Log likelihood	−1,593.8	−1,400.7	−1,241.7	−1,350.6
Pseudo-R^2	.12	.02	.09	.05
N	2,723	1,503	1,511	1,511

Source: Calculations based on data from 2002 and 2004 National Election Study surveys.

chapter 5.[51] I use those measures to investigate the extent to which better-informed people had different views about the 2001 tax cut than those who were otherwise similar but less well-informed.

I begin by considering the impact of political information on attention to and knowledge about the tax cut. Perhaps unsurprisingly, better-informed people were much more likely to express an opinion for or against the tax cut, much more likely to consider the issue important, and much more likely to recognize the respective positions of the Republican and Democratic parties. For example, the statistical results presented in table 6.3 imply that someone at the bottom of the distribution of political information had only a 29% chance of having "thought about" the 2001 tax cut; but that probability increased to 87% at the top of the distribution.[52] Conservatives, more affluent

[51] In the 2004 NES survey, the information scale is based on respondents' answers to a series of factual questions about politics; in the 2002 survey the information scale is based on subjective ratings of general political knowledge supplied by the NES interviewers at the end of the pre- and post-election interviews. Detailed descriptions of the scales appear in chapter 5.

[52] These calculations are for an ideological moderate with average family income. They split the difference between the statistical results reported in the table for the tax cut "President

people, and those who were asked about the tax cut "President Bush signed" (rather than the tax cut "Congress passed") were also more likely to express an opinion for or against the 2001 tax cut; but all those differences were modest by comparison with the difference due to general political information.

Better-informed people also attached a good deal more importance to the 2001 tax cut; someone at the highest information level was about twice as likely as someone at the lowest information level to say that the issue was "very important" (40% versus 17%). However, in this case there was a strong interaction evident between information and ideology: well-informed conservatives were actually *less* likely than uninformed conservatives to say that the tax cut was "very important" (30% versus 43%), while well-informed liberals were vastly *more* likely than uninformed liberals to say so (51% versus 4%).

Better-informed people were also much more likely to recognize the parties' positions on the tax-cutting issue; the probability of recognizing that the Democratic Party opposed the tax cut increased from 21% at the lowest information level to 64% at the highest information level, while the probability of recognizing that the Republican Party favored the tax cut increased from 21% to 82%. (In addition, people who were asked about the tax cut "President Bush signed" were significantly more likely to be able to characterize the parties' positions correctly than people who were asked about the tax cut "Congress passed," with no cues provided by the question wording about who was on which side of the issue.)

It should not be surprising that better-informed people were more attentive to the tax-cutting issue. What is more consequential is that they developed markedly different opinions about the issue than those who were less well-informed. That fact is evident from the statistical results presented in table 6.4, which focus on the relationship between political information and support for the 2001 tax cut. For the sample as a whole, the estimated probability of supporting the tax cut for a person with average income declined markedly with increasing information, from 75% at the bottom of the information scale to 66% in the middle of the information scale to 57% at the top of the information scale.[53]

Bush signed" and the tax cut "Congress passed." Similarly, in the case of having "thought about" the tax cut—where the analysis includes responses from both the 2002 and 2004 NES surveys—the calculations split the difference between the two years.

[53] These estimated information effects are smaller than those reported in my previously published analysis of support for the Bush tax cuts (Bartels 2005). The difference primarily reflects the inclusion here of additional data from the 2004 NES survey, which were unavailable when that piece was written. The estimated information effects corresponding to the estimate of −.510 in the first column of table 6.4 are −.849 (with a standard error of .166) for the 2002 data alone and −.299 (with a standard error of .157) for the 2004 data alone. The decline is concentrated among Republicans (from −1.01 in 2002 to −.00 in 2004); the estimated information effect among Democrats actually increased in magnitude, from −1.48 in 2002 to −1.72 in 2004.

TABLE 6.4
Partisanship, Political Information, and Support for the 2001 Tax Cut

Ordered probit parameter estimates (with standard errors in parentheses) for probability of (strongly or not strongly) favoring the 2001 tax cut. Additional response thresholds are included in the analyses but not shown here.

	Total sample	Republicans	Independents	Democrats
Political information (0 to 1)	−.510 (.112)	−.384 (.230)	−.359 (.182)	−1.572 (.207)
Family income (0 to 1)	.268 (.105)	.221 (.205)	−.019 (.177)	.018 (.186)
"President Bush" wording	.030 (.078)	.008 (.149)	.017 (.135)	−.216 (.134)
2004 survey	−.192 (.065)	.148 (.119)	−.346 (.109)	−.317 (.124)
Intercept	.624 (.093)	1.507 (.208)	.601 (.155)	.969 (.158)
Log likelihood	−2,216.7	−487.0	−812.0	−665.8
Pseudo-R^2	.01	.01	.01	.06
N	1,767	599	621	547

Source: Calculations based on data from 2002 and 2004 National Election Study surveys.

Arthur Lupia and his colleagues have pointed out that this impact of political information on support for the 2001 tax cut differed dramatically between conservatives and liberals and between Republicans and Democrats.[54] Their finding is echoed in the second, third, and fourth columns of table 6.4, which provide separate estimates of the impact of political information on support for the tax cut among Republicans, Independents, and Democrats, respectively.[55] These results suggest that information had *some* negative effect on support for the tax cut even among Republicans and Independents, but that the effect was much more powerful among Democrats. Even among the best-informed Republicans, 90% supported the tax cut. So did a bare majority (53%) of the best-informed Independents. However, among Democrats, support for the tax cut declined from 76% at the bottom of the information distribution to only 19% at the top of the information distribution.

[54] Lupia et al. (2006).

[55] The separate analyses for the three partisan groups capture some other interesting differences in patterns of support for the tax cut. First, family income—insofar as it mattered at all—probably only mattered among Republicans. Second, the question wording associating the tax cut with President Bush produced a noticeable decline in support among Democrats, but no corresponding increase in support among Republicans or Independents. And third, both Independents and Democrats showed a significant decline in support for the tax cut between 2002 and 2004; however, Republicans became, if anything, more likely to support the tax cut in 2004 than they had been in 2002.

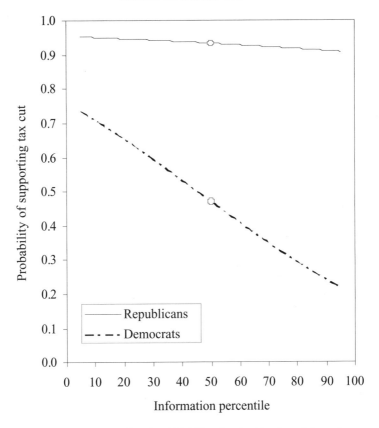

Figure 6.2 Support for the 2001 Tax Cut by Partisanship and Information Level

Figure 6.2 provides a graphical representation of the distinct information effects for Republicans and Democrats implied by the statistical results in table 6.4. The general pattern here is reminiscent of the pattern of ideological polarization evident in figures 5.2, 5.3, and 5.4—but with two notable differences. First, there is a sizable partisan difference in support for the tax cut even among people at the bottom of the information distribution. Thus, whereas the implications of political ideology for views about inequality seem to have been entirely opaque to the least-informed citizens, even they seem to have recognized that their partisan loyalties were of some relevance in thinking about whether they favored or opposed the tax cut—especially when the wording of the question associated the tax cut with President Bush.

Second, and more importantly, whereas the patterns of polarization in figures 5.2, 5.3, and 5.4 were roughly symmetrical, the pattern in figure 6.2 is highly asymmetrical. While increasing information produced a steep decline in support for the tax cut among Democrats, it produced no corresponding increase in support for the tax cut among Republicans—because even very uninformed Republicans were already virtually certain to say they supported the tax cut, if they expressed any view at all. Rather than simply blurring the partisan differences evident among better-informed people, political ignorance had a marked effect on the overall level of support for the tax cut.

These results suggest that, had the public as a whole been better-informed, public support for the tax cut would have been significantly lower than it actually was. Indeed, projections based on the statistical results in tables 6.3 and 6.4 imply that more than 80% of the *net* majority in favor of the tax cut in 2002 and 2004 (among people who took a position one way or the other) would have disappeared had the entire public been fully-informed, reducing the actual 32-point margin of support to a six-point margin.[56] Thus, to a remarkable degree, popular support for the 2001 tax cut seems to have been grounded in the political ignorance of ordinary citizens.

CHUMP CHANGE

In his first three years as president, George W. Bush presided over two of the biggest tax cuts in American history. In both cases the benefits went disproportionately to the wealthy while the costs were put off to the future, presumably to be borne a good deal more equally in the form of eventual tax increases, cuts in government programs, and deficit economics. And in both cases the views of ordinary Americans, insofar as those views could be said to exist, were largely supportive of Bush's policy initiatives.

Some observers have inferred from these facts that ordinary people are simply confused about what is in their own interests. For example, in the course of

[56] These figures are derived from the separate parameter estimates for Republicans, Independents, and Democrats reported in table 6.4. Actual values of the explanatory variables (for each respondent in the 2002 and 2004 NES surveys who expressed a view for or against the tax cut) imply a 66–34 margin of support. Substituting a "perfect" information score of 1.0 for each respondent's actual information score produces a 55–45 margin of support. However, that calculation takes no account of the fact that many of the people who said they "haven't thought about" the tax cut would have done so had they been better informed. Using the parameter estimates reported in the first column of table 6.3 to capture this effect reduces the margin of support for the tax cut from 55–45 to 53–47 (since the people who *would have* taken a position had they been better informed would have been somewhat less likely than those who *did* take a position to support the tax cut). In terms of the total population, the actual margin of support to opposition was 41% to 22% (with 37% taking no position), while the fully-informed margin of support to opposition would have been 47% to 41% (with 12% taking no position).

describing 2004 presidential candidate Richard Gephardt's proposal to repeal President Bush's tax cuts and spend the money on universal health care, *New York Times* columnist (and Princeton economist) Paul Krugman wrote that "if American families knew what was good for them, then most of them—all but a small, affluent minority—would cheerfully give up their tax cuts in return for a guarantee that health care would be there when needed."[57]

Other observers, while a bit more circumspect about stipulating what people would do if they knew what was good for them, have raised similar doubts about the capacity of the American public to reason effectively about tax policy. For example, in the course of reflecting on the Bush era of "'Let Them Eat Cake' economics," *Newsweek* columnist Jonathan Alter worried that "even if the tax cuts help stimulate a modest recovery, we have dug ourselves a deep hole." He added that "explaining all this politically is a 'bank shot,' to use a billiards term. It requires trusting the voters with complexity. Will they see that their new $400 child credits are chump change compared with all the new fee hikes and service cuts? Will they understand that they're paying more in state and local taxes so that a guy with a Jaguar putting up a McMansion down the block can pay less in federal taxes? Will they connect those 30 kids cramming their child's classroom to decisions in far-away Washington?"[58]

One way to answer Alter's questions is to see how well public support for the Bush tax cuts has held up as their implementation has proceeded and their effects have been felt—or not. The 2004 NES survey repeated the question from the 2002 survey asking respondents whether they favored or opposed the 2001 tax cut. Figure 6.3 compares the responses in the two years.[59]

On one hand, there is clear evidence here of a decline in public support for the 2001 tax cut. By 2004 only 27% of the public said they strongly favored the tax cut, down from 32% in 2002; 17% strongly opposed the tax cut, up from 13% in 2002. In this light, it is interesting to note that the public perceptions of tax burdens documented in table 5.6 also shifted perceptibly between 2002 and 2004. By 2004, people were less likely to say that they are asked to pay more than they should (by 8.5 percentage points) and more likely to say that rich people are asked to pay less than they should (by 6.6 percentage points). These changes seem to reflect some recognition of the fact that the 2001 and 2003 Bush tax cuts significantly reduced overall federal tax rates, especially for the wealthiest taxpayers.

Despite these shifts, however, supporters of the 2001 tax cut continued to outnumber opponents by 38% to 25% in the 2004 NES survey—a 3–2 margin

[57] Paul Krugman, "Roads Not Taken," *New York Times*, April 25, 2003, A31.

[58] Jonathan Alter, "'Let Them East Cake' Economics," *Newsweek*, July 28, 2003, 36.

[59] Since respondents in 2004 were asked about the tax cut "President Bush signed," their responses are compared with responses from the random half of the 2002 sample that answered the same version of the question.

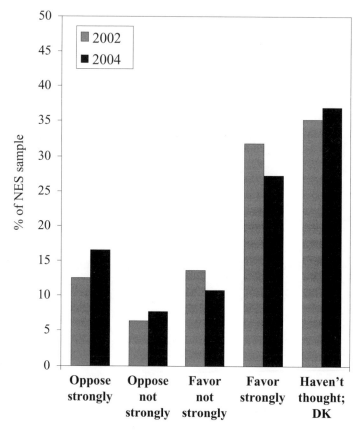

Figure 6.3 Public Support for the 2001 Tax Cut in 2002 and 2004

among those who expressed a view one way or the other. Another 37% of the public still had not thought about whether they favored or opposed the tax cut. More than three years after the tax cut began to take effect, Alter's "bank shot" seemed to have missed the pocket.

Not surprisingly, opposition to the tax cut was most common among people who expressed strong support for egalitarian values—especially among those who were generally well-informed about politics. The statistical analyses presented in table 6.5 summarize the relationship between egalitarian values, political information, and support for the tax cut among the 63% of respondents in the 2004 NES survey who favored or opposed the tax cut. The results indicate that political information had a significant negative effect on support for the tax cut, just as in table 6.4. However, the subgroup analyses presented in the second, third, and fourth columns of the table show that the impact of

TABLE 6.5
Egalitarian Values, Political Information, and Support
for the 2001 Tax Cut in 2004

Ordered probit parameter estimates (with standard errors in parentheses) for probability of
(strongly or not strongly) favoring the 2001 tax cut. Additional response thresholds are included
in the analyses but not shown here.

	Total sample	*Non-egalitarian*	*Moderately egalitarian*	*Strongly egalitarian*
Political information				
(0 to 1)	−.367 (.167)	.398 (.315)	−.219 (.263)	−1.314 (.328)
Family income				
(0 to 1)	.337 (.170)	.889 (.321)	.402 (.265)	−.250 (.337)
Intercept	.319 (.120)	.003 (.251)	.358 (.182)	.390 (.222)
Log likelihood	−896.3	−254.0	−350.4	−221.0
Pseudo-R²	.00	.02	.00	.05
N	705	229	282	194

Source: Calculations based on data from 2004 National Election Study survey.

information on support for the tax cut was mostly limited to the most egalitarian segment of the public—the minority of people (fewer than 30%) with
scores above +.5 on the −1 to +1 scale of egalitarian values introduced in
chapter 5.

The patterns of support and opposition implied by these results are presented graphically in figure 6.4. Among strong egalitarians, the average level of
support for the tax cut declined sharply with political information, from almost
60% among the least-informed to less than 20% among the best-informed.
Conversely, among the roughly similar-sized group of people with scores less
than or equal to zero on the egalitarian values scale in chapter 5, support for the
tax cut *increased* modestly with political information, from a bit less than 70%
among the least-informed to about 80% among the best-informed.

What is most striking in figure 6.4, however, is the pattern of support for
the 2001 tax cut among the 40% of NES respondents who expressed moderate support for egalitarian values (scale scores between zero and +.5). Their
views differed only modestly from those of outright opponents of egalitarian
values; even when they were highly informed about politics, almost two-
thirds favored the tax cut, if they took any position at all. Thus, even by 2004,
consistent opposition to the tax cut was concentrated among the relatively
small minority of people who were politically well-informed *and* strongly
committed to egalitarian values.

Of course, the fact that relatively few people had come around to opposing
the Bush tax cuts by 2004 does not rule out the possibility that more people
will do so in the years to come. Nor does it imply public support for *further*

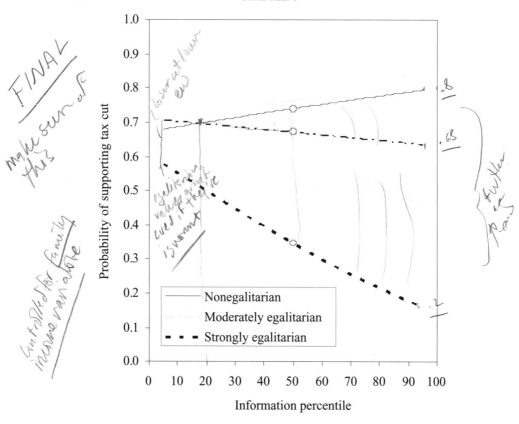

Figure 6.4 Support for the 2001 Tax Cut by Egalitarian Values and Information Level, 2004

tax cuts. In addition to asking people how they felt about the "big tax cut a few years ago," the 2004 NES survey included questions focusing on possible trade-offs among future tax cuts, domestic spending, and deficit reduction. Two of these questions asked people whether they favored or opposed increasing the federal budget deficit or reducing spending "on domestic programs like Medicare, education, and highways," respectively, in order to "cut the taxes paid by ordinary Americans." A few minutes later, another pair of questions asked people whether they favored increasing taxes in order to cut the budget deficit or increase domestic spending, respectively.

Responses to these trade-off questions suggest that in the wake of the Bush tax cuts there was much less public support for further tax-cutting than for increasing domestic spending. About 37% of the NES respondents said they favored increasing taxes in order to increase domestic spending, while only 21% favored cutting domestic spending in order to cut taxes (table 6.6).

TABLE 6.6
Public Priorities: Taxes and Domestic Spending

"Do you favor cuts in spending on domestic programs like Medicare, education and highways in order to cut the taxes paid by ordinary Americans?" "Do you favor increases in the taxes paid by ordinary Americans in order to increase spending on domestic programs like Medicare, education and highways?"

	Oppose tax increases in order to increase spending	Favor tax increases in order to increase spending	Total
Oppose spending cuts in order to cut taxes	44.4%	31.6%	76.0%
Favor spending cuts in order to cut taxes	15.8%	5.1%	20.8%
Total	60.1%	36.7%	96.8%

$N = 1,066$.
Source: 2004 National Election Study survey.

However, the largest single group—almost 45%—rejected *both* spending cuts and tax increases, presumably favoring the status quo to further movement in either direction. (Five percent of the respondents rather illogically favored *both* spending cuts in order to cut taxes and tax increases in order to increase spending; another 3% declined to take a position on one or both questions and are omitted from the table.)

Tax cuts were more popular (and tax increases were less popular) when the proposed trade-offs involved the budget deficit rather than domestic spending. The results for these trade-offs, presented in table 6.7, reveal twice as much support for tax cuts as in table 6.6 (43% versus 21%) and only about half as much support for tax increases (21% versus 37%). People who favored tax increases in order to cut the budget deficit *and* opposed increasing the budget deficit in order to cut taxes—logically consistent "deficit hawks"—made up only 15% of the public. These results imply that the budget deficit was of less pressing concern to the public than domestic spending, notwithstanding the salience of the budget deficit in elite debate regarding tax policy.[60]

Yet, a slim plurality of people in table 6.7, as in table 6.6, opposed movement in *either* direction from the status quo. One possible interpretation of this pattern is that current fiscal policy has been carefully tailored to suit public preferences, forestalling sentiment for significant policy shifts of any kind.

[60] This impression is confirmed by responses to a third pair of questions in the 2004 NES survey pitting domestic spending against deficit reduction. Almost 55% of the respondents favored increasing the budget deficit in order to increase domestic spending, while only 20% favored reducing domestic spending in order to reduce the budget deficit.

TABLE 6.7
Public Priorities: Taxes and the Budget Deficit

"Do you favor an increase in the federal budget deficit in order to cut the taxes paid by ordinary Americans?" "Do you favor increases in taxes paid by ordinary Americans in order to cut the federal budget deficit?"

	Oppose tax increases in order to cut deficit	Favor tax increases in order to cut deficit	Total
Oppose deficit increase in order to cut taxes	38.5%	15.0%	53.5%
Favor deficit increase in order to cut taxes	37.0%	5.9%	42.9%
Total	75.5%	20.9%	96.4%

$N = 1,028$.
Source: 2004 National Election Study survey.

Another possibility—much more likely, in my view—is that ordinary citizens are simply unaccustomed to thinking about trade-offs of this sort, and thus are disinclined to go out on a limb by endorsing *any* proposed policy changes.

The latter interpretation is supported by John Mark Hansen's analysis of public thinking about budget trade-offs in the mid-1990s. Faced with similar pairings of policy options, from 49% to 64% of Hansen's survey respondents opposed deviations from the status quo in order to cut taxes, increase domestic spending, or reduce the budget deficit (corresponding to the upper left cells in tables 6.6 and 6.7). No more than 30% favored any one of the six possible departures from prevailing fiscal policy proposed in these questions (corresponding to the upper right and lower left cells in tables 6.6 and 6.7).[61]

Considered in isolation, these results do not seem inconsistent with the notion that fiscal policy faithfully reflects public preferences. However, the illusion of responsiveness evaporates quickly when we examine the pattern of congruence between public sentiment and actual policy over the subsequent decade. The implausibility of supposing that public preferences drive policy is especially evident in the trade-off between taxes and the federal budget deficit. In 1995, 19% of the public favored tax increases to reduce the budget deficit, while only 12% favored increasing the budget deficit in order to cut taxes (and 64% opposed both). Nevertheless, taxes were cut substantially over

---

[61] Hansen (1998). Hansen's analysis, based on data from the 1995 NES Pilot Study survey, included additional trade-off questions involving defense spending as well as domestic spending, tax cuts, and deficit reduction. Defense spending was a good deal less popular than domestic spending or tax cuts or deficit reduction; from 51% to 59% of the respondents favored cutting defense spending in these trade-off scenarios, while from 7% to 11% favored increasing defense spending.

the next decade. In 2004, after massive tax cuts and a significant run-up in the budget deficit, only 15% favored tax increases to reduce the budget deficit, while 37% favored increasing the deficit even further in order to cut taxes even further (and only 38% opposed both).

Of course, it is possible that public preferences shifted markedly between 1995 and 2001, precipitating the massive tax cuts engineered by the Bush administration and leaving some significant public support for further cuts. However, it seems much more likely that the public's views about appropriate fiscal policy were a *consequence*, rather than a *cause*, of elite action. Had the extremely close and bitterly contested 2000 presidential election turned out differently, President Al Gore would have been able to draw on as much or more public support for his radically different taxing-and-spending agenda as President Bush did for his. In either case, it would be a mistake to characterize public opinion as a primary *impetus* for major shifts in tax policy. At most, public opinion was a *resource* to be used—and shaped—by elites in their own policy struggles.

INTO THE SUNSET

The scope of action of partisan political elites will be further tested by the struggle over extending the 2001 and 2003 tax cuts. Having relied on aggressive "sun-setting" provisions to fit these tax cuts within the parameters of the congressional budget reconciliation process, President Bush and his allies now face a major political challenge to get them extended indefinitely. Whether they do get extended is one of the most consequential policy choices facing the United States over the next few years.

Republican leaders and conservative interest groups have attempted to frame this debate by portraying resistance to extending the Bush tax cuts as support for tax *increases*. Within a week of the passage of EGGTRA in 2001, White House spokesman Ari Fleischer told reporters that President Bush expected the tax cuts to be extended and that "to do anything other than that is to raise taxes on the American people."[62] That viewpoint has subsequently filtered even into official budget calculations. As *Washington Post* columnist David Broder noted, the federal budget submitted by President Bush in February 2006 "simply assumes that the tax cuts have been made permanent—and thus includes them in the 'baseline' for all future years." This bit of creative bookkeeping is intended to hide the long-term cost of extending the Bush tax cuts—$1.6 trillion over the next decade, according to the Congressional Budget Office.

[62] Daniel J. Parks with Bill Swindell, "Tax Debate Assure a Long Life as Bush, GOP Press for New Cuts," 1304.

The key passage [in the documentation accompanying the president's budget] says, without elaboration, that "the 2001 Act and 2003 Act provisions were not intended to be temporary, and not extending them in the baseline raises inappropriate procedural roadblocks to extending them at current rates." . . . Translation: If you tell Congress the cost of making those tax cuts permanent, lawmakers might have second thoughts about doing it. . . . Bush tried to get Congress to go along with this bookkeeping switch back in 2004, actually submitting legislation to authorize the change. The House refused to accept it. He put it back in his budget last year, with the same result. But this year he's back again, with more urgency, as he presses the case to make these tax cuts permanent.[63]

In 2006, the Senate voted, largely along party lines, to extend some elements of the Bush tax cuts at a cost of nearly $70 billion. However, one reporter noted that "even as Senate Republicans celebrated, they failed to reach agreement with House Republicans on scores of other tax breaks," and warned that even this limited extension "could set the stage for budgetary heartburn in the years ahead," while full-scale extension "would cost hundreds of billions of dollars a year, posing excruciating budget choices for the next president."[64]

By the time of the 2006 midterm election, it was by no means clear that even a Republican-controlled Congress would have much appetite to address the long-term problems raised by a full-scale extension of the Bush tax cuts. Economic conservatives were becoming increasingly disgruntled as the Bush administration's fiscal policies showed no evidence that huge tax cuts would spur spending discipline. Brian Riedl, a budget analyst at the conservative Heritage Foundation, complained that "the political will to make the difficult decisions on spending is lacking." Bruce Bartlett, a prominent supply-sider who helped shape economic policy under President Reagan and the first President Bush, advocated a substantial new value-added tax to cope with inevitable increases in the cost of federal entitlement programs. "Whose beast was being starved?" Bartlett asked. "There's no evidence that it was working. We need to deal with reality."[65]

When Democrats won majorities in both chambers of Congress in 2006, the prospects for further changes in tax policy became even more circumscribed. According to a *New York Times* report, the new chairmen of the House and Senate tax-writing committees, Charles Rangel and Max Baucus, "said Democrats would be making a mistake to pursue rescinding the income tax cuts" due

---

[63] David Broder, "Trillion-Dollar Gimmick: Extending Bush's Tax Cuts Through Sleight of Hand," *Washington Post*, February 19, 2006, B7.

[64] Edmund L. Andrews, "Senate Approves 2-Year Extension of Bush Tax Cuts," *New York Times*, May 12, 2006, A1.

[65] Eduardo Porter, "When Even Supply-Siders Say Taxes Must Rise, an Unpopular Policy Looks Inevitable," *New York Times*, December 5, 2005, C10.

to expire in 2010. However, it was clear that they had little interest in extending those cuts. "Why should we be talking now about 2010?" Rangel asked. "I'm 76 years old, and I don't buy green bananas." Instead, Democrats "hoped to forge an agreement with the Republicans in limiting the growing reach of the alternative minimum tax, which has started to hit many middle-class Americans who claim deductions for state taxes and other expenses." However, the *Times'* reporters cautioned that "reducing that tax could involve a loss of hundreds of millions of dollars in revenue and Democrats are loath to propose alternative ways of raising the money."[66]

If the short-term prospects for a bipartisan agreement to fix the Alternative Minimum Tax seem doubtful, the long-term fate of the Bush tax cuts looks equally bleak, at least in their current form. In 2007, Senate Democrats proposed a five-year budget extending the tax cuts through 2011 and 2012, but with one slight hitch: the extensions would only go into effect if $400 billion could be found to pay for them. "Now given that the current Congress is having trouble coming up with $40 billion–$50 billion for a temporary fix to the alternative minimum tax," one business journalist noted, "finding a spare $200 billion a year seems like a tall order indeed." He predicted that "the Bush capital gains, dividend, and marginal rate tax cuts would be left to die with only the social policy tax cuts—such as increased child tax credit—standing any chance of surviving." In the same vein, a prominent financial columnist wrote that Democrats "will almost certainly want to renew Bush's middle-class tax breaks, such as tuition credits. But the wealthy will find themselves in the cross hairs."[67]

Just as Republican control of the White House and Congress paved the way for the Bush tax cuts, the outcome of the 2008 election may have a major impact on whether and how they survive. The major contenders for the 2008 Democratic presidential nomination have all proposed rolling back the cuts for high-income taxpayers, which would reduce the projected $1.6 trillion cost of the tax cuts in the next decade by about half.[68] In contrast, the major Republican candidates—including John McCain, who was one of his party's most consistent opponents of the Bush tax-cutting agenda while it was being implemented—"say they intend to preserve the cuts if elected, but if

[66] Stephen Labaton and Steven R. Weisman, "Talking about Common Ground: Victorious Democrats Vow Cooperative Approach on Taxes and Economy," *New York Times*, November 9, 2006, C1.

[67] James Pethokoukis, "President Bush's Tax Cut Suicide," *U.S. News & World Report* Capital Commerce Blog, March 20, 2007; Jane Bryant Quinn, "The Economic Perception Gap," *Newsweek*, November 20, 2006, 59.

[68] According to a report in the *New York Times*, John Edwards has proposed repealing the tax cuts for households earning more than $200,000; Hillary Rodham Clinton favors letting those cuts expire in 2010; and Barack Obama wants to let the tax cuts for households earning more than $250,000 expire. Edmund L. Andrews, "2008 Democratic Hopefuls Propose a Ceiling on the President's Tax Cuts," *New York Times*, April 21, 2007, A10.

Democrats also control the next Congress, they will have a tough time doing so."[69]

The fact of the matter is that even a Democratic president seeking to extend the most popular elements of the Bush tax cuts would face considerable procedural hurdles. As one observer noted, "the presidential candidates are on a collision course with congressional Democratic leaders who have adopted rules that require paying for new tax cuts with savings or tax increases elsewhere, a stance that would presumably apply to an extension of the existing tax cuts." Of course, a Democratic Congress might take a more lenient stance toward middle-class tax cuts championed by a Democratic president. In the meantime, congressional Democrats are themselves "latching on to the most populist, politically easiest-to-defend tax cuts and then advocating higher taxes for wealthier Americans to pay for new spending programs."[70]

If significant portions of the 2001 and 2003 tax cuts are allowed to expire, America may begin to extricate itself from the "deep hole" referred to by Alter—or at least stop digging successively deeper holes with every budget cycle. If that happens, however, the change will have more to do with the procedural technicalities of congressional budget reconciliation, and with the outcome of the 2008 election, than with any fundamental shift in the values or policy preferences of the American public.

Meanwhile, the next president and Congress will also face the question of what to do about the estate tax, which is similarly enmeshed in the "sunsetting" provisions of the 2001 EGTRRA tax cut. Since it only affects the very wealthiest taxpayers, the estate tax hardly looks on its face like a populist, easy-to-defend form of taxation. Nevertheless, it turns out to be remarkably popular. Chapter 7 addresses the fascinating question of why that is—and the even more important question of whether that matters.

[69] James Pethokoukis, "Democrats Spoil GOP Strategy," *U.S. News & World Report* Capital Commerce Blog, May 10, 2007. McCain was one of only two Republican senators who opposed the 2001 EGTRRA tax cut and one of only three who opposed the 2003 JGTRRA tax cut.
[70] Andrews, "2008 Democratic Hopefuls Propose a Ceiling on the President's Tax Cuts," A10; Pethokoukis, "Democrats Spoil GOP Strategy."

CHAPTER 7

The Strange Appeal of Estate Tax Repeal

FOR MANY LIBERALS, the most egregious feature of the Bush tax cuts was the gradual phaseout and temporary repeal of the federal estate tax. The fiscal impact of the estate tax phase-out is relatively modest in the overall scheme of the Bush tax cuts; the Joint Committee on Taxation has estimated that it will cost the federal government $186 billion through 2011, less than 15% of the total cost of the 2001 EGTRRA legislation alone. However, the fight over estate tax repeal seems uniquely symbolic of the skewed class politics of the New Gilded Age. Eliminating what one prominent economist has called "the closest thing to a perfect tax we have"[1] in order to protect the inherited wealth of multimillionaires seems perversely contrary to the interests of the 98% of American families whose estates will never reach the threshold for taxation. How could a democratic political system arrive at such a policy?

In 2002 the estate tax was only assessed on estates worth $1 million or more, and many of those were exempted. Under the provisions of the 2001 EGTRRA tax cut, the estate tax threshold gradually increased to $3.5 million in 2009, while the tax rate gradually declined. The estate tax will be totally repealed in 2010; however, as with other elements of the 2001 tax cut, it will be reinstated in its pre-2002 form in 2011—absent further action by Congress.

Paul Krugman mocked the apparent illogic of this off-again, on-again scheme: "If your ailing mother passes away on Dec. 30, 2010, you inherit her estate tax-free. But if she makes it to Jan. 1, 2011, half the estate will be taxed away. That creates some interesting incentives. Maybe they should have called it the Throw Momma From the Train Act of 2001."[2] Whether wealthy ailing mothers will, in fact, be put at risk remains to be seen. Legislation providing for permanent repeal of the estate tax has cleared the House of Representatives on more than one occasion, only to fall short of garnering the 60 votes necessary to overcome a Democratic filibuster in the Senate.

But why is Congress even considering estate tax repeal? In their comprehensive account of the repeal effort, Michael Graetz and Ian Shapiro portrayed the threat to the estate tax as a "political mystery":

---

[1] Robert H. Frank, "The Estate Tax: Efficient, Fair and Misunderstood." *New York Times*, May 12, 2005.

[2] Paul Krugman, "Bad Heir Day," *New York Times*, May 30, 2001.

A law that constituted the blandest kind of common sense for most of the twentieth century was transformed, in the space of little more than a decade, into the
supposed enemy of hardworking citizens all over this country. How did so many
people who were unaffected by the estate tax—the most progressive part of the
tax law—and who might ultimately see their own taxes increased to replace the
revenues lost if the estate tax disappeared, come to oppose it? Who made this
happen?

   The answers to these questions reveal a great deal about how American politics actually works in the age of polls, sound bites, think tanks, highly organized
membership organizations, and single-issue coalitions.[3]

   Graetz and Shapiro assumed as a matter of course that if ordinary people
oppose the estate tax, *someone*—as it turns out, conservative think tanks, interest groups, and propagandists—must have "made this happen." In this
chapter, I propose another possibility—one that is less conspiratorial but in
some ways even more troubling. My account suggests that the estate tax was
quite unpopular with the American public long before conservative think
tanks, interest groups, and propagandists came along. Thus, if public sentiment determined public policy, the estate tax would probably have been
repealed long ago.

   From this perspective, the real "political mystery" of the estate tax is not
why the repeal movement has enjoyed so much success in recent years, but
why such an unpopular tax has lasted as long as it has. The answer to that
question reveals a great deal about how American politics has actually worked
through most of the past century. It is not a story of "polls, sound bites, think
tanks, highly organized membership organizations, and single-issue coalitions," as Graetz and Shapiro would have it. Rather, it is a story of powerful
public officials pursuing their own ideological impulses, ignorant or heedless
of public sentiment. Ironically, in this case the powerful public officials happen to have been on the side of ordinary people, while public sentiment has
been on the side of the multimillionaires.

PUBLIC SUPPORT FOR ESTATE TAX REPEAL

If the extent of public support for the Bush tax cuts documented in chapter 6
is remarkable, the extent of public support for estate tax repeal is even more
remarkable. For example, the 2002 National Election Study survey included
questions focusing on the ongoing controversy about "doing away with the tax
on large inheritances." These questions were asked in two forms, one referring

[3] Graetz and Shapiro (2005), 3.

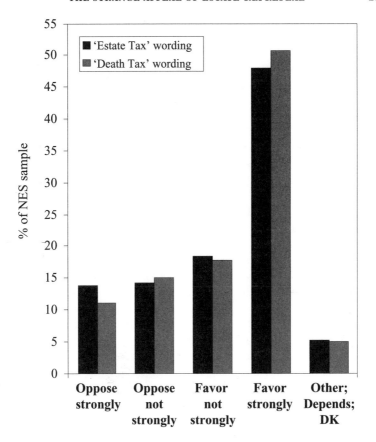

Figure 7.1 Public Support for Repealing the Estate Tax

to the "estate tax" and the other to the "death tax." Figure 7.1 shows the distributions of public opinion for both versions.[4]

Since the "death tax" label has been aggressively championed by proponents of repealing the tax, it might be expected to generate more public support for repeal than the "estate tax" wording. It did, but only by a few percentage points. What is more significant is that, regardless of the wording, a substantial majority of survey respondents favored repealing the tax. Combining the results for both versions of the question, 49% of the public "strongly" favored repeal while another 18% were less strong supporters. Only 27%

[4] "There has been a lot of talk recently about doing away with the tax on large inheritances, the so-called ['estate tax'/'death tax']. Do you FAVOR or OPPOSE doing away with the [estate tax/death tax]? Do you [favor/oppose] doing away with the [estate tax/death tax] STRONGLY or NOT STRONGLY?"

opposed repeal, and they were slightly more likely to be "not strong" opponents than "strong" opponents. (They were also less likely than supporters of repeal to say that this issue was "very important" to them personally.)

These results are broadly consistent with those of other surveys that have asked about repealing the estate tax. For example, the 2003 survey conducted by National Public Radio, the Kaiser Foundation, and Harvard's Kennedy School of Government found 54% of the public in favor of repealing the "federal estate tax" and 16% opposed (with 29% saying they "don't know enough to say"); 60% favored repealing the tax when the phrase "death tax" was mentioned in the question (with 15% opposed and 26% saying they "don't know enough to say").[5]

Some analysts have cast doubt on the depth of public support for repealing the estate tax implied by survey results like these. For example, the NPR/Kaiser Foundation/Kennedy School survey included a series of additional questions proposing various exemption levels for the estate tax; a total of 52% of the sample favored keeping the current tax (15%) or raising the exemption level to $1 million (26%) or to $5 million (11%), while only 26% continued to support repeal even if the tax was "collected only on estates worth $25 million or more."[6] Similarly, a 2001 survey conducted by Mark Penn for the Democratic Leadership Council found substantial support for continuing to apply the estate tax to very large estates; when Penn offered respondents the choice of eliminating the estate tax, leaving it as is, or "exempting small family farms and small businesses from the estate tax, but not multimillionaires," 56% chose the third option, while fewer than one in four continued to favor eliminating the tax.[7] Findings like these suggest that *some* form of continued estate tax could conceivably win substantial public sup-

[5] National Survey of Americans' Views on Taxes, April 2003, www.kff.org, www.npr.org. As in the 2002 NES survey, the two questions were asked of random half-samples. "There is a federal estate tax—that is, a tax on the money people leave when they die. Do you favor or oppose eliminating this tax, or don't you know enough to say?" Favor, 54%—Oppose, 16%—Don't know enough to say, 29%. "There is a federal estate tax that some people call the death tax. This is a tax on the money people leave when they die. Do you favor or oppose eliminating this tax, or don't you know enough to say?" Favor, 60%—Oppose, 15%—Don't know enough to say, 26%.

[6] "Would you (still) favor eliminating the federal estate tax if it were collected only on estates worth $1 million or more? . . . $5 million or more? . . . $25 million or more?" Keep estate tax, 15%—Keep tax but only on estates of $1 million or more, 26%—Keep tax but only on estates of $5 million or more, 11%—Keep tax but only on estates of $25 million or more, 7%—Eliminate tax even on estates of $25 million or more, 26%—Don't know/Refused, 15%.

[7] Mark J. Penn, "What Americans Really Think about Bush's Tax Cut," March 2001, www.ndol.org/blueprint/spring2001/penn.html. "A key feature of President Bush's tax cut proposal is the elimination of the estate tax. The estate tax is now levied against estates of more than $600,000. That exemption will soon rise to $1 million. Only the top 2 percent of estates are now subject to the tax. Which is closer to your view?" "We should eliminate the estate tax," 23%—"We should leave it as it is," 16%—"We should exempt small family farms and small businesses from the estate tax, but not multimillionaires," 56%—Don't know, 5%.

TABLE 7.1
Obtuse Support for Repealing the Estate Tax

"There has been a lot of talk recently about doing away with the tax on large inheritances, the so-called ['estate tax'/'death tax']. Do you FAVOR or OPPOSE doing away with the [estate tax/death tax]?"

	Favor repeal	Oppose repeal	N
Total sample	67.6%	27.2%	1,346
Among those who . . .			
have family incomes of less than $50,000	62.9%	29.9%	620 (46%)
want more spending on most government programs	66.3%	28.3%	1,232 (92%)
say income gap has increased *and* that is a bad thing	64.9%	31.9%	596 (40%)
say government policy contributes to differences in income	64.6%	30.1%	813 (63%)
say rich people pay less than they should in federal income taxes	65.2%	31.4%	674 (50%)
All of the above	63.4%	32.8%	134 (10%)

Source: Calculations based on data from 2002 National Election Study survey.

port. Nevertheless, what is most striking in the survey data is that a great many people with no material stake in repealing the estate tax seem remarkably eager to get rid of it.

The depth of public antipathy toward the estate tax is vividly demonstrated in table 7.1, which shows how support for repeal in the 2002 NES survey varied with seemingly relevant circumstances and political views of the respondents. In the sample as a whole, almost 68% of the respondents favored repeal. Even among people with family incomes of less than $50,000 (about half the sample), 63% favored repeal. Among people who wanted to spend more money on a variety of federal government programs, 66% favored repeal.[8] Among

[8] Respondents who were interviewed in both waves of the 2002 NES survey were asked whether federal spending in each of 17 specific areas should be increased, decreased, or kept about the same. I counted those who favored more increases than decreases as wanting more government spending. The 17 spending items focused on "building and repairing highways," "AIDS research," "welfare programs," "public schools" (or "big-city schools"), "dealing with crime," "child care," "homeland security" (or "the war on terrorism"), "unemployment insurance," "defense," "environmental protection," "aid to poor people" (or "aid to the working poor"), "foreign aid," "Social Security," "tightening border security to prevent illegal immigration," "aid to blacks," "preventing infant mortality," and "pre-school and early education for poor children" (or "pre-school and early education for black children").

people who said that the difference in incomes between rich and poor had increased in the past 20 years *and* that that is a bad thing, 65% favored repeal. Among those who said that government policy is a "very important" or "somewhat important" cause of economic inequality (almost two-thirds of the sample), 65% favored repeal. Among those who said that the rich are asked to pay too little in federal income taxes (half the sample), 65% favored repeal. Most remarkably, among those with family incomes of less than $50,000 who want more spending on government programs *and* said income inequality had increased *and* said that is a bad thing *and* said that government policy contributes to income inequality *and* said that rich people pay less than they should in federal income taxes—the 10% of the sample with the strongest conceivable set of reasons to support continuation of the estate tax—63% favored repeal.

The persistence of overwhelming public support for repeal in the face of such a variety of seemingly contrary considerations is quite impressive. As in the case of the Bush tax cuts more generally, this pattern of support leads one to wonder what considerations have led so many people to embrace policies that are so clearly contrary to their material interests.

The statistical analyses reported in table 7.2 relate support for estate tax repeal in the 2002 NES survey to a variety of indicators of respondents' political values and perceived self-interest.[9] Since the primary direct effect of repealing the estate tax would be to reduce the long-run tax burden of the wealthiest 1–2% of American taxpayers, it seems plausible to suppose that people who believed the rich pay too much in taxes should have been much more likely to favor repealing the estate tax, while those who believed the rich pay too little in taxes should have been much more likely to oppose repeal. Since repealing the estate tax would have no direct effect on people's own tax burdens (for all but the wealthiest handful) or on the tax burden of the poor, opinions about whether these taxes are too high or too low are less obviously relevant. However, if people recognized that repealing the estate tax is likely to lead, eventually, to increases in other, broader-based taxes (in some combination with reductions in government services and larger budget deficits), those who believed their own taxes (or the taxes paid by the poor) are too high might be inspired to oppose repealing the estate tax.

Attitudes regarding the tax burden borne by the rich did have a modest positive effect on support for repealing the estate tax. The results presented

[9] As with the parallel analyses presented in table 6.3, the parameter estimates reported in table 7.2 are from instrumental variables regression analyses. Since the question on estate tax repeal appeared in the post-election wave of the 2002 NES survey, I use perceived tax burdens in the pre-election survey as instruments for the corresponding perceived tax burdens in the post-election survey.

TABLE 7.2
Self-Interest, Political Values, and Support for Estate Tax Repeal

Parameter estimates from instrumental variables regression analyses (with standard errors in parentheses). Support for estate tax repeal ranges from −1 (oppose strongly) to +1 (favor strongly).

	{1}	{2}	{3}
Own tax burden (−1 to +1)	.332 (.093)	.225 (.092)	.226 (.105)
Rich tax burden (−1 to +1)	.150 (.070)	.009 (.074)	−.003 (.076)
Poor tax burden (−1 to +1)	.101 (.107)	.101 (.106)	.104 (.131)
Republican Party identification (−1 to +1)	—	.189 (.092)	.168 (.113)
Conservative ideology (−1 to +1)	—	.379 (.157)	.454 (.173)
Government spending preferences (−1 to +1)	—	—	.024 (.247)
Perceived government waste (0 to 1)	—	—	−.119 (.256)
Family income (0 to 1)	.195 (.079)	.102 (.079)	.104 (.081)
"Death tax" wording	.061 (.041)	.039 (.040)	.030 (.041)
Intercept	.143 (.058)	.166 (.063)	.233 (.216)
Standard error of regression	.740	.716	.724
Adjusted R²	.01	.07	.05
N	1,346	1,346	1,346

Source: Calculations based on data from 2002 National Election Study survey.

in the first column of table 7.2 suggest that people who thought the rich pay too much in federal income taxes were somewhat more likely to favor repeal, while those who thought the rich pay too little were somewhat less likely to favor repeal. So far, so good. However, this effect is dwarfed by the much larger effect of respondents' attitudes about their *own* tax burdens. The latter effect is also positive, meaning that people who thought *they* are asked to pay too much in federal income taxes were substantially more likely to support repealing the estate tax—despite the fact that the vast majority of them never have been or would be subject to the tax.

Separate analyses by income class indicate that the effect of respondents' own perceived tax burdens was about equally powerful among upper- and middle-income people. However, people whose incomes put them in the bottom third of the income distribution seem to have attached no weight one way or the other to their own tax burdens. Their views about estate tax repeal seem to have been strongly related to their own income levels, and perhaps also to their views about the tax burdens of poor people—with support for repeal perversely higher among low-income respondents who thought the poor are asked to pay too much.[10]

It is possible that the apparent effects of perceived tax burdens in the first column of table 7.2 are really attributable to more general political dispositions that shape people's views about tax burdens as well as their specific opinions about the estate tax. In order to test that possibility, the analysis reported in the second column of table 7.2 includes party identification and political ideology as explanatory factors in addition to perceived tax burdens.[11] The results of this more elaborate analysis indicate, not surprisingly, that Republicans and (especially) conservatives were a good deal more likely than Democrats and liberals to favor estate tax repeal. Meanwhile, the apparent effect of people's perceptions of the tax burden of the rich disappears entirely, while the apparent effect of their perceptions of their own tax burdens is reduced by one-third and the apparent effect of family income is reduced by one-half.

The analysis reported in the third column of table 7.2 adds two more potential explanatory factors: government spending preferences and perceived government waste.[12] The statistical results presented in table 6.3 implied that these factors influenced people's support for the 2001 tax cut; but the results presented in table 7.2 suggest that they had no perceptible impact on support for estate tax repeal. Here, as in the analysis presented in the second column, support for estate tax repeal seems to have been most strongly affected by political ideology, party identification, and people's perceptions of their own tax burdens.

In assessing the substantial effects of ideology and party identification, it is important to bear in mind that the distributions of ideology and partisanship in the American public are not sufficiently skewed for their impact in table 7.2 to imply much *net* support for estate tax repeal. Instead, as with the

[10] The parameter estimates for *Own tax burden* are .37 (with a standard error of .11) for the 36% of the NES sample with family incomes over $65,000, .38 (.16) for the 33% of the sample with family incomes between $35,000 and $65,000, and .03 (.33) among the 31% with family incomes under $35,000. The parameter estimates for family income are .41 (.41), .75 (.49), and 1.38 (.51), respectively. The perceived tax burdens of poor people had no perceptible effect among upper- and middle-income respondents, but a parameter estimate of .39 (with a standard error of .34) among low-income respondents.

[11] As in the analyses reported in table 6.3, I employ the difference in "thermometer ratings" assigned to conservatives and liberals as an instrument for *Conservative ideology* and the respondents' 2000 presidential vote as an instrument for *Republican party identification*.

[12] I employ an index derived from eight government spending items in the pre-election wave of the 2002 NES survey as an instrument for the corresponding index of *Government spending preferences* in the post-election wave of the survey, and perceptions of trust in government (whether government can be trusted to do what is right, whether government is run for the benefit of all, and whether government officials are crooked) as instruments for *Perceived government waste*.

Bush tax cuts more generally, the most important single factor in accounting for the predominance of public support for estate tax repeal was respondents' attitudes about their own tax burdens. People who said *they* are asked to pay too much in federal income taxes were substantially more likely to support repealing the estate tax—even though almost none of them would ever be subject to the tax. Even after allowing for the effects of family income, partisanship, ideology, government spending preferences, and perceptions of government waste, those who said they are asked to pay too much were significantly more likely to favor repeal. Since respondents were much more likely to think that they are asked to pay too much in taxes rather than too little, the impact of these views on the overall distribution of opinion about repealing the estate tax was substantial, accounting for about one-fourth of the *net* public support for repeal.[13]

While support for estate tax repeal was strongly related to people's views about their own tax burdens, their views about whether the rich pay too much or too little in taxes had no apparent effect. Since the sole effect of repealing the estate tax would be to reduce the long-run tax burden of the wealthiest 1–2% of American taxpayers, it seems logical to expect that people who wanted the rich to bear a larger share of the tax burden would be especially likely to oppose repeal. They were not. Nor were people who said that the poor are overburdened by the tax system more likely to oppose repeal, notwithstanding the likelihood that repealing the estate tax would lead to increases in other, broader-based taxes, reductions in government services, and larger budget deficits.

IS PUBLIC SUPPORT FOR REPEAL A PRODUCT OF MISINFORMATION?

As with support for tax cuts more generally, support for estate tax repeal seems to be oddly unconnected to some considerations that would seem on their face to be quite relevant (such as whether rich people pay too much in taxes) and misconnected to some considerations that ought logically to be irrelevant, or even to imply opposition rather than support (such as whether people think their own taxes are too high). Peculiarities like these presumably help to account for why so many of Graetz and Shapiro's Washington informants "attributed the unexpected public support for repeal to misinformation and semantics."[14]

---

[13] The sample mean value for the (−1 to +1) estate tax variable was .387. Multiplying the sample mean value for *Own tax burden*, .410, by the parameter estimate in the third column of table 7.2, .226, accounts for 24% of this net support for repealing the estate tax.

[14] Graetz and Shapiro (2005), 253.

Proponents of estate tax repeal have not hesitated to rely on specious arguments to make their case. One is the notion that the estate tax poses a mortal threat to small businesses and family farms. A 2005 study by the Congressional Budget Office found that fewer than 5% of taxable estates in 2000 belonged to farmers or family-owned businesses, and that the vast majority of these had sufficient liquid assets (stocks, bonds, bank accounts, and insurance) to cover their estate tax liability. The study identified a total of 138 farm estates that may have lacked sufficient liquid assets (not counting trusts) to cover their estate tax liability; but they would have been able to spread their estate tax payments over a period of up to 14 years. And if the $3.5 million exemption scheduled to take effect in 2009 had been in effect in 2000, only 65 farm estates would have owed any tax at all.[15]

Another common argument of supporters of estate tax repeal is that it unfairly taxes assets that were already taxed as income. For example, a television ad aired in North Dakota by the American Family Business Institute paired images of the D-Day invasion with a claim that "The I.R.S. hits this greatest generation with an unjust double tax, the death tax." However, the reality is that much of the wealth subject to estate taxation consists of "unrealized"— and therefore untaxed—capital gains resulting from increases in the value of stock, real estate, and other assets.[16]

The powerful factual myths bolstering support for estate tax repeal show no sign of losing traction. They continue to be retailed by such prominent figures as Connie Mack, the chairman of President Bush's blue-ribbon tax reform panel. In a brief interview published a week before the panel filed its report (and a few months after the Congressional Budget Office published its report on the effects of the estate tax on farms and small businesses), Mack was asked about the possibility of repealing the estate tax:

> I think there is a likelihood that Congress will deal with that issue before this term comes to an end. I would vote to eliminate, as we refer to it, the death tax. I think it's an unfair tax.
>
> *(Really? I think it's a perfect tax. The idea behind it was to allow people to postpone paying taxes until they die, at which point they presumably no longer care. Why do you call it unfair?)*
>
> Well, let's say, if you are in the farming business and you have the desire to pass this farm on to your children. The problem is that when your parents die, you

[15] Congressional Budget Office, "The Effects of the Federal Estate Tax on Farms and Small Businesses," July 2005.

[16] Edmund L. Andrews, "Death Tax? Double Tax? For Most, It's No Tax," *New York Times*, August 14, 2005; Jacob Freedman, "Rough Accounting Ahead for Inheritors," *CQ Weekly*, June 16, 2006, 1672.

have to come up with cash to pay the estate tax. One thing you don't have is cash. You've got plenty of land. So I just don't believe it's a fair tax.

(That strikes me as a red herring. The issue is not really small farms, but zillion-dollar estates made up of stocks and bonds.)

I don't know what the percentage breakdown is. I still go back to the same notion that these individuals who have accumulated these resources have paid taxes on them many times in their life, and then to say, when you die, now you pay more taxes on it? There is a limit.[17]

Maybe the chairman of the president's tax reform panel—a veteran of the Senate Appropriations, Finance, and Joint Economic committees—really had no idea how many of the people burdened by the estate tax are family farmers, despite the CBO's report on the subject a few months earlier. Maybe he believes that their wealth has already been taxed "many times." Maybe he knows but does not care. Of course, the fact that specious arguments circulate in elite political discourse does not necessarily imply that they penetrate the thinking of ordinary citizens, or that they have significant effects on policy preferences. Nevertheless, the brazenness of conservative efforts to impugn the "death tax" reinforces the suspicion in some quarters that public support for estate tax repeal is largely a product of widespread misunderstanding of how the estate tax actually works.

Opinion surveys provide plenty of support for the notion that public misunderstanding of the estate tax is widespread. For example, the 2003 NPR/Kaiser Foundation/Kennedy School survey asked respondents who favored eliminating the estate tax (57% of the sample) about their reasons for doing so. All four of the reasons proposed in the survey were endorsed by substantial majorities, including "It affects too many people" (62%) and "It might affect YOU someday" (69%).[18] These results suggest that a very substantial number of people who supported repealing the estate tax mistakenly believed that their own taxes would be lower as a result. Another question in the same survey asked whether "most families have to pay the federal estate tax when someone dies or only a few families have to pay it." Almost half the respondents said that most families have to pay, and an additional 18% said they did not know. Thus, two-thirds of the American public apparently failed

[17] Deborah Solomon, "Taxing Issues," *New York Times Magazine*, October 23, 2005, 23.

[18] "Why do you favor eliminating the estate tax as it is now? Is this a reason or not?" "The money was already taxed once and it shouldn't be taxed again." Yes, a reason, 92%—No, not a reason, 7%—Don't know, 2%. "It affects too many people." Yes, a reason, 62%—No, not a reason, 34%—Don't know, 3%. "It might affect YOU someday." Yes, a reason, 69%—No, not a reason, 30%—Don't know, 1%. "It might force the sale of small businesses and family farms." Yes, a reason, 74%—No, not a reason, 22%—Don't know, 4%.

to recognize the single most important fact about the estate tax: that it is paid only by very wealthy people.[19]

Economist Joel Slemrod has shown that confusion on this score contributed to public support for estate tax repeal. He estimated that, other things being equal, support for repeal was 10.3 percentage points higher among people who thought most families have to pay than among those who recognized that only a few families pay estate taxes. (People who said they didn't know were slightly *more* supportive than those who were misinformed.) Slemrod concluded that "popular misunderstanding . . . contributes to the widespread opposition to the tax, although a majority would oppose it even in the absence of this particular misconception."[20]

Unlike the NPR/Kaiser Foundation/Kennedy School survey analyzed by Slemrod, the 2002 National Election Study survey did not include specific factual questions about the estate tax or its effects. However, it is possible to examine the effects of political information more generally on support for estate tax repeal among the NES respondents. The analysis in chapter 6 showed that support for the 2001 tax cut was significantly weaker among better-informed people than among those who were less well-informed. Is that true as well of the strong support for repealing the estate tax evident in figure 7.1?

The answer is no. In the case of estate tax repeal, the statistical results presented in table 7.3 indicate that better-informed people in the 2002 NES survey were actually slightly *more* likely than those who were less well-informed to favor repeal.[21] Separate analyses for Republicans, Independents, and Democrats show somewhat stronger positive effects of political information on support for repeal among Republicans and Independents. Among Democrats the estimated effect is negative, but only slightly so.[22]

---

[19] "Do you think that most families have to pay the federal estate tax when someone dies or only a few families have to pay it?" Most families have to pay, 49%—Only a few families have to pay, 33%—Don't know, 18%.

[20] Slemrod (2006), 69. Krupnikov et al. (2006) repeated Slemrod's analysis separately for Democrats and Republicans; they found that the effect of misinformation was about twice as large for Democrats as for Republicans.

[21] As in table 6.5, these analyses allow for additional differences in support for estate tax repeal due to differences in family income and question wording ("estate tax" versus "death tax"). Income had a positive effect on support for repeal, especially among Republicans; the "death tax" question wording produced somewhat more support for repeal among Republicans but had no apparent effect on Independents or Democrats.

[22] Krupnikov et al. (2006) reported qualitatively similar results from their analysis of the same data using a different statistical procedure, instrumental variables regression, paralleling and elaborating the analysis of Bartels (2004). The magnitudes of their estimated information effects are larger than for those reported here—in part because the instrumental variables procedure mitigates bias due to measurement error in political information, in part because it ignores ceiling effects in support for estate tax repeal, and in part because Krupnikov et al. classified Democratic and Republican "leaners" as partisans, whereas I classify them here as Independents. (Oddly, the apparent information effect is about twice as large for Republican leaners as for full-fledged Republican identifiers.)

TABLE 7.3

Partisanship, Political Information, and Support for Estate Tax Repeal

Ordered probit parameter estimates (with standard errors in parentheses) for probability of (strongly or not strongly) favoring estate tax repeal. Additional response thresholds are included in the analyses but not shown here.

	Total sample	Republicans	Independents	Democrats
Political information				
(0 to 1)	.287 (.143)	.538 (.273)	.589 (.241)	−.268 (.252)
Family income				
(0 to 1)	.455 (.117)	.629 (.217)	.135 (.202)	.352 (.201)
"Death tax"				
wording	.086 (.062)	.255 (.115)	−.015 (.105)	.063 (.105)
Intercept	.048 (.091)	.052 (.188)	.178 (.151)	.097 (.151)
Log likelihood	−1,807.4	−485.9	−631.2	−638.6
Pseudo-R²	.01	.02	.01	.00
N	1,346	434	471	441

Source: Calculations based on data from 2002 National Election Study survey.

The contrasting effects of political information on support for estate tax repeal among Republicans and Democrats are represented graphically in figure 7.2. Among Democrats, support for repeal declined from 62% for the least well-informed to 51% for the most well-informed. Among Republicans, however, support for repeal increased from 69% for the least well-informed to 85% for the most well-informed. Thus, while increasing levels of political information clearly bolstered the relationship between partisanship and views about the estate tax, there is no indication here that a better-informed public would, on balance, be any less enthusiastic about estate tax repeal.

Table 7.4 provides additional perspective on the interaction between political information and political values in producing support for estate tax repeal. The first and second columns of the table show the impact of political information on support for repeal separately among people who said that rich people pay too little federal income tax and among those who said that the tax burden of rich people is about right or too high. The results suggest that increasing political awareness had a substantial positive effect on support for estate tax repeal in the latter group but no effect at all in the former group. Even very well informed people who said that the tax burden of rich people is too low were more likely than not to support estate tax repeal. Among people who lacked this reason for opposing repeal, however, uninformed people were about equally divided between support and opposition, but highly informed people were very likely to favor repeal.

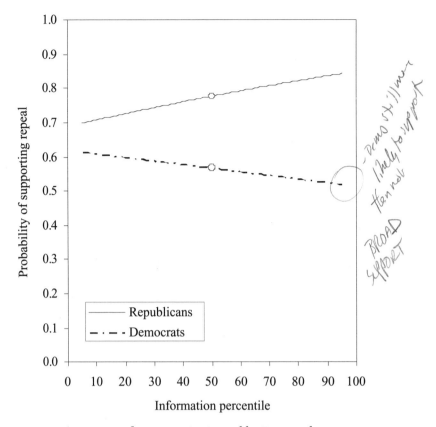

Figure 7.2 Support for Estate Tax Repeal by Partisanship
and Information Level

The third and fourth columns of table 7.4 present the results of parallel
analyses among two more subgroups of NES respondents. The results presented in the third column are based on the views of people who said that
the difference in incomes between rich people and poor people in the
United States today is larger than it was 20 years ago, *and* that that is a bad
thing; these are the people for whom growing economic inequality might
provide a reason to oppose repealing the estate tax. (In 2002, these respondents made up slightly more than 40% of the NES sample.) The results
presented in the fourth column are based on the responses of people who
said that the difference in incomes between rich people and poor people
has not increased (about 25% of the total sample), *or* that the larger income
gap is a good thing (about 5%), *or* that they did not know or had not
thought about whether the larger income gap is a good thing or a bad thing
(about 28%). What these three groups have in common is that they lack

TABLE 7.4
Attitudes about Inequality, Political Information, and Support
for Estate Tax Repeal

Ordered probit parameter estimates (with standard errors in parentheses) for probability of (strongly or not strongly) favoring estate tax repeal. Additional response thresholds are included in the analyses but not shown here.

	Rich people pay too little federal income tax	Tax burden of rich people is about right or too high	Income gap is larger and that is a bad thing	Income gap is is not larger or larger gap is not bad
Political information				
(0 to 1)	−.099 (.184)	.915 (.233)	−.439 (.212)	1.011 (.204)
Family income (0 to 1)	.297 (.153)	.588 (.182)	.359 (.171)	.512 (.162)
"Death tax" wording	.033 (.080)	.189 (.098)	.103 (.092)	.083 (.083)
Intercept	.294 (.121)	−.290 (.140)	.394 (.155)	−.238 (.117)
Log likelihood	−1,081.6	−702.7	−810.1	−974.5
Pseudo-R²	.00	.03	.01	.03
N	784	562	594	752

Source: Calculations based on data from 2002 National Election Study survey.

either a factual basis or a moral basis (or both) for thinking of growing economic inequality as a problem that might be exacerbated by repealing the estate tax.

Dividing the survey respondents in this way produces dramatically different estimates of the effect of political information on views about estate tax repeal.[23] Among those who had reason to be concerned about growing economic inequality, politically informed respondents were significantly more likely than those who were less well-informed to oppose estate tax repeal. However, among those who did not recognize or did not care about increasing inequality, those who were better-informed were substantially more likely to *favor* repeal.

For people of average political awareness these results imply very little difference in support for repeal between those who were concerned about inequality and those who were not. For people of less-than-average political awareness, those who were concerned about increasing inequality were actually

---

[23] We saw in chapter 5 that better-informed respondents were more likely to recognize that the income gap between rich and poor has grown, and more likely to think that that is a bad thing. Thus, it should not be surprising that the average level of political information is higher for the subgroup of respondents analyzed in the third column of table 7.4 than for the subgroup analyzed in the fourth column. Nevertheless, the variation in political information *within* each subgroup is sufficient to estimate the effects of information on policy preferences with tolerable precision.

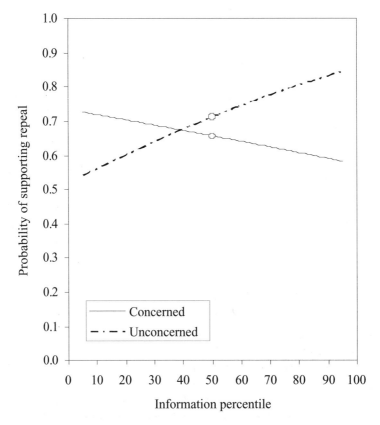

Figure 7.3 Support for Estate Tax Repeal by Concern about
Income Inequality and Information Level

somewhat *more* likely to favor repeal than those who did not know or did not
care that inequality has increased. Only among the best-informed citizens did
concern about inequality produce significant resistance to the allure of estate
tax repeal—and even the best-informed people who recognized and regretted the fact that inequality has increased were more likely than not to favor
repeal (figure 7.3).

The pattern of support for estate tax repeal in figure 7.3 highlights the extent to which the political effects of information may hinge on a conjunction
between specific bits of policy-relevant knowledge and specific moral interpretations of policy-relevant facts.[24] Among people who happened not to

---

[24] On the significance of specific policy-relevant facts see Gilens (2001); on moral interpretations, see Stoker (1992).

know or care that economic inequality has increased, the best informed about politics and public affairs were, by far, the most likely to *support* repealing the estate tax. Both recognition of the economic trend and a moral judgment that it is "a bad thing" were necessary to make well-informed, politically sophisticated people more likely to *oppose* repeal.

These results highlight the depressing limits of political information as a potential transformative force. In the case of the estate tax, the most powerful effect of greater political awareness was to significantly *bolster* support for repeal among people who did not recognize, or did not care, that income inequality has increased. The countervailing effect among people who *did* recognize and regret the fact that inequality has increased, while significant, was a good deal weaker.

It is important to consider an additional, indirect effect of information on support for estate tax repeal: the evidence presented in table 5.12 suggests that increasing political information would tend, overall, to produce a substantial increase in public recognition of and concern about increasing inequality. In effect, increasing political information would not only produce shifts to the right along the dotted and solid lines in figure 7.3, but also a shift *from* the dotted line *to* the solid line, producing some additional reduction in support for estate tax repeal. However, the overall impact of the direct and indirect effects of increasing political information implied by my analysis remains quite modest.

For people who assume that public support for estate tax repeal must be a product of ignorance or misinformation, these results should be triply disheartening. They suggest, first, that even if every person in America could be made to see that economic inequality has increased *and* made to feel that that is a bad thing, the overall distribution of public opinion about estate tax repeal would change rather little, since declining support for repeal among better-informed people would be largely offset by increasing support for repeal among those who were less well-informed. Second, even if the entire public somehow became splendidly well-informed about politics and public affairs, the overall distribution of public opinion about estate tax would change rather little, since declining support among people concerned about inequality (and an increase in their numbers) would be largely offset by increasing support among people who continued to be unconcerned about inequality. Finally, since even very well-informed citizens who recognized and regretted the fact that inequality has increased were more likely to support estate tax repeal than to oppose it, it seems very likely that a majority of the public would persist in favoring repeal even if they were splendidly well-informed *and* concerned about inequality. In short, there is no ground here for imagining that the strange appeal of estate tax repeal could be overcome simply by making citizens better informed.

DID INTEREST GROUPS MANUFACTURE PUBLIC
ANTIPATHY TO THE ESTATE TAX?

The analysis presented here seems consistent with Slemrod's analysis in indicating that public ignorance and misinformation play a relatively modest role in accounting for the strange appeal of estate tax repeal. Slemrod estimated that eliminating public misconceptions about the reach of the estate tax would only decrease public support for repeal from 79% to 72%.[25] Similarly, the analysis here suggests that even universal public recognition of increasing economic inequality would only decrease public support for repeal from 68% (the overall level of support in the 2002 NES sample) to 57% (reflecting the estimated probability of support among people at the top of the distribution of political awareness who both recognized and regretted increasing economic inequality). As Graetz and Shapiro put it, "folk wisdom in Washington, which attributes the widespread support for repeal to the gap between belief, rhetoric, and reality, misses the real story."[26]

But what is that real story? Graetz and Shapiro's account emphasized the role of conservative political entrepreneurs in framing and selling estate tax repeal as a moral issue rather than an economic issue. These entrepreneurs

> understood that tax debates are not won by giving the public more information. The trick is giving them the right kind of information from your point of view, shaping the lens through which they come to see the issue at hand.... The death tax label added moral momentum to the case for repeal, turning the taxman into a pimp for the grim reaper.... Jonathan Weisman was not exaggerating when he wrote in *USA Today* ... that the repeal movement had become "a massive lobbying effort that has swayed public opinion, altered the terms of the debate and proven unstoppable."[27]

In Graetz and Shapiro's account, conservative think tanks played a key role in this propaganda effort: the "growing think tank gap strengthened the hand of the repeal forces considerably.... In bringing the conservative tax-cutting agenda from the margins to the mainstream, the new think tanks have ...

[25] Slemrod (2006). Slemrod's 79% figure represents support for repeal among people who took a position one way or the other—the 28% of the sample in the 2003 NPR/Kaiser Foundation/Kennedy School survey who said they "don't know enough to say" are excluded. The estimated 7-point effect of misinformation combines a 10-point decrease in support for estate tax repeal among the 49% of respondents who thought most families pay estate tax and a 12-point decrease among the 20% who did not know. By comparison, Slemrod estimated that eliminating public misconceptions about the progressivity of the current tax system would decrease public support for a flat-rate tax from 53% to 42% (a decrease of 24 percentage points among the 44% of the public who thought rich people would pay more under a flat-rate system).

[26] Graetz and Shaprio (2005), 254.

[27] Ibid., 254, 253, 129–130.

transformed the limits of acceptable conduct." In particular, the Heritage Foundation, a "colossus of ideologically focused conservatism, with an annual operating budget in excess of $30 million, would play a major role in moving estate tax repeal into the realm of the politically thinkable." They portrayed estate tax repeal as "an early and intense preoccupation at Heritage," which generated a "flood of activity" on the issue. (Along the way, they found space to describe in loving detail the foundation's headquarters, with its "well-manicured lawn," "dark wood paneling," "gilt mirror," and "gold-etched names of donors.")[28]

Eventually, 240 pages into their account, Graetz and Shapiro mentioned in passing that the Heritage Foundation's total spending on estate tax repeal "from the mid-1990s through 1999" amounted to $250,000. Even with some allowance for the effects of "placing Heritage's considerable resources at the repeal coalition's disposal" in ways that are not reflected in that figure, it strains credibility to imagine that an expenditure of that magnitude—roughly 0.2% of the foundation's total spending during the years in which it pursued the issue of estate tax repeal—could reflect an "intense preoccupation" or produce a "flood of activity," much less constituting "a major role in moving estate tax repeal into the realm of the politically thinkable."[29]

If the observed political action in this case seems too modest to produce the alleged political reaction, perhaps that is because public opinion did not really need to be "swayed" or "manipulated" into supporting estate tax repeal. The fact of the matter is that Americans have always found the juxtaposition of death and taxes peculiarly unsettling, even before the Heritage Foundation and other conservative groups began to mount a vigorous attack on the supposed iniquities of the "death tax" in the 1990s.

Although major survey organizations seem to have ignored the issue before the mid-1990s,[30] vivid evidence of that antipathy is available from an unlikely source: in-depth interviews with ordinary Americans on the subject of distributive justice. Summarizing the results of these interviews, which she conducted in New Haven in the mid-1970s, Jennifer Hochschild noted that "almost everyone, rich and poor, is incensed that the very wealthy do not pay their fair share of taxes." At the same time, however, she noted that "no one is enthusiastic about, and very few even accept, inheritance taxes. On this point, the sanctity of private property overwhelms the principle of equality in the political domain. Policymakers who seek revenues and support for government expenditures should not publicize inheritance taxes, even for the very wealthy."[31]

[28] Ibid., 85, 241–242, 89, 94, 98, 92–93.
[29] Ibid., 242, 358.
[30] The Roper Center's *iPOLL* database includes 82 survey questions mentioning the estate tax, death tax, or inheritance tax; but none of those questions was asked before 1996.
[31] Hochschild (1981), 280.

The examples Hochschild provided of her working people's views about inheritance taxes sound uncannily similar to the focus-group-tested rhetoric of the repeal effort described by Graetz and Shapiro 25 years later:[32]

> If I'm working and I'm banking my money, I'm planning for *their* [his children's] future. So hey, if I turn around and pass away, they got every right in the world to get what I worked for.

> It's wrong, taking away money from somebody that has earned it. You pay taxes all your life on the money you earn, and then when you pass away and you leave some money to your relatives, you gotta take *more* money out of it. It seems like tax on top of tax.

> Awful, because it's in the family, and the family has a perfect right to hand it down to their children if they want to.

> Why should I work all my life and run the risk that three idiots that got jobs out of patronage are going to decide whether my daughter is going to get my money? No way. Before I'll do that, I'll stop working.

> Probably shouldn't be one. It's his money, he can do what he wants.

None of these ordinary working people was spurred to indignation by right-wing think tanks, sound bites, or well-organized political activists. They opposed the estate tax because it violated their deeply held views about family, work, and economic opportunity.

Even more surprising evidence of long-standing public antipathy to government interference with inheritance comes from an opinion survey commissioned by *Fortune* magazine in 1935.[33] In the midst of the most catastrophic economic depression in American history, *Fortune* asked survey respondents "How much money do you think any one person should be allowed to inherit?" The results are presented in table 7.5.

Over half the respondents in the *Fortune* survey said there should be "no limit" on inheritances; fewer than one-third favored limits of less than $1 million (almost $15 million in current dollars). The editors of *Fortune* characterized these results as "astonishing" and an indication "that the nature of Public Opinion in this country is still all but unknown":

> Despite the various noises made by the Doctors Townsend, Long, and Coughlin, and despite, again, five long years of economic hardship, 44 per cent of the people supported the right of millionaires (constituting probably no more

---

[32] Ibid., 152, 183, 201, 206, 221. The quotations come, respectively, from an unskilled worker, an assembly-line maintenance man, a widowed housewife, a chemical manufacturer, and a 19-year-old living with his parents and working in his father's corner store.

[33] *Fortune*, October 1935, 56–57. I am indebted to Adam Berinsky for calling this survey to my attention.

US ppl just don't like the estate tax [handwritten]

TABLE 7.5

Views on the Right to Inherit, by Income Class, 1935

"How much money do you think any one person should be allowed to inherit?"

	$100,000 or less[a]	$100,000 to $1,000,000	Over $1,000,000[b]	No limit	Don't know
Total sample	15.1%	15.5%	2.3%	51.7%	15.4%
Prosperous	8.9%	16.1%	2.5%	58.9%	13.6%
Upper middle	13.8%	15.6%	2.8%	51.1%	16.7%
Lower middle	16.0%	16.3%	2.5%	51.2%	14.0%
Poor	17.8%	15.3%	1.9%	47.1%	17.9%
Negro	15.0%	12.0%	1.3%	58.0%	13.7%

[a] Includes "None" responses ranging from 0.4% to 1.0%.
[b] Includes "Over $10,000,000" responses ranging from 0 to 0.7% *over half* [handwritten]
Source: *Fortune* Quarterly Survey, 1935.

revenue Q but same issue [handwritten]

than .004 of 1 per cent of the people) to continue to possess a million invested dollars, subject only to present taxation. It was concluded that this phenomenon was partly due to the fear of a half of the people that any measure destroying the millionaire might come too close to touching their own prospects for attaining what they would consider modest wealth. But there is a difference between self-made wealth, a tradition to which many Americans continue to aspire, and inherited wealth, for which few have well-founded hopes. (In 1933 about 1,300,000 Americans died, of whom only 10,000, or .77 of 1 per cent, left taxable estates—$50,000 or more—with a net average value of $80,000.)

If Hochschild's New Haven working people sound like participants in Heritage Foundation focus groups, the editors of *Fortune* here sound like irritated twenty-first century liberals lecturing ordinary Americans about the actual workings of the estate tax and the unreality of their faith in economic opportunity. The lectures have never been very effective. Yet, it is hard to see any evidence here that the right-wing activism described by Graetz and Shapiro has been particularly effective either. Hochschild recognized 25 years ago that, from the perspective of "policymakers who seek revenues and support for government expenditures," estate tax repeal was a train wreck waiting to happen. At best, the Heritage Foundation helped draw the attention of conservative elites to public antipathy that had gone unrecognized for decades.

ELITE IDEOLOGY AND THE POLITICS OF ESTATE TAX REPEAL

According to Graetz and Shapiro, "no repeal effort ever got off the ground during the Ronald Reagan and George H. W. Bush administrations largely because most Washington insiders assumed that abolishing the estate tax was politically impossible. According to the orthodox wisdom, the vast majority of Americans would oppose repealing a steeply progressive tax that they would never themselves pay. It was not until the Gephardt-Waxman fiasco in 1992, when their gambit to cut the threshold to $200,000 blew up in Democrats' faces, that conservatives became alert to the possibility that they might have missed something."[34]

My analysis strongly suggests that the "orthodox wisdom" described by Graetz and Shapiro was quite mistaken through much of the twentieth century: far from opposing estate tax repeal, "the vast majority of Americans" would probably have been happy to support it. Thus, for partisans of popular sovereignty, the real "political mystery" is not why the estate tax was phased out in 2001, but why it lasted as long as it did. The answer to that question has little to do with conservative elites' grasp of public opinion, but much to do with the political leverage of liberal Democratic elites whose own ideological values made them eager to retain "a steeply progressive tax."

This interpretation is indirectly bolstered by Graetz and Shapiro's own account of the last serious attempt to repeal the estate tax, by President Calvin Coolidge and Treasury Secretary Andrew Mellon in the mid-1920s. Mellon— himself one of the wealthiest men in America at the time—proposed abolishing the federal estate tax as part of a proposed $250 million post-war tax cut. As in 2001, estate tax repeal competed with a wide variety of other potentially popular tax cuts. The House of Representatives passed a $336 million tax cut, well in excess of the $250 million proposed by the administration. However, the chair and ranking minority member of the Ways and Means Committee, William Green (R-Iowa) and John Nance Garner (D-Texas), both strongly opposed estate tax repeal, and they succeeded in keeping it out of the House tax package, though the bill did cut the top estate tax rate in half and substantially increased the credit for state inheritance taxes. According to Graetz and Shapiro, "Green and Garner each faced strong constituent pressures to repeal the tax, but neither budged." In contrast, on the Senate side Finance Committee chair Reed Smoot (R-Utah) supported repeal and managed to win his committee's support for a $362 million tax cut "by trading Republican support for lower income tax rates on middle-income people for Democratic votes for estate tax repeal." A conference committee appointed to reconcile the House and Senate plans ended up producing an even bigger aggregate tax cut than either chamber had originally voted, $381 million. Green succeeded in preventing total repeal of the estate tax; nevertheless, the final bill cut estate tax rates, increased the credit for state estate taxes, and increased the exemption to $100,000.[35]

[34] Graetz and Shapiro (2005), 118.
[35] My account of the 1920s repeal effort follows that of Graetz and Shapiro (2005), 221–225.

Nothing in this episode suggests that estate tax repeal was politically un-thinkable in the 1920s. Quite to the contrary, it was intensely debated in the context of a broader tax-cutting initiative, it passed in the Senate, and it seems to have fallen by the wayside in conference committee primarily due to the strong opposition of a single strategically placed committee chair who refused to budge in the face of "strong constituent pressures to repeal the tax."

Having narrowly failed to repeal the estate tax in the 1920s, only a decade after its inception, Republicans would have to wait a long time for another opportunity. The Great Depression, though it could not produce significant public enthusiasm for inheritance taxes, did produce something even more important—durable Democratic majorities in Congress. The House re-mained in Democratic hands for 60 of the 64 years between 1931 and 1994, and the only instance of unified Republican control for the remainder of the century was a tenuous two-year period at the beginning of the first Eisen-hower administration, when the Republicans held a 10-seat margin in the House and a one-seat margin in the Senate.

Republicans won control of the House in 1994 and soon began pushing es-tate tax repeal. By the late 1990s predominantly Republican majorities in both houses of Congress favored repeal but were far from being able to over-ride a veto by Democratic president Bill Clinton. When the bitterly contested 2000 election left the White House in Republican hands, producing the first unified Republican government in almost half a century, it took less than five months for the estate tax phaseout to be passed and signed into law.

The lesson I draw from this history is that strong public support for estate tax repeal was certainly not sufficient, and probably not necessary, for repeal to happen. When conservative Republicans controlled the levers of power in Washington in the 1920s, they came close to engineering repeal but were stymied by the opposition of a single obstinate committee chair. When De-mocrats were in control, through much of the rest of the twentieth century, estate tax repeal was the furthest thing from any sensible politician's mind, regardless of what the public thought of the idea. During periods of divided government, including the Reagan and George H. W. Bush administrations, it would have been quite reasonable for "Washington insiders" to continue to assume "that abolishing the estate tax was politically impossible"—not be-cause "the vast majority of Americans would oppose repealing a steeply pro-gressive tax that they would never themselves pay," but because liberal Democratic lawmakers were willing and able to prevent it.

The most recent episodes in estate tax policy making underscore the impor-tance of both elite partisanship and institutional checks on majoritarian policy making in the contemporary American political system. In 2006, the Senate narrowly failed on two separate occasions to enact a permanent repeal or ma-jor reform of the estate tax. In June, Republican leaders mustered a 53–2 ma-jority for repeal in their own caucus but attracted only four of 43 Senate

Democrats to their cause (Max Baucus, Blanche Lincoln, Ben Nelson, and Bill Nelson), and thus fell three votes short of the 60 needed to cut off a Democratic filibuster. According to one press report, "Republicans are now debating whether to give up on their goal and attack Democrats in the coming midterm elections as obstructionists on a measure that they say has considerable support, or settle for a bipartisan measure that would stop short of eliminating the tax entirely."[36]

House Republican leaders facilitated a compromise by constructing a new bill that would retain the estate tax for estates worth more than $5 million ($10 million for couples). As a further sweetener to key Democratic moderates in the Senate, the bill included a special tax break for timber industries worth $900 million over three years. The bill duly passed the House, and Senate Majority Leader Bill Frist pledged to bring it to a quick vote, but "facing opposition from Democrats who oppose any big reduction in the estate tax and conservative Republicans who want nothing less than total repeal," Frist changed course and "announced that he was postponing action."[37]

A few weeks later, House Republican leaders constructed an even more audacious package by combining the estate tax reduction and other tax breaks with a long-standing Democratic priority, a $2.10 per hour increase in the federal minimum wage. Again, the compromise measure passed the House (with 34 Democrats joining 196 Republicans in favor). Frist lined up all but two Senate Republicans; one supporter said of the compromise, "It helps a lot of different people with real problems. It's politics at its best. Everybody gives and everybody takes." According to a press report, "Mr. Frist and his allies in business viewed the wage increase, stretched over three years, as an acceptable trade-off for a permanent reduction in the estate tax and $38 billion in tax breaks and federal aid that constituted the third part of the measure. But they could not overcome intense opposition from Democrats and organized labor." Despite the attractive packaging—and a warning from Frist that senators would not get an opportunity to vote on the popular provisions separately—"Democrats did not back off," and the bill fell three votes short of the 60 votes needed to cut off debate. Frist "noted that the major provisions of the measure—the wage increase, the estate tax reduction and the package of tax breaks—all enjoyed majority

[36] Edmund L. Andrews, "G.O.P. Fails in Attempt to Repeal Estate Tax," *New York Times*, June 9, 2006, C1.
[37] Edmund L. Andrews, "Timber Becomes Tool in Effort to Cut Estate Tax," *New York Times*, June 21, 2006, C1; Rachel Van Dongen, "House Backs Compromise Estate Tax Cut," *CQ Weekly*, June 23, 2006, 1788; Rachel Van Dongen, "Frist Lets Estate Tax Revision Simmer as He Looks for Support," *CQ Weekly*, July 7, 2006, 1876.

Senate support yet could not clear the procedural hurdles" imposed by the body's filibuster rule.[38]

The fact that Republicans saw potential electoral gains in attacking Democrats as "obstructionists" for opposing estate tax repeal clearly implies that public opinion is not entirely irrelevant in this story. However, it is equally clear that public support for estate tax repeal has been far from sufficient to make it happen. Indeed, Frist's final failed attempt to push a significant estate tax reduction through the Senate demonstrated that even the combination of public support, majority support in the House, majority support in the Senate, an enthusiastic president, and an attractive package of popular add-ons could not overcome the disciplined resistance of Democratic elites to permanent estate tax repeal.

Although the Bush administration has been stymied in its efforts to permanently repeal the estate tax, it has faced fewer hurdles in softening estate tax enforcement, underlining the capacity of those who execute the laws to shape policy through quiet shifts in priorities and procedures. A deputy commissioner of the Internal Revenue Service, Kevin Brown, ordered staff cuts reducing the agency's complement of estate tax lawyers from 345 to 188, saying that "careful analysis showed that the I.R.S. was auditing enough returns to catch cheats" and that "auditing a greater percentage of gift and estate tax returns would not be worthwhile because 'the next case is not a lucrative case'." Six of the lawyers whose jobs were likely to be eliminated "said in interviews that the cuts were just the latest moves behind the scenes at the I.R.S. to shield people with political connections and complex tax-avoidance devices from thorough audits," but "Mr. Brown dismissed as preposterous any suggestion that the I.R.S. was soft on rich tax cheats."[39]

As with the Bush tax cuts more generally, the legislative fate of estate tax repeal will be powerfully shaped by the power of the status quo in American politics. In light of the looming automatic reinstatement of the pre-2002 estate tax in 2011, permanent repeal seems very unlikely regardless of which party holds the reins of government in the wake of the 2008 election. A Republican president and Congress bent on repeal would face the same problem Frist faced in 2006—an intransigent minority willing and able to block action in the Senate. At best, the result might be a negotiated compromise reducing the estate tax rate and the number of estates subject to taxation from their pre-2002 levels. On the other hand, a Democratic president and

[38] David Nather, "Bills Merged in Pre-Recess Flurry," *CQ Weekly*, July 29, 2006, 2110; Carl Hulse, "House Approves Wage Increase Linked to Tax Breaks," *New York Times*, July 30, 2006; David Nather and Rachel Van Dongen, "Frist Loses Estate Tax Showdown," *CQ Weekly*, August 4, 2006, 2176; Carl Hulse, "Wage Bill Dies; Senate Backs Pension Shift," *New York Times*, August 4, 2006.

[39] David Cay Johnston, "I.R.S. Will Cut Tax Lawyers Who Audit the Richest," *New York Times*, July 23, 2006, A16.

Congress would have the tempting option of doing nothing, letting the estate tax resume in its pre-2002 form, and deploying the resulting incremental tax revenue to preserve or expand popular government programs. Alternatively, Democrats could barter a continuation of the much-reduced 2009 estate tax for the acquiescence of moderate Republicans in less palatable revenue-raising initiatives. In any case, it seems very likely that some version of the estate tax will be back in place in 2011. Notwithstanding the strange public appeal of estate tax repeal, America's wealthiest families will once again be subject to what liberal economist Robert Frank identified as "the closest thing to a perfect tax we have."[40]

The prospect of a revived estate tax highlights not only the power of the status quo in the legislative process, but also the limited force of public sentiment when it happens to conflict with the ideological convictions of strategically placed political elites. In the context of the broader politics of inequality, it is ironic that public sentiment in this instance is on the side of multimillionaires, while elite intransigence is centered among liberal Democrats. However, that specific configuration of political forces is neither typical nor essential to the story.

To demonstrate that point, I turn in chapter 8 to a parallel case drawn from the opposite end of the American income spectrum and featuring a very different configuration of political forces—the evolution of the federal minimum wage. In that policy domain, the power of the status quo and the limited force of public sentiment are both even more striking than they are in the case of estate tax repeal, but with very different political ramifications. Whereas liberal Democrats have employed the power of the status quo to frustrate public sentiment opposing a tax on America's wealthiest inheritors, conservative Republicans have used the power of the status quo to frustrate strongly egalitarian public sentiment favoring wage hikes for America's poorest workers.

[40] Robert H. Frank, "The Estate Tax: Efficient, Fair and Misunderstood," *New York Times*, May 12, 2005.

The Eroding Minimum Wage

IN MAY 2007, overwhelming majorities in both chambers of Congress passed the Fair Minimum Wage Act of 2007, which increased the federal minimum wage from $5.15 per hour to $7.25 per hour in three annual 70-cent increments. The liberal Economic Policy Institute estimated that 5.3 million workers would be directly affected by the increase, with another 7.2 million indirectly benefiting from "spillover effects." House Speaker Nancy Pelosi hailed the outcome as a victory for "the hardest-working Americans." It was also a victory for Pelosi and the Democratic Party, since they had made a minimum wage increase one of the most salient planks in their 2006 midterm campaign platform. When the first phase of the increase took effect two months later, Democratic National Committee Chairman Howard Dean announced that, "Because Democrats kept their promise, America's working families will receive a long-overdue pay raise today."[1]

Low-wage workers were, no doubt, very grateful for the raise. However, from a broader historical perspective, the 2007 increase looks less like a major advance in the economic status of the working poor than like an isolated break in a long downward trend. Even after the full increase takes effect in 2009, the real value of the minimum wage will be less than it had been 50 years earlier, while average real hourly wages for all American workers will have increased by about two-thirds over that period.[2] Moreover, absent further legislative action, the real value of the minimum wage will resume eroding the moment the new $7.25 wage rate takes effect.

In this chapter I attempt to account both for the substantial increase in the real value of the minimum wage in the first two decades of the post-war era and for its subsequent decline. From the standpoint of democratic responsiveness, the decline is much more puzzling than the increase, since the public has been broadly and consistently supportive of minimum wage increases throughout this period. How has the real value of the minimum wage fallen by almost 45% since the late 1960s, despite this strong public support? As in the case of estate tax repeal, the politics of the minimum wage seem to be driven much more by partisanship and ideology than by public opinion or, for that matter, economics.

The dramatic rise and fall of the minimum wage over the past 70 years is one of the most remarkable aspects of the political economy of inequality. The original federal minimum wage was one of the major policy innovations of the New Deal era. In 1938, Congress enacted a minimum wage of 25 cents per hour (about $3.60 in 2006 dollars) for "employees engaged in interstate commerce or in the production of goods for interstate commerce"—about 20% of the U.S. labor force. Subsequent legislation gradually expanded coverage to include most workers in large retail and service enterprises, construction, hospitals and nursing homes, hotels and restaurants, farms, and state and local governments, eventually encompassing about 90% of all nonsupervisory workers.[3]

While the scope of minimum wage coverage gradually increased, so did the minimum wage rate. By 1950 the minimum was 75 cents per hour, by

[1] "EPI Issue Guide: Minimum Wage," April 2007, table 1, http://www.epi.org/issueguides/minwage/table1.pdf; Stephen Labaton, "Congress Passes Increase in the Minimum Wage," New York Times, May 25, 207, A12; "Governor Dean's Statement," http://www.democrats.org/a/2007/07/minimum_wage_in.php.

[2] The real value of the minimum wage in 1959 (in 2006 dollars) was $6.95. If inflation averages 3% per year, the corresponding real value of a $7.25 hourly wage in 2009 will be $6.63. Average hourly pay (in 2006 dollars) was $15.95 in 1959 and $25.28 in 2004; if the rate of increase over that 45-year period persists for another five years, it will be $26.61 in 2009, a 67% increase over 1959.

[3] U.S. Department of Labor, "History of Federal Minimum Wage Rates under the Fair Labor Standards Act, 1938–1996"; Page and Simmons (2000), 225. Earlier, President Roosevelt established voluntary federal wage standards under the National Industrial Recovery Act, but it was invalidated by the Supreme Court.

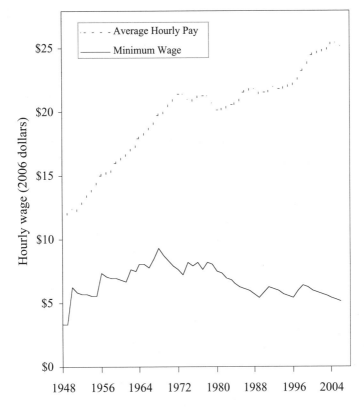

Figure 8.1 The Real Value of the Minimum Wage, 1948–2006

1968 it was $1.60 per hour, and in 1981 it was $3.35 per hour; the current rate of $5.15 per hour took effect in 1997. These periodic increases in the nominal minimum wage rate have of course been eroded by inflation. (Unlike Social Security benefits, for example, which are automatically adjusted to reflect changing price levels, the minimum wage rate has not been indexed to counteract the effects of inflation.) Figure 8.1 shows how the real value of the federal minimum wage has changed over the past half-century. For purposes of comparison, the figure also shows how the average hourly compensation of American workers has changed over the same period.[4]

The history of minimum wage policy, which is summarized in figure 8.1, can be divided into two distinct periods. During the first two decades of the post-war

[4] The minimum wage values in figure 8.1 do not reflect the fact that some states have set higher minimums. Average hourly wage rates are calculated from data provided by the Bureau of Economic Analysis, dividing "Wage and Salary Accruals" (table 6.3) by "Hours Worked by Full-Time and Part-Time Employees" (table 6.9). Both wage series are deflated by the Census Bureau's consumer price index for urban consumers, CPI-U.

era, periodic upward adjustments in the nominal minimum wage rate produced substantial increases in its real value, generally keeping pace with real wage gains in the economy as a whole. The average value of the minimum wage in the 1950s was $6.34 (in 2006 dollars), which was 45% of average hourly pay. The average minimum in the 1960s was $7.94—44% of average hourly pay. The real value of the minimum wage peaked in 1968, at $9.30 per hour.

When real wage growth stalled in the economy as a whole in the 1970s, the real value of the minimum wage began to decline, both in absolute terms (to $7.96) and in relative terms (to 38% of the average hourly wage). The Reagan era saw a modest increase in average wages but a sharp and steady decline in the real value of the minimum wage, from $7.45 in 1981 to $5.46 in 1989. (The nominal minimum wage remained unchanged throughout this period, at $3.35.) Since then, average compensation has continued to grow (by 17% between 1989 and 2006), while the value of the minimum wage has remained relatively constant. By 2006, the real value of the minimum wage had declined by 45% from its peak in 1968 (from $9.30 to $5.15 in 2006 dollars), while average hourly pay had increased by 28% (from $19.70 to $25.18). In relative terms, whereas minimum wage workers in the 1950s and 1960s earned 45% of the average wage in the economy as a whole, by 2006 the minimum wage was less than 21% of the average wage.

In this chapter I examine a variety of possible explanations for the substantial erosion in the real value of the minimum wage over the past 40 years. I consider but reject the possibility that economic evidence has persuaded policy makers that maintaining the minimum wage is counterproductive. On the contrary, recent economic research suggests that the negative effects of minimum wage laws on employment are much less significant than has often been assumed, while declines in the real value of the minimum wage have contributed substantially to increasing inequality in the bottom half of the income distribution. Similarly, I consider but reject the possibility that public opinion has turned against the minimum wage. In fact, every opinion survey conducted over the past 40 years has found majorities of the public favoring minimum wage increases, and in recent years supporters have outnumbered opponents by margins of about four to one.

The declining political strength of labor unions seems to be a much more important aspect of minimum wage politics. Indeed, the massive decline in union membership since the late 1940s has probably depressed the real value of the minimum wage by about 40%. Partisan politics has also played a key role. Republican presidents and Republican members of Congress have generally opposed minimum wage increases, and they have utilized the complexities of the legislative process to block or moderate policy changes reflecting majority sentiment on this issue. The result is that the real value of the minimum wage has risen significantly under Democrats but fallen significantly under Republicans. In response, proponents of minimum wage increases have turned to statehouses and ballot measures to pursue their policy goals, while the federal government has increasingly come to rely on an alternative policy, the Earned Income Tax Credit, as a partial substitute for a robust minimum wage in providing income support to low-wage workers.

THE ECONOMIC EFFECTS OF THE MINIMUM WAGE

Orthodox economic theory has long held the minimum wage in disrepute, making it (literally) a textbook example of a fruitless attempt to repeal the law of supply and demand. According to the 1992 edition of the *MIT Dictionary of Modern Economics*, for example, "minimum wage legislation has been shown in almost all cases to have had an adverse effect upon employment, particularly that of teenagers. This demonstrates the difficulty of formulating a specific wage that eliminates exploitation without causing unemployment."[5]

A dozen years later, in an election-year editorial blasting the Democratic presidential candidate's proposal to raise the minimum wage to $7 an hour, the editors of the *Wall Street Journal* asked. "How many low-wage workers does John Kerry want to throw out of work?" "Force the price of labor too high," they warned, "and suddenly businesses hire fewer workers, especially those at the lower rungs of the skill ladder. This is one of the most settled propositions in economics, second only perhaps to free trade. Sure, Mr. Kerry has found a few economists willing to lend their credibility to his proposal, but even they don't deny that some people may lose their jobs—which is why they don't want to raise the minimum *too high*."[6]

Notwithstanding the *Wall Street Journal*'s view, the effect of minimum wage laws on employment seems to be an increasingly unsettled proposition in economics. A 2000 survey of 308 members of the American Economic Association found only 46% agreeing with the statement, "Minimum wages increase unemployment among young and unskilled workers," while 27% disagreed. (The corresponding figures 10 years earlier had been 62% and 18%.)[7] According to one academic observer, "here's what most labor economists believe: The minimum wage kills very few jobs, and the jobs it kills were lousy jobs anyway. It is almost impossible to maintain the old argument that minimum wages are bad for minimum-wage workers."[8]

[5] *The MIT Dictionary of Modern Economics*, 4th ed., David W. Pearce, ed. (Cambridge, MA: MIT Press, 1992), 279.

[6] "The Wages of Politics: How Many Low-Wage Workers Does John Kerry Want to Throw Out of Work?" *Wall Street Journal* editorial page, June 24, 2004.

[7] Fuller and Geide-Stevenson (2003), 378.

[8] Steven E. Landsburg, "The Sin of Wages: The *Real* Reason to Oppose the Minimum Wage," *Slate*, July 9, 2004. (Landsburg argued that the minimum wage concentrates the burden of income maintenance unfairly on low-wage employers, and that an expanded Earned Income Tax Credit would be fairer and more efficient.)

The heretical-sounding view that raising the minimum wage may have no discernible negative effect on employment was bolstered by the research of economists David Card and Alan Krueger in the early 1990s. Card and Krueger exploited a "natural experiment"—an 80-cent increase in the New Jersey minimum wage in 1992—to examine the impact of minimum wage laws on employment and prices. They surveyed 399 fast-food restaurants in New Jersey and neighboring areas of Pennsylvania (where the prevailing minimum wage remained unchanged). Comparing the two sets of restaurants before and after the New Jersey wage increase, they found that employment declined by almost 10% in Pennsylvania but *increased* slightly in New Jersey. Moreover, they found that the increase in employment in New Jersey was concentrated among the restaurants that had previously been paying the lowest wages—those presumably most affected by the minimum wage increase. Restaurants where the starting wage already equaled or exceeded the new minimum experienced declines in employment comparable to those observed in Pennsylvania. A parallel survey of fast-food restaurants in Texas before and after the national minimum wage increase in 1991 showed a similar increase in employment in low-wage restaurants and a similar decrease in employment in restaurants that had already been paying the new minimum wage.[9]

Card and Krueger were careful to note that their work did *not* imply "that the employment losses from a much higher minimum wage would be small: the evidence at hand is relevant only for a moderate range of minimum wages, such as those that prevailed in the U.S. labor market during the past few decades."[10] Presumably there is *some* minimum wage level so high that it actually harms minimum-wage workers by reducing their prospects for employment more than it increases their wages. Another economist, Russell Sobel, used a time-series model of labor demand to estimate the value of the minimum wage that would maximize the total transfer of income to minimum wage workers: $5.36 in 1996 dollars, or $6.76 in 2006 dollars.[11]

The actual value of the federal minimum wage fell below Sobel's estimate of the income-maximizing wage level in the early 1980s and has not approached that level since. Interestingly, the $7.00 minimum wage rate advocated by John Kerry in the 2004 presidential campaign, and pilloried by the editors of the *Wall Street Journal*, matches Sobel's estimate almost exactly. (Assuming five years between nominal wage increases and 3% annual inflation, adopting a $7.00 wage in 2005 would produce an average real minimum wage, in 2006 dollars, of $6.88.) The state minimum wage adopted by Florida voters in 2004 ($6.40 in 2006, adjusted annually to keep pace with the regional consumer price index) is also quite consistent with Sobel's estimated optimal level.

---

[9] Card and Krueger (1995), 38, 60. Additional analysis and responses to criticism appear in Card and Krueger (2000).

[10] Card and Krueger (1995), 393.

[11] Sobel (1999), 768–775.

In addition to studying the impact of minimum wage laws on employment, economists have investigated the broader question of how minimum wage laws have affected the overall shape of the income distribution. Card and Krueger used aggregate data on the proportion of workers in each state directly affected by the 1990–1991 minimum wage increase to estimate the impact of that increase on the distribution of earnings. They concluded that "more than 35 percent of the earnings gains generated by the 1990 and 1991 minimum wage hikes were concentrated among families in the bottom 10 percent of the family-earnings distribution," and that raising the minimum wage "rolled back some 30 percent of the previous decade's accumulated increase in wage dispersion."[12]

Card and Krueger noted that their finding regarding the impact on wage dispersion of raising the minimum wage in the early 1990s closely matched an independent estimate of the share of wage dispersion attributable to the decline in the real value of the minimum wage through the 1980s. A subsequent study along similar lines by David Lee produced even more dramatic results, suggesting that "a great majority of the observed growth in inequality in the lower tail of the [income] distribution is attributable to the erosion of the real value of the federal minimum wage rate during the 1980s."[13]

In a recent summary of the economic literature and its implications for policy making, Krueger urged elected officials to focus on political issues of distribution rather than economic issues of efficiency:

> I think it is becoming increasingly difficult to support the position that a modest minimum wage hike would have even a noticeable impact on employment. . . . The issue, in my view, comes down to questions of fairness: Whether it is fair to workers to allow the value of the minimum wage, after adjusting for inflation, to fall to its lowest level in 50 years; and whether it is fair to impose the costs of meeting a higher minimum wage on business owners and possibly on customers. These are not questions for which economists have any advantage in answering over politicians or the general public.[14]

PUBLIC SUPPORT FOR THE MINIMUM WAGE

How have politicians and the general public answered Krueger's questions? In very different ways.

The Roper Center's *iPOLL* archive of opinion surveys includes several dozen instances over the past 60 years in which national samples of the public were asked whether they favored or opposed increasing the minimum wage.

[12] Card and Krueger (1995), 308, 297.

[13] DiNardo, Fortin, and Lemieux (1996); Lee (1999).

[14] Alan B. Krueger, "The Economic Effects of New Jersey's Last Minimum Wage Increase," prepared statement before the Labor Committee, New Jersey Senate, January 24, 2005.

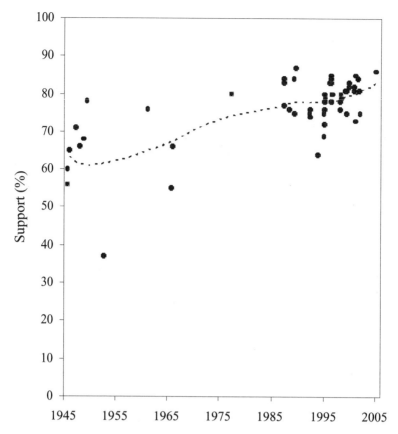

Figure 8.2 Public Support for Minimum Wage Increases, 1945–2006

The surveys were conducted by a variety of survey organizations using a variety of different question wordings; some asked about specific proposed increases, while others left the amount unspecified. The results of these surveys are summarized in figure 8.2, which shows the proportion of each survey sample favoring a minimum wage increase.[15]

Although the survey data are quite sparse for the period between 1950 and 1985, there seems to have been a gradual growth in support for minimum wage increases over that period. In 1965, when the real value of the minimum wage was nearing its peak, two Gallup Polls found 55% and 66% of the public supporting further increases. By 1987, with the real value of the minimum wage

---

[15] The dotted line in the figure is a smoothed trend line generated by a locally weighted regression model. Question wording and data for each survey are available from the Roper Center's *iPOLL* archive.

having declined by more than one-third over the preceding two decades, three separate surveys found even stronger support for an increase, with percentages in favor ranging from 77% to 84%. In the past 20 years, while the real value of the minimum wage has declined modestly, public support for increasing the minimum wage has been consistent and overwhelming, with only two surveys finding less than 70% support and most finding 80% or more of the public favoring an increase.

In a survey conducted by the Pew Research Center in March 2006, half the respondents were asked whether they favored or opposed raising the minimum wage to $6.45 per hour (a 25% increase from the current value of $5.15); the other half were asked about an even larger increase to $7.15 per hour. Their responses are presented in table 8.1. In both cases there was overwhelming support for the proposed increase, with almost half the respondents strongly in favor and fewer than 15% opposed. What is more, public support for a minimum wage hike appears to be largely unaffected by the magnitude of the proposed increase; the results were virtually identical for the two versions of the question, with a margin of support approaching six to one even for a $2.00 increase in the current minimum wage rate.

Public support for raising the minimum wage also seems to be relatively impervious to counterargument. For example, a survey conducted by the Service Employees International Union in May 1987 asked a national sample of registered voters whether they supported or opposed raising the minimum wage. Eighty-three percent of the respondents said they supported an increase (59% "strongly"), while 14% opposed it. Respondents were then asked to agree or disagree with a variety of claims about the minimum wage—for

TABLE 8.1

Public Support for Raising the Minimum Wage, 2006

"As I list some programs and proposals that are being discussed in this country today, please tell me whether you strongly favor, favor, oppose, or strongly oppose each. . . . An increase in the minimum wage, from $5.15 an hour to $6.45 [$7.15] an hour."

	Increase to $6.45 per hour		Increase to $7.15 per hour	
Strongly favor	49%	86%	49%	83%
Favor	37%		34%	
Oppose	8%	11%	10%	14%
Strongly oppose	3%		4%	
Don't know	3%		3%	

$N = 1,405$.
Source: March 2006 News Interest Index Poll.

example, "Wages should be set by the market and not by the government" (69% agreed) and "Raising the minimum wage might result in some job loss" (54% agreed). Then they were asked again whether they supported or opposed an increase. Despite the respondents' apparent willingness to accept strong counterarguments, their support for a minimum wage increase was virtually unchanged, with 84% supporting an increase (57% "strongly") and only 13% opposing it. Nor did support for a minimum wage increase seem to vary with knowledge of the current minimum wage rate. Among respondents who knew the current rate, 84% thought that amount was too low and only 3% thought it was too high; when respondents who did not know (most of whom overestimated the current value) were told the current rate, 85% of them thought it was too low and only 1% thought it was too high.

Finally, public support for minimum wage increases is substantial even in groups that might not be expected to be enthusiastic. While it may not be surprising to find high levels of support among Democrats and poor people, strong majorities of Republicans and wealthy people also favor minimum wage increases. Martin Gilens has tabulated public support for raising the minimum wage in 13 opinion surveys from the 1990s. His tabulations show support averaging 88% among Democrats and 86% among people at the 10th percentile of the income distribution. However, 64% of Republicans and 70% of people at the 90th percentile of the income distribution also said they favored minimum wage increases.[16]

Figure 8.3 provides a more detailed look at the relationship between income and support for minimum wage increases in three recent opinion surveys.[17] In the two cases where the income data are detailed enough to isolate respondents with incomes of $10,000 or less, about 95% of those respondents said they favored an increase in the minimum wage. People with higher incomes were somewhat less supportive; but even people in the top quintile of the income distribution favored a minimum wage increase by margins approaching three to one.

THE POLITICS OF INACTION

The breadth and consistency of public support for raising the minimum wage make it all the more surprising that the real value of the minimum wage has

[16] I am indebted to Gilens for sharing these unpublished tabulations. The figures for survey respondents at the 10th and 90th percentiles of the income distribution are his imputations based on quadratic regressions of support for minimum wage increases on categorical income data in each opinion survey.

[17] Gallup/CNN/USA Today Poll, October 2001; Los Angeles Times Polls, January 1999 and January 1998. The 1999 Los Angeles Times Poll asked about "President Clinton's proposal to increase the minimum wage one dollar over the next two years." The 2001 and 1998 surveys asked about raising the minimum wage without specifying the amount.

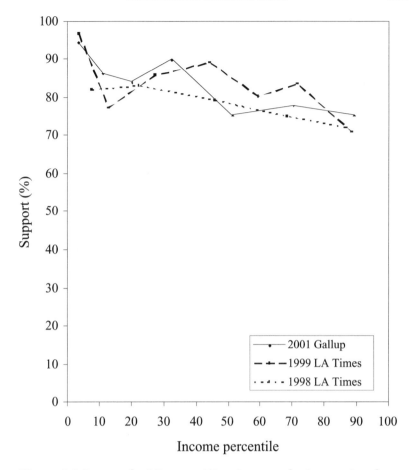

Figure 8.3 Support for Minimum Wage Increases by Income Level

declined so substantially since the 1960s. With even Republicans and rich people strongly in favor of minimum wage increases, and with mounting evidence from economists of negligible effects on employment and positive effects on incomes, how and why have elected officials in Washington allowed the minimum wage to erode?

One promising solution to this political puzzle is that setting the minimum wage rate in nominal dollars produces a strong policy bias: without periodic action to increase the minimum wage, inflation produces a steady decline in its real value. Nolan McCarty, Keith Poole, and Howard Rosenthal have stressed the particular significance of this fact in the American legislative context, where institutional checks and balances often make it impossible for a simple majority to produce policy change. "The veto powers of minorities," they wrote, "are particularly important when status quo policies are not indexed for inflation. Federal minimum wages are fixed in nominal dollars. A conservative minority has been able to block substantial increases in the minimum, even when the Democrats had unified control of Congress under Jimmy Carter and in the early Clinton administration. Therefore, the real minimum wage has fallen."[18]

This explanation seems compelling as far as it goes. However, it begs the question of *why* minimum wage rates have been set in nominal dollars. After all, many other federal benefits and income thresholds are automatically adjusted to take account of inflation. So are some state minimum wages, including the one approved by Florida voters in 2004. (Florida's first annual automatic minimum wage increase, from $6.25 to $6.40 per hour, took effect on January 1, 2006; there were no reports of economic dislocation or social unrest.)[19] Meanwhile, Congress has repeatedly considered and rejected proposals to index the federal minimum wage rate.[20]

In discussing the pros and cons of indexing, Card and Krueger pointed out that "a debate over the minimum wage gives politicians a clear opportunity to take a stand on a simple and well-understood issue, and to signal their positions to various constituency groups. Indexation of the minimum wage would eliminate these potentially valuable opportunities."[21] However, the political value of opportunities for position-taking hardly seems sufficient to explain why the minimum wage continues to be set in nominal dollars. Given the breadth and consistency of popular support for raising the minimum wage, elected officials might be expected to take frequent advantage of opportunities to go on the record in favor of increasing the minimum wage. But that is not what we observe; if it was, the real value of the minimum wage would not have eroded so drastically over the past 40 years. The fact that most elected officials seem remarkably uninterested in championing minimum wage increases brings us back to our basic puzzle: why has overwhelming public support for raising the minimum wage made so little headway against the forces of gridlock in Washington?

Both the significance and the limits of gridlock are illustrated by the sole minimum wage increase of the Reagan-Bush era. In 1989, Democratic congressional leaders engineered passage of a bill that would have increased the minimum wage from $3.35 to $4.55 over a three-year period. President Bush vetoed the bill immediately but used his veto message to reiterate his support for a more moderate increase: "As I have said many times, I could sign into law an increase in the hourly minimum wage to $4.25, phased in over 3 years, which

[18] McCarty, Poole, and Rosenthal (2006), 13–14; see also chapter 6 and Rosenthal (2004). Their analysis builds on Krehbiel's (1998) influential model of "gridlock" in legislative politics.

[19] Agency for Workforce Innovation, "Florida Minimum Wage Raise Calculation Announced," September 30, 2005.

[20] Indexing seems to have come closest to implementation in 1977, when the House defeated an indexing provision by a vote of 223 to 193.

[21] Card and Krueger (1995), 395.

preserves job opportunities through a 6-month training wage for all new hires." Given this clear signal—and having already maneuvered the president into exercising a politically unpopular veto—labor leaders and congressional Democrats decided to take what they could get. As the chief lobbyist for the AFL-CIO put it, "It's clear Bush will veto anything over $4.25. . . . At this particular point, we're not interested in playing politics. We want an increase."[22]

For their part, "senior members of the Bush administration were growing increasingly concerned that it would be politically difficult and unpopular to again turn back minimum-wage legislation" once the proposed wage increase was scaled back from the bill Bush had vetoed. Bush's chief of staff, John Sununu, and AFL-CIO President Lane Kirkland negotiated what one press account referred to as "a face-saving compromise" raising the minimum to $4.25, but over two years rather than three, and with a temporary subminimum "training wage" for teenagers. The bill passed by large majorities in the House (382–37) and Senate (89–8).[23]

In this case, although President Bush used his veto power to moderate the minimum wage increase favored by Congress, his willingness to accept a smaller increase seems to have owed something to a concern that "it would be politically difficult and unpopular" to appear too intransigent on the issue. More often, though, public pressure has been insufficient to overcome legislative gridlock, even in instances where action seemed likely. Another minimum wage hike looked all but certain in the run-up to the 2000 election. One lobbyist called a wage increase "a bullet train coming down the tracks. . . . The leadership in the Republican Party was saying that it was going to happen." As a congressional reporter explained, Republicans "are seeking to minimize their political losses on a perilous issue by moving quickly to arrange a compromise that could allow them to simultaneously claim an accomplishment, neuter a Democratic issue and mollify the GOP base of support." Rather than attempting to forestall an increase, Republican leaders hoped to add significant tax benefits for small businesses. House majority leader Dick Armey told reporters that "the GOP would try and do the 'wrong thing in the least hurtful manner.' "[24]

Four months later, *CQ Weekly* was still reporting that "GOP leaders have resigned themselves to passing a minimum wage increase, an idea many of them dislike but recognize as paramount to some Republicans' political survival." However, packaging a minimum wage hike with benefits for small

---

[22] "Bush Sends Congress Veto of Minimum-Wage Bill," *CQ Weekly*, June 17, 1989, 1501.

[23] Alyson Pytte, "Ending Minimum Wage Standoff Took Give from Both Sides," *CQ Weekly*, November 4, 1989, 2942; Paul Starobin, "Democrats Rework Strategy on Minimum-Wage Hike," *CQ Weekly*, July 8, 1989, 1692; Alyson Pytte, "Minimum-Wage Bill Cleared, Ending 10-Year Stalemate," *CQ Weekly*, November 11, 1989, 3053.

[24] Gebe Martinez, "House GOP's Pliancy on Minimum Wage Rooted in Election Concerns," *CQ Weekly*, May 8, 1999, 1073.

businesses "proved more difficult than expected," as House and Senate Republicans disagreed with each other and with Democrats about how much tax-cutting was enough. Finally, President Clinton and House Speaker Dennis Hastert "agreed in principle on a plan to provide a two-year minimum wage increase and $76 billion in tax breaks over 10 years." But when the House attached the wage increase to a $240 billion tax cut, Clinton threatened a veto, and with "the minimum wage not emerging as a major campaign issue for Democrats . . . the issue did not come up again in the lame duck session."[25] With public pressure seeming to have evaporated, the "perilous issue" for opponents of a minimum wage increase was suddenly easy to ignore.

Additional rounds of congressional inaction in 2005 and 2006 underline the insufficiency of procedural hurdles to account for the continuing erosion of the minimum wage. In 2005, veteran Democratic Senator Edward Kennedy proposed a three-stage increase in the minimum wage to $7.25 per hour. As a press account by Marilyn Geewax put it, "Kennedy should have had plenty of support. An estimated 10 million low-income workers would get pay increases if the wage floor were to rise, and polls consistently show four of five Americans want Congress to act. In the midst of the legislative battle, Hurricane Katrina highlighted the problems of low-income families. But the Senator lost."[26]

Kennedy's plan was to offer the minimum wage hike as an amendment to the major bankruptcy reform bill then making its way through Congress. A similar strategy had worked in 1996, when Kennedy "tied the Senate in knots for months" by "trying to attach his wage increase to any moving legislative vehicle and confronting Republicans with the issue at every turn." In that case, once Democrats succeeded in forcing a floor vote on the minimum wage increase, Republicans were loath to appear "friendlier to wealthy business interests than to the working poor," and most of them ended up voting in favor.[27]

By 2005, the real value of the minimum wage was even lower than it had been in 1996, but a newly reelected Republican president and Congress had their own business to do. Senate leaders were intent on preventing the

[25] Lori Nitschke, "GOP Hopes Minimum Wage Bill with Tax Benefits Will Lure Votes and Disarm Democrats," *CQ Weekly*, September 25, 1999, 2227; Lori Nitschke, "Minimum Wage Bill Stalls over Issue of Business Offsetts," *CQ Weekly*, November 13, 1999, 2711. House Republicans proposed $30.2 billion in tax cuts over five years, Senate Republicans $18.4 billion, Senate Democrats $11.5 billion, and House Democrats $9.5 billion. "2000 Legislative Summary: Minimum Wage," *CQ Weekly*, December 16, 2000, 2901.

[26] Marilyn Geewax, "Minimum Wage Odyssey: A Yearlong View from Capitol Hill and a Small Ohio Town," *Trenton Times*, November 27, 2005, A11.

[27] Allison Stevens, "Sen. Kennedy: Tactics of a Minimum Wage Champion," *CQ Weekly*, April 10, 2004, 855.

bankruptcy bill from getting "bogged down with amendments" that would make it unacceptable to the House, and "set the rules to require a hard-to-reach 60-vote supermajority." The same rules applied to an alternative amendment offered by a Republican senator facing a tough race for reelection, Rick Santorum, which proposed a smaller wage hike along with tax relief for small businesses. In effect, as Geewax put it, "Kennedy and Santorum will be allowed to engage in a little political theater . . . but they won't be given a realistic chance of slowing the underlying bill." As one lobbyist told her, "The bankruptcy bill is important to a lot of interests."

In the end, neither amendment attracted even a simple majority on the Senate floor. Kennedy's proposal attracted only four Republican votes and was defeated 46–49. Four key moderates (Democrats Max Baucus, Kent Conrad, and Barbara Mikulski and Republican Arlen Specter) did not vote, while two others (Republicans Olympia Snowe and Susan Collins) came down against Kennedy's plan. Santorum's amendment received only 38 votes, all from Republicans.

Two months later, Kennedy introduced his minimum wage proposal as a free-standing bill. "The Republican leadership will never allow it to get an up-or-down vote," Geewax wrote, "But Kennedy announces his bill to tweak Republicans. His press release is headlined: 'As Republicans pick fights over judges, Kennedy fights for hard-working Americans.'"

After five more months of inaction, Kennedy found another promising-looking vehicle for a minimum wage amendment—the Transportation-Treasury-Housing appropriations bill. The result was "déjà vu all over again." As in March, a Republican alternative packaged the minimum wage increase with tax and regulatory relief for small businesses. As in March, the Senate leadership maneuvered to require 60 votes for passage. And despite having lowered his proposed minimum wage from $7.25 to $6.25, Kennedy attracted only one more vote than he had in March, while the Republican alternative failed by a 15-vote margin.

One possible reading of these episodes is that they demonstrate the importance of the antimajoritarian features of the American legislative process: Senate Republican leaders refused to bring Kennedy's stand-alone bill increasing the minimum wage to a vote, and when he offered minimum wage amendments to bills that could not be shelved, they used parliamentary tactics to raise the threshold for passage from 51 votes to 60. What that reading overlooks is how modest the underlying support for Kennedy's proposals seems to have been, quite aside from the procedural hurdles they faced. Neither of Kennedy's amendments garnered even a simple majority on the Senate floor.

This outcome is especially significant in light of Card and Krueger's suggestion that elected officials might relish "a clear opportunity to take a stand on a simple and well-understood issue" like the minimum wage. With about

80% of the public—and almost two-thirds of Republicans—favoring a minimum wage increase, members of Congress might have been expected to leap
at the opportunity to signal their support. With procedures in place to ensure
that the roll calls would amount to nothing more than "a little political theater," as Geewax put it—and with a Republican majority in the House of
Representatives unlikely to act even if the Senate approved a higher minimum wage—senators had a golden opportunity to cast entirely symbolic
votes in favor of either or both increases. In each case, however, moderate
Republicans and even some Democrats let these putatively valuable position-
taking opportunities go unexploited.

For their part, Democrats have frequently passed up opportunities to compromise on modest minimum wage increases. When Kennedy's first ($7.25)
amendment was defeated, Santorum's ($6.25) alternative attracted not a
single Democratic vote. Even after Kennedy's second ($6.25) amendment
failed, Democratic senators unanimously sided with conservatives Trent Lott
and John Sununu in opposing the Republican amendment packaging the
same $6.25 wage with tax breaks for small businesses. Meanwhile, Kennedy
pledged to "continue to raise this as long as I'm in the United States Senate,"
while Democratic National Committee Chairman Howard Dean complained
that "Republicans in Washington continue to undermine the economic security of our nation's working families," and Democratic presidential candidate
John Edwards called the erosion of the minimum wage "a perfect example of
the Republican leadership in Congress, combined with the powerful presence of lobbies in Washington, thwarting the will of the people."[28]

Senator Kennedy's proposal for a $7.25 minimum wage reappeared in
Congress in June 2006, attached to the fiscal 2007 Defense appropriations
bill. This time the amendment attracted 52 supporters, still well short of the
60 votes needed to keep the amendment alive under a special agreement.
When the House Appropriations Committee voted 32–27 to attach a similar
minimum wage increase to the State-Justice-Commerce appropriations bill,
House Speaker Dennis Hastert shelved the measure. A week later, the committee rejected the minimum wage provision by a vote of 28–34; five Republican committee members changed their votes, while two others "left the
room during voting," according to a press report.[29]

Several weeks later, legislative maneuvering on the minimum wage took an
even stranger turn. Republican leaders eager to curtail the estate tax decided

[28] Kathryn A. Wolfe, "No Winner in Minimum Wage Fight As Competing Plans Fail in Senate," *CQ Weekly*, October 21, 2005, 2855; Democratic Party, "Dean on the Need to Raise the
Federal Minimum Wage," April 6, 2006, http://www.democrats.org/a/2006/04/dean_on_the_nee
.php; John M. Broder, "States Take Lead in Push to Raise Minimum Wages," *New York Times*,
January 2, 2006, A1.

[29] Sue Kirchhoff, "Increase to Minimum Wage Fails in Senate," *USA Today*, June 21, 2006;
Kim Chipman, "Bid to Boost Minimum Wage Suffers Setback," *Bloomberg News*, June 20, 2006.

to package a major reduction in the estate tax with a $2.10 increase in the minimum wage—the same increase Kennedy had been proposing. Moderate Republican members of Congress had been "clamoring" for a minimum wage vote in the run-up to the midterm election, arguing that "Republican support for an increase in the federal wage is essential to shore up the party's strength among blue-collar and low-income workers who could decide critical House contests in the Northeast and Midwest." One Republican told *CQ Weekly*, "A minimum of 30 members need that vote so that they don't get skewered and barbecued over the summer break. They know the 30-second commercials have already been cut."[30]

Observers were divided on the question of whether Republican leaders actually wanted this package to become law. Some claimed that House Republican leaders merely wanted to put their members on record in favor of a minimum wage increase that they knew Senate Democrats would kill. Kennedy called the measure "a cynical game of politics with the lives of millions of hard-working American families. I am confident the Senate will reject this political blackmail, as the House leadership is banking on."[31]

If Republican leaders intended the so-called trifecta package as a poison pill, they were not to be disappointed. Kennedy's Democratic colleagues and liberal commentators denounced the package as "the height of hypocrisy," "an insult to the intelligence of the American people," and a product of "the G.O.P.'s corrosive culture of deceit." When the package came to the Senate floor, it attracted only one more Democratic vote than the estate tax bill alone had attracted several weeks earlier, leaving Republicans three votes short of the 60 votes necessary to overcome a Democratic filibuster.[32]

DEMOCRATS, UNIONS, AND THE ERODING MINIMUM WAGE

Partisan politics has loomed large in every recent effort to raise the minimum wage, including the successful effort of 2007. Aside from the strange reversal of partisan roles on the 2006 "trifecta," the consistent pattern has been for

[30] Carl Hulse, "Republicans Near a Vote to Increase U.S. Wage," *New York Times*, July 28, 2006, A18; David Nather, "Bills Merged in Pre-Recess Flurry," *CQ Weekly*, July 29, 2006, 2110.

[31] Carl Hulse, "Wage Bill Dies; Senate Backs Pension Shift," *New York Times*, August 4, 2006; Carl Hulse, "House Approves Wage Increase Linked to Tax Breaks," *New York Times*, July 30, 2006.

[32] Hulse, "House Approves Wage Increase Linked to Tax Breaks"; Bob Herbert, "Deceit Beyond Bounds," *New York Times*, August 10, 2006, A23. The additional Democratic vote came from Robert Byrd of West Virginia, who was apparently less swayed by the chance to support a minimum wage increase than by provisions in the package that would have funded cleanups of abandoned coal mines and health care for retired miners. David Nather and Rachel Van Dongen, "Frist Loses Estate Tax Showdown." *CQ Weekly*, August 4, 2006, 2176.

Democrats to support significant increases in the minimum wage while Republicans have gone along infrequently and reluctantly. Thus, it might be tempting to attribute the marked rise and fall of the real value of the minimum wage in figure 8.1 to a parallel rise and fall in the political strength of the Democratic Party in Washington.

A simple tabulation of changes in the real value of the minimum wage provides strong support for that explanation. In the 25 years between 1949 and 2004 in which Democrats controlled the White House, the real value of the minimum wage increased by $4.08—a little more than 16 cents per year. In the 31 years in which Republican presidents were in office, the real value of the minimum wage *declined* by $1.93—about six cents per year.

Statistical analyses of fluctuations in the real minimum wage over the past half-century provide more systematic evidence of significant partisan differences. They also suggest that the fate of the minimum wage has hinged even more crucially on the fortunes of the Democratic Party's most important ally in this policy domain, organized labor. The statistical analyses reported in table 8.2 indicate that the real value of the minimum wage has been strongly related to the political strength of labor unions, as measured by the percentage of workers who are union members. Thus, the declining unionization of the American workforce over the past half-century seems to have contributed greatly to the decline in the real value of the minimum wage. The implied long-term decline in the real value of the minimum wage attributable to the decline in unionization since the late 1940s ranges from $3.25 to $4.25 (in 2006 dollars).[33]

There is also a strong tendency for the minimum wage rate to track changes in average wages. Allowing for the persistence of the minimum wage level from year to year, the implied long-term effect of a $1 increase in average hourly pay is to raise the minimum wage by almost 30 cents. Since average hourly pay (in 2006 dollars) has increased by more than $13 since the late 1940s, the responsiveness of minimum wage levels to average wage levels has significantly bolstered the real value of the minimum wage, contributing to its increase in the 1950s and 1960s and moderating its decline since then. Over the entire post-war era, the cumulative increase in the real

---

[33] The algebra of partial adjustment in dynamic models of this sort is presented in many elementary econometrics textbooks (e.g., Gujarati 1995, 599–601; Kennedy 1998, 156). The estimated long-run effect of each explanatory variable on the real value of the minimum wage is equal to the estimated short-run effect divided by the proportion of the lagged minimum wage rate that does *not* persist in the current period. For the statistical model in the first column of table 8.2, for example, the estimated long-run effect of unionization is $1/(1 - .558) = 2.26$ times as large as the estimated short-run effect. Unionization declined from 31.8% of the labor force in 1948 to 12.9% in 2003, producing an estimated long-run effect of $2.26 \times .096 \times (12.9 - 31.8) = -\$4.10$. The corresponding estimates for the models in the second, third, and fourth columns of table 8.2 are −$4.26, −$3.25, and −$3.48.

TABLE 8.2

Partisan Politics and the Minimum Wage, 1949–2004

Ordinary least squares regression parameter estimates (with standard errors in parentheses) for real value of the federal minimum wage (in 2006 dollars). Explanatory variables lagged one year.

	{1}	{2}	{3}	{4}
Democratic president	—	.26 (.13)	—	.21 (.13)
Democratic Congress (%)	—	—	.032 (.013)	.028 (.013)
Prevailing minimum wage ($)	.558 (.102)	.530 (.101)	.482 (.102)	.468 (.101)
Average pay ($)	.131 (.054)	.153 (.054)	.131 (.052)	.149 (.052)
Union membership (%)	.096 (.029)	.106 (.029)	.089 (.028)	.098 (.028)
Intercept	−1.83 (1.21)	−2.42 (1.21)	−2.93 (1.23)	−3.27 (1.23)
Standard error of regression	.49	.47	.47	.46
Adjusted R²	.81	.82	.83	.84
N	56	56	56	56

Source: Calculations based on data from U.S. Department of Labor ("History of Federal Minimum Wage Rates under the Fair Labor Standards Act, 1938–2007") and *Statistical Abstract of the United States* (various years).

value of the minimum wage attributable to rising average wages almost exactly counterbalanced the cumulative decline attributable to declining unionization.[34]

Although these economic and social trends have had powerful effects on the minimum wage, partisan politics has had its own significant impact: Democratic presidents and Democratic strength in Congress have contributed importantly to increasing and maintaining the real value of the minimum wage. The statistical analyses reported in the second, third, and fourth columns of table 8.2 include partisan control of the White House, Congress, or both as explanatory factors.[35] When both indicators are included in the analysis, in the fourth column of the table, the results imply that the long-run real value of the minimum wage declined by about $1.05 due to the shift in the partisan composition of Congress from the mid-1960s (when Democrats held 68% of the seats) to 2004 (when Democrats held 48% of the

[34] The average wage level (in 2006 dollars) increased from $11.47 in 1948 to $24.94 in 2003. The estimated long-run effect of this cumulative increase was to increase the real value of the minimum wage by about $3.50; the effects implied by the four distinct models in table 8.2 are $3.99, $4.38, $3.41, and $3.77.

[35] As in chapters 2 and 4, I measure partisan control beginning one year after a new president or Congress takes office. My measure of congressional partisanship is a simple average of the Democratic percentages of seats in the House and Senate in each year.

seats). Shifting from a Democratic president to a Republican president implies an additional 40-cent decline. Together, these two partisan effects account for more than half of the observed decline in the real value of the minimum wage since the mid-1960s.

The estimated effects of changes in average wages and union membership on the real value of the minimum wage remain quite powerful even after taking account of partisan control of the White House and Congress. The analysis presented in the fourth column of table 8.2 implies that the cumulative increase in average wages since the 1940s has raised the real value of the minimum wage by about $3.80, while the cumulative decline in union membership over the same period has depressed the real value of the minimum wage by about $3.50. Even making separate allowance for the possibility of a secular trend in the real value of the minimum wage has very little impact on the magnitude of these estimates, though it does make them a good deal less precise, since both average wages and union membership are themselves strongly trended.[36]

The statistical analyses presented in table 8.2 are based on the assumption that the policy effects of having a Democratic president and Democratic strength in Congress are constant, regardless of the broader policy-making environment. That assumption is relaxed in table 8.3, which examines interactions between presidential partisanship and the other important determinants of minimum wage levels. The first column of the table reports estimates of the impact of each of these other factors when a Democrat is in the White House; the second column reports parallel estimates for Republican administrations, and the third column reports the differences between the estimates for Democratic and Republican administrations.

Although all of the partisan differences in the third column of table 8.3 are estimated rather imprecisely, they suggest some quite plausible elaborations of the partisan effects evident in table 8.2. First, the real value of the minimum wage has been much less stable under Democratic presidents, since they have often pursued and sometimes achieved significant increases in the prevailing rate. In contrast, Republican presidents have generally preferred lower minimum wage rates, and given the political difficulty of reducing the nominal minimum wage they have had little choice but to wait for inflation to gradually erode the real value of the existing minimum.

Second, the minimum wage rate has tracked the level of average wages in the economy much more closely under Democratic presidents than it has

[36] Adding a linear trend term to the regression analysis reported in the fourth column of table 8.2 reduces the apparent impact of union membership by about 3% (from .096 to .093, with a standard error of .070) and increases the apparent impact of average wages by about 6% (from .149 to .158, with a standard error of .126). The corresponding long-term estimates are similarly affected, since the inclusion of a linear trend term leaves the estimated persistence of the prevailing minimum wage rate unchanged.

TABLE 8.3

Minimum Wage Levels under Democratic and Republican Presidents, 1949–2004

Ordinary least squares regression parameter estimates (with standard errors in parentheses) for real value of the federal minimum wage (in 2006 dollars). Explanatory variables lagged one year.

	Democratic president	Republican president	Partisan difference
Democratic Congress (%)	.039 (.026)	.013 (.015)	.026 (.028)
Prevailing minimum wage ($)	.269 (.184)	.475 (.132)	−.205 (.223)
Average pay ($)	.296 (.126)	.103 (.051)	.193 (.122)
Union membership (%)	.161 (.070)	.086 (.029)	.075 (.068)
Intercept	−6.71 (2.69)	−1.34 (1.26)	−5.37 (2.73)
Standard error of regression	.54	.37	
Adjusted R²	.85	.83	
N	25	31	

Source: Calculations based on data from U.S. Department of Labor ("History of Federal Minimum Wage Rates under the Fair Labor Standards Act, 1938–2007") and *Statistical Abstract of the United States* (various years).

under Republican presidents, reflecting the traditional aspiration of liberal policy makers to link the economic fortunes of the middle class and the working poor.

Third, the strength of labor unions has been about twice as consequential under Democratic presidents as under Republican presidents, reflecting the traditional political alliance between union leaders and the Democratic Party and the greater scope for activism enjoyed by each when the other wields significant political influence. Finally, the partisan balance in Congress has been about three times as important under Democratic presidents as under Republican presidents. When Republicans control the White House, minimum wage increases are rare regardless of which party controls Congress, but Democratic presidents are a good deal more likely to succeed in engineering minimum wage increases when there are enough Democrats in Congress to overcome the blocking tactics of their Republican adversaries.

The explanatory factors included in tables 8.2 and 8.3 do a surprisingly good job of accounting for the pronounced rise and fall of the real value of the minimum wage evident in figure 8.1. As I have already noted, the upward pressure exerted by rising average pay and the downward pressure exerted by declining unionization almost exactly counterbalanced each other over the entire half-century. However, average pay rose fastest in the 1950s and 1960s, while unionization remained fairly stable, and unionization declined most dramatically in the late 1970s and 1980s, when real wage levels were stagnant. Those intersecting trends, together with the rising and falling fortunes of the

Democratic Party in Washington, account for the major shifts in the real value of the minimum wage over the post-war period.[37]

The broad patterns of minimum wage policy making evident in the statistical analyses reported in tables 8.2 and 8.3 are generally consistent with detailed case studies of congressional votes to raise the minimum wage. For example, a study of Senate votes on the 1977 minimum wage increase found "substantial party, regional, and unionization effects." Even after allowing for differences in union strength and other factors, the estimated difference in preferred minimum wage levels between Democratic and Republican senators was 22 cents (73 cents in 2006 dollars).[38]

The striking unresponsiveness of actual minimum wage rates to the high levels of public support recorded in opinion surveys over the past 40 years also finds a parallel in more detailed individual-level analysis. The NES Senate Election Study surveyed an average of 185 people in each of the 50 states in connection with the 1988, 1990, and 1992 elections.[39] The state-by-state opinion data make it possible to investigate the responsiveness of individual senators to the preferences of their constituents. Although the survey did not include specific questions about the minimum wage, it does make it possible to assess the extent to which senators' votes on this issue were influenced by the more general ideological tenor of public opinion in their states.

The Senate's most consequential minimum wage vote during this period occurred in April 1989, on a bill that would have raised the minimum wage from \$3.35 to \$4.55 per hour.[40] Sixty-three senators voted in favor of the increase, while 37 opposed it. Table 8.4 reports the results of a series of statistical analyses relating their votes to the ideological views of their constituents and to the senators' own partisan affiliations.

The analysis presented in the first column of table 8.4 shows that senators' minimum wage votes were virtually unrelated to their constituents' ideological views. In marked contrast, the analysis presented in the second column of the table indicates that there was a very strong relationship between senators' votes and their own partisan affiliations: Democratic senators were much more likely than Republicans to vote in favor of increasing the minimum wage. The analysis

---

[37] For the regression analysis presented in the second column of table 8.2, adding linear and quadratic trend terms reduces the standard error of the regression by about 1%. Adding linear and quadratic trend terms to each of the other seven regression analyses *increases* the standard errors of the regressions by almost 2%, on average. The only instances in which the estimated trend effects are substantial in magnitude are the first two models reported in table 8.3, for Democratic administrations; however, those parameter estimates are too imprecise to be informative due to the small number and uneven spacing of Democratic presidents over the past 40 years.

[38] Krehbiel and Rivers (1988), 1163.

[39] The design of the NES Senate Election Study is described in more detail in chapter 9.

[40] This is the bill President Bush vetoed before accepting a smaller increase several months later. The Senate vote on the bill Bush signed was too lopsided to shed any light on the responsiveness of individual senators to the ideological views of their constituents.

TABLE 8.4
Constituency Opinion, Partisanship, and Senate Support for a
Minimum Wage Increase

Probit parameter estimates (with standard errors in parentheses) for Senate vote on final
passage of the Minimum Wage Restoration Act, April 1989.

	{1}	{2}	{3}
Liberal constituency opinion (−1 to +1; AL=−.333, MA=−.012)	.84 (1.76)	—	3.99 (2.90)
Democratic senator	—	2.56 (.38)	2.71 (.43)
Intercept	−.46 (.30)	−1.79 (.32)	−2.53 (.67)
Log likelihood	−65.78	−32.43	−31.42
Pseudo-R²	.00	.51	.52
N	100	100	100

Source: Calculations based on data from Senate Legislative Information System and NES
Senate Election Study.

presented in the third column of the table takes simultaneous account of constituency opinion and partisanship. Here, both factors appear to matter, but the magnitude of the estimated effect of constituency opinion is quite modest, while the estimated effect of partisanship remains very strong.

The political significance of these statistical results may be gleaned by comparing the implied probabilities of supporting the minimum wage increase for hypothetical Democratic and Republican senators representing exactly the same ideologically moderate constituents: 97% for the Democrat, 21% for the Republican. (These predicted probabilities closely match the actual pattern of roll call votes: 53 of 55 Democratic senators voted in favor, while only 10 of 45 Republican senators did so.) By comparison, even extreme constituency opinion had relatively little impact on senators' votes. For example, the predicted probability of a Democratic senator supporting the minimum wage increase was 90% even if he represented the most conservative state in the country (Arkansas), whereas the predicted probability of a Republican senator opposing the minimum wage increase was 62% even in the most liberal state (Massachusetts).

As in the case of estate tax repeal, it would be an exaggeration to suggest that minimum wage politics is entirely a matter of elites pursuing their own ideological convictions. Nevertheless, it seems clear that policy making in this domain has had much more to do with partisan politics and ideology than with public sentiment. When Democrats have controlled the White House and Congress and labor unions have been strong, the minimum wage has generally flourished. When Democrats and labor unions have been weaker, Republican presidents and legislators have usually managed to block significant increases.

Overwhelming public support for a higher minimum wage may have prevented its real value from eroding even faster; but it has not been sufficient to forestall substantial declines during periods of conservative ascendancy in Washington.

THE EARNED INCOME TAX CREDIT

While the real value of the minimum wage has eroded substantially over the past 40 years, the government has embraced a very different policy to bolster the incomes of low-wage workers: the Earned Income Tax Credit (EITC). Implemented on a modest scale in 1975 and significantly expanded in 1986, 1990, 1993, and 2001, by 2004 the EITC generated more than $35 billion in additional income for 21 million poor families. From the perspective of the working poor, the growth of the EITC has by no means fully compensated for the erosion of the minimum wage; the effective wage subsidy provided by the EITC amounts to less than $1 per hour, whereas the real value of the minimum wage has declined by more than $4 per hour since the late 1960s. Nevertheless, the EITC has rather unobtrusively evolved into "one of the most important federal antipoverty programs," surpassing the federal contribution to state and local welfare programs and rivaling federal spending on Food Stamps and other nutrition programs.[41]

From the perspective of policy makers, the EITC has been an admirably flexible program. In the 1970s it provided an appealing alternative to the Nixon administration's proposed "negative income tax"; moreover, "by putting money in the hands of low-income consumers, it complemented President Ford's pledge to stimulate the flagging economy." In the 1980s it "provided the glue that held together" President Reagan's ambitious tax reform package, counterbalancing tax cuts for high-income taxpayers and allowing policy makers to honor an agreement between the president and congressional leaders to "achieve distributional and revenue neutrality" in the overall package. In the 1990s, another significant expansion "eased the transition" from traditional welfare to the more restrictive Temporary Assistance for Needy Families (TANF) program while fulfilling President Clinton's campaign promise to "make work pay."[42]

The EITC has a variety of significant political advantages. Probably most importantly, tying the income subsidy to wages encourages work and sidesteps the association of traditional welfare programs with the "undeserving poor." This aspect of the program is reinforced by the designation of EITC as a "tax credit," despite the fact that most recipients have little or no income tax liability to offset.[43] Moreover, whereas the minimum wage raises the cost of

[41] Slemrod and Bakija (2004), 43.

[42] Ventry (2000), 995, 1015, 1008.

[43] According to Slemrod and Bakija (2004, 43), "In 2000, the total dollar value of the EITC was $32 billion, with $28 billion of that representing the refundable portion" not offset by recipients' tax liability.

doing business for employers of low-wage workers, the EITC lowers that cost by stimulating low-wage labor supply.[44]

The EITC, however, is much more complicated than the minimum wage—"so complex that the IRS publishes more than 50 pages of instructions" for would-be beneficiaries. Filing procedures were tightened in the wake of a controversial IRS study suggesting that about 30% of EITC benefits claimed in 1999 should not have been paid; and "Congress has appropriated more than $1 billion for audits of low-income taxpayers" since 1998.[45] Meanwhile, the General Accounting Office has estimated that between 15% and 25% of those who are eligible—and more than half of those without children—fail to claim the credit.

The EITC is also a good deal less salient than the minimum wage to ordinary citizens and a good deal less popular. In the 2003 survey sponsored by National Public Radio, the Kaiser Family Foundation, and Harvard University's Kennedy School of Government, almost 40% of respondents admitted that they had never heard of the Earned Income Tax Credit or did not know what it was.[46] In 1995, when Republicans floated the possibility of reducing the EITC, only a bare majority of survey respondents opposed doing so, while 25% said they favored eliminating it.[47] These survey results leave little doubt that, if policy makers were guided solely by manifest public enthusiasm for specific government programs, they would not have embraced the EITC in preference to a robust minimum wage.

REVERSING THE TIDE

In October 2005, just five days after one more proposal for a minimum wage increase went down to defeat in the Senate, the CEO of Wal-Mart told his company's directors and executives that "the U.S. minimum wage . . . is out

[44] Leigh (2004).

[45] Dorothy A. Brown, "A Tax Credit or a Handout?" *New York Times*, April 18, 2006, A27; Internal Revenue Service, *Compliance Estimates for Earned Income Tax Credit Claimed on 1999 Returns* (February 28, 2002); General Accounting Office, *Earned Income Tax Credit Eligibility and Participation* (GAO-02-290R, 2001); Scholz (1994).

[46] "Earned Income Tax Credit . . . Have you heard the term and know what it means, have you heard the term but don't know what it means, or have you not heard the term?" Heard the term and know what it means, 61%—Heard the term but don't know what it means, 28%—Have not heard the term, 11%.

[47] Gallup/CNN/USA Today Poll, November, 1995: "(Based on what you have read or heard, please tell me if you favor or oppose each of the following Republican proposals.). . . . Reducing the Earned Income Tax Credit for the working poor." Favor, 39%—Oppose, 53%—Mixed (vol.), 2%—Don't know/Refused, 6%. News Interest Index Poll, September, 1995: "Some leaders in Washington are talking about getting rid of the Earned Income Tax Credit, which reduces or cancels out income taxes for poor people who work, but make very little money. Would you favor or oppose ending this tax credit?" Favor, 25%—Oppose, 68%—Don't know, 6%.

of date with the times. . . . We can see first-hand . . . how many of our customers are struggling to get by. We have seen an increase in spending on the 1st and 15th of each month and less spending at the end of the month, letting us know that our customers simply don't have the money to buy basic necessities between paychecks."[48]

Some liberal activists and observers expressed skepticism about the sincerity of Wal-Mart's concern for America's struggling working poor; the company's public support for a minimum wage increase came only days before the release of a hard-hitting documentary focusing on the "sweatshop conditions in which thousands of employees of Wal-Mart's suppliers routinely work, and the depressive effect that Wal-Mart has on working-class living standards here in the United States."[49] Nevertheless, the addition of the retailing giant to a coalition that already included the AFL-CIO, the Episcopal Church, and dozens of other organizations supporting a minimum wage increase seemed to mark an important turning point in national recognition that the federal minimum wage was indeed "out of date with the times."

Despite the breadth of apparent support for a minimum wage increase in late 2005, another year and a half would pass before an increase actually made it through Congress. Both the delay and the end result shed important light on the politics of the minimum wage, and on the difficulties and possibilities of egalitarian policy making more generally.

In attempting to account for the Senate's failure to vote a minimum wage hike in 2005, reporter Marilyn Geewax noted that "relatively few voters ever contacted their elected representatives" to express support for a minimum wage increase. Public opinion in favor of raising the minimum wage is consistent and impressively broad, the argument goes, but also quite shallow. "In contrast," Geewax wrote, "restaurateurs and small-business owners were organized, energized and informed by top-notch lobbyists who never stopped telling Congress that higher wages would cut profits and limit the ability to create jobs." Given the mismatch in organization and lobbying effort, one public interest advocate told her, "To get something through this Congress that corporate interests don't like would be a Herculean task."[50]

Given these political and institutional hurdles to policy change in Washington, it should not be surprising that minimum wage activists have increasingly taken their case to the states. "The end goal of minimum wage advocates," one observer has suggested, "is for Congress to act soon on a truly significant increase with indexation. But if that doesn't happen, and it

[48] H. Lee Scott, quoted in Peter Katel, "Minimum Wage," *CQ Researcher 15* (December 16, 2006), 1053–1076.

[49] Harold Meyerson, "Trouble in Wal-Mart's America," *Washington Post*, October 26, 2005, A19.

[50] Marilyn Geewax, "Minimum Wage Odyssey: A Yearlong View from Capitol Hill and a Small Ohio Town," *Trenton Times*, November 27, 2005, A11.

probably won't, then it's likely that it will be done piecemeal out in the country."[51]

By 2005, 18 states, including almost half the country's total population, had state minimum wage rates that exceed the federal minimum. Most of these are relatively wealthy, politically liberal states. A striking exception is Florida, a conservative Republican state with one of the highest levels of economic inequality in the nation. In 2004, 71% of Florida voters approved an amendment to the state constitution establishing a minimum wage of $6.15 per hour, with automatic annual increases to keep pace with inflation. A year after the measure took effect, one journalist noted that the negative economic consequences predicted by opponents of raising the minimum wage "haven't appeared yet"—the state added 248,000 new jobs, while unemployment fell to a 30-year low.[52]

Inspired by Florida's successful minimum wage amendment, and spurred by repeated frustration in Washington, grass-roots campaigns sprang up to push for minimum wage initiatives in several additional states and localities. According to a 2005 press report, "Liberal activists say they're using the minimum wage to put Republicans on the defensive. They hope to put minimum wage initiatives on the ballots next year in nine states, including Ohio, Michigan and Arizona, says Kristina Wilfore, head of the liberal Ballot Strategy Initiative Center. 'This is going to take off like wildfire,' she says. 'It will pull progressive voters to the polls. The way the gay marriage amendment lured conservative voters to the polls (in November) was a wake-up call for us.'"

According to Senator Charles Schumer, the coordinator of the Democratic Party's 2006 Senate campaign strategy, "The average American thinks that the minimum wage ought to be raised, even if they are making more than the minimum wage. Far more importantly, from a political viewpoint, it appeals to certain groups of people who don't usually turn out to vote."[53]

Measures to raise state minimum wage rates appeared on the 2006 ballot in six states—Arizona, Colorado, Missouri, Montana, Ohio, and Nevada. All six measures passed, with an average vote margin of almost two to one. Whether the presence of these measures on the ballot actually succeeded in "pull[ing] progressive voters to the polls" is unclear. However, in view of the closeness of many key races it seems likely that minimum wage advocates will claim credit for providing Democrats with a crucial edge in their narrow midterm victory, especially in two pivotal races for partisan control of the Senate. In Missouri, proponents spent over $2 million on mobilizing turnout in

[51] Peter Harkness, "States & Localities: War on Wqaages Goes Local," *CQ Weekly*, Feburary 6, 2006, 320; John M. Broder, "States Take Lead in Push to Raise Minimum Wages," *New York Times*, January 2, 2006, A1.

[52] Harkness, "States & Localities: War on Wages Goes Local," 320.

[53] Dennis Cauchon, "States Say $5.15 an Hour Too Little," *USA Today*, May 31, 2005; Edmund L. Andrews, "Democrats Link Fortunes to Rise in Minimum Wage," *New York Times*, July 13, 2006, A18.

urban areas, and Democratic challenger Claire McCaskill defeated Republican incumbent Jim Talent by a margin of fewer than 50,000 votes. In Montana, a minimum wage increase passed by more than 175,000 votes, while Democratic challenger Jon Tester unseated Republican incumbent Conrad Burns by fewer than 3,000 votes.[54]

During the campaign, House Democratic leader Nancy Pelosi promised that if her party gained a majority in the election, a minimum wage increase would be on the House floor within 24 hours of the new Congress starting work. However, introducing a bill is not the same thing as passing it. With only a modest majority in the House and an even slimmer majority in the Senate, Democrats recognized that they would need significant Republican cooperation to overcome a Senate filibuster and avoid a presidential veto. In a post-election press conference, President Bush signaled a willingness to compromise, calling a minimum wage increase "an area where I believe we can make some—find common ground." As it turned out, however, that common ground took several months to find, and it was littered with billions of dollars in sweeteners in the form of tax breaks for small businesses.[55]

In the first weeks of the new Democratic Congress, the House passed a "clean" bill raising the minimum wage to $7.25 per hour. Senate Democrats, intent on forestalling a Republican filibuster, coupled a similar minimum wage hike with $8.3 billion in tax cuts for small businesses. The House responded by passing a $1.3 billion tax cut for small businesses. The U.S. Chamber of Commerce supported the House package; small-business groups led by the National Federation of Independent Business insisted on more generous tax write-offs, while some Republicans continued to oppose any increase in the minimum wage. After three further months of wrangling, a compromise emerged as part of a larger deal on spending for the war in Iraq. The compromise package coupled a three-step increase in the mini-

[54] John Atlas and Peter Dreier, "Waging Victory," *American Prospect Online*, November 10, 2006. Minimum wage increases garnered 76% of the vote in Missouri, 73% in Montana, 69% in Nevada, 66% in Arizona, 56% in Ohio, and 53% in Colorado.

[55] James Parks, "Kennedy, Pelosi Promise Quick Action on Minimum Wage If Democrats Win Congress," AFL-CIO Now, October 24, 2006, http://blog.aflcio.org/2006/10/24/kennedy-pelosi-promise-quick-action-on-minimum-wage-if-democrats-win-congress/; Press Conference by the President, November 8, 2006, http://www.whitehouse.gov.edgesuite.net/news/releases/2006/11/20061108-2.html. Even after the Democrats' midterm victory, many conservatives hoped to extract major policy concessions in exchange for acquiescing in a minimum wage hike. For example, prominent conservative commentator William Safire used his old spot on the *New York Times* Op-Ed page to float the possibility of reviving the minimum-wage-for-estate-tax deal that congressional Democrats had already rejected before the election. Safire suggested that "the window of bipartisan compromise can . . . fit a minimum wage increase tied to inheritance tax reduction," but warned that "the window won't be open long" once liberal congressional committee chairmen got bogged down in partisan "posturing." William Safire, "After the Thumpin'," *New York Times*, November 9, 2006.

mum wage—from $5.15 to $5.85 in July 2007, to $6.55 in July 2008, and to $7.25 in July 2009—with $4.84 billion in tax breaks. It was approved by margins of 348–73 in the House and 80–14 in the Senate, and signed into law by President Bush the following day. While Democrats declared the compromise a long-delayed victory for working people, House minority leader John Boehner called it "a sneaky way to do business."[56]

A few days after the first installment of the 2007 minimum wage hike took effect, Senator Kennedy announced that he would introduce further legislation raising the minimum wage to $9.50 per hour. Presidential candidate John Edwards proposed a similar increase by 2012, along with a "national goal" of maintaining a minimum wage equal to half the average wage thereafter.[57] For the moment, however, the political momentum for further increases seems to have ebbed. Whether it will be revived in the context of the 2008 campaign, or by the advent of a new administration in 2009, remains to be seen.

Near the end of their 400-page study of the effects of minimum wage laws, economists Card and Krueger argued that "the intensity of the political debate surrounding the minimum wage—on both sides of the issue—is out of proportion to its real importance to the economy."[58] They may be right. Nevertheless, the symbolic importance of this "modest transfer program," as they call it, is considerable. The substantial erosion of the minimum wage over the past 40 years stands as a dramatic example of the American political system's unresponsiveness to public sentiment. Faced with consistent, overwhelming public support for minimum wage increases—and in a context of accelerating economic inequality—politicians in Washington have mostly procrastinated, obfuscated, impeded, and grandstanded. The 2007 minimum wage hike is an important exception to this pattern; but there is no reason to believe that it represents anything other than a brief respite in the long-term erosion of the minimum wage.

Still, one may wonder how much light policy making in this domain sheds on the broader workings of the American political system. Is the erosion of the minimum wage a rare exception to a general pattern of democratic responsiveness, perhaps reflecting the peculiar political dynamics of a policy domain in which the balance of economic power between employers and low-wage workers is so strongly tilted in favor of employers? Or is unresponsiveness endemic in a policy-making process where intense interests have numerous avenues of influence, and where the political ramifications of unequal economic power are pervasive? Those are the questions I explore in chapter 9.

[56] Edmund L. Andrews, "Familiar Problem Stalls Minimum Wage Bill," *New York Times*, February 17, 2007, A10; Stephen Labaton, "Congress Passes Increase in the Minimum Wage," *New York Times*, May 25, 207, A12.

[57] Broder, "States Take Lead in Push to Raise Minimum Wages," A1; "Edwards Calls for Minimum Wage Increase As Part of Plan to Build One America," July 5, 2007, http://johnedwards.com/news/headlines/20070705-minimum-wage/.

[58] Card and Krueger (1995), 395.

CHAPTER 9

Economic Inequality and Political Representation

> I assume that a key characteristic of a democracy is
> the continued responsiveness of the government to
> the preferences of its citizens, considered as political
> equals.
>
> —Robert Dahl, 1971[1]

ONE OF THE most basic principles of democracy is the notion that every citizen's preferences should count equally in the realm of politics and government. But there are a variety of good reasons to suspect that policy makers in
real political systems do *not* consider citizens as political equals. Wealthier
and better-educated citizens are more likely than the poor and less-educated
to have clearly formulated and well-informed preferences, and significantly
more likely to turn out to vote, to have direct contact with public officials,
and to contribute money and energy to political campaigns.

Given the salience of these disparities, and the importance attached to political equality in American political culture, one might suppose that political
scientists have been hard at work documenting the ways in which resource inequalities shape political representation and public policy. Alas, that supposi-
tion would be quite mistaken. According to the American Political Science
Association's recent Task Force on Inequality and American Democracy, "we
know little about the connections between changing economic inequality and
changes in political behavior, governing institutions, and public policy."[2]

One aspect of political inequality that *has* been unusually well-documented
is the disparity between rich and poor citizens in political participation.[3] The
extent to which scholarly attention has focused on disparities in participation
probably reflects, in part, the simple fact that those disparities are relatively
easy to measure. As Sidney Verba and Gary Orren put it, "Political equality
cannot be gauged in the same way as economic inequality. There is no metric
such as money, no statistic such as the Gini index, and no body of data comparing countries. There are, however, relevant data on political participation."[4]

---

[1] Dahl (1971), 1.

[2] Task Force on Inequality and American Democracy (2004), 661–662.

[3] Prominent examples include Verba, Nie, and Kim (1978), Wolfinger and Rosenstone (1980),
and Verba, Schlozman, and Brady (1995). For a recent overview, see Schlozman et al. (2005).

[4] Verba and Orren (1985), 15.

The mere availability of relevant data would probably not be sufficient to inspire much interest in participatory inequality if analysts did not believe that participation has important consequences for representation. As it happens, that presumption seems to be quite common. For example, Verba, Kay Schlozman, and Henry Brady motivated their monumental study of *Voice and Equality* by arguing that "inequalities in activity are likely to be associated with inequalities in governmental responsiveness."[5] It is striking, though, how little political scientists have done to *test* the presumption that inequalities in participation have political consequences. For the most part, scholars of political participation have treated actual patterns of governmental responsiveness as someone else's problem.

Meanwhile, statistical studies of political representation dating back to Warren Miller and Donald Stokes's classic analysis in the early 1960s have found strong statistical connections between constituents' policy preferences and their representatives' policy choices. However, those studies have almost invariably treated constituents in an undifferentiated way, using simple averages of opinions in a given district, on a given issue, or at a given time to account for representatives' policy choices. Thus, they shed little or no light on the fundamental issue of political equality.[6]

This chapter provides a more nuanced analysis of political representation, which recognizes that the weight attached to constituents' views in the policy-making process may depend on those constituents' politically relevant resources and behavior—primarily on their incomes, and secondarily on a variety of other resources and behaviors that might mediate the relationship between income and political representation, including electoral turnout, political information, and contact with public officials.

My analysis focuses on representation by U.S. senators in the late 1980s and early 1990s. That focus is inspired not by any particular substantive feature of the time period or of the Senate as a representative body, but by the availability of unusual data facilitating systematic analysis of the relationship between senators' policy choices and the views of their constituents. Using both summary measures of senators' voting patterns and specific roll call votes on the minimum wage, civil rights, government spending, and abortion, I find that senators in this period were vastly more responsive to affluent constituents than to constituents of modest means. Indeed, my analyses indicate that the

---

[5] Verba, Schlozman, and Brady (1995), 14.

[6] Miller and Stokes (1963). Among subsequent studies in the same tradition, articles by Page and Shapiro (1983), Bartels (1991), and Stimson, MacKuen, and Erikson (1995) provide examples of varying approaches. Rivers's (n.d.) unpublished analysis of differential congressional responsiveness to the views of political independents (by comparison with incumbent- or opposition-party identifiers) was a pioneering examination of unequal representation. More recent studies of differential responsiveness include Gilens (2005), Griffin and Newman (2005), and Jacobs and Page (2005).

views of constituents in the upper third of the income distribution received about 50% more weight than those in the middle third, with even larger disparities on specific salient roll call votes. Meanwhile, the views of constituents in the bottom third of the income distribution received no weight at all in the voting decisions of their senators. Far from being "considered as political equals," they were entirely *un*considered in the policy-making process.

IDEOLOGICAL REPRESENTATION

Empirical analyses of representation are typically grounded in a simple statistical model relating elite policy choices to mass preferences. Variation in mass preferences and policy choices may be observed across districts or other geographical units, across issues, or over time. The (usually implicit) assumption is that elected officials are equally responsive to the views of all their constituents, so that *average* opinion for each district, issue, or time period provides an adequate reflection of mass preferences. The focus of analysis is on how these mass preferences influence observed policy choices.[7]

Here, my analysis of representation employs estimates of constituency opinion in each of the 50 states from the Senate Election Study conducted by the National Election Studies (NES) research team.[8] The Senate Election Study was a national survey conducted in the weeks just after the November 1988, 1990, and 1992 general elections; the combined sample for all three years includes 9,253 U.S. citizens of voting age.[9] A key advantage of the

[7] In the context of the analysis here, the basic model takes the form

$$Y_k = \alpha + (\Sigma_{i \in k} \beta X_i)/N_k + \gamma Z_k + \varepsilon_k,$$

where Y_k is an observed roll call vote (or summary of roll call votes) cast by senator k, X_i represents the opinion of a specific survey respondent i in senator k's state, N_k is the number of survey respondents from senator k's state for whom opinion data are available, Z_k is a dummy variable indicating senator k's party affiliation, ε_k is a stochastic term representing other influences on representative k's legislative behavior, and α, β, and γ are constant parameters to be estimated. The key parameter in this model is β, which captures the statistical relationship between constituency opinion and senators' roll call votes.

[8] Data, codebooks, and a more detailed description of the study design are available from the NES Web site, http://www.umich.edu/~nes.

[9] As is commonly the case with telephone surveys, the Senate Election Study sample significantly underrepresented young people, racial and ethnic minority groups, and people with little formal education. Since these sample biases are especially problematic in a study of economic inequality, I post-stratified the sample within each state on the basis of education, race, age, sex, and work status. The highest average sample weights were 1.76 for respondents without high school diplomas, 1.40 for blacks, 1.37 for Hispanics, 1.28 for 18- to 24-year-olds, and 1.14 for working males; the lowest average sample weights were .76 for nonworking females, .83 for college graduates, and .88 for people 65 and older. For a more detailed account of the post-stratification procedure see Bartels (2002b).

study, for my purposes here, is that it was designed to provide a fairly large representative sample of adult citizens in each of the 50 states—the state-by-state sample sizes range from 151 to 223.[10] Thus, it is possible to estimate constituency opinion in each state with considerable precision.

I begin by relating the voting behavior of senators to the general ideological views of their constituents as measured by the conservatism scale in the NES Senate Election Study surveys. I recoded the seven-point conservatism scale in the surveys to range from −1 to +1, with negative values reflecting liberal opinion and positive values reflecting conservative opinion. The balance of opinion, by this measure, was at least slightly conservative in every state, ranging from .012 in Massachusetts and .034 in California to .320 in Alabama and .333 in Arkansas.

I use the resulting data on constituents' opinions to account for the roll call votes of senators on issues that reached the Senate floor during the period covered by the Senate Election Study: the 101st (1989–1990), 102nd (1991–1992), and 103rd (1993–1994) Congresses. Keith Poole and Howard Rosenthal's W-NOMINATE scores provide a convenient summary measure of senators' ideological positions based on all the votes they cast in each Congress.[11] The W-NOMINATE scores are scaled to range from −1 for the most liberal member of each Senate to +1 for the most conservative member.

The overall relationship between constituency opinion and the ideological tenor of senators' voting records is displayed in figure 9.1. The figure shows roll call scores for each senator in each of the three Congresses covered by my analysis, as well as regression lines summarizing the relationship between constituency opinion and senators' conservatism for each party's senators in each Congress. The positive slopes of the regression lines show that, as expected, more conservative states tended to get more conservative representation in the Senate.[12] The responsiveness of senators to constituency opinion was roughly similar for both parties and for each of the three Congresses, except that Democrats representing conservative states were somewhat more

[10] Although some details of the sample design and questionnaire varied across the three election years, the basic design remained unchanged, and a substantial core of questions was repeated in similar form in all three years. In the absence of any marked changes in constituency opinion from year to year, I combined the responses from all three years to produce more precise estimates of public opinion in each state.

[11] Data and documentation are available from the Voteview Web site, http://voteview.com/. I use W-NOMINATE scores rather than the more familiar D-NOMINATE or DW-NOMINATE scores because the W-NOMINATE scores are estimated separately for each Congress, avoiding any danger of artificial consistency or redundancy in the results of my separate analyses of voting patterns in three successive Congresses. In practice, however, the various NOMINATE scales are very highly intercorrelated (and, for that matter, highly correlated with other general measures of legislative voting patterns). On the calculation and specific properties of the W-NOMINATE scores, see Poole and Rosenthal (1997), 249–251.

[12] The t-statistics for the six slope coefficients range from 2.2 to 5.8.

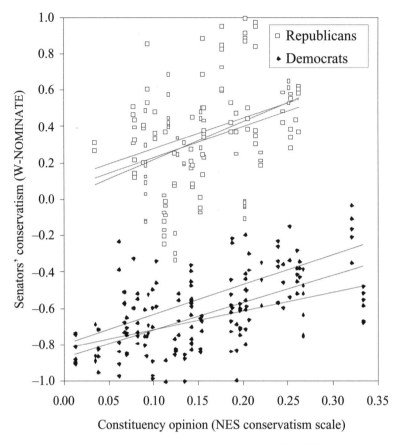

Figure 9.1 Constituency Opinion and Senators' Roll Call Votes, by Party

liberal in the 103rd Congress (the first two years of Bill Clinton's presidency) than in the 101st and 102nd Congresses (with George H. W. Bush in the White House).[13]

Figure 9.1 also reveals very substantial differences in the voting behavior of Republican and Democratic senators representing constituents with similar ideological views. Indeed, Republican and Democratic senators representing exactly the same constituents frequently exhibited markedly different ideological behavior. These differences were somewhat smaller in the early 1990s than in more recent congresses, but even then they were much larger

[13] The estimated slope for Democratic senators in the 103rd Congress is 1.03 (with a standard error of .20). The other five estimated slopes range from 1.50 to 2.07.

than the differences between senators of the same party representing liberal and conservative states. For example, the Republican senators representing California in the 101st and 102nd Congresses were a great deal closer in their voting patterns to their Republican colleagues from Texas and Mississippi than to their Democratic colleague from California.[14] These findings underscore the immense significance of elite ideology in the making of American public policy.

UNEQUAL RESPONSIVENESS

The overall pattern of representation displayed in figure 9.1 has two salient features: substantial partisan differences in the voting behavior of Republican and Democratic senators, and a fairly strong relationship within each party between the ideological behavior of senators and the ideological views of their constituents. My primary aim in this chapter is to explore the extent to which the apparent responsiveness of senators to liberal or conservative public opinion in their states reflects *differential* responsiveness to the views of senators' affluent constituents.

Examining unequal responsiveness requires us to relax the usual assumption that the behavior of elected officials reflects a simple *average* of their constituent's views. Here, I allow for the possibility that senators respond unequally to the views of rich, middle-class, and poor constituents.[15] To test that possibility, I separated respondents in the Senate Election Study surveys into three income groups: a low-income group with family incomes below $20,000 (about $30,000 in 2006 dollars), a middle-income group with family incomes ranging from $20,000 to $40,000, and a high-income group with family incomes above $40,000 (about $60,000 in 2006 dollars).[16] Averaging

[14] The average W-NOMINATE score for Senators Wilson (R-CA) and Seymour (R-CA) was .29. The average score for Senator Cranston (D-CA) in these two Congresses was −.87, while the average score for Senators Gramm (R-TX), Cochrane (R-MS), and Lott (R-MS) was .51. When Cranston retired and Seymour was defeated, they were replaced by two new Democratic senators, Boxer and Feinstein, whose average score in the 103rd Congress was −.78.

[15] The elaborated model takes the form

$$Y_k = \alpha + (\Sigma_{i \in kL}\, \beta_L\, X_i\,)/N_k + (\Sigma_{i \in kM}\, \beta_M\, X_i\,)/N_k + (\Sigma_{i \in kH}\, \beta_H\, X_i\,)/N_k + \gamma Z_k + \varepsilon_k,$$

where the additional subscripts L, M, and H partition the sample of constituents within each state into low-, middle-, and high-income groups. The fact that these groups have separate responsiveness parameters β_L, β_M, and β_H allows for the possibility that senators respond differentially to their respective views. (However, nothing in the model prevents these separate responsiveness parameters from turning out to be equal, in which case this more elaborate model reduces to the simpler model in note 7.)

[16] These thresholds are chosen to make the three income groups as similar as possible in size, given the categorization of family incomes in the Senate Election Study surveys.

across states, these groups constitute 30.7%, 40.2%, and 29.1%, respectively, of the (weighted) Senate Election Study sample. I estimated the average opinion of survey respondents within each income group in each state, multiplied by the proportion of the state's sample with incomes in the relevant range.[17]

Relating the voting behavior of senators to the preferences of their high-, middle-, and low-income constituents considered separately provides a more flexible account of political responsiveness than the standard model of representation in which only *average* constituency opinion matters. Obviously, this elaborated model still falls far short of being a realistic causal model of legislative behavior. A good many factors may influence senators' roll call votes in addition to the senators' own partisanship and the policy preferences of their constituents. Equally obviously, "responsiveness" in the statistical sense captured by an analysis of this sort may or may not reflect a direct causal impact of constituents' preferences on their senators' behavior. Nevertheless, the relationship between constituency opinion and legislative behavior in this simple model reflects an important feature of the policy-making process in any democratic political system, regardless of whether that relationship is produced by conscious political responsiveness on the part of legislators, selective retention of like-minded legislators by voters, shared backgrounds and life experiences, or other factors.[18]

Table 9.1 reports the results of a series of statistical analyses relating senators' roll call votes, as summarized by their w-NOMINATE scores in the 101st, 102nd, and 103rd Congresses, to constituency opinion measures computed separately for low-, middle-, and high-income constituents and to the senators' own party affiliations. The first three columns of the table report separate results for each Congress, while the final column reports

---

[17] In the notation of note 15, the average ideology of the low-income group within each state is

$$(\Sigma_{i \in kL} X_i)/N_{kL},$$

where N_{kL} is the number of low-income constituents in that state's survey sample. Multiplying that average ideology by N_{kL}/N_k, the proportion of low-income constituents in the state, reproduces the income-specific summation $(\Sigma_{i \in kL} X_i)/N_k$ in note 15 (and similarly for the middle- and high-income groups). The parameters attached to these weighted averages of constituency opinion reflect the responsiveness of senators to an entire constituency made up of each income group (or, equivalently, the relative responsiveness to a single constituent in each income group), *not* the aggregate responsiveness to each income group given its actual share of the state's constituency, which varies somewhat from state to state. I have also explored versions of the analysis in which survey respondents in each state are grouped on the basis of their place in the state income distribution rather than the national income distribution; the empirical results are generally quite similar.

[18] On the theoretical significance of "responsiveness" among other aspects of the relationship between representatives' behavior and their constituents' views, see Achen (1978).

TABLE 9.1
Differential Responsiveness of Senators to Constituency Opinion

Ordinary least squares regression coefficients (with standard errors in parentheses) for Poole-Rosenthal w-NOMINATE scores.

	101st Congress	102nd Congress	103rd Congress	1989–1994 (Pooled)
Low-income constituency opinion	−.11 (.61)	−.50 (.59)	−.39 (.55)	−.33 (.44)
Middle-income constituency opinion	2.47 (.72)	2.91 (.71)	2.58 (.65)	2.66 (.60)
High-income constituency opinion	4.73 (1.03)	4.43 (.99)	3.22 (.92)	4.15 (.85)
Republican senator	.91 (.04)	.95 (.04)	.99 (.04)	.95 (.04)
Intercept	−.87 (.06)	−.96 (.06)	−.92 (.05)	Congress-specific intercepts; observations clustered by senator
Standard error of regression	.216	.213	.195	.207
adjusted R^2	.83	.84	.88	.85
N	100	102	101	303
High- vs. Low-income responsiveness gap	4.84 (1.30)	4.92 (1.25)	3.61 (1.17)	4.48 (1.04)

Source: Calculations based on data from Voteview.com and NES Senate Election Study.

the results of a combined analysis employing the roll call data from all three Congresses.[19]

In each case, senators' voting patterns are strongly and consistently related to their party affiliations, as one would expect from the partisan differences in voting behavior summarized graphically in figure 9.1. As in figure 9.1, the expected difference in voting behavior between Republican and Democratic senators representing the same state amounted to about half of the total ideological distance between the most conservative senator and the most liberal senator in each Congress.

In addition, senators seem to have been quite responsive to the ideological views of their middle- and high-income constituents. For example, the estimated impact of middle-income constituency opinion in the analysis combining data

[19] Since unmeasured influences on the roll call votes cast by the same senator in three successive Congresses are very unlikely to be statistically independent, the standard errors reported in the rightmost column of table 9.1 (and in my subsequent pooled regression analyses) allow for arbitrary patterns of correlation in the disturbances for each senator.

from all three Congresses (2.66 in the rightmost column of table 9.1) implies enough responsiveness to shift a senator's ideological position by .34 (on the −1 to +1 roll call scale) as his middle-income constituents moved from the liberal end to the conservative end of the ideological spectrum in figure 9.1 (that is, from the ideological climate of Massachusetts to that of Arkansas).[20] The senators' apparent responsiveness to the views of high-income constituents was even greater, despite their smaller numbers; the estimate of 4.15 in the combined analysis implies a shift of .39 in a senator's roll call score in response to an equivalent shift in high-income constituency opinion.[21]

These results imply that senators' roll call votes were quite responsive to the ideological views of their middle- and high-income constituents. In contrast, the views of low-income constituents had *no* discernible impact on the voting behavior of their senators.[22] Whether we consider the three Congresses separately or together, the statistical results are quite consistent in suggesting that the opinions of constituents in the bottom third of the income distribution were utterly irrelevant.[23]

These patterns of differential responsiveness are summarized graphically in figure 9.2, which shows the estimated weights attached to the ideological

[20] I assume here, for purposes of illustration, that middle-income constituents constitute 40.2% of the public (their average proportion in the Senate Election Study sample). Thus, the estimated effect of shifting middle-income opinion by .321 units (the ideological distance between Massachusetts and Arkansas in figure 9.1) is $.402 \times .321 \times 2.66 = .34$. Since upper-income constituents made up 29.1% of the Senate Election Study sample, the analogous calculation for the estimated effect of shifting upper-income opinion by .321 units is $.291 \times .321 \times 4.15 = .39$.

[21] The last row of table 9.1 presents the difference in estimated responsiveness to high- and low-income constituents in each of the statistical analyses. The *t*-statistics for these differences range from 3.1 (for the 103rd Congress) to 4.3 (for the pooled analysis including all three Congresses). Thus, we can reject with a great deal of confidence the hypothesis that senators were equally sensitive to the views of rich and poor constituents. Even the differences in responsiveness between the middle- and low-income groups are much too large to be coincidental, with *t*-statistics (not shown) ranging from 2.0 to 3.0.

[22] The estimated impact of low-income constituency opinion is actually negative in each case, but quite small both in absolute terms and in comparison to the standard error of the estimate. More generally, the estimated effects of low-income constituency opinion throughout this chapter are often negative, occasionally positive, but never large enough to rule out zero as a plausible value.

[23] Achen (1978) pointed out that Miller and Stokes's (1963) pioneering analysis of congressional representation was plagued by measurement error in constituency opinions due to the small number of survey respondents in each congressional district (13, on average). Because the Senate Election Study included at least 150 respondents in each state, measurement error is likely to be a much less serious problem in my analysis. However, in order to gauge the effect of measurement error on the results reported here, I repeated the regression analyses presented in table 9.1 using an instrumental variables estimator, which is less efficient than ordinary regression analysis but produces consistent parameter estimates in spite of measurement errors in the explanatory variables (see, for example, Fuller 1987, 50–59, 148–163). Instrumental variables estimation is facilitated here by the availability of independent measures of state ideology generated from separate, roughly contemporaneous surveys by Erikson, Wright, and McIver (1993)

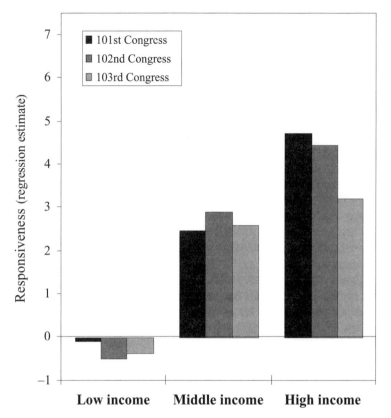

Figure 9.2 Senators' Responsiveness to Income Groups (W-NOMINATE Scores)

and Park, Gelman, and Bafumi (2002). Using these independent estimates of state ideology, an indicator variable for southern states, the average income of each state's respondents in the Senate Election Study surveys, and interactions between average income and each of the other variables as instruments for the income-specific measures of ideology in the Senate Election Study surveys produced generally similar, though much less precise, results. The estimated gap in responsiveness to high- and low-income groups is 45% larger than in table 9.1; however, that difference is not large enough to reach conventional standards of statistical significance, since the standard errors attached to the estimates of constituency responsiveness from the instrumental variables regression are two to three times as large as the corresponding standard errors in table 9.1. The party-specific results paralleling those presented in tables 9.6 and 9.7 below are in closer agreement—the estimated responsiveness gap for Republican senators differs by less than 20%, while the two estimates for Democratic senators are virtually identical. These results suggest that measurement error in constituency opinion probably has only a modest effect on the estimates of responsiveness reported in the text—and that the reduced bias of the instrumental variables estimates is almost certainly outweighed by their greater imprecision.

views of low-, middle-, and high-income constituents in each of the three Congresses covered by my analysis. The roughly linear increase in apparent responsiveness across the three income groups, with those in the bottom third getting no weight and those in the middle and top thirds getting substantial weight, suggests that the modern Senate comes a good deal closer to equal representation of *incomes* than to equal representation of *citizens*.[24]

The roll call scores analyzed in table 9.1 are summary measures of senators' ideological positions on the whole range of issues that reached the floor of the Senate in the 101st, 102nd, and 103rd Congresses. In order to test the robustness of the statistical results I also examined senators' votes on four specific roll calls on salient issues during this period.[25] One of these is the same 1989 vote to increase the federal minimum wage analyzed in table 8.4. The other three votes are a 1990 cloture vote on an amendment strengthening the Civil Rights Act, a 1991 vote on a Budget Act waiver shifting $3.15 billion in budget authority from the Defense Department to domestic programs, and a 1992 cloture vote on removing the "firewall" between defense and domestic appropriations.[26] Descriptions of these roll call votes are presented in table 9.2.

The behavior of senators on these four specific, salient roll call votes reveals disparities in responsiveness to the views of wealthy, middle-class, and poor constituents even more extreme than for the broader range of issues represented by senators' W-NOMINATE scores. The results of statistical analyses relating senators' votes to their constituents' preferences and their own partisan affiliations are presented in table 9.3. The analyses parallel those in table 9.1, with separate estimates for the effects of low-, middle-, and high-

[24] In an earlier version of the analysis reported here (Bartels 2002b) I included direct measures of average constituency opinion and income-weighted constituency opinion in each state, rather than separate measures of opinion among low-, middle-, and high-income constituents. That linear specification of differential responsiveness produced results quite consistent with those reported here. Pooling the data from all three Congresses produced a parameter estimate for unweighted constituency opinion of −.20 (with a standard error of .62), while the parameter estimate for income-weighted constituency opinion (with family incomes measured in thousands of dollars) was .062 (with a standard error of .021). Thus, even more literally than here, the results of that analysis suggested that senators represent *income* rather than *constituents*.

[25] I selected salient roll call votes from among the "key votes" featured in *Congressional Quarterly* and the *Almanac of American Politics*, avoiding lopsided roll calls and those on which either party was unanimous. For each roll call, I counted senators who paired or announced in favor as "yea" votes and those who paired or announced against as "nay" votes; senators who paired without taking a position, voted "present," or did not vote are excluded from my analysis.

[26] I chose roll call votes that were relatively close and widely regarded as politically consequential. Senate support for the conservative position on these four roll calls ranged from 37 votes on the minimum wage to 69 votes on the 1991 budget waiver. As it happens, a "yea" vote on each of these roll calls represented a liberal ideological position; however, I reversed the coding of the votes so that, as in table 9.1, the coefficients for Republican senators and conservative constituencies are expected to be positive.

TABLE 9.2
Selected Ideological Roll Call Votes, 1989–1994

Minimum Wage. HR2. Minimum Wage Restoration Act of 1989. Amends the Fair Labor Standards Act of 1938 to increase the federal minimum wage per hour from $3.35 to $3.85 in FY 1990, $4.25 in FY 1991, and $4.55 in FY 1992 and thereafter. Vote on final passage.
    Record Vote No. 39; April 12, 1989. 63–37.

Civil Rights. S2104. Civil Rights Act of 1990. To invoke cloture on the Kennedy (D-MA) amendment restoring and strengthening civil rights laws banning discrimination in employment and for other purposes.
    Record Vote No. 158; July 17, 1990. 62–38 (60 required to invoke cloture).

Budget Waiver. HR2707. Fiscal 1992 Labor, Health and Human Services, and Education Appropriations. Harkin (D-IA) motion to waive the Budget Act, to rescind $3.15 billion in budget authority from unobligated balances in Defense Department accounts and transfer the budget authority to domestic programs including Head Start, Low-Income Home Energy Assistance, State Legalization Impact Assistance Grants, and Pell Grants.
    Record Vote No. 182; September 10, 1991. 28–69 (60 required to waive).

Budget Cloture. S2399. Appropriations Category Reform Act of 1992. To invoke cloture on the motion to proceed to the bill to modify the 1990 Budget Enforcement Act to eliminate firewalls prohibiting shifting of funds between defense and domestic appropriations.
    Record Vote No. 56; March 26, 1992. 51–48 (60 required to invoke cloture).

Sources: *Congressional Quarterly*; Senate Legislative Information System.

income constituents' ideological views as well as each senator's own partisan affiliation.[27]

On one of the four issues considered in table 9.3, the budget cloture vote, the apparent sensitivity of senators to the ideological views of high-income constituents was comparable in magnitude to the corresponding estimates in table 9.1. However, for each of the other three issues senators seem to have been a good deal more sensitive to the views of high-income constituents

[27] Since each senator's vote is a dichotomous outcome, table 9.3 reports probit coefficients rather than ordinary regression coefficients. Since the scale on which probit coefficients is estimated is essentially arbitrary, I rescaled the results for each roll call (setting the coefficient for senators' partisan affiliations to 1.0) in order to facilitate comparison of the probit results across roll calls. As it happens, this normalization also makes the probit results roughly comparable to the ordinary regression results reported in table 9.1 (where the coefficients for senators' partisan affiliations range from .91 to .99). Conventional probit results can be recovered by dividing each of the parameter estimates and standard errors in table 9.3 by the estimated value of σ (the standard deviation of the stochastic disturbances in the underlying probit relationship) in the same column of the table.

TABLE 9.3
Differential Responsiveness on Salient Ideological Roll Call Votes

Rescaled probit coefficients (with standard errors in parentheses) for conservative positions on roll call votes.

	Minimum wage	Civil rights	Budget waiver	Budget cloture
Low-income constituency opinion	−.70 (1.61)	−1.64 (1.52)	1.54 (2.99)	−1.67 (1.77)
Middle-income constituency opinion	.95 (1.77)	2.22 (1.96)	7.43 (3.75)	4.42 (2.31)
High-income constituency opinion	14.63 (4.40)	10.52 (4.04)	10.71 (4.86)	3.98 (3.09)
Republican senator	1.00 (.20)	1.00 (.19)	1.00 (.25)	1.00 (.15)
Intercept	−1.29 (.34)	−1.15 (.32)	−.87 (.30)	−.78 (.20)
σ	.252	.254	.689	.362
Log likelihood	−22.97	−20.57	−41.51	−30.70
Pseudo-R²	.65	.69	.29	.55
N	100	100	97	99
High- vs. Low-income responsiveness gap	15.33 (4.72)	12.16 (4.46)	9.17 (6.19)	5.65 (3.95)

Source: Calculations based on data from Senate Legislative Information System and NES Senate Election Study.

than on the day-to-day business summarized in the w-NOMINATE scores. In the case of the civil rights and budget waiver votes, the statistical results presented in table 9.3 imply that the effect of a senator's own party affiliation would be entirely neutralized by a shift in the views of his affluent constituents from one extreme to the other of the observed distribution of ideological opinion. For the minimum wage vote an even smaller shift in opinion among high-income constituents—say, from the average opinion in California to the average opinion in West Virginia—would have been sufficient to counteract the effect of senators' own partisan loyalties.[28]

In contrast, the ideological views of low-income constituents seem to have been just as irrelevant for these salient roll call votes as they were for the day-to-day business of the Senate. Three of the four estimates for low-income

[28] The average opinion of Californians on the −1 to +1 ideology scale was .034; the average opinion of West Virginians was .266. An ideological shift of (.266−.034 =) .232 units by high-income constituents (29.1% of the total Senate Election Study sample) would produce a shift on the underlying probit scale for the Minimum Wage vote of .291 × .232 × 14.63 = .99, exactly counterbalancing the difference between Democratic and Republican senators. Analogously, .291 × .321 × 10.52 = .98 for the Civil Rights vote and .291 × .321 × 10.71 = 1.00 for the Budget Waiver vote, again matching the estimated impact of senators' own partisanship.

opinion in table 9.3 are negative, and all four are small enough to be statistically indistinguishable from zero. The results for the vote on raising the minimum wage reflect the political plight of low-income constituents with special poignancy. Those results suggest that senators attached no weight at all to the views of constituents in the bottom third of the income distribution—the constituents whose economic interests were obviously most directly at stake—even as they voted to approve a minimum wage increase. The views of middle-income constituents seem to have been only slightly more influential. On this issue, even more than the others considered in table 9.3, senators' voting decisions were largely driven by the ideological predilections of their affluent constituents and by their own partisan inclinations.

UNEQUAL RESPONSIVENESS ON SOCIAL ISSUES: THE CASE OF ABORTION

The results presented in tables 9.1 and 9.3 provide strong evidence of senators' differential responsiveness to the views of rich and poor constituents. However, there is some reason to wonder whether economic inequality might be less consequential in the domain of social issues, which tend to be "easier" for constituents to grasp than ideological issues and less directly tied to economic interests.[29] The civil rights vote analyzed in table 9.3 is something of a hybrid in this respect, since it taps both general ideology (the federal government's role in preventing discrimination) and the partially distinct issue of race.[30] However, a more extensive analysis of representation in the domain of social issues requires focusing on an issue that figured more prominently on the congressional agenda than civil rights did in the late 1980s and early 1990s. The obvious choice is abortion.

Here, I examine four key roll call votes touching on various controversial aspects of abortion policy in the period covered by the NES Senate Election Study: requiring parental notification prior to abortions performed on minors, overturning the Bush administration's "gag rule" on abortion counseling, prohibiting federal funding of most abortions, and criminalizing efforts to obstruct access to abortion clinics. Descriptions of these roll call votes are presented in table 9.4.

I measure constituency opinion in each state using the same NES abortion question introduced in chapter 3. As with the more general liberal-conservative

[29] The distinction between "easy" and "hard" issues is due to Carmines and Stimson (1980). More prosaically, it is also possible that the results presented in tables 9.1 and 9.3 might reflect some idiosyncratic feature of the NES conservatism scale, which I use to measure constituency ideology.

[30] On the relationship between racial issues and general ideology, see Carmines and Stimson (1989) and Poole and Rosenthal (1997), 109–112.

TABLE 9.4
Selected Abortion Roll Call Votes, 1989–1994

Parental Notification. HR5257. Fiscal 1991 Labor, Health and Human Services, Education, and Related Agencies Appropriations. Harkin (D-IA) motion to table the Armstrong (R-CO) amendment to the committee amendment to HR 5257 requiring notification of a parent or legal guardian prior to an abortion on a minor.
Record Vote No. 266; October 12, 1990. 48–48.

Counseling Ban. S323. Family Planning Amendments Act of 1992. Overriding presidential veto of the bill to reauthorize Title X of the Public Health Service Act for five years; the bill would overturn the Bush administration's "gag rule" and thus allow abortion counseling at federally funded family planning clinics.
Record Vote No. 254; October 1, 1992. 73–26 (66 required to override).

Public Funding. HR2518. Fiscal 1994 Labor, Health and Human Services, and Education Appropriations. Committee amendment to strike the Hyde amendment provisions included in the House bill that prohibit federal funds from covering abortions except in cases of rape, incest or when the life of the woman is endangered.
Record Vote No. 290; September 28, 1993. 40–59.

Clinic Access. S636. Freedom of Access to Clinic Entrances Act of 1994. Adoption of the conference report to establish federal criminal and civil penalties for people who use force, the threat of force or physical obstruction to block access to abortion clinics.
Record Vote No. 112; May 12, 1994. 69–30.

Sources: Congressional Quarterly; Senate Legislative Information System.

scale, responses are recoded to range from −1 to +1, with negative values reflecting pro-life opinion and positive values reflecting pro-choice opinion.[31] Table 9.5 presents the results of statistical analyses relating senators' votes on the four abortion roll calls to their constituents' views about abortion and their own partisan affiliations.[32]

Every one of the four abortion roll call votes analyzed in table 9.5 provides additional evidence of senators' differential responsiveness to the views of affluent constituents. In general, the disparities are smaller than those for the ideological roll call votes considered in table 9.3. Moreover, for two of the

[31] Given my coding of the response options in the NES abortion question, the estimated balance of opinion is pro-choice in all but four states (Kentucky, Mississippi, West Virginia, and Louisiana). Not surprisingly, public opinion about abortion is correlated with more general ideological views. The correlation between conservatism and pro-choice opinion at the individual level is −.25, and the corresponding correlation between state-level conservatism and pro-choice opinion is −.69.

[32] Because a "yea" vote represented the pro-choice position on each of these roll calls, both abortion opinion and Democratic partisanship are expected to have positive effects on the probability of casting a "yea" vote. Senate support for the pro-choice position on these four roll calls ranged from 40 votes in support of public funding to 73 votes in favor of overturning the abortion counseling ban.

TABLE 9.5
Differential Responsiveness on Abortion Roll Call Votes

Rescaled probit coefficients (with standard errors in parentheses) for pro-choice positions on roll call votes.

	Parental notification	Counseling ban	Public funding	Clinic access
Low-income constituency opinion	−.20 (2.04)	1.09 (1.69)	−1.24 (2.32)	−2.14 (1.74)
Middle-income constituency opinion	1.94 (2.29)	−.75 (2.51)	5.13 (2.47)	2.85 (2.29)
High-income constituency opinion	4.79 (1.85)	6.35 (2.40)	3.48 (1.83)	2.23 (1.74)
Democratic senator	1.00 (.18)	1.00 (.20)	1.00 (.20)	1.00 (.18)
Intercept	−1.08 (.22)	−.53 (.16)	−1.39 (.26)	−.49 (.17)
σ	.545	.432	.603	.488
Log likelihood	−42.30	−31.94	−44.67	−37.55
Pseudo-R²	.36	.44	.33	.38
N	96	99	99	99
High- vs. Low-income responsiveness gap	4.99 (2.87)	5.26 (2.66)	4.72 (3.15)	4.38 (2.51)

Source: Calculations based on data from Senate Legislative Information System and NES Senate Election Study.

four votes the parameter estimate for middle-income opinion is larger than the corresponding parameter estimate for high-income opinion (though these estimates are far too imprecise for the differences to be statistically reliable). Thus, the overall pattern of responsiveness is somewhat more egalitarian in table 9.5 than in table 9.3. However, the political irrelevance of constituents in the bottom third of the income distribution is just as apparent for abortion votes as for economic issues; and the estimated responsiveness gaps (in the last row of table 9.5) provide strong, consistent evidence of affluent advantage. These results make it clear that differential responsiveness was not limited to ideological issues or to the specific measure of general ideological opinion in the Senate Election Study. Even on abortion—a social issue with little or no specifically economic content—economic inequality produced substantial inequality in political representation.

PARTISAN DIFFERENCES IN REPRESENTATION

My analysis thus far provides considerable evidence that senators were more responsive to the opinions of affluent constituents than of middle-class

TABLE 9.6
Differential Responsiveness of Republican Senators

Ordinary least squares regression coefficients (with standard errors in parentheses) for Poole-Rosenthal W-NOMINATE scores.

	101st Congress	102nd Congress	103rd Congress	1989–1994 (Pooled)
Low-income constituency opinion	−.36 (1.07)	−.52 (1.07)	.19 (1.11)	−.24 (.75)
Middle-income constituency opinion	2.78 (1.45)	2.95 (1.45)	2.45 (1.37)	2.72 (1.26)
High-income constituency opinion	6.59 (2.22)	6.91 (2.21)	6.79 (2.24)	6.77 (2.02)
Intercept	−.04 (.13)	−.10 (.13)	−.10 (.12)	Congress-specific intercepts; observations clustered by senator
Standard error of regression	.263	.262	.257	.255
Adjusted R^2	.20	.22	.23	.24
N	45	44	44	133
High- vs. Low-income responsiveness gap	6.95 (2.50)	7.43 (2.50)	6.59 (2.57)	7.01 (2.20)

Source: Calculations based on data from Voteview.com and NES Senate Election Study.

constituents. More surprisingly, it provides strong evidence that senators were totally unresponsive to the opinions of constituents in the bottom third of the income distribution. In this section I examine whether these patterns of differential responsiveness were similar for Republican and Democratic senators. Given the distinct class bases of the parties' electoral coalitions, one might expect Republican senators to be especially sensitive to the opinions of affluent constituents and Democrats to attach more weight to the opinions of less affluent constituents. However, votes, campaign contributions, and the various other political resources associated with higher income are clearly valuable to politicians of both parties. Thus, Democrats as well as Republicans may be especially responsive to the views of resource-rich constituents, notwithstanding the historical association of the Democratic Party with the political interests of the working class and the poor.

I look for partisan differences in responsiveness by repeating the analyses of differential responsiveness reported in table 9.1 separately for senators in each party. The results are summarized in table 9.6 for Republicans and in table 9.7

TABLE 9.7

Differential Responsiveness of Democratic Senators

Ordinary least squares regression coefficients (with standard errors in parentheses) for Poole-Rosenthal w-NOMINATE scores.

	101st Congress	102nd Congress	103rd Congress	1989–1994 (Pooled)
Low-income constituency opinion	.32 (.68)	−.28 (.65)	−.55 (.44)	−.18 (.44)
Middle-income constituency opinion	2.20 (.75)	2.85 (.73)	2.69 (.51)	2.59 (.63)
High-income constituency opinion	3.76 (1.01)	3.33 (.96)	1.84 (.66)	2.98 (.66)
Intercept	−.84 (.05)	−.93 (.05)	−.87 (.03)	Congress-specific intercepts; observations clustered by senator
Standard error of regression	.173	.170	.116	.155
Adjusted R^2	.42	.40	.47	.44
N	55	58	57	170
High- vs. Low-income responsiveness gap	3.44 (1.38)	3.62 (1.30)	2.39 (.89)	3.16 (.83)

Source: Calculations based on data from Voteview.com and NES Senate Election Study.

for Democrats. Not surprisingly, the statistical results for each party's senators considered separately—especially for Republicans—are much less precise than those for the entire Senate.[33] Despite that imprecision, three facts emerge. First, Republican senators were about twice as responsive as Democrats to the views of high-income constituents. Second, Democrats and Republicans were about equally responsive to the views of middle-income constituents; thus, the roughly linear increase in apparent responsiveness from one income group to the next in figure 9.2 seems to overstate the gap in influence between the middle and upper classes for Democratic senators while un-

---

[33] The greater imprecision of the statistical results for Republican senators is not only due to the fact that there were fewer Republicans than Democrats in the Senate during the period covered by my analysis. It also reflects the fact, evident in figure 9.1, that constituency opinion was considerably less variable for Republicans than for Democrats (or for the Senate as a whole) in an era when very conservative voters in states like Alabama, Arkansas, Georgia, and West Virginia were still routinely electing Democratic senators. For both these reasons, my estimates of the impact of constituency ideology on senators' voting behavior are much less precise for Republican senators than for Democrats, with standard errors about twice as large.

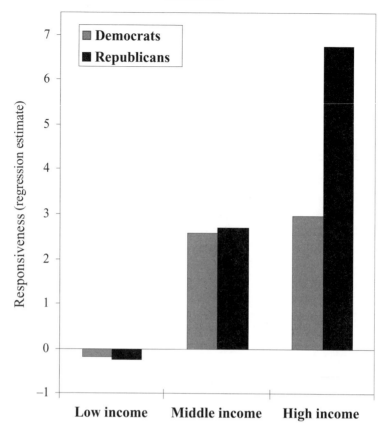

Figure 9.3 Democratic and Republican Senators' Responsiveness to Income Groups

derstating the gap for Republican senators. Finally, there is still no evidence here of any responsiveness to the views of constituents in the bottom third of the income distribution, even from Democratic senators.

The patterns of differential responsiveness implied by these results is summarized in figure 9.3, which shows separate estimates of responsiveness for senators in each party (from the analysis combining data from all three Congresses) comparable to the overall estimates presented in figure 9.2. The figure makes clear both the similar responsiveness of Republican and Democratic senators to low- and middle-income constituents and their divergent responsiveness to high-income constituents.[34]

Table 9.8 reports estimates of responsiveness for the entire Senate and

---

[34] The *t*-statistic for the estimated partisan difference in responsiveness to high-income constituents is 1.8, suggesting that the true difference is more than 95% likely to be positive.

TABLE 9.8

Responsiveness on Salient Ideological Votes, by Party

Rescaled probit coefficients (with standard errors in parentheses) for conservative positions on minimum wage, civil rights, budget waiver, and budget cloture votes (pooled).

	All senators	Republicans	Democrats
Low-income constituency opinion	−.92 (1.30)	−.36 (2.19)	−1.28 (1.44)
Middle-income constituency opinion	2.87 (1.23)	−.37 (2.23)	5.98 (1.64)
High-income constituency opinion	7.91 (2.53)	18.90 (4.34)	4.18 (2.54)
Republican senator	1.00 (.13)	—	—
Intercept	Roll call–specific intercepts; observations clustered by senator	Roll call–specific intercepts; observations clustered by senator	Roll call–specific intercepts; observations clustered by senator
σ	.374		
Log likelihood	−129.42	−50.01	−62.81
Pseudo-R^2	.53	.29	.41
N	396	175	221
High- vs. Low-income responsiveness gap	8.84 (2.93)	19.26 (5.05)	5.46 (2.84)

Source: Calculations based on data from Senate Legislative Information System and NES Senate Election Study.

separately for Republican and Democratic senators on the four salient ideological roll call votes analyzed in table 9.3. Table 9.9 does the same for the four abortion roll call votes analyzed in table 9.5. In each case, the analyses combine data from all four roll call votes in order to generate more precise estimates of differential responsiveness for each party's Senate delegation.[35]

The results presented in table 9.8 are qualitatively similar to those presented in tables 9.6 and 9.7 but even more striking in magnitude. For Republican senators there is no evidence of responsiveness to middle-income constituents, much less low-income constituents. The views of high-income

[35] As with the issue-by-issue analyses presented in tables 9.3 and 9.5, I normalize the probit coefficients to produce a coefficient of 1.00 on party affiliation. I apply the same normalization to the separate analyses for Republican and Democratic senators. Thus, I assume that the same scale factor σ represents the magnitude of unobserved stochastic influences on the voting behavior of Republicans and Democrats on all four roll calls in each table. (Allowing distinct scale factors for each roll call would make party-specific estimation untenable in cases whether either party's delegation was nearly unanimous.) However, I allow for the possibility of different choice thresholds (that is, probit intercepts) for each roll call (and, in the party-specific analyses, for each party).

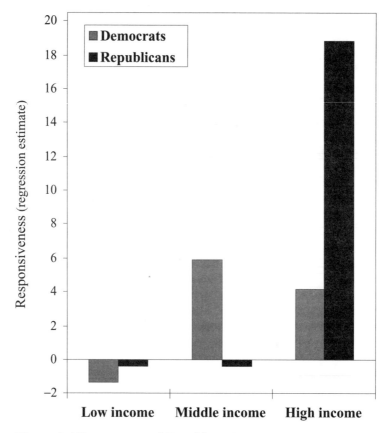

Figure 9.4 Democratic and Republican Senators' Responsiveness on Ideological Roll Call Votes

constituents, however, seem to have received a great deal of weight from Republican senators on these four issues—almost three times as much as in table 9.6, and more than four times as much as for Democrats in the right-most column of table 9.8. Meanwhile, Democrats seem to have responded at least as strongly to the views of middle-income constituents as to the views of high-income constituents—though, once again, there is no evidence of any responsiveness to the views of low-income constituents. These patterns of responsiveness are displayed graphically in figure 9.4.

The results for abortion votes presented in table 9.9 reflect a generally similar pattern. Again, neither party's senators seem to have attached any weight at all to the views of low-income constituents. Again, Democrats seem to have been somewhat more responsive to the views of middle-income constituents, while Republicans were more responsive to the views of upper-

TABLE 9.9
Responsiveness on Abortion Votes, by Party

Rescaled probit coefficients (with standard errors in parentheses) for pro-choice positions on parental notification, counseling ban, public funding, and clinic access votes (pooled).

	All senators	Republicans	Democrats
Low-income constituency opinion	−.77 (1.28)	−1.00 (1.49)	−.45 (2.04)
Middle-income constituency opinion	2.61 (1.59)	1.19 (2.34)	4.44 (2.28)
High-income constituency opinion	3.93 (1.19)	4.34 (1.77)	3.27 (1.46)
Democratic senator	1.00 (.13)	—	—
Intercept	Roll call–specific intercepts; observations clustered by senator	Roll call–specific intercepts; observations clustered by senator	Roll call–specific intercepts; observations clustered by senator
σ	.526		
Log likelihood	−160.32	−85.20	−72.62
Pseudo-R²	.40	.19	.31
N	393	173	220
High- vs. Low-income responsiveness gap	4.70 (1.71)	5.33 (2.20)	3.71 (2.39)

Source: Calculations based on data from Senate Legislative Information System and NES Senate Election Study.

income constituents. However, these differences between the two parties were much more modest for abortion votes than for the ideological votes examined in table 9.8. It is also worth noting that senators were generally less responsive to the opinions of affluent constituents on abortion votes than on ideological votes. This difference is evident in figure 9.5, which presents the estimated effects of constituency opinion for each party's senators on the same scale employed in figure 9.4.

The intraparty analyses summarized in figures 9.3, 9.4, and 9.5 indicate that upper-income constituents got a good deal less responsiveness from Democratic senators than from Republican senators. It seems natural to wonder whether they also got less responsiveness from Democrats than from Republicans in the White House. The fortuitous fact that the roll call votes analyzed here spanned the partisan turnover from the first President Bush to President Clinton allows for a rough test of that possibility. The statistical results presented in table 9.1 imply that senators were considerably more responsive to upper-income constituents when a Republican was in the White House (during the 101st and 102nd Congresses) than they were with a Democrat in the

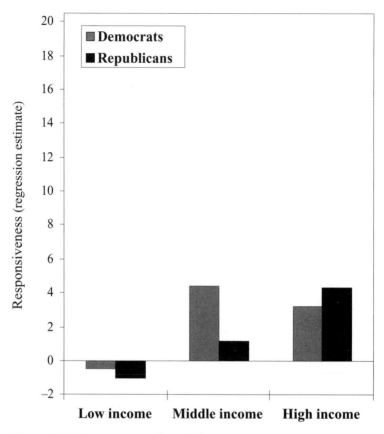

Figure 9.5 Democratic and Republican Senators' Responsiveness on Abortion Roll Call Votes

White House (during the 103rd Congress). Constituents in the upper third of the income distribution got 52% and 91% more weight than those in the middle third in the two Congresses of the Bush administration, but only 25% more under Clinton. The results for individual roll call votes are generally consistent with this pattern. (The only two votes on which estimated responsiveness to the middle class exceeded estimated responsiveness to the upper class by more than 11% were the two from Clinton's presidency—the abortion funding vote in 1993 and the clinic access vote in 1994. On the other hand, for the six roll call votes selected from the Bush administration, senators' average responsiveness to upper-income constituents was more than three times their average responsiveness to middle-income constituents.) These comparisons, though obviously far from definitive, suggest that differential responsiveness may stem not only from the partisan values of senators themselves, but also from the partisan values of presidents whose agenda-setting and lobbying activities may mitigate or exacerbate economic biases in congressional representation.

WHY ARE THE POOR UNREPRESENTED?

The evidence presented here indicates that senators are consistently responsive to the views of affluent constituents but entirely *un*responsive to those with low incomes. In this section I turn to a brief consideration of the bases of this unequal responsiveness.

One common reaction to the evidence presented here is: "Of course the poor don't get represented; they don't vote!" This reaction is a natural reflection of the appealing idea that elected representatives are disciplined by a desire to get reelected. The flip side of that appealing idea, as V. O. Key Jr. observed, is that "politicians and officials are under no compulsion to pay much heed to classes and groups of citizens that do not vote."[36] While that may be true, it is by no means obvious that politicians *would* pay much heed to the views of the poor if they *did* vote. It may be naïve to put so much faith in the responsiveness of elected representatives to the preferences of voters—and unfair to push the blame for unresponsiveness, at least implicitly, onto poor nonvoters.

The actual magnitude of disparities in turnout across income groups casts some doubt on the notion that nonresponsiveness to the poor is due to their failure to vote. For example, 80% of the high-income respondents in the Senate Election Study surveys reported having voted in the most recent election; but so did 60% of the low-income respondents. Even with considerable allowance for overreporting of turnout, it is obvious that tens of millions of low-income citizens are showing up at the polls. Nevertheless, low-income citizens as a group seem to be getting *no* representation, whereas high-income people are getting considerable of representation. Income-related disparities in turnout simply do not seem large enough to provide a plausible explanation for the income-related disparities in responsiveness documented here.

Of course, poor people are less engaged in the political process in other potentially relevant ways besides voting. Perhaps their views are ignored because they are less knowledgeable about politics; uninformed constituents are less likely to have crystallized preferences on specific political issues and are less likely to be able to monitor their representatives' behavior.[37] Perhaps the

[36] Key (1949), 527. The implications of this logic for disparities in the "voting power" of citizens are elaborated in Bartels (1998).

[37] Converse (1990); Delli Carpini and Keeter (1996). I constructed a four-point political knowledge scale measuring respondents' ability to name their senators (or Senate candidates) and identify which party they represented. "And how about the two U.S. Senators from your state. Do you happen to remember what their names were? . . . What is [NAME]'s party affiliation?" I assigned

views of poor people are ignored because they are less likely to communicate those views to elected officials; personal contact with elected officials and their staffs provides potentially important signals regarding both the content and intensity of constituents' political views.[38]

To test these possibilities, I used survey questions in the NES Senate Election Study to measure inequalities in political knowledge and contacting as well as turnout. Not surprisingly, knowledge and contact with public officials, like turnout, were much more prevalent among affluent people than among poor people. Indeed, income-related differences in knowledge and contact were considerably larger, in proportional terms, than income-related differences in turnout; the average levels of knowledge and contacting among low-income respondents were less than half the average levels among high-income respondents. These differences are summarized in table 9.10, which reports average levels of turnout, knowledge, and contact for the entire Senate Election Study sample and for low-, middle-, and high-income respondents separately.

I used these measures of individual citizens' turnout, knowledge, and contacting behavior from the Senate Election Study to construct resource-weighted measures of constituency opinion for each state. For example, turnout-weighted constituency opinion in each state reflects the ideological views of survey respondents in that state who reported voting in the most recent election, but ignores the views of those who said they did not vote. Insofar as the views of voters differ from the views of nonvoters, turnout-weighted constituency opinion should be expected to push senators in somewhat different directions than if they were responsive to overall constituency opinion.

These resource-weighted measures of constituency opinion make it possible to explore the bases of the disparities in responsiveness evident in tables 9.1, 9.3, and 9.5. If those disparities are attributable to differences between

---

one point for knowing each senator's name and one point for knowing each senator's party affiliation. In states with just-concluded Senate elections, I averaged the knowledge ratings for both candidates. The resulting information scale was recoded to range from zero (for people who recalled neither senator's name) to one (for people who recalled both senators' names and party affiliations).

[38] Verba, Schlozman, and Brady (1995). I measured contact using a six-point scale derived from respondents' reports of having met with senators or members of their staffs. "U.S. Senators can have contact with the people from their state in many ways. I will read a list of some of these ways. Think of [NAME], who has been a U.S. Senator in Washington. Have you met [him/her] personally? . . . Have you talked to a member of [his/her] staff or to someone in [his/her] office? . . . Do you know anyone, any of your family, friends, or people at work, who have had some contact with [him/her]?" I assigned one point for a positive response to each of these three questions for each senator. (Since the questions were not asked about retiring senators, in those cases I counted a positive response for *either* candidate in the just-concluded campaign.) The six-point scale was recoded to range from zero (for no reported contacts) to one (for all three contacts with both senators).

TABLE 9.10

Turnout, Knowledge, and Contact, by Income Group

Mean (with standard error in parentheses) and standard deviation of turnout, knowledge, and contact in NES Senate Election Study, by income groups. Sample post-stratified within states by education, race, age, sex, and work status.

		Turnout	Knowledge	Contact
Total sample	Mean	.694 (.005)	.282 (.004)	.184 (.003)
(N=9,253)	Standard deviation	.461	.365	.255
Low income	Mean	.598 (.010)	.171 (.006)	.123 (.004)
(N=2,628)	Standard deviation	.490	.293	.206
Middle income	Mean	.684 (.008)	.275 (.006)	.177 (.004)
(N=3,738)	Standard deviation	.465	.360	.248
High income	Mean	.810 (.007)	.409 (.007)	.256 (.005)
(N=2,887)	Standard deviation	.392	.398	.292

Source: Calculations based on data from NES Senate Election Study.

rich and poor constituents in turnout, information, or contacting, including direct measures of constituency preferences weighted by turnout, information, and contacting in my analyses should capture those effects. For example, if senators were more responsive to the views of affluent constituents because affluent constituents were more likely to vote, including turnout-weighted constituency opinion in analyses paralleling those presented in tables 9.1, 9.3, and 9.5 should drive the remaining disparities in responsiveness to different income groups to zero. But if significant disparities in responsiveness to rich and poor constituents still appear even after allowing for differences attributable to turnout, the implication is that the effect of income works through mechanisms other than differential turnout—or perhaps that money matters in its own right (for example, through responsiveness of elected officials to potential campaign contributors).

Significant disparities in responsiveness to rich and poor constituents *do* still appear even after allowing for differences attributable to turnout, knowledge, and contacting. These disparities are reported in table 9.11, which presents the results of my elaborated analyses, including turnout-weighted, knowledge-weighted, and contact-weighted constituency opinion. The analysis reported in the first column of the table combines roll call scores from the 101st, 102nd, and 103rd Congresses (as in the fourth column of table 9.1). The analysis reported in the second column is based on the four salient ideological votes (elaborating the analysis reported in the first column of table 9.8). The analysis reported in the third column is based on the four abortion votes (elaborating the analysis reported in the first column of table 9.9).

TABLE 9.11
Income, Political Resources, and Differential Responsiveness

Ordinary least squares regression coefficients (with standard errors in parentheses) for Poole-Rosenthal W-NOMINATE scores in 101st, 102nd, and 103rd Congresses (pooled). Rescaled probit coefficients (with standard errors in parentheses) for conservative positions on minimum wage, civil rights, budget waiver, and budget cloture votes (pooled). Rescaled probit coefficients (with standard errors in parentheses) for pro-choice positions on parental notification, counseling ban, public funding, and clinic access votes (pooled).

	W-NOMINATE scores	Ideological votes	Abortion votes
Low-income constituency opinion	−.74 (.65)	−.98 (1.72)	−2.15 (1.48)
Middle-income constituency opinion	2.04 (.67)	2.13 (1.66)	1.23 (1.77)
High-income constituency opinion	2.66 (1.31)	5.03 (3.24)	2.44 (1.42)
Turnout-weighted constituency opinion	.25 (.82)	−.96 (1.75)	2.50 (1.53)
Knowledge-weighted constituency opinion	−1.30 (1.13)	−2.84 (2.52)	−.98 (2.62)
Contact-weighted constituency opinion	4.14 (1.51)	10.99 (3.72)	.32 (3.48)
Republican senator	.94 (.04)	1.00 (.08)	1.00 (.12)
Intercept	Congress-specific intercepts; observations clustered by senator	Roll call–specific intercepts; observations clustered by senator	Roll call–specific intercepts; observations clustered by senator
σ	—	.364	.511
Standard error of regression	.201	—	—
Log likelihood	—	−121.42	−158.36
Adjusted R^2	.86	—	—
Pseudo-R^2	—	.56	.41
N	303	396	393
High- vs. Low-income responsiveness gap	3.41 (1.13)	6.00 (2.74)	4.58 (1.74)

Source: Calculations based on data from Voteview.com, Senate Legislative Information System, and NES Senate Election Study.

With all three additional resource-weighted opinion measures included in these analyses, the only one that has a consistent positive effect is contact-weighted opinion.[39] Even in this case, the substantive significance of the apparent effect is modest. The statistical results suggest that each reported contact with a senator or his staff increased the weight attached to the contacting constituent's views by somewhere between 1% (in the case of abortion votes) and 21% (in the case of ideological votes) of the original estimated gap between high- and low-income respondents.[40] Meanwhile, neither turnout nor political knowledge seems to have increased the influence of constituents' views on their senators' roll call votes.[41]

Allowing for differences in turnout, knowledge, and contacting reduces only modestly the substantial income-based disparities in responsiveness evident in my preceding analyses. Comparing the estimated effects reported in the first column of table 9.11 with those in the fourth column of table 9.1 suggests that accounting for differences in turnout, knowledge, and contacting reduces the gap in representation between high-income and low-income constituents by only one-fourth (from 4.48 to 3.41). Similar comparisons between the parameter estimates in the second and third columns of table 9.11 and those in the first columns of tables 9.8 and 9.9 suggest that differences in turnout, knowledge, and contacting account for only one-third of the original disparity in responsiveness on ideological roll call votes and only 3% of the original disparity in responsiveness on abortion votes. In each case the disparities in responsiveness are quite substantial and statistically reliable even with three additional (and strongly correlated) measures of constituency opinion included in the analysis.[42] These results provide surprisingly strong and consistent evidence that the biases I have identified in senators' responsiveness to rich and poor constituents are *not* primarily due

---

[39] The average *t*-statistic for the three separate parameter estimates for contact-weighted opinion is 1.9. The corresponding average *t*-statistics for turnout-weighted opinion and knowledge-weighted opinion are 0.5 and −0.9.

[40] The Senate Election Study allowed respondents to report up to six separate contacts with senators or their staffs. The average constituent reported about one contact (for an average score of .184 on the 0-to-1 contact scale); most reported none at all.

[41] The apparent noneffect of turnout-weighted opinion in table 9.11 contrasts with John Griffin and Brian Newman's (2005) finding that voters are better represented than nonvoters. However, their analysis did not take account of the income-based disparities in responsiveness considered here, or of alternative resource-based explanations for differential responsiveness. Simplifying my analysis to parallel theirs—replacing the separate opinion measures for high-, middle-, and low-income constituents with a single measure of undifferentiated constituency opinion, and including turnout-weighted opinion but not contact-weighted opinion or knowledge-weighted opinion measures—generally produces positive and statistically significant coefficients on turnout-weighted opinion. The fact that these apparent effects disappear when we differentiate the views of high-, middle-, and low-income constituents suggests that voters get more representation because they are affluent, not because they vote.

[42] The *t*-statistics for the remaining gaps in responsiveness range from 2.2 to 3.0.

to differences between rich and poor constituents in turnout, political knowledge, or contacting.

A tempting alternative hypothesis is that the disproportional influence of affluent constituents reflects their disproportional propensity to contribute money to political campaigns. It is impossible to investigate that possibility directly here, since the Senate Election Study did not include questions on political giving. As it happens, however, a contemporaneous survey focusing in detail on various forms of political participation provides the data necessary for a very rough test of the hypothesis. Verba, Schlozman, and Brady reported that almost three-fourths of the total value of campaign contributions reported by their respondents came from people in the top quarter of the income distribution (with 1989 family incomes exceeding $50,000). People in the broad middle of the income distribution (with family incomes between $15,000 and $50,000) accounted for almost all of the rest; people in the bottom quintile (with family incomes below $15,000) accounted for only 2% of total campaign contributions.[43]

These figures suggest that if senators *only* responded to campaign contributions they would attach about six times as much importance to the views of a typical affluent constituent as to the views of a typical middle-income constituent—and virtually no importance to the views of low-income constituents. All of the disparities in representation documented in this chapter are consistent with the latter implication; regardless of how the data are sliced, there is no discernible evidence that the views of low-income constituents had any effect on their senators' voting behavior. In contrast, the estimated gaps in representation between high-income and middle-income constituents are generally less extreme than the disparity in their campaign contributions would suggest, especially for the day-to-day Senate business reflected in the Poole-Rosenthal w-NOMINATE scores. Nevertheless, it is striking that two of the eight salient roll call votes considered here (raising the minimum wage and overturning limitations on abortion counseling) produced estimated disparities in representation between high-income and middle-income constituents large enough to match or exceed the disparities in campaign giving reported by Verba, Schlozman, and Brady. For these specific issues at least, the data are consistent with the hypothesis that senators represented their campaign contributors to the exclusion of other constituents.

There is clearly a great deal more to be learned about the mechanisms by which economic inequality gets reproduced in the political realm. The simple assumption that the rich are more influential than the poor because they are more likely to vote receives no support in my analysis. The idea that they are more influential because they are better informed about politics and govern-

---

[43] Verba, Schlozman, and Brady (1995), 194, 565.

ment fares equally poorly. The notion that they are more influential because they are more likely to contact government officials receives some support but is far from being the whole story. The even simpler assumption that the rich are more influential than the poor because they provide the contributions that fuel contemporary campaigning and lobbying activities receives somewhat stronger support; but that support is quite indirect, and the role of money in shaping public policy clearly deserves much more careful empirical examination.[44]

It is important to reiterate here that I have been using the terms *responsiveness* and *representation* loosely to refer to the statistical association between constituents' opinions and their senators' behavior. Whether senators behave the way they do *because* their constituents have the opinions they do is impossible to gauge using the research design employed here. It is plausible to imagine that senators consciously and intentionally strive to represent the views of (especially) affluent constituents. However, as Lawrence Jacobs and Benjamin Page have observed in the context of national foreign policy making, public opinion may *seem* to be influential only because it happens to be correlated with the opinion of influential elites, organized interest groups, or the policy makers themselves.[45]

The correlation between public opinion and elite opinion, in turn, may reflect conscious efforts by elites, interest groups, or policy makers to shape public opinion in support of their views, or it might reflect the patterns of political recruitment and advancement that put some kinds of people rather than others in positions of influence in the first place. In the present context, it seems unlikely that affluent constituents are sufficiently well-informed about the policy views of their senators, specifically, for the statistical connection to reflect affluent constituents' responsiveness to senators rather than senators' responsiveness to affluent constituents. However, the fact that senators are themselves affluent, and in many cases extremely wealthy, hardly seems irrelevant to understanding the strong empirical connection between their voting behavior and the preferences of their affluent constituents.[46]

Whatever their basis, the massive disparities in responsiveness documented here are impressively consistent across a variety of political contexts,

---

[44] Hall and Wayman (1990); Ansolabehere, de Figueiredo, and Snyder (2003).

[45] Jacobs and Page (2005).

[46] The salary of U.S. senators increased during the period covered by my analysis from $89,500 to $133,600. The cutoff for the top 5% of the family income distribution over the same period ranged from $99,000 to $120,000. The Senate's financial disclosure forms do not allow for precise estimates of senators' overall financial status, much less their economic backgrounds. However, CNN reported on the basis of 2003 disclosure forms that "at least 40" members of that year's Senate were millionaires, while "[a]t least 10 senators reported net worths of less than $100,000." Sean Loughlin and Robert Yoon, "Millionaires Populate U.S. Senate," CNN, June 13, 2003, http://www.cnn.com/2003/ALLPOLITICS/06/13/senators.finances.

issues, and opinion measures. They are even more impressive in their sheer magnitude. In particular, the fact that senators consistently appear to pay *no* attention to the views of millions of constituents in the bottom third of the income distribution must be profoundly troubling to anyone who accepts Dahl's stipulation that "a key characteristic of a democracy is the continued responsiveness of the government to the preferences of its citizens, considered as political equals."[47]

Do these results imply that it is fruitless for poor people to participate in the electoral process? Not necessarily. Although the evidence presented in this chapter suggests that their views are very unlikely to have a significant *direct* impact on the behavior of their elected officials, whether or not they participate, it also underscores the powerful *indirect* effect of public opinion through the electoral process. In every analysis presented here, the differences in voting behavior between Democratic and Republican senators representing similar constituents are substantial, often dwarfing the differences among Democrats (or Republicans) representing constituents with very different political views. Thus, whenever the votes of those poor people who do turn out make the difference between electing a Democratic senator or a Republican, they will clearly be enormously consequential for the course of public policy, despite the fact that the views of poor people have no *direct* effect on the behavior of Democrats or Republicans after they get elected.

More affluent citizens, however, have significant direct *and* indirect effects on the behavior of elected officials. Although their choices at the polls affect the partisan composition of Congress, their political views also have a substantial direct impact on the day-to-day policy choices of their representatives. That impact is a testament to the ubiquitous sway of economic inequality in the American political system.

[47] Dahl (1971), 1.

CHAPTER 10

Unequal Democracy

Hurricane Katrina evacuation. Photographer: David J. Phillip.
Used with the permission of AP Images.

THE IMPACT OF wealth on political life has been a subject of concern at least
since the time of Aristotle, who surveyed and critiqued the laws of the various Greek city-states regarding limitations on wealth, inheritance, communal
ownership of property, and the extension of citizenship rights to the working
class. Indeed, Aristotle made the relationship between wealth and political
status the fundamental basis for classifying regimes: "what differentiates

oligarchy and democracy is wealth or the lack of it. The essential point is that where the possession of political power is due to the possession of economic power or wealth, whether the number of persons be large or small, that is oligarchy, and when the unpropertied class have power, that is democracy."[1]

In the early modern period, the Italian republics viewed their wealthy citizens as constant threats to political stability and liberty. According to political theorist John McCormick,

> Unless formally restrained, the richest citizens tended to use their privilege to molest fellow citizens with impunity and direct the workings of government toward their own benefit rather than toward that of the general citizenry. . . . If a popular government or republic is not to veer dangerously toward an unaccountable oligarchy, natural or not, institutional affirmative action for common citizens is necessary. In this light, contemporary democracies could do worse than reconsider the extra-electoral practices that earlier republics, their partisans and their theorists often thought were crucial to insure the genuine liberty of citizens.[2]

American history, too, has been marked by periodic popular backlashes against the political effects of concentrated wealth. According to Kevin Phillips, public opinion "has distrusted economic elites and periodically used democratic politics to curb their abuses. Banks, special corporations, railroads, the giant trusts, the 'money power,' Wall Street, and the 'malefactors of great wealth' have all spent decades in the firing zone of angry electorates." The escalating economic inequality and political corruption of the Gilded Age and the Roaring Twenties stimulated the institutional reforms of the Progressive Era and the New Deal. Louis Brandeis, a significant figure in both the Progressive Era and the New Deal, famously wrote that "We can have a democratic society or we can have great concentrated wealth in the hands of a few. We cannot have both."[3]

The economic trends documented in chapter 1 once again raise the question of whether democracy can flourish in the midst of great concentrated wealth. One way of framing this question is to ask, with Sidney Verba and Gary Orren, whether the economic and political "spheres of justice" can be kept "autonomous and their boundaries intact." On that score there seems to me to be little basis for optimism in my examination of the political economy of the New Gilded Age. Economic inequality clearly has pervasive, corrosive effects on political representation and policy making in contemporary America.

[1] Aristotle, *Politics*, T. A. Sinclair, trans. (Harmondsworth: Penguin Books, 1962), books II and III, 117.

[2] McCormick (2006), 147, 161. McCormick's suggestions for "institutional affirmative action for common citizens" included a wealth ceiling on eligibility to serve in the House of Representatives, a modified version of California's "recall referendum," and a citizens' assembly selected by lot to monitor and, if necessary, sanction elected officials.

[3] Phillips (2002), 294, 418.

In light of these effects, the liberal hope for distinct "spheres of justice" with "their boundaries intact" seems naively fastidious and quite probably ineffectual.

Verba and Orren recognized that porous boundaries may allow "transmutation" in both directions: while economic power may be convertible into political power, political power may also be used to alter or mitigate the effects of developments in the economic realm—as it *has* been used more or less effectively in the Progressive Era, the New Deal, and other pivotal moments in American history. Of course, there are substantial risks to justice on that side as well. Still, if economic inequality seriously compromises the values of democracy, it seems worth recalling and assessing the ways and means by which democracy might realistically be employed to constrain economic inequality.[4]

WHO GOVERNS?

This book began with the question Robert Dahl asked nearly half a century ago: "In a political system where nearly every adult may vote but where knowledge, wealth, social position, access to officials, and other resources are unequally distributed, who actually governs?"[5] I suggested that the answer Dahl provided for New Haven in the 1950s might be obsolete in the vastly more unequal America of the twenty-first century, where the share of national income controlled by the wealthiest stratum of "economic notables" is three times as large as it was 50 years ago. However, the remarkable fact is that political scientists have done little to illuminate how the economic and social changes of the New Gilded Age have affected American democracy.

Insofar as Dahl's question is interpreted as asking whose preferences influence policy outcomes, the answer suggested by my analysis in chapter 9 is that affluent people have considerable clout, while the preferences of people in the bottom third of the income distribution have *no* apparent impact on the behavior of their elected officials. Whether we consider the day-to-day business of the Senate in three successive Congresses or specific salient roll call votes on government spending, the minimum wage, civil rights, and abortion, the statistical results are remarkably consistent in suggesting an utter lack of responsiveness to the views of millions of people whose only distinguishing characteristic is their low incomes. Observers of contemporary American politics may be unsurprised to hear that elected officials attached more weight to the preferences of affluent and middle-class constituents than of low-income constituents. However, only the most cynical critic of

[4] Verba and Orren (1985), 8.
[5] Dahl (1961), 1.

American democracy could be unsurprised to learn that low-income constituents seem to have been entirely ignored in the policy-making process.

This pessimistic conclusion finds a parallel in a separate study conducted by Martin Gilens. Gilens collected almost 2,000 survey questions measuring Americans' preferences regarding a wide variety of national policy issues. For each issue, he examined whether a policy change supported or opposed by various segments of the public was subsequently adopted. He found a strong statistical relationship between the views of affluent citizens and the subsequent course of public policy. However, for less affluent citizens the relationship was weaker; and when the analysis was limited to issues on which rich and poor people had divergent preferences, Gilens found that the well-off were vastly more likely to see their views reflected in subsequent policy changes. Gilens concluded that "influence over actual policy outcomes appears to be reserved almost exclusively for those at the top of the income distribution."[6]

What do these findings suggest about the state of American democracy? Political leaders appear to be responding significantly to the policy preferences of millions of middle- and upper-income citizens. This crucial popular element in the American political system is aptly reflected in a term coined by Dahl: *polyarchy*. However, the pattern of responsiveness portrayed in chapter 9, and by Gilens, is a very far cry from approximating Dahl's loftier *democratic* ideal of "continued responsiveness of the government to the preferences of its citizens, considered as political equals." Indeed, Gilens has suggested that "representational biases of this magnitude call into question the very democratic character of our society."[7]

These disparities in representation are especially troubling because they suggest the potential for a debilitating feedback cycle linking the economic and political realms: increasing economic inequality may produce increasing inequality in political responsiveness, which in turn produces public policies that are increasingly detrimental to the interests of poor citizens, which in turn produces even greater economic inequality, and so on. If that is the case, shifts in the income distribution triggered by technological change, demographic shifts, or global economic development may in time become augmented, entrenched, and immutable.

Of course, the patterns of responsiveness documented in chapter 9 are for a single governmental institution in a single six-year period, now more than a decade in the past. Gilens's work is broader in scope, and he has subsequently been gathering and analyzing data that may provide a clearer picture of how disparities in representation have, or have not, varied over decades. Perhaps future scholarly investigation will demonstrate that the disparities in repre-

[6] Gilens (2005), 794.
[7] Dahl (1971); Gilens (2005), 778.

sentation portrayed here are somehow anomalous or otherwise misleading. In the meantime, however, the available evidence is striking and sobering. In Aristotle's terms, our political system seems to be functioning not as a "democracy" but as an "oligarchy." If we insist on flattering ourselves by referring to it as a democracy, we should be clear that it is a starkly *unequal* democracy.

In another sense, the evidence presented in chapter 9 suggests a different answer to Dahl's question. The patterns of responsiveness to constituency opinion documented there were set against a pervasive pattern of divergence in the behavior of Democratic and Republican officials, even when they "represented" the very same constituents. In most cases, even massive differences in the preferences of middle- and upper-income constituents had less effect on senators' policy choices than their own partisan ideologies. Whatever elections may be doing, they are *not* forcing elected officials to cater to the policy preferences of the "median voter." Thus, in a very real sense, the answer to the question of "who actually governs" is: whoever makes a successful claim to have won an election. As Joseph Schumpeter noted more than half a century ago, "collectives act almost exclusively by accepting leadership—this is the dominant mechanism of practically any collective action which is more than a reflex. . . . Democracy does not mean and cannot mean that the people actually rule in any obvious sense of the terms 'people' and 'rule.' Democracy means only that the people have the opportunity of accepting or refusing the men who are to rule them."[8]

The scope for independent action by elected leaders may be especially great in cases where public sentiment is divided, unstable, confused, or simply nonexistent. In the midst of a generally optimistic survey of the policy preferences of *The Rational Public*, political scientists Benjamin Page and Robert Shapiro portrayed tax policy as "a highly technical realm that is ripe for concealment and mystification." My analysis in chapters 6 and 7 provides ample evidence of confusion, uncertainty, and "unenlightened self-interest" in public opinion about tax policy. Thus, it should perhaps not be surprising to find public officials relying less on citizens' attitudes than on their own ideological convictions for policy direction in this domain. It is tempting to take comfort in the belief that, as Jacob Hacker and Paul Pierson put it, "Not all issues make voters' eyes glaze over in the way that details of tax policy do."[9]

It is important to note, however, that the paucity of elite responsiveness to public opinion extends even to issues on which public opinion seems to be unusually firm and stable. In the case of estate tax repeal, for example, the relevant evidence is extremely fragmentary, but insofar as it exists at all it suggests that

[8] Schumpeter (1950), 270, 284–285.
[9] Page and Shapiro (1992), 166; Hacker and Pierson (2005a), 49.

the estate tax has been quite unpopular for at least 70 years. For most of that time, the only real obstacle to estate tax repeal was the ideological conviction of Democratic presidents and members of Congress. Within months of the arrival of a Republican president with Republican majorities in the House and Senate in 2001, an estate tax phaseout was passed and signed into law.

The case of the eroding minimum wage, which I examined in chapter 8, is even more remarkable. There is abundant evidence of strong, consistent public support for minimum wage increases throughout the past 40 years—a period in which the real value of the federal minimum wage has declined by more than 40%. Here, too, the most important hurdle to the public getting what it says it wants seems to be the conviction of policy makers—in this case, primarily conservative Republican policy makers—that a higher minimum wage would have significant adverse consequences unrecognized by the substantial public majority that supports it.

Democratic victories in the 2006 midterm election provided the impetus for a long-overdue increase in the minimum wage in 2007. However, there is less to that apparent triumph of popular sentiment than meets the eye. For one thing, the new minimum wage rate will still be far lower, in real terms, than it was 40 years ago, despite the substantial increase in average wages and collective wealth in the intervening decades. Moreover, low-wage workers owe their good fortune, such as it is, less to overwhelming public support for a minimum wage increase than to the perceived failure of President Bush's war in Iraq and the indiscretions of a Republican congressman with an unhealthy interest in teenage interns. For partisans of democracy, neither the end nor the means can be entirely edifying.

PARTISAN POLITICS AND THE "HAVE-NOTS"

Scholars of political participation and liberal activists often seem to suppose that the cure for political inequality is to educate and mobilize the disadvantaged in support of specific progressive policies. However, the evidence of unresponsiveness to the views of low-income citizens presented in chapter 9 and in Gilens's work suggests that that strategy is very unlikely to be politically effective. As one energetic critic of the "burgeoning 'democratic inequality studies' field," Robert Weissberg, has argued, political activism "does perform as advertised, but only *sometimes*, and even then usually for those who already enjoy many advantages." Weissberg added that, "shouting louder ('voice') is likely to be futile . . . for those mired in poverty."[10]

If "voice" is "likely to be futile" for people on the losing end of economic inequality, is there any hope for progress? My analysis points to two related

[10] Weissberg (2004), 36–37.

bright spots in an otherwise gloomy picture. First, the correlation between class positions and political views is not so substantial that support for egalitarian policies is limited to "those mired in poverty." Just as many poor people espouse antipathy to redistribution and the welfare state, many affluent people support egalitarian policies that seem inconsistent with their own narrow material interests. Insofar as the political activism of affluent egalitarians "does perform as advertised," policy makers may be much more generous toward the poor than the political clout of the poor themselves would seem to warrant.

In any case, my analyses suggest that the specific policy views of citizens, whether rich or poor, have less impact in the policy-making process than the ideological convictions of elected officials. Whether we consider broad patterns of economic distribution, as in chapter 2, major changes in the tax system, as in chapters 6 and 7, income support for the poor, as in chapter 8, or specific roll call votes on a wide range of issues, as in chapter 9, policy choices seems to depend more on the partisan ideologies of key policy makers than on the details of public opinion. Thus, even if poor people have negligible *direct* influence on the day-to-day decisions of elected officials, they—and their more affluent ideological allies—may have substantial *indirect* influence by altering the balance of power between Democrats and Republicans in the making of public policy.

The prominent role of political parties in my account of the political economy of inequality calls to mind a famous suggestion by V. O. Key Jr. in his monumental analysis of *Southern Politics in State and Nation*, that "over the long run the have-nots lose in a disorganized politics." Key's assertion was inspired by his close study of the one-party politics of the South in the Jim Crow era, which suggested that the southern states with the most stable, cohesive factional structures had more genuine competition between "ins" and "outs," a greater "sense of corporate responsibility" among elected officials, less "favoritism and graft" in the conduct of government business, and more "power to discipline wild-eyed men" on the explosive issue of race—all factors contributing, in Key's view, to rational public consideration of the "crucial issues" of "taxation and expenditure."

By comparison, less stable factional structures only sporadically facilitated "the old Populist battle of the poor, white farmer against the plantation regions." States with the most "discontinuous and kaleidoscopic" factional structures were marked by "issueless politics" lacking even "a semblance of factional responsibility," placing "a high premium on demagogic qualities of personality," and providing "great negative power to those with a few dollars to invest in legislative candidates." The implication Key drew from these observations was that stable, organized factional competition—which he thought of as approximating, under the peculiar historical conditions of the one-party South, "the role assigned elsewhere to political parties"—is the most promising "institutionalized mechanism for the expression of lower-bracket viewpoints."[11]

Key's assertion regarding the importance of organized political competition for the fortunes of the economically disadvantaged fits neatly in a broader scholarly literature on party competition and democratic government. The intellectual tradition associated most closely with E. E. Schattschneider—and expressed most famously in the 1950 report of the American Political Science Association's Committee on Political Parties, which he chaired—emphasized the constructive role of political parties and party competition in structuring and adjudicating political conflict. Progressive observers of mid-century American politics bemoaned the obstacles to policy change created by federalism, boss rule, and the institutional separation of powers in Washington. Their favorite prescription for reform was a more "responsible" party system modeled on the British parliamentary system, with voters choosing between cohesive party teams offering distinct platforms and empowered to implement those platforms once elected.[12]

If the analysis and prescription offered by midcentury political scientists were correct, the contemporary American party system would seem to meet the requirements for party government—and, by extension, for progressive policy making—rather well. In Congress, ideological moderates have largely disappeared, turning the two parties' delegations into increasingly distinct liberal and conservative camps. Party unity and party-line voting increased steadily through the 1970s and 1980s, reaching levels by the 1990s exceeding those of the 1950s and spurring analyses of "conditional party government." Meanwhile, the proportion of "strong" party identifiers in the electorate increased substantially beginning in the 1970s, while the proportion of "independents" declined. At the same time, the strength of the relationship between partisanship and voting behavior also increased markedly, with partisan voting in the past four presidential elections reaching levels surpassing those prevailing in the 1950s. These behavioral manifestations of increasing partisanship have been accompanied by attitudinal manifestations, with citizens increasingly seeing important differences between the parties, recognizing their relative ideological positions, and volunteering more reasons for liking one party and disliking the other.[13]

Schattschneider should have been delighted by these developments. The hitch, of course, is that responsible parties may do little for the "have-nots" if the wrong party wins. Thus, while organized party competition may be a *necessary* condition for progressive policy making, it is not a *sufficient* condition.

[11] Key (1949), 307, 298–310.

[12] Schattschneider (1942); Committee on Political Parties (1950).

[13] McCarty, Poole, and Rosenthal (2006); Rohde (1991); Miller (1991); Bartels (2000); Hetherington (2001).

Indeed, one recent study of American politics suggests that "the unmatched coordination and cohesion" of the contemporary Republican Party has resulted in "tilting the balance of benefits and protections away from ordinary Americans and toward the well off, the well connected, and the Republican base."[14]

Interestingly, Key himself seems to have abandoned the "have-nots" hypothesis over the course of the 1950s, as southern state politics evolved in unexpected ways and his own scholarly focus broadened to include one-party systems in non-southern states. As Key's most distinguished student, David Mayhew, noted that in his book on *American State Politics*, published only seven years after *Southern Politics in State and Nation*, "Key entirely abandoned the 'have-nots' claim. Or at least he carefully refrained from restating it." This shift seems to reflect both the "precarious" relationship between dual factionalism and progressive politics in the South—as Mayhew observed, "dual factionalism hardly qualified as a *sufficient* condition for government attention to 'have-nots'"—and the apparent counterexamples of progressive politics in the one-party systems of New England.[15]

Subsequent scholars of state politics have taken Key's hypothesis as an influential starting point. However, most of their analyses have focused not on the *structure* of party competition but on the *closeness* of the electoral division between Democrats and Republicans as measured by vote shares or seats in the state legislature. Early analyses of this sort found little impact of party competition on state policy outcomes.[16] The results of more recent studies are also mixed, but they suggest, if anything, that an even partisan division between Democrats and Republicans may produce policy outcomes generally considered harmful to the political interests of "have-nots." For example, one study found inconsistent but generally negative effects of party competition on the size of state governments, while another found that evenly divided state legislatures produced lower taxes and lower levels of workers' compensation benefits.[17]

Edward Jennings offered a different interpretation of Key's "have-nots" hypothesis, in which the *class basis* of party competition rather than the *closeness* of party competition affects the political fortunes of the economically disadvantaged (as measured by the generosity of state welfare benefits). His comparison of social policy in eight states showed that the six states with class-based party systems from the New Deal through the 1960s (Connecticut, Louisiana, Massachusetts, Michigan, Minnesota, and Wisconsin) spent more on welfare than the two that did not (Indiana and Virginia). He also found that the states with class-based party systems spent more on welfare

[14] Hacker and Pierson (2005b), 3, 14.
[15] Mayhew (1988), 24, 34; Key (1956).
[16] Lockard (1959); Dye (1966); Winters (1976).
[17] Rogers and Rogers (2000); Besley and Case (2003).

when Democrats controlled state politics than when Republicans were in charge, suggesting that class-based politics is especially good for "have-nots" when their side wins.[18]

Robert Brown's broader analysis of all 50 states failed to support Jennings's assertion that class-based party systems generally produced progressive policy outcomes; on average, states characterized by a class-based "New Deal" cleavage structure provided no more generous welfare benefits than southern or "post–New Deal" states. However, Brown's analysis did confirm that a class-based cleavage structure raised the policy stakes for "have-nots": Democratic control of state governments had a strong positive effect on welfare spending in the "New Deal" states but little or no impact in southern or "post–New Deal" states.[19]

Although there seems to be relatively little empirical support for the proposition that party competition per se produces progressive social policy, Jennings's and Brown's findings are part of a substantial empirical literature establishing the political importance of *which* party controls the reins of government at any given time. Within the past decade or so, political scientists and economists have found significant partisan differences in state revenues and expenditures, taxes and spending patterns, and Medicaid spending. They have also demonstrated that welfare benefits tend to be more generous in states with higher absolute or relative turnout rates among low-income voters.[20]

These state-level findings are strongly echoed by my findings regarding partisan patterns of policy making and economic distribution at the national level. In case after case, Democratic officials have provided strong support for policies favoring the "have-nots"—expanding the economy, increasing funding for domestic programs, raising the minimum wage—while Republican officials have pursued policies favoring the "haves"—fighting inflation, cutting taxes, repealing the estate tax. These consistent, long-standing differences in the class interests embodied in the two parties' governing philosophies are revealed most dramatically in the patterns of income growth documented in chapter 2. Over the past half-century, Democratic presidents have generally presided over robust income growth for families across the economic spectrum, while Republican administrations have generally been bad for the economic fortunes of middle-class families and even worse for the economic fortunes of the working poor. The political significance of these stark partisan differences can only be gainsaid by supposing that they are the result of a massive (and highly improbable) historical coincidence.

[18] Jennings (1979).

[19] Brown (1995).

[20] Rogers and Rogers (2000); Besley and Case (2003); Knight (2000); Grogan (1994). Hill, Leighley, and Hinton-Andersson (1995); Husted and Kenney (1997). Besley and Case (2003) provide a comprehensive review of these and other relevant studies.

Large-scale historical analysis of "the macro polity" underscores the impact of political parties on the broad course of American public policy. In the context of a complex analysis relating economic conditions, liberal or conservative shifts in "public mood," partisan loyalties in the electorate, presidential approval, election outcomes, and policy making in the White House, Congress, and the Supreme Court, Robert Erikson, Michael MacKuen, and James Stimson found that partisan control of government was by far the most important determinant of policy outputs. For example, the estimated effect on White House policy activity of replacing a Republican president with a Democrat was more than three times as large as the estimated direct effect of moving from the most conservative public mood on record (in 1952) to the most liberal public mood on record (in 1961); the estimated effects of partisan control on congressional policy activity were even larger. Although the authors themselves did not stress these findings, it is difficult to read their work without being mightily impressed by how substantially the course of public policy over the past half-century has altered with changes in partisan control of the reins of national government.[21]

The United States is by no means unique in this regard. Writing in the late 1990s, Carles Boix criticized comparative political economists for "the rather tangential role they have ascribed to electoral politics and the impact of partisanship" in accounting for cross-national differences in economic policies and performance. Summarizing his own research on Europe, Boix asserted that "conservative governments cut taxes, slash public investment programs, sell most public businesses, and revamp the labor market to increase the profitability of capital and to induce the unemployed to actively search for jobs. Socialist cabinets, instead, raise tax rates on high-income brackets and boost public spending on infrastructure and human capital in order to ease the transition from an unskilled population profile to a well-educated workforce without having to lower the social wage."[22]

What may be surprising, both to Americans and to foreigners, is the extent to which the supposedly tame partisan politics of the post-war United States mimic the contrast Boix portrayed between European socialists and conservatives. Notwithstanding the popular perception that there's "not a dime's worth of difference" between Democrats and Republicans, as George Wallace used to say—and notwithstanding the strong emphasis on the moderating effects of electoral competition in formal theories of majoritarian politics—the fact of the matter is that partisan control of government has been of consistent, substantial importance to the economic fortunes of "have-nots" over the past half-century.

---

[21] Erikson, MacKuen, and Stimson (2002), 204, 305, 308, 310.
[22] Boix (1998), 219, 202.

The current configuration of the American party system features a highly competitive balance between Republicans and Democrats in the electorate, in Congress, and in the Electoral College. But the parties are not evenly matched because they are indistinguishable; in fact, they are now more ideological, more cohesive, and more distinct in their supporting coalitions than at any time in recent memory. While a large segment of the public remains politically disengaged, attentive citizens have increasingly responded to these developments by choosing up sides, adopting more or less consistent packages of policy positions and partisan loyalties.

The implications of increasing economic and ideological polarization of the parties and their supporting coalitions appear to depend primarily on the outcome of the partisan struggle for political dominance. Political scientists have found rather little evidence that intense partisan competition per se benefits "have-nots," but considerable evidence that "have-nots" benefit when their party wins. For most of the past century, when Democrats have controlled the reins of government, they have consistently pursued high employment, high taxes, and economic redistribution from the rich to the poor. When Republicans have governed, they have consistently done the opposite. The partisan tenor of the contemporary political environment seems likely, if anything, to reinforce those tendencies, making the stakes for "haves" and "have-nots" alike even higher than in the past—and the political struggle correspondingly more intense.

POLITICAL OBSTACLES TO ECONOMIC EQUALITY

The temptation to suppose that organized political competition must work to the advantage of "have-nots" is grounded in the natural-seeming assumption that "have-nots" will use the power of the ballot to restrain the privileges of the less numerous "haves," if not to expropriate their wealth. Certainly that has happened from time to time in the course of American history. Kevin Phillips noted that the American public "has distrusted economic elites and periodically used democratic politics to curb their abuses." Likening the economic circumstances of the current era to the most conspicuous past eras of escalating inequality, the original Gilded Age and the Roaring Twenties, Phillips observed that those periods of concentrated wealth and political corruption ended with the Progressive Era and the New Deal, respectively, and suggested that "A politics in this tradition is unlikely to blink at confronting twenty-first century elites."[23]

Today, however, ordinary Americans display rather little desire to curb the abuses of "malefactors of great wealth," much less to expropriate their vast

[23] Phillips (2002), 294.

fortunes. Even the collapse of Enron and other spectacularly fraudulent and pernicious specimens of American entrepreneurship has generated only modest public consternation and no concerted political response.

Perhaps the process of reaction and reform has simply not reached its critical stage. Phillips suggested that "the early twenty-first century should see another struggle" reminiscent of the Progressive and New Deal eras "because corporate aggrandizement in the 1980s and 1990s went beyond that of the Gilded Age—the parallels of political corruption and concentrated wealth—to frame issues of abandoning American workers, communities, and loyalties."[24] Perhaps. In the meantime, however, most of the same people who think the rich are asked to pay less than they should in taxes have been happy to endorse the Bush tax cuts and estate tax repeal.

One explanation for these facts is simply that people are confused about what is in their own interest. My analysis in Chapter 3 provides rather little support for the most popular assertion of false consciousness in current punditry—the notion that working-class whites have been drawn to the Republican Party by the "hallucinatory appeal" of "cultural wedge issues like guns and abortion," as Thomas Frank put it.[25] Nevertheless, there is plenty of raw material here for an account of contemporary politics emphasizing ordinary Americans' misperceptions, myopia, and missing connections between values and interests on one hand and policy preferences and votes on the other.

Perhaps most importantly, my analysis in Chapter 4 suggests that Republicans have benefited greatly from myopic voters' reactions to the fortunate electoral timing of income gains under Republican presidents—and the even more remarkable unfortunate electoral timing of income slumps under Democratic presidents. Despite the superior historical performance of Democratic presidents in generating income growth for middle-class and poor families over the past half-century, American voters have shown a strong tendency to punish Democrats and reward Republicans based on the very unrepresentative sliver of economic performance that happens to fall within their narrow focus on "present advantages," as Ostrogorski put it more than a century ago.

According to Jennifer Hochschild, the ambiguities and contradictions in American public opinion regarding issues of distributive justice reflect, in part, the conflicting "patterns of demand and reward" associated with the "separate arenas" of economics and politics:

> In other Western nations, socialist parties have developed a world view that overcomes this separation; but Americans see class relations, if at all, as only one among many components of public life. . . . When they view redistribution as an

---

[24] Ibid., 413.
[25] Frank (2004), 245.

economic question, they argue from a principle of differentiation and oppose it. When they view it as a political question, they argue from a principle of equality and sometimes favor it. . . . People who feel torn between two views are unlikely to act forcefully to promote either; therefore by default, they end up "supporting" the status quo.[26]

Reliance on a "principle of differentiation" in moral judgments about inequality is reinforced by a tendency to think of the economic sphere as existing prior to and apart from the political sphere. Thus, a Treasury secretary can insist that when "market forces work to provide the greatest rewards to those with the needed skills," the resulting escalation of economic inequality "is simply an economic reality, and it is neither fair nor useful to blame any political party." Here, "market forces" are impersonal but beneficent, "economic reality" is simple and inexorable, and political blame "is neither fair nor useful." As one heterodox economist put it, "Economics functions in a theological role in our society . . . to justify the ways of the market to men."[27]

Even a cursory examination of trends in other countries provides strong evidence that technological change and globalization do not *have* to produce the glaring disparities in economic fortunes experienced by Americans over the past three decades. Government action can ensure that the economic benefits stemming from these historic developments are widely shared. A recent study of income redistribution in affluent democracies found that the United States has simply done less than other countries to mitigate the effects of increasingly unequal market incomes. Ten of the 11 countries for which data are available (all except the Netherlands) experienced increases in income inequality among working-age households in the 1980s and 1990s. Of these 10 countries, nine engaged in more aggressive redistribution at the end of this period than at the beginning; in general, the increase in redistribution was greatest in countries where the increase in inequality of market incomes was greatest. The glaring exception was the United States, which experienced a larger-than-average increase in income inequality but no corresponding increase in redistribution.[28]

Insofar as Americans have any understanding of the alternative policies pursued by other affluent democracies, they mostly seem to reject those alternatives as inconsistent with America's core cultural values of economic opportunity and self-reliance: European welfare states, they tell themselves, are

[26] Hochschild (1981), 20, 48, 249.
[27] Remarks Prepared for Delivery by Treasury Secretary Henry H. Paulson at Columbia University, August 1, 2006, http://www.treas.gov/press/releases/hp41.htm; Duncan K. Foley, quoted in Peter Steinfels, "Economics: The Invisible Hand of the Market," *New York Times*, November 25, 2006, B5.
[28] Kenworthy and Pontusson (2005).

bloated, ossified, and hidebound. The reality seems to be that European economies have performed about as well as the American economy in generating long-term growth and that economic mobility is at least as extensive in contemporary Europe as in the United States. However, it seems quite unlikely that most Americans would acknowledge those facts. As Hochschild has observed, the "dominant American world view . . . is complex and flexible, has a long history and deep roots, and has withstood or absorbed great shocks and vehement opposition."[29]

The survey results presented in chapter 5 suggest that Americans' perceptions of economic and social reality are strongly colored by their political predispositions. Democrats and Republicans differ much more than rich people and poor people do in their perceptions of the extent of economic opportunity in American society. And political awareness sometimes exacerbates rather than mitigates ideological biases in perceptions of economic and social reality. For example, conservatives who are generally well-informed about politics and public affairs are significantly more likely than less well-informed conservatives to *deny* that differences in incomes between rich people and poor people have increased.

There are also significant partisan differences in attributions of responsibility for national economic conditions. In one recent study, for example, about 35% of survey respondents chose the president or Congress as "most responsible for the economic conditions in our country in the last few years." (The remaining 65% chose "working people," "business people," or "national and international business cycles.") However, Democrats were much more likely than Republicans or Independents to attribute economic responsibility to the president specifically and to government more generally.[30]

Finally, and perhaps most importantly, it seems very likely that political pressure for redistribution is curtailed by the increasing social isolation of winners and losers in the free-market economy of the New Gilded Age. As economic inequality increased in the United States after 1970, economic segregation increased as well. Moreover, "As Americans migrated to the suburbs . . . rich and poor have become separated not just by neighborhood but also by municipal boundaries. With suburbanization, wealth has come to differentiate not just America's citizens but its cities as well."[31]

The remarkable insulation of America's comfortable class from the realities of economic inequality was highlighted by the response of critics and readers to *Nickel and Dimed*, journalist Barbara Ehrenreich's colorful first-person

---

[29] Perotti (1996); Wilensky (2002), chapter 12; Pontusson (2005); Solon (2002); Osberg and Smeeding (2003); Hochschild (1981), 281.

[30] Hellwig, Ringsmuth, and Freeman (2007).

[31] Massey and Denton (1993); Jargowsky (1996); Mayer (2001); Oliver (2001), 69.

account of a few months spent working at a series of low-wage jobs. "I grew up hearing over and over, to the point of tedium, that 'hard work' was the secret of success," Ehrenreich wrote. "No one ever said that you could work hard—harder even than you ever thought possible—and still find yourself sinking ever deeper into poverty and debt." Reviewers called Ehrenreich's account "illuminating," "jarring," "explosive," "frightening," and "unforgettable."[32] Perhaps it had never occurred to them that waitresses, housecleaners, and sales clerks work hard, endure myriad petty abuses and indignities from employers and customers, and struggle to make ends meet. It seems hard to imagine that the parents and grandparents of Ehrenreich's readers and reviewers would have been so shocked by these glimpses of the practical and moral ramifications of inequality in the everyday lives of the working poor.

The class divide in contemporary America is no doubt exacerbated by the fact that the people on the losing end of the free-market economy often have different skin colors and accents than those that predominate among the affluent and comfortable. Martin Gilens has documented the importance of racial discrimination in accounting for *Why Americans Hate Welfare*. Alberto Alesina and Edward Glaeser have used cross-national data to show that racially and ethnically heterogeneous societies generally have much less generous social policies than those that are more homogeneous. According to one recent study, even (white) Americans' support for the Bush tax cuts stemmed in significant part from "racial resentments and attachments rooted in the history of slavery and discrimination." Since these resentments and attachments are not going to disappear anytime soon—and since American society will become even more diverse in the coming decades—racial and ethnic divisions will continue to be a major obstacle to greater economic equality.[33]

THE CITY OF UTMOST NECESSITY

In a recent book-length examination of *Democratic Faith*, political theorist Patrick Deneen found a compelling basis for political equality in an unlikely source: Plato's *Republic*. Before presenting his famous account of an ideal city ruled by philosopher-kings, Plato described a more rudimentary "city of utmost necessity" in which the farmer, the builder, the weaver, and the cobbler band together to provide for their common needs. Their division of labor reflects the fact that "each of us is naturally not quite like anyone else, but

---

[32] Ehrenreich (2001), 220; reviews from *New York Times Book Review*, *Newsweek*, *New York Times*, *San Francisco Chronicle*, and *Newsweek*, respectively.

[33] Gilens (1999); Alesina and Glaeser (2004); Kinder, Burns, and Vieregge (2005), 2.

rather differs in his nature; different men are apt for the accomplishment of different work." But if that sounds remarkably like Adam Smith's economic rationale for market capitalism, Plato grounded his account of just collective life in the even more basic fact that "each of us isn't self-sufficient but is in need of much."

As Deneen put it,

> We are to engage in that form of work for which we have special talent explicitly to avoid *neglect* of our fellow citizens," and out of a fundamental recognition that "no one of us is capable of creating the good things of life by ourselves alone. . . . Equality's self-evidence is demonstrated every day by the simple existence and permanent persistence of politics. Democracy is not premised upon the eventual perfection of our imperfect city nor the citizens who reside therein but precisely upon the permanent presence of imperfect humans who must, by dint of their equal insufficiency and the permanency of need, inhabit, and govern together, cities of men.[34]

In Plato's account, the "city of utmost necessity" with its just and healthy division of labor is apt to fall prey to man's appetite for luxuries, resulting in the gradual evolution of a "feverish" city of myrrh and incense and girls and cakes—and a professional army to defend these luxuries from the predations of jealous neighbors. Of course, modern citizens of rich democracies know much more than Plato could possibly have imagined about man's appetite for luxuries. Our cities are so wealthy, complex, and "feverish" that we are very apt to lose sight of their fundamental basis in our common needs. Only in moments of extremity are we likely to see beyond what Deneen referred to as "our apparent difference of position in the shadow of gleaming skyscrapers."[35]

One such moment of extremity occurred in August 2005, when floods triggered by Hurricane Katrina inundated much of the city of New Orleans. Many Americans were shocked and shamed by the televised images of the aftermath of the flooding. Scenes of physical devastation were juxtaposed with even more disturbing scenes of human devastation. Thousands of residents, mostly black and poor, seemed to be trapped in a Hobbesian state of nature, abandoned by government and civilized society. On August 31, as "a major American city all but disintegrated," according to one news account, President Bush flew over New Orleans and the Gulf Coast in Air Force One on his way from Texas to Washington, DC. When he finally arrived on the ground in New Orleans some two weeks later, he acknowledged in a dramatic televised address from Jackson Square that America had "witnessed the kind

[34] Deneen (2005), 115–116; Plato, *Republic*, Allan Bloom, trans. (New York: Basic Books, 1968).
[35] Deneen (2005), 116.

of desperation no citizen of this great and generous nation should ever have to know—fellow Americans calling out for food and water, vulnerable people left at the mercy of criminals who had no mercy, and the bodies of the dead lying uncovered and untended in the street."[36]

It would be hard to imagine a starker reminder of the extent to which each of us lives every day in a "city of utmost necessity." Those who escaped the devastation of Katrina may have congratulated themselves on their self-sufficiency; but the truth of the matter is that they differed from those left behind primarily in their access to the collective resources of civilized society. As one reporter wrote, attempting to explain why so many poor people remained in the flooded city, "Evacuation, if you don't have a car, a credit card or a place to go, sounds like trading the deep sea you know for the devil you don't."[37] He might have added, but did not, that having a car would have been of little use without public highways and bridges, that the magical efficacy of credit cards rests on a complex web of legally enforced financial arrangements, and that having "a place to go" was largely a matter of knowing someone with a spare bedroom out of reach of the floodwaters.

According to one press report, "What a shocked world saw exposed in New Orleans . . . wasn't just a broken levee. It was a cleavage of race and class, at once familiar and startlingly new, laid bare in a setting where they suddenly amounted to matters of life and death." Another asserted that "Katrina's whirlwind has laid bare the fault lines of race and class in America. For a lightning moment, the American psyche was singed."[38]

The aftermath of the storm provided an even starker reminder that access to the collective resources of civilized society is vastly unequal, notwithstanding our Platonic equality of need. In his Jackson Square address, President Bush promised "bold action" to "confront" poverty, racial discrimination, and "the legacy of inequality." "These trials," he said, "remind us that we're tied together in this life, in this nation—and that the despair of any touches us all."[39] In a special report on "The Other America," *Newsweek* columnist Jonathan Alter suggested that the shock and shame of Katrina might "strip away the old evasions, hypocrisies and not-so-benign neglect" surrounding issues of inequality in America. "For the moment, at least, Americans are ready

[36] David Ovalle, Phil Long, and Martin Merzer, "Lawlessness, Floating Bodies as New Orleans Deteriorates," *Seattle Times*, September 1, 2005; "President Discusses Hurricane Relief in Address to the Nation," September 15, 2005, http://www.whitehouse.gov/news/releases/2005/09/20050915-8.html.

[37] Jonathan Tilove, " 'Our Society Is So Uneven': Katrina Exposes Inequalities of Race, Wealth," *Trenton Times*, September 4, 2005, B1.

[38] Jason DeParle, "Broken Levees, Unbroken Barriers: What Happens to a Race Deferred," *New York Times*, September 4, 2005, sect. 4, 1; Tilove, " 'Our Society Is So Uneven'," B1.

[39] "President Discusses Hurricane Relief in Address to the Nation."

to fix their restless gaze on enduring problems of poverty, race and class that have escaped their attention," and policy makers in Washington might "think harder about why part of the richest country on earth looks like the Third World."[40]

Alas, the hope for a silver lining proved to be short-lived. Less than a month after the president's stirring speech, amid reports of ideological wrangling over federal and local responsibilities, tax cuts and budget deficits, labor law and housing policy, the lightning moment seemed to have passed.[41] A year after the hurricane, Alter wrote a chagrined admission that the "cynical" critics who called his earlier piece "naïve" were "largely right":

> Not only has the president done much less than he promised on the financing and logistics of Gulf Coast recovery, he has dropped the ball entirely on using the storm and its aftermath as an opportunity to fight poverty. Worker recovery accounts and urban homesteading never got off the ground, and the new enterprise zone is mostly an opportunity for Southern companies owned by GOP campaign contributors to make some money in New Orleans. The mood in Washington continues to be one of not-so-benign neglect of the problems of the poor.

Alter quoted Senator John Kerry's claim that President Bush's Jackson Square speech "ought to stand as one of the all-time monuments to hollow rhetoric and broken promises."[42]

The process of rebuilding in the wake of Katrina has continued to expose "fault lines of race and class in America." Eight months after the storm, one reporter contrasted the pace of rebuilding in Eastover, "a gated subdivision that was home to some of this city's wealthiest black residents," and the Lower Ninth Ward, "a predominantly black working-class community where some of New Orleans's poorest people lived." The Eastover Property Owners Association "was so well organized and financed that it recently retained a professional planner to help respond to the city's requirement that devastated neighborhoods devise their own revival blueprints." In contrast, the Lower Ninth Ward—"a community rich in history, home to families whose roots date back generations"—had no neighborhood association until several months after the storm, and struggled to find planning assistance when the federal government declined to provide it. As one resident said, "People [here] don't have the same training and background and schooling and experience at working the system."[43]

---

[40] Jonathan Alter, "The Other America," *Newsweek*, September 19, 2005, 42–48.

[41] Jason DeParle, "Liberal Hopes Ebb in Post-Storm Poverty Debate," *New York Times*, October 11, 2005, A1.

[42] Jonathan Alter, "Still Blind to the Poverty," *Newsweek*, September 4, 2006, 38.

[43] Gary Rivlin, "In Rebuilding as in the Disaster, Wealth and Class Help Define New Orleans," *New York Times*, April 25, 2006, A24.

As is often the case, these significant social disadvantages were compounded by significant material disadvantages:

> Even today, nearly eight months after the storm, there are no FEMA trailers in the Lower Ninth Ward because the area is still without gas and drinkable water. . . . Just as disparities between rich and poor were exposed in the days after Hurricane Katrina, class and wealth seem to be playing a significant role as elected officials struggle to determine which neighborhoods will be rebuilt and which should revert to swampland, if not bulldozed and sold en masse to a developer. While Eastover is full of the sound of saws ripping wood and the pneumatic punch of nail guns, the sound of the Lower Ninth Ward is mainly silence.[44]

While class and wealth have played a significant role in the disparate fates of New Orleans homeowners, they have weighed even more heavily in the fates of people too poor to have owned their own homes. For thousands of them, as a press account almost two years after the original disaster put it, "the shock of evacuation has hardened into the grim limbo of exile." With rebuilding aid targeted to homeowners, "the local and federal governments have done almost nothing to make it possible for low-income renters" to return to New Orleans. As a result, "Hardly any of the 77,000 rental units destroyed in New Orleans have been rebuilt," and "there were still more than 30,000 families displaced by Hurricanes Katrina and Rita spread across the country in apartments paid for by the Federal Emergency Management Agency, and another 13,000 families, down from a peak of nearly 18,000, marooned in trailer or mobile home parks, where hunger is so prevalent that lines form when the truck from the food bank appears."[45]

No doubt it was naïve to suppose that a moment of extremity would trigger "bold action" to overcome "the legacy of inequality," as President Bush promised in Jackson Square. Both the legacy of inequality and the present reality of inequality are pervasive and powerful.

Pervasive and powerful, but not entirely immutable. The most important lesson of this book is a very simple one: politics matters. The rising tide of economic inequality in contemporary America has myriad economic and social causes, including technological change, demographic trends, and global competition. Some of these we can influence; others we can only adapt to. But however high the tide of economic forces may rise, we are not condemned to wait behind our levees for disaster to engulf us.

[44] Ibid.

[45] Shaila Dewan, "Road to New Life after Katrina is Closed to Many," *New York Times*, July 12, 2007, A1.

Imperfect as they are, the processes and institutions of American democracy provide us with consequential choices. We can reinforce the levees; we can divert some of the fastest-running waters; and we can insist that the most vulnerable among us not be abandoned when the affluent flee to higher ground.

We *can* make these choices. Whether we *will* make them remains to be seen.

Selected References

Aaronson, Daniel, and Bhashkar Mazumder. 2005. "Intergenerational Economic Mobility in the United States: 1940–2000." Working Paper 05-12, Federal Reserve Bank of Chicago.

Abramson, Paul R., John H. Aldrich, and David W. Rohde. 1994. *Change and Continuity in the 1992 Election*. Washington, DC: CQ Press.

———. 2002. *Change and Continuity in the 2000 Election*. Washington, DC: CQ Press.

Achen, Christopher H. 1978. "Measuring Representation." *American Journal of Political Science* 22: 475–509.

Achen, Christopher H., and Larry M. Bartels. 2004. "Musical Chairs: Pocketbook Voting and the Limits of Democratic Accountability." Paper presented at the annual meeting of the American Political Science Association, Chicago.

———. 2006. "It Feels Like We're Thinking: The Rationalizing Voter and Electoral Democracy." Paper presented at the annual meeting of the American Political Science Association, Philadelphia.

Adams, Greg D. 1997. "Abortion: Evidence of an Issue Evolution." *American Journal of Political Science* 41: 718–737.

Alesina, Alberto. 1988. "Macroeconomics and Politics." In Stanley Fischer, ed., *National Bureau of Economic Research Macroeconomics Annual*, vol. 3, 11–55. Cambridge, MA: MIT Press.

Alesina, Alberto, and Edward L. Glaeser. 2004. *Fighting Poverty in the US and Europe: A World of Difference*. Oxford: Oxford University Press.

Alesina, Alberto, John Londregan, and Howard Rosenthal. 1993. "A Model of the Political Economy of the United States." *American Political Science Review* 87: 12–33.

Alesina, Alberto, and Dani Rodrik. 1994. "Distributive Politics and Economic Growth." *Quarterly Journal of Economics* 109: 465–490.

Alesina, Alberto, and Howard Rosenthal. 1989. "Partisan Cycles in Congressional Elections and the Macroeconomy." *American Political Science Review* 83: 373–398.

Alesina, Alberto, and Jeffrey Sachs. 1988. "Political Parties and the Business Cycle in the United States, 1948–1984." *Journal of Money, Credit and Banking* 20: 63–82.

Alexander, Herbert E. 1980. *Financing Politics*. Washington, DC: Congressional Quarterly Press.

Althaus, Scott L. 1998. "Information Effects in Collective Preferences." *American Political Science Review* 92: 545–558.

Ansolabehere, Stephen, John M. de Figueiredo, and James M. Snyder Jr. 2003. "Why Is There So Little Money in U.S. Politics?" *Journal of Economic Perspectives* 17: 105–130.

Arrow, Kenneth J. 1963. *Social Choice and Individual Values*, 2nd ed. New Haven, CT: Yale University Press.

Atkinson, A. B. 1997. "Bringing Income Distribution in from the Cold." *Economic Journal* 107: 297–321.

Autor, David H., Lawrence F. Katz, and Meissa S. Kearney. 2005. "Trends in U.S. Wage Inequality: Re-assessing the Revisionists." Working Paper 11627, National Bureau of Economic Research. http://www.nber.org/papers/w11627.

Bartels, Larry M. 1990. "Public Opinion and Political Interests." Paper presented at the annual meeting of the Midwest Political Science Association, Chicago.

———. 1991. "Constituency Opinion and Congressional Policy Making: The Reagan Defense Buildup." *American Political Science Review* 85: 457–474.

———. 1996. "Uninformed Votes: Information Effects in Presidential Elections." *American Journal of Political Science* 40: 194–230.

———. 1998. "Where the Ducks Are: Voting Power in a Party System." In John G. Geer, ed., *Politicians and Party Politics*, 43–79. Baltimore: Johns Hopkins University Press.

———. 2000. "Partisanship and Voting Behavior, 1952–1996." *American Journal of Political Science* 44: 35–50.

———. 2002a. "Beyond the Running Tally: Partisan Bias in Political Perceptions." *Political Behavior* 24: 117–150.

———. 2002b. "Economic Inequality and Political Representation." Paper presented at the annual meeting of the American Political Science Association, Boston.

———. 2003. "Democracy with Attitudes." In Michael B. MacKuen and George Rabinowitz, eds., *Electoral Democracy*, 48–82. Ann Arbor: University of Michigan Press.

———. 2004. "Unenlightened Self-Interest: The Strange Appeal of Estate Tax Repeal." *The American Prospect* (June): A17–A19.

———. 2005. "Homer Gets a Tax Cut: Inequality and Public Policy in the American Mind." *Perspectives on Politics* 3: 15–31.

———. 2006a. "A Tale of Two Tax Cuts, a Wage Squeeze, and a Tax Credit." *National Tax Journal* 59: 403–423.

———. 2006b. "What's the Matter with *What's the Matter with Kansas?*" *Quarterly Journal of Political Science* 1: 201–226.

Bartels, Larry M., and Henry E. Brady. 2003. "Economic Behavior in Political Context." *American Economic Review* 93: 156–161.

Bartels, Larry M., Hugh Heclo, Rodney E. Hero, and Lawrence R. Jacobs. 2005. "Inequality and American Governance." In Lawrence R. Jacobs and Theda Skocpol, eds., *Inequality and American Democracy: What We Know and What We Need to Learn*, 88–155. New York: Russell Sage Foundation.

Bartels, Larry M., and John Zaller. 2001. "Presidential Vote Models: A Recount." *PS: Political Science and Politics* 34: 9–20.

Beck, Nathaniel. 1982. "Parties, Administrations, and American Macroeconomic Outcomes." *American Political Science Review* 76: 83–93.

Beller, Emily, and Michael Hout. 2006. "Intergenerational Social Mobility: The United States in Comparative Perspective." *Future of Children* 16: 19–36.

Bénabou, Roland. 1996. "Inequality and Growth." In Ben S. Bernanke and Julio J. Rotemberg, eds., *National Bureau of Economic Research Macroeconomics Annual*, vol. 11, 11–76. Cambridge, MA: MIT Press.

Besley, Timothy, and Anne Case. 2003. "Political Institutions and Policy Choices: Evidence from the United States." *Journal of Economic Literature* 41: 7–73.

Bibby, John F. 1996. *Politics, Parties, and Elections in America*, 3rd ed. Chicago: Nelson-Hall.

Biven, W. Carl. 2002. *Jimmy Carter's Economy: Policy in an Age of Limits*. Chapel Hill: University of North Carolina Press.

Blanchard, Oliver J., and Roberto Perotti. 2002. "An Empirical Characterization of the Dynamic Effects of Changes in Government Spending and Taxes on Output." *Quarterly Journal of Economics 117*: 1329–1368.

Blank, Rebecca, and Alan Blinder. 1986. "Macroeconomics, Income Distribution, and Poverty." In Sheldon Danziger and Daniel Weinberg, eds., *Fighting Poverty: What Works and What Doesn't*, 180–208. Cambridge, MA: Harvard University Press.

Boix, Carles. 1998. *Political Parties, Growth and Equality: Conservative and Social Democratic Economic Strategies in the World Economy*. Cambridge: Cambridge University Press.

Bradbury, Katharine, and Jane Katz. 2002. "Women's Labor Market Involvement and Family Income Mobility When Marriages End." *New England Economic Review* Q4: 41–74.

Brown, Robert D. 1995. "Party Cleavages and Welfare Effort in the American States." *American Political Science Review 89*: 23–33.

Burtless, Gary. 1999. "Growing American Inequality: Sources and Remedies." In Henry J. Aaron and Robert D. Reischauer, eds., *Setting National Priorities: The 2000 Election and Beyond*, 137–165. Washington, DC: Brookings Institution Press.

Campbell, Angus, Philip E. Converse, Warren E. Miller, and Donald E. Stokes. 1960. *The American Voter*. New York: John Wiley & Sons.

Card, David, and Alan B. Krueger. 1995. *Myth and Measurement: The New Economics of the Minimum Wage*. Princeton, NJ: Princeton University Press.

———. 2000. "Minimum Wages and Employment: A Case Study of the Fast-Food Industry: Reply." *American Economic Review 90*: 1397–1420.

Carmines, Edward G., and James A. Stimson. 1980. "The Two Faces of Issue Voting." *American Political Science Review 74*: 78–91.

———. 1989. *Issue Evolution: Race and the Transformation of American Politics*. Princeton, NJ: Princeton University Press.

Carmines, Edward G., and James Woods. 1997. "The Role of Party Activists in the Evolution of the Abortion Issue." *Political Behavior 24*: 361–377.

Christiano, Lawrence J., Martin Eichenbaum, and Charles L. Evans. 1999. "Monetary Policy Shocks: What Have We Learned and to What End?" In John B. Taylor and Michael Woodford, eds., *Handbook of Macroeconomics*, vol. 1A, 65–148. Amsterdam: North-Holland.

Committee on Political Parties. 1950. "Toward a More Responsible Two-Party System." *American Political Science Review 44*, Supplement: v–ix, 1–96.

Conover, Pamela Johnston, Stanley Feldman, and Kathleen Knight. 1987. "The Personal and Political Underpinnings of Economic Forecasts." *American Journal of Political Science 31*: 559–583.

Converse, Philip E. 1964. "The Nature of Belief Systems in Mass Publics." In David E. Apter, ed., *Ideology and Discontent*, 206–261. New York: Free Press.

———. 1990. "Popular Representation and the Distribution of Information." In John A. Ferejohn and James H. Kuklinski, eds., *Information and Democratic Processes*, 369–388. Chicago: University of Illinois Press.

Cutler, David M., and Lawrence F. Katz. 1991. "Macroeconomic Performance and the Disadvantaged." *Brookings Papers on Economic Activity 1*: 1–74.

Dahl, Robert A. 1961. *Who Governs? Democracy and Power in an American City*. New Haven, CT: Yale University Press.

———. 1971. *Polyarchy: Participation and Opposition*. New Haven, CT: Yale University Press.

———. 1982. *Dilemmas of Pluralist Democracy: Autonomy vs. Control*. New Haven, CT: Yale University Press.

———. 2006. *On Political Equality*. New Haven, CT: Yale University Press.

Danziger, Sheldon, and Peter Gottschalk. 1995. *America Unequal*. New York: Russell Sage Foundation and Harvard University Press.

Delli Carpini, Michael X., and Scott Keeter. 1996. *What Americans Know about Politics and Why It Matters*. New Haven, CT: Yale University Press.

Deneen, Patrick J. 2005. *Democratic Faith*. Princeton, NJ: Princeton University Press.

Dew-Becker, Ian, and Robert J. Gordon. 2005. "Where Did the Productivity Growth Go? Inflation Dynamics and the Distribution of Income." Paper presented at the 81st meeting of the Brookings Panel on Economic Activity, Washington, DC, September 8–9.

DiNardo, John, Nicole M. Fortin, and Thomas Lemieux. 1996. "Labor Market Institutions and the Distribution of Wages, 1973–1992: A Semi-Parametric Approach." *Econometrica* 64: 1001–1044.

Downs, Anthony. 1957. *An Economic Theory of Democracy*. New York: Harper & Row.

Dye, Thomas. 1966. *Politics, Economics, and the Public: Policy Outcomes in the American States*. Chicago: Rand McNally.

Edsall, Thomas Byrne, and Mary D. Edsall. 1991. *Chain Reaction: The Impact of Race, Rights, and Taxes on American Politics*. New York: W. W. Norton.

Ehrenreich, Barbara. 2001. *Nickel and Dimed: On (Not) Getting By in America*. New York: Henry Holt and Company.

Erikson, Robert S. 1989. "Economic Conditions and the Presidential Vote." *American Political Science Review* 83: 567–573.

———. 1990. "Economic Conditions and the Congressional Vote: A Review of the Macrolevel Evidence." *American Journal of Political Science* 34: 373–399.

———. 2004. "Economic Voting: Micro vs. Macro Perspectives." Paper presented at the annual Political Methodology Summer Meeting, Stanford University.

Erikson, Robert S., Joseph Bafumi, and Bret Wilson. 2002. "Was the 2000 Presidential Election Predictable?" *PS: Political Science & Politics* 35: 815–819.

Erikson, Robert S., Michael B. MacKuen, and James A. Stimson. 2002. *The Macro Polity*. Cambridge: Cambridge University Press.

Erikson, Robert S., Gerald C. Wright, and John P. McIver. 1993. *Statehouse Democracy: Public Opinion and Policy in the American States*. Cambridge: Cambridge University Press.

Feldman, Stanley. 1988. "Structure and Consistency in Public Opinion: The Role of Core Beliefs and Values." *American Journal of Political Science* 32: 416–440.

———. 2003. "A Conflicted Public? Equality, Fairness, and Redistribution." Paper presented at the conference on Inequality and American Democracy, Princeton University, November 7–8.

Fenno, Richard F., Jr. 1978. *Home Style: House Members in Their Districts*. Boston: Little, Brown.

Fiorina, Morris P. 1981. *Retrospective Voting in American National Elections*. New Haven, CT: Yale University Press.

Fishkin, James S. 1997. *The Voice of the People: Public Opinion and Democracy*. New Haven, CT: Yale University Press.

Frank, Thomas. 2004. *What's the Matter with Kansas? How Conservatives Won the Heart of America*. New York: Henry Holt and Company.

———. 2005. "Class Is Dismissed." Unpublished manuscript. http://www.tcfrank .com/dismissed.pdf.

Fuller, Dan, and Doris Geide-Stevenson. 2003. "Consensus among Economists: Revisited." *Journal of Economic Education* 34: 369–387.

Fuller, Wayne A. 1987. *Measurement Error Models*. New York: John Wiley & Sons.

Gilens, Martin. 1999. *Why Americans Hate Welfare*. Chicago: University of Chicago Press.

———. 2001. "Political Ignorance and Collective Policy Preferences." *American Political Science Review* 95: 379–396.

———. 2005. "Inequality and Democratic Responsiveness." *Public Opinion Quarterly* 69: 778–796.

Glazer, Nathan. 2003. "On Americans & Inequality." *Dædalus* 132: 111–115.

Goren, Paul. 2005. "Party Identification and Core Political Values." *American Journal of Political Science* 49: 881–896.

Gottschalk, Peter, and Timothy M. Smeeding. 2000. "Empirical Evidence on Income Inequality in Industrialized Countries." In Anthony B. Atkinson and François Bourguignon, eds., *Handbook of Income Distribution*, vol. 1, 261–308. Amsterdam: Elsevier.

Graetz, Michael J., and Ian Shapiro. 2005. *Death by a Thousand Cuts: The Fight over Taxing Inherited Wealth*. Princeton, NJ: Princeton University Press.

Griffin, John D., and Brian Newman. 2005. "Are Voters Better Represented?" *Journal of Politics* 67: 1206–1227.

Grogan, Coleen M. 1994. "Political-Economic Factors Influencing State Medicaid Policy." *Political Research Quarterly* 47: 589–623.

Gujarati, Damodar N. 1995. *Basic Econometrics*, 3rd ed. New York: McGraw-Hill.

Hacker, Jacob S., Suzanne Mettler, and Dianne Pinderhughes. 2005. "Inequality and Public Policy." In Lawrence R. Jacobs and Theda Skocpol, eds., *Inequality and American Democracy: What We Know and What We Need to Learn*, 156–213. New York: Russell Sage Foundation.

Hacker, Jacob S., and Paul Pierson. 2005a. "Abandoning the Middle: The Bush Tax Cuts and the Limits of Democratic Control." *Perspectives on Politics* 3: 33–53.

———. 2005b. *Off Center: The Republican Revolution and the Erosion of American Democracy*. New Haven, CT: Yale University Press.

Hall, Richard, and Frank Wayman. 1990. "Buying Time: Moneyed Interests and the Mobilization of Bias in Congressional Committees." *American Political Science Review* 84: 797–820.

Hansen, John Mark. 1998. "Individuals, Institutions, and Public Preferences over Public Finance." *American Political Science Review* 92: 513–531.

Harding, David J., Christopher Jencks, Leonard M. Lopoo, and Susan E. Mayer. 2005. "The Changing Effects of Family Background on the Incomes of American Adults." In Samuel Bowles, Herbert Gintis, and Melissa Osborne Groves, eds., *Unequal*

Chances: Family Background and Economic Success, 100–144. New York: Russell Sage Foundation; Princeton, NJ: Princeton University Press.

Heckman, James. 1979. "Sample Selection Bias as a Specification Error." *Econometrica 46*: 153–161.

Hellwig, Timothy, Eve Ringsmuth, and John R. Freeman. "The American Public and the Room to Manuever: Responsibility Attributions and Policy Efficacy in an Era of Globalization." Paper presented at the annual meeting of the Midwest Political Science Association, Chicago.

Hershey, Marjorie Randon. 2005. *Party Politics in America*, 11th ed. New York: Pearson Longman.

Hetherington, Marc J. 1996. "The Media's Role in Forming Voters' National Economic Evaluations in 1992." *American Journal of Political Science 40*: 372–395.

———. 2001. "Resurgent Mass Partisanship: The Role of Elite Polarization." *American Political Science Review 95*: 619–631.

Hibbs, Douglas A., Jr. 1977. "Political Parties and Macroeconomic Policy." *American Political Science Review 71*: 1467–1487.

———. 1987. *The American Political Economy: Macroeconomics and Electoral Politics*. Cambridge, MA: Harvard University Press.

———. 2006. "Voting and the Macroeconomy." In Barry R. Weingast and Donald Wittman, eds., *The Oxford Handbook of Political Economy*, 565–586. Oxford: Oxford University Press.

Hibbs, Douglas A., Jr., and Christopher Dennis. 1988. "Income Distribution in the United States." *American Political Science Review 82*: 467–490.

Hill, Kim Quaile, Jan E. Leighley, and Angela Hinton-Andersson. 1995. "Lower-Class Mobilization and Policy Linkage in the United States." *American Journal of Political Science 39*: 75–86.

Hines, James R., Jr., Hilary Hoynes, and Alan B. Krueger. 2001. "Another Look at Whether a Rising Tide Lifts All Boats." Working Paper #454, Industrial Relations Section, Princeton University.

Hochschild, Jennifer L. 1981. *What's Fair? American Beliefs about Distributive Justice*. Cambridge, MA: Harvard University Press.

———. 2001. "Where You Stand Depends on What You See: Connections among Values, Perceptions of Fact, and Political Prescriptions." In James H. Kuklinski, ed., *Citizens and Politics: Perspectives from Political Psychology*, 313–340. New York: Cambridge University Press.

Hout, Michael. 2004. "How Inequality May Affect Intergenerational Mobility." In Kathryn M. Neckerman, ed., *Social Inequality*, 969–987. New York: Russell Sage Foundation.

Huber, John D., and Piero Stanig. 2006. "Voting Polarization on Redistribution across Democracies." Unpublished paper presented at the annual meeting of the American Political Science Association, Philadelphia.

Huckfeldt, R. Robert, and Carol Weitzel Kohfeld. 1989. *Race and the Decline of Class in American Politics*. Urbana: University of Illinois Press.

Husted, Thomas A., and Lawrence W. Kenney. 1997. "The Effect of the Expansion of the Voting Franchise on the Size of Government." *Journal of Political Economy 105*: 54–82.

Jacobs, Lawrence R., and Benjamin I. Page. 2005. "Who Influences U.S. Foreign Policy?" *American Political Science Review* 99: 107–124.

Jacobs, Lawrence R., and Theda Skocpol. 2005. *Inequality and American Democracy: What We Know and What We Need to Learn.* New York: Russell Sage Foundation.

Jargowsky, Paul A. 1996. "Take the Money and Run: Economic Segregation in U.S. Metropolitan Areas." *American Sociological Review* 61: 984–998.

Jencks, Christopher. 2002. "Does Inequality Matter?" *Dædalus* 131: 49–65.

Jennings, Edward T., Jr. 1979. "Competition, Constituencies, and Welfare Policies in American States." *American Political Science Review* 73: 414–429.

Jost, John T., and Mahzarin R. Banaji. 1994. "The Role of Stereotyping in System-Justification and the Production of False Consciousness." *British Journal of Social Psychology* 33: 1–27.

Jost, John T., Sally Blount, Jeffrey Pfeffer, and György Hunyady. 2003. "Fair Market Ideology: Its Cognitive-Motivational Underpinnings." *Research in Organizational Behavior* 25: 53–91.

Karier, Thomas. 1997. *Great Experiments in American Economic Policy: From Kennedy to Reagan.* Westport, CT: Praeger Publishers.

Keech, William R. 1980. "Elections and Macroeconomic Policy Optimization." *American Journal of Political Science* 24: 345–367.

Kennedy, Peter. 1998. *A Guide to Econometrics*, 4th ed. Cambridge, MA: MIT Press.

Kenworthy, Lane, and Jonas Pontusson. 2005. "Rising Inequality and the Politics of Redistribution in Affluent Countries." *Perspectives on Politics* 3: 449–471.

Key, V. O., Jr. 1949. *Southern Politics in State and Nation.* New York: Alfred A. Knopf.

———. 1956. *American State Politics: An Introduction.* New York: Alfred A. Knopf.

———. 1964. *Politics, Parties, & Pressure Groups*, 5th ed. New York: Thomas Y. Crowell Company.

———. 1966. *The Responsible Electorate: Rationality in Presidential Voting 1936–1960.* Cambridge, MA: Harvard University Press.

Kinder, Donald R. 1983. "Diversity and Complexity in American Public Opinion." In Ada Finifter, ed., *Political Science: The State of the Discipline*, 389–428. Washington, DC: American Political Science Association.

Kinder, Donald R., Nancy Burns, and Dale B. Vieregge. 2005. "Liberalism, Race, and Exceptionalism: Understanding the American Appetite for Tax Reduction." Paper presented at the annual meeting of the American Political Science Association, Washington, DC.

Kluegel, James R., and Eliot R. Smith. 1986. *Beliefs about Inequality: Americans' Views of What Is and What Ought to Be.* New York: Aldine de Gruyter.

Knight, Brian. 2000. "Supermajority Voting Requirements for Tax Increases: Evidence from the States." *Journal of Public Economics* 76: 41–67.

Kramer, Gerald H. 1971. "Short-Term Fluctuations in U.S. Voting Behavior, 1896–1964." *American Political Science Review* 65: 131–143.

———. 1983. "The Ecological Fallacy Revisited: Aggregate- versus Individual-Level Findings on Economics and Elections, and Sociotropic Voting." *American Political Science Review* 77: 92–111.

Krehbiel, Keith. 1998. *Pivotal Politics: A Theory of U.S. Lawmaking.* Chicago: University of Chicago Press.

Krehbiel, Keith, and Douglas Rivers. 1988. "The Analysis of Committee Power: An Application to Senate Voting on the Minimum Wage." *American Journal of Political Science* 32: 1151–1174.

Krugman, Paul. 2002. "For Richer: How the Permissive Capitalism of the Boom Destroyed American Equality." *New York Times Magazine*, October 20, 62–142.

Krupnikov, Yanna, Adam Seth Levine, Markus Prior, and Arthur Lupia. 2006. "Public Ignorance and Estate Tax Repeal: The Effect of Partisan Differences and Survey Incentives." *National Tax Journal* 59: 425–437.

Ladd, Everett Carll, Jr., with Charles D. Hadley. 1975. *Transformations of the American Party System: Political Coalitions from the New Deal to the 1970s.* New York: W. W. Norton.

Lee, David S. 1999. "Wage Inequality in the United States during the 1980s: Rising Dispersion or Falling Minimum Wage?" *Quarterly Journal of Economics* 114: 977–1023.

Lee, Woojin, and John E. Roemer. 2006. "Racism and Redistribution in the United States: A Solution to the Problem of American Exceptionalism." *Journal of Public Economics* 90: 1027–1052.

Leege, David C., Kenneth D. Wald, Brian S. Krueger, and Paul D. Mueller. 2002. *The Politics of Cultural Differences: Social Change and Voter Mobilization Strategies in the Post–New Deal Period.* Princeton, NJ: Princeton University Press.

Leigh, Andrew. 2004. "Who Benefits from the Earned Income Tax Credit? Incidence among Recipients, Coworkers and Firms." Unpublished manuscript, Research School of Social Sciences, Australian National University, November.

Lenz, Gabriel S. 2004. "The Consequences of Income Inequality for Redistributive Policy in the United States." In Kathryn M. Neckerman, ed., *Social Inequality*, 797–820. New York: Russell Sage Foundation.

Lerner, Melvin J. 1980. *The Belief in a Just World: A Fundamental Delusion.* New York: Plenum Press.

Levy, Frank. 1998. *The New Dollars and Dreams: American Incomes and Economic Change.* New York: Russell Sage Foundation.

Levy, Frank, and Richard J. Murnane. 1992. "U.S. Earnings Levels and Earnings Inequality: A Review of Recent Trends and Proposed Explanations." *Journal of Economic Literature* 30: 1333–1381.

Levy, Frank, and Peter Temin. 2007. "Inequality and Institutions in 20th Century America." Working Paper 13106, National Bureau of Economic Research. http://www.nber.org/papers/w13106.

Lippmann, Walter. 1922. *Public Opinion.* Reprint, New York: Penguin Books, 1946.

Lockard, Duane. 1959. *New England State Politics.* Chicago: Henry Regnery.

Lupia, Arthur, Adam Seth Levine, Jesse O. Menning, and Gisela Sin. 2006. "Were Bush Tax Cut Supporters 'Simply Ignorant?' A Second Look at Conservatives and Liberals in 'Homer Gets a Tax Cut.'" Unpublished manuscript, University of Michigan.

Massey, Douglas, and Nancy Denton. 1993. *American Apartheid: Segregation and the Making of the Underclass.* Cambridge, MA: Harvard University Press.

Mayer, Susan E. 2001. "How the Growth in Income Inequality Increased Economic Segregation." JCPR Working Paper 230, Joint Center for Poverty Research, Northwestern University/University of Chicago.

Mayhew, David R. 1988. "Why Did V. O. Key Draw Back from His 'Have-Nots' Claim?" In Milton C. Cummings Jr., ed., *V. O. Key Jr. and the Study of American Politics*, 24–38. Washington, DC: American Political Science Association.

McCall, Leslie. 2005. "Do They Know and Do They Care? Americans' Awareness of Rising Inequality." Paper presented at the Russell Sage Foundation Social Inequality Conference, University of California, Berkeley, May.

McCarty, Nolan, Keith T. Poole, and Howard Rosenthal. 2006. *Polarized America: The Dance of Ideology and Unequal Riches*. Cambridge, MA: MIT Press.

McClosky, Herbert. 1958. "Conservatism and Personality." *American Political Science Review* 52: 27–45.

McClosky, Herbert, and John Zaller. 1984. *The American Ethos: Public Attitudes toward Capitalism and Democracy*. Cambridge, MA: Harvard University Press.

McCormick, John P. 2006. "Contain the Wealthy and Patrol the Magistrates: Restoring Elite Accountability to Popular Government." *American Political Science Review* 100: 147–163.

Mead, Lawrence M. 2004. "The Great Passivity." *Perspectives on Politics* 2: 671–675.

Meltzer, Allan H., and Scott F. Richard. 1981. "A Rational Theory of the Size of Govenrment." *Journal of Political Economy* 89: 914–927.

Miller, Warren E. 1991. "Party Identification, Realignment, and Party Voting: Back to the Basics." *American Political Science Review* 85: 557–568.

Miller, Warren E., and Donald E. Stokes. 1963. "Constituency Influence in Congress." *American Political Science Review* 57: 45–56.

Mishel, Lawrence, Jared Bernstein, and Heather Boushey. 2003. *The State of Working America 2002/2003*. Ithaca, NY: ILR Press.

Neckerman, Kathryn M., ed. 2004. *Social Inequality*. New York: Russell Sage Foundation.

Oliver, J. Eric. 2001. *Democracy in Suburbia*. Princeton, NJ: Princeton University Press.

Osberg, Lars, and Timothy Smeeding. 2003. "An International Comparison of Preferences for Leveling." Unpublished manuscript, Dalhousie University and Syracuse University; version 2.1.

Osberg, Lars, Timothy M. Smeeding, and Jonathan Schwabish. 2004. "Income Distribution and Public Social Expenditure: Theories, Effects, and Evidence." In Kathryn M. Neckerman, ed., *Social Inequality*, 821–859. New York: Russell Sage Foundation.

Ostrogorski, Moiseide. 1902. *Democracy and the Organization of Political Parties*. New York: Macmillan.

Page, Benjamin I., and Robert Y. Shapiro. 1983. "Effects of Public Opinion on Policy." *American Political Science Review* 77: 175–190.

———. 1992. *The Rational Public: Fifty Years of Trends in Americans' Policy Preferences*. Chicago: University of Chicago Press.

Page, Benjamin I., and James R. Simmons. 2000. *What Government Can Do: Dealing with Poverty and Inequality*. Chicago: University of Chicago Press.

Park, David K., Andrew Gelman, and Joseph Bafumi. 2002. "State-Level Opinions from National Surveys: Poststratification using Hierarchical Logistic Regression." Paper prepared for presentation at the annual meeting of the Society for Political Methodology, Seattle.

Parker, Jonathan A., Yacine Ait-Sahalia, and Motohiro Yogo. 2004. "Luxury Goods and the Equity Premium." *Journal of Finance* 59: 2959–3004.

Perotti, Roberto. 1996. "Growth, Income Distribution, and Democracy: What the Data Say." *Journal of Economic Growth* 1: 149–187.

Persson, Torsten, and Guido Tabellini. 1994. "Is Inequality Harmful for Growth?" *American Economic Review* 84: 600–621.

Phillips, Kevin. 1969. *The Emerging Republican Majority*. New Rochelle, NY: Arlington House.

———. 1990. *The Politics of Rich and Poor: Wealth and the American Electorate in the Reagan Aftermath*. New York: Random House.

———. 2002. *Wealth and Democracy: A Political History of the American Rich*. New York: Broadway Books.

Piketty, Thomas, and Emmanuel Saez. 2003. "Income Inequality in the United States, 1913–1998." *Quarterly Journal of Economics* 118: 1–39.

Pontusson, Jonas. 2005. *Inequality and Prosperity: Social Europe vs. Liberal America*. Ithaca, NY: Cornell University Press.

Poole, Keith T., and Howard Rosenthal. 1997. *Congress: A Political-Economic History of Roll Call Voting*. New York: Oxford University Press.

Prior, Markus, and Arthur Lupia. 2006. "What Citizens Know Depends on How You Ask Them: Opportunities, Incentives and Political Knowledge." Unpublished manuscript, Princeton University and the University of Michigan.

Putterman, Louis, John E. Roemer, and Joaquim Silvestre. 1998. "Does Egalitarianism Have a Future?" *Journal of Economic Literature* 36: 861–902.

Rawls, John. 1971. *A Theory of Justice*. Cambridge, MA: The Belknap Press of Harvard University Press.

Remnick, David, ed. 2000. *The New Gilded Age: The New Yorker Looks at the Culture of Affluence*. New York: Random House.

Riker, William H. 1982. *Liberalism against Populism: A Confrontation between the Theory of Democracy and the Theory of Social Choice*. San Francisco: W. H. Freeman and Company.

Rivers, Douglas. N.d. "Partisan Representation in Congress." Unpublished paper, Department of Political Science, University of California, Los Angeles.

Rodriguez, Francisco R. 1999. "Does Distributional Skewness Lead to Redistribution? Evidence from the United States." *Economics and Politics* 11: 171–199.

———. 2004. "Inequality, Redistribution, and Rent-Seeking." *Economics and Politics* 16: 287–320.

Roemer, John E. 1999. "The Democratic Political Economy of Progressive Income Taxation." *Econometrica* 67: 1–19.

———. 2001. *Political Competition: Theory and Applications*. Cambridge, MA: Harvard University Press.

Rogers, Diane Lim, and John H. Rogers. 2000. "Political Competition and State Government Size: Do Tighter Elections Produce Looser Budgets?" *Public Choice* 105: 1–21.

Rohde, David W. 1991. *Parties and Leaders in the Postreform House*. Chicago: University of Chicago Press.

Rosenthal, Howard. 2004. "Politics, Public Policy, and Inequality: A Look Back at the Twentieth Century." In Kathryn M. Neckerman, ed., *Social Inequality*, 861–892. New York: Russell Sage Foundation.

Schattschneider, E. E. 1942. *Party Government*. New York: Holt, Rinehart, and Winston.

Schlozman, Kay Lehman, Benjamin I. Page, Sidney Verba, and Morris P. Fiorina. 2005. "Inequalities of Political Voice." In Lawrence R. Jacobs and Theda Skocpol, eds., *Inequality and American Democracy: What We Know and What We Need to Learn*, 19–87. New York: Russell Sage Foundation.

Scholz, John Karl. 1994. "The Earned Income Tax Credit: Participation, Compliance, and Antipoverty Effectiveness." *National Tax Journal* 47: 63–87.

Schultz, Kenneth A. 1995. "The Politics of the Political Business Cycle." *British Journal of Political Science* 25: 79–99.

Schumpeter, Joseph R. 1950. *Capitalism, Socialism and Democracy*, 3rd ed. New York: Harper Colophon Books.

Shani, Danielle. 2006. "Knowing Your Colors: Can Knowledge Correct for Partisan Bias in Political Perceptions?" Paper presented at the annual meeting of the Midwest Political Science Association, Chicago.

Slemrod, Joel. 1994. *Tax Progressivity and Income Inequality*. New York: Cambridge University Press.

———. 2006. "The Role of Misconceptions in Support for Regressive Tax Reform." *National Tax Journal* 59: 57–75.

Slemrod, Joel, and Jon Bakija. 2004. *Taxing Ourselves: A Citizen's Guide to the Debate over Taxes*, 3rd ed. Cambridge, MA: MIT Press.

Sobel, Russell S. 1999. "Theory and Evidence on the Political Economy of the Minimum Wage." *Journal of Political Economy* 107: 761–785.

Solon, Gary. 2002. "Cross-Country Differences in Intergenerational Earnings Mobility." *Journal of Economic Perspectives* 16: 59–66.

Stenner, Karen. 2005. *The Authoritarian Dynamic*. New York: Cambridge University Press.

Stimson, James A., Michael B. MacKuen, and Robert S. Erikson. 1995. "Dynamic Representation." *American Political Science Review* 89: 543–565.

Stoker, Laura. 1992. "Interests and Ethics in Politics." *American Political Science Review* 86: 369–380.

Stonecash, Jeffrey M. 2000. *Class and Party in American Politics*. Boulder, CO: Westview Press.

———. 2005. "Inequality and a Conflicted Public." In *The Maxwell Poll: Civic Engagement and Inequality*, 1–10. Campbell Public Affairs Institute, Maxwell School of Citizenship and Public Affairs, Syracuse University.

Task Force on Inequality and American Democracy. 2004. "American Democracy in an Age of Rising Inequality." *Perspectives on Politics* 2: 651–666.

Tobin, James, and Murray Weidenbaum, eds. 1988. *Two Revolutions in Economic Policy: The First Economic Reports of Presidents Kennedy and Reagan*. Cambridge, MA: MIT Press.

Tocqueville, Alexis de. 2003. *"Democracy in America" and "Two Essays on America."* London: Penguin Books.

Tufte, Edward R. 1978. *Political Control of the Economy*. Princeton, NJ: Princeton University Press.

Twain, Mark, and Charles Dudley Warner. 1873. *The Gilded Age: A Tale of Today*. Reprint, New York: Penguin Books, 2001.

Ventry, Dennis J., Jr. 2000. "The Collision of Tax and Welfare Politics: The Political History of the Earned Income Tax Credit, 1969–99." *National Tax Journal* 53: 983–1026.

Verba, Sidney, Norman H. Nie, and Jae-on Kim. 1978. *Participation and Political Equality: A Seven-Nation Comparison*. Cambridge: Cambridge University Press.

Verba, Sidney, and Gary R. Orren. 1985. *Equality in America: The View from the Top*. Cambridge, MA: Harvard University Press.

Verba, Sidney, Kay Lehman Schlozman, and Henry E. Brady. 1995. *Voice and Equality: Civic Voluntarism in American Politics*. Cambridge, MA: Harvard University Press.

Weissberg, Robert. 2004. "Politicized Pseudo Science." *PS: Political Science & Politics* 39: 33–37.

Wilensky, Harold L. 2002. *Rich Democracies: Political Economy, Public Policy, and Performance*. Berkeley: University of California Press.

Winters, Richard. 1976. "Party Control and Policy Change." *American Journal of Political Science* 20: 597–636.

Wolff, Edward N. 2002. *Top Heavy: The Increasing Inequality of Wealth in America and What Can Be Done about It*. New York: The New Press.

Wolfinger, Raymond E., and Steven J. Rosenstone. 1980. *Who Votes?* New Haven, CT: Yale University Press.

Zaller, John. 1985. "Pre-Testing Information Items on the 1986 NES Pilot Survey." Report to the National Election Study Board of Overseers.

———. 1992. *The Nature and Origins of Mass Opinion*. New York: Cambridge University Press.

Zellner, Arnold. 1962. "An Efficient Method of Estimating Seemingly Unrelated Regressions and Tests for Aggregation Bias." *Journal of the American Statistical Association* 57: 348–368.

Index

Aaronson, Daniel, 16n
abortion (opinion), 79–83; and senators' votes, 265–267; and voting behavior, 84–94
Abramson, Paul, 70–71n
Achen, Christopher, 100n, 157n, 258n, 260n
Adams, Greg, 93n
AFL-CIO, 235; support for minimum wage increase, 248
aid to blacks (opinion), 82–83; and egalitarianism, 134–135; and voting behavior, 84–94
Ait-Sahalia, Yacine, 14n
Aldrich, John, 70–71n
Alesina, Alberto, 14n, 31n, 52, 298
Almanac of American Politics, 262n
Alter, Jonathan, 187, 300–301
Alternative Minimum Tax (AMT), 195
Althaus, Scott, 181n
American Economic Association, 227
American Family Business Institute, 206
American State Politics (Key), 291
Anderson, Nick (cartoon), 162
Andrews, Edmund L., 168n, 194n, 195n, 196n, 206n, 220n, 249n, 251n
Ansolabehere, Stephen, 281n
Aristotle, 283–284
Armey, Dick, 235
Arrow, Kenneth, 175n
Atkinson, A. B., 26–27, 31n
Atlas, John, 250n

Bafumi, Joseph, 100n, 261n
Bai, Matt, 95n
Bakija, Jon, 246n
Ballot Strategy Initiative Center, 249
Banaji, Mahzarin, 149n
Barshay, Jill, 167n, 168n, 169n

Bartels, Larry, 99n, 100n, 111n, 127n, 157n, 175n, 179n, 181n, 183n, 208n, 253n, 254n, 262n, 275n
Bartlett, Bruce, 194
Baucus, Max, 165, 166, 194–195, 220, 237
Beck, Nathaniel, 31n
Beller, Emily, 16n
Bénabou, Roland, 14n, 27n
Berinsky, Adam, 216n
Bernasek, Anna, 14n
Bernstein, Jared, 8n
Besley, Timothy, 291n, 292n
Bibby, John, 70n
Bivin, W. Carl, 46n
Blanchard, Oliver, 33n
Boehner, John, 251
Boix, Carles, 293
Borgman, Jim (cartoon), 223
Boushey, Heather, 8n
Boxer, Barbara, 257n
Bradbury, Katherine, 16n
Brady, Henry, 116n, 252n, 253, 276n, 280
Brandeis, Louis, 284
Breaux, John, 166
Brenner, Lynn, 21n, 22n
Broder, David, 169, 193–194
Broder, John, 238n, 249n, 251n
Brooks, David, 16, 67–68, 71, 74
Brown, Dorothy, 247n
Brown, Kevin, 221
Brown, Robert, 292
budget reconciliation process, 164–165, 196
budget surplus and tax cuts, 171, 173
Burns, Arthur, 105
Burns, Conrad, 250
Burns, Nancy, 298n
Bush, George H. W.: minimum wage veto, 234–235; and Senate

Bush, George H. W. (*continued*)
responsiveness to income groups,
273–275

Bush, George W., 20, 29, 110; economic
policies, 55; and income growth, 63;
minimum wage increase, 250–251; in
New Orleans, 299–301

Bush tax cuts, 164–170; bases of public
support, 176–181; extent of public
support, 170–176; information and
public support, 181–186; prospects
for extension, 193–196; "sun-setting"
provisions, 164–165, 193, 196

campaign contributions: and
election-year economy, 116; by
income level, 280

campaign spending, 116–119; and
election outcomes, 120–125; and
voting behavior, 120–121

Campbell, Angus, 111n

Card, David, 228–229, 234, 237, 251

Carmines, Edward, 93n, 265n

Carnahan, Jean, 166

Carter, Jimmy, economic policies, 45–46

Case, Anne, 291n, 292n

Cauchon, Dennis, 249n

CBS News/*New York Times* Poll, 172,
174–175

Census Bureau: Current Population
Survey, 7n, 42; Historical Income
Tables, 6, 32, 55–56n

Center on Budget and Policy Priorities,
163n, 167

Chafee, Lincoln, 166, 168

Chamber of Commerce, U.S., 167, 250

Cheney, Richard, 168, 169

child tax credit, JGTRRA, 169

Chipman, Kim, 238n

Christiano, Lawrence, 33n

church attendance and voting behavior,
90–94

Citizens for Tax Justice, 163n, 166–167

class polarization in voting behavior,
cross-national comparison, 95–96

Cleland, Max, 166

Clinton, Bill, 20, 29, 36; and Earned

Income Tax Credit, 246; economic
policies, 55; proposed minimum wage
increase, 236; and senate
responsiveness to income groups,
273–275

Clinton, Hillary Rodham, 195n

Cochrane, John, 168n

Cochrane, Thad, 257n

college graduates, voting patterns, 68–71

Collins, Susan, 166, 237

Committee on Political Parties,
American Political Science
Association, 290

Comprehensive Employment and
Training Act (CETA), 46–47

Congress and income inequality, 34

Congressional Budget Office (CBO),
193, 206

Congressional Quarterly, 262n

Conover, Pamela, 100n

Conrad, Kent, 167, 237

contact with senators (in NES Senate
Election Study), 276; and senators'
responsiveness, 276–279

Converse, Philip, 79n, 136n, 275n

Coolidge, Calvin, 218

CQ Weekly, 235, 239

Cranston, Alan, 257n

cultural issues and voting behavior,
83–93

Cutler, David, 25n

Dahl, Robert, 1, 2, 19, 27, 252, 282,
285–287

Danziger, Sheldon, 47n, 54

Daschle, Tom, 165

Dean, Howard, 223, 238

death penalty (opinion) and voting
behavior, 87–90

"death tax," public support for repeal,
198–199

defense spending (opinion), 82–83; and
voting behavior, 84–94

DeLay, Tom, 170

Delli Carpini, Michael, 181n, 275n

Democratic Faith (Deneen), 298–299

Deneen, Patrick, 298–299

Dennis, Christopher, 31–32
Denton, Nancy, 297n
DeParle, Jason, 300n
Dewan, Shaila, 302n
Dew-Becker, Ian, 17–18
Dilemmas of Pluralist Democracy (Dahl), 2n
DiNardo, John, 229n
Dowd, Maureen, 65
Downs, Anthony, 26n
Dreier, Peter, 250n
Dye, Thomas, 291n

Earned Income Tax Credit (EITC), 55, 60, 227n, 246–247
economic growth and inequality, 14
Economic Growth and Tax Relief Reconciliation Act (EGTRRA), 164–167, 193, 196, 197
economic issues and voting behavior, 83–93
economic mobility, 15–16
Economic Policy Institute, 223
Economist, The, 20, 143
"econophysics," 19
Edsall, Mary, 67, 79
Edsall, Thomas, 67, 79
Edwards, John, 22, 195n, 238, 251
egalitarian values, 23–24, 27, 127–128, 130–132; and policy preferences, 134–135; social bases, 132–133; and support for Bush tax cuts, 188–190
Ehrenreich, Barbara, 297–298
Eisenhower, Dwight, 107n, 110; campaign spending, 119; economic policies, 43
electoral cycles in income growth, 104–109
Emerging Republican Majority, The (Phillips), 66
Enron, 295
environment (opinion) and voting behavior, 88–90
Episcopal Church support for minimum wage increase, 248
Erikson, Robert, 99n, 100n, 127n, 253n, 260n, 293

estate tax, 27; congressional deliberations, 218–221; interest group opposition, 214–215; and minimum wage increase, 238–239; prospects for permanent repeal, 221–222; public support for repeal, 198–213, 215–217
explanations for economic inequality (public opinion), 147–148

Fair Minimum Wage Act of 2007, 223, 250–251
Federal Emergency Management Agency (FEMA), 302
Federal Reserve Board, 55, 58, 105
"feeling thermometer" ratings, 136–139
Feinstein, Diane, 166, 257n
Feldman, Stanley, 100n, 128, 130n
Figueiredo, John de, 281n
Fiorina, Morris, 100
Firestone, David, 168n, 169n
Fishkin, James, 181n
Fleischer, Ari, 193
Florida minimum wage, 228, 234, 249
Foley, Duncan, 296n
Forbes 400, 11, 15
Ford, Gerald: and Earned Income Tax Credit, 246; economic policies, 45
Fortin, Nicole, 229n
Fortune magazine, 216–217
Frank, Robert, 14, 197n, 222
Frank, Thomas, 65, 71, 79, 84, 85n, 90, 97, 295
Freedman, Jacob, 206n
Freeman, John, 297n
Frist, Bill, 220, 221
Fuller, Dan, 227n
Fuller, Wayne, 260n

Gallup Poll, 230
Garner, John Nance, 218
gay marriage, 65; opinion and voting behavior, 87–90
Geewax, Marilyn, 236–237, 238, 248
Geide-Stevenson, Doris, 227n
Gelman, Andrew, 261n
General Accounting Office, 247
General Social Surveys, 14n

Gephardt, Richard, 187

Gilded Age, 24, 284, 294–295

Gilens, Martin, 181n, 212n, 232, 253n, 286, 298

Glaeser, Edward, 298

Glazer, Nathan, 128

Gordon, Robert, 17–18

Gore, Al, 63, 74, 193

Goren, Paul, 133n

Gottschalk, Peter, 47n, 54

government jobs (opinion), 79–83; and egalitarianism, 134–135; and voting behavior, 84–94

government services (opinion), 82–83; and egalitarianism, 134–135; and voting behavior, 84–94

government spending preferences: measurement, 201n; and support for estate tax repeal, 204–205; and support for 2001 tax cut, 178–179

Graetz, Michael, 197–198, 205, 214–218

Gramm, Phil, 257n

Grassley, Charles, 165, 166, 168

Green, William, 218

Greenstein, Robert, 167

Griffin, John, 253n, 279n

Grogan, Coleen, 292n

Gross, Daniel, 18n

Gujarati, Damodar, 240n

gun control (opinion) and voting behavior, 87–90

Hacker, Jacob, 27n, 173–175, 287, 291n

Hadley, Charles, 67

Hall, Richard, 281n

Hansen, John Mark, 192

Harding, David, 16n

Harkness, Peter, 249n

Harris Poll, 144–146, 173

Harvard University Kennedy School of Government (survey), 176, 200, 207–208, 247

Hastert, Dennis, 236, 238

"have-nots" and party competition, 289–294

health care (opinion) and voting

behavior, 88–90; and egalitarianism, 134–135

Heckman, James, 179n

Hellwig, Timothy, 297n

Heritage Foundation, 215, 217

Hershey, Marjorie, 70n

Hibbs, Douglas, 31–32, 43, 45n, 47–49, 54–55, 100

Hill, Kim, 292n

Hines, James, 25n

Hinton-Andersson, Angela, 292n

Hochschild, Jennifer, 128, 146–147, 160, 175n, 215–216, 295–296, 297

"honeymoon" period in presidential administrations, 52–54, 57, 99

House Appropriations Committee, 238

House Ways and Means Committee, 167, 218

Hout, Michael, 16n

Hoynes, Hilary, 25n

Hubbard, R. Glenn, 167

Huber, John, 95–96

Huckfeldt, Robert, 67

Hulse, Carl, 221n, 239n

Humphrey, Hubert, 74

Hurricane Katrina, 236, 283 (photograph), 299–302

ideology: and attitudes toward rich people and poor people, 138–139; and egalitarian values, 133; and perceived tax burdens, 141–142; and perceptions of economic inequality, 151–161; and policy preferences, 134–135

immigration (opinion) and voting behavior, 87–90

income differences: perceived, 143–147; and support for estate tax repeal, 210–212

income growth: under Democratic and Republican presidents, 31–42; historical pattern, 7–13, 41; post-tax, 54–60; and presidential election outcomes, 101–104; related to macroeconomic performance, 50–52; and voting behavior, 111–115

incumbent party tenure: and election outcomes, 103; and voting behavior, 112

information, political (in National Election Study surveys), 153, 182n, 275–276; and perceptions of economic inequality, 153–159; and senators' responsiveness, 276–279; and support for Bush tax cut, 181–186; and support for estate tax repeal, 208–213

Institute on Taxation and Economic Policy, 163

interest groups and antipathy to estate tax, 214–215

Internal Revenue Service (IRS), 221; and Earned Income Tax Credit, 247

International Social Survey Program (ISSP), 14n, 147–148

iPOLL archive, 174n, 215n, 229

Jackson Square, New Orleans, 299–301

Jacobs, Lawrence, 253n, 281

Jargowsky, Paul, 297n

Jeffords, James, 165, 166

Jennings, Edward, 291–292

Jim Crow era, 77, 94, 289

Jobs and Growth Tax Relief Reconciliation Act (JGTRRA), 168–169, 196n

Job Training and Partnership Act (JTPA), 47

Johnson, Lyndon, economic policies, 44

Johnson, Tim, 166

Johnston, David Cay, 13n, 221n

Joint Committee on Taxation, U.S. Congress, 164, 168n, 197

Jost, John, 149n, 152n

Kaiser Foundation (survey), 176, 200, 207–208, 247

Karier, Thomas, 54n

Katel, Peter, 248n

Katz, Jane, 16n

Katz, Lawrence, 25n

Keech, William, 31n

Keeter, Scott, 181n, 275n

Kennedy, Edward, 236–237, 238–239, 251

Kennedy, John, 74; economic policies, 43–44, 54

Kennedy, Peter, 240n

Kenworthy, Lane, 296n

Kerry, John, 29, 73, 74, 227, 301

Key, V. O., Jr., 77, 100, 125–126, 275, 289–291

Kim, Jae-on, 252n

Kim, Walter, 18n

Kinder, Donald, 136n, 298n

Kinsley, Michael, 16, 28

Kirchhoff, Sue, 238n

Kirkland, Lane, 235

Knight, Brian, 292n

Knight, Kathleen, 100n

Kohfeld, Carol, 67

Kohl, Herbert, 166

Kramer, Gerald, 99n, 100

Krehbiel, Keith, 234n, 244n

Kristof, Nicholas, 66

Krueger, Alan, 25n, 228–229, 234, 237, 251

Krugman, Paul, 13n, 17, 25, 187, 197

Krupnikov, Yanna, 208n

Labaton, Stephen, 195n, 224n, 251n

labor force participation and income inequality, 40

Ladd, Everett, 67

Landrieu, Mary, 166

Landsburg, Steven, 227n

Lee, David, 229

Leege, David, 90n

Leigh, Andrew, 247n

Leighley, Jan, 292n

Lemieux, Thomas, 229n

Leonhardt, David, 15n

Lerner, Melvin, 149n

Levy, Frank, 13, 25n

Lincoln, Blanche, 165, 166, 230

Lippmann, Walter, 143

Lockard, Duane, 291n

Londregan, John, 52n

Long, Phil, 300n
Los Angeles Times Poll, 174
Lott, Trent, 169, 238, 257n
Loughlin, Sean, 166n, 281n
Lupia, Arthur, 184
Luxembourg Income Study, 15

Mack, Connie, 206
MacKuen, Michael, 127n, 253n, 293
macroeconomic policies, partisan,
    43–47, 54–60
Marshall, Ray, 46n
Martinez, Gebe, 235n
Massey, Douglas, 297n
Maxwell Poll on Civic Engagement and
    Inequality, 150
Mayer, Susan, 297n
Mayhew, David, 291
Mazumder, Bhashkar, 16n
McCain, John, 165, 166, 195–196
McCall, Leslie, 14n, 144–145
McCarty, Nolan, 26n, 67, 96n, 233–234
McCaskill, Claire, 250
McClosky, Herbert, 128, 149n
McConnell, Mitch, 170
McCormick, John, 284
McIver, John, 260n
Mead, Lawrence, 30
measurement error (in survey
    responses), 178n; in perceived tax
    burdens, 180n; in senators'
    constituency opinion, 260n
median voter, 26, 287
Medicare versus tax cuts, 173–174
Mellon, Andrew, 218
Meltzer, Allan, 26n
Merzer, Martin, 300n
Meyerson, Harold, 248n
Mikulski, Barbara, 237
military intervention (opinion) and
    voting behavior, 89–90
Miller, Warren, 253, 260n
Miller, Zell, 166
minimum wage, 25, 27; congressional
    deliberations, 234–239; under
    Democrats and Republicans,
    240–244; economic effects, 227–229;

historical trajectory, 224–226;
    indexation, 233–234; public support,
    229–232; state initiatives, 248–250;
    and 2006 campaign, 249–250
Mishel, Lawrence, 8n
MIT Dictionary of Modern Economics,
    227
Munk, Nina, 11n, 15n
Murnane, Richard, 25n
myopia, economic, 99–104; and election
    outcomes, 109–110, 124–125

Nather, David, 170n, 221n, 239n
National Election Study (NES), 68–69,
    79–80, 82, 84, 87, 89, 90, 111, 130,
    139, 143, 147, 150–152, 170, 176, 179,
    187, 198–199, 201–202, 208; Senate
    Election Study, 244, 254–255,
    257–258, 275, 276; weighted data,
    69n, 254n
National Federation of Independent
    Business, 250
National Public Radio (survey), 176,
    200, 207–208, 247
Nature and Origins of Mass Opinion
    (Zaller), 156
NBC News/Wall Street Journal Poll,
    172, 174, 175
Nelson, Ben, 166, 220
Nelson, Bill, 220
New Deal: cleavage structure, 292;
    coalition, 93–94, institutional
    reforms, 284, 285, 294–295
Newman, Brian, 253n, 279n
New York Times Magazine, 22–23
Nickel and Dimed (Ehrenreich),
    297–298
Nie, Norman, 252n
Nitschke, Lori, 165n, 166n, 167n, 236n
Nixon, Richard, 104–105, 107n, 110;
    and Earned Income Tax Credit, 246;
    economic policies, 44
Norquist, Grover, 170

Obama, Barack, 195n
oil price shocks and income inequality,
    38–40, 45, 46

Oliver, Eric, 297n
On Political Equality (Dahl), 2n
opportunity to succeed, perceived, 150
Orren, Gary, 5–6, 23–24, 135, 252, 284–285
Osberg, Lars, 15n, 148n, 297n
Ostrogorski, Moiseide, 98, 295
Ota, Alan, 168n, 169n, 170n
Ovalle, David, 300n

Page, Benjamin, 55n, 224n, 253n, 281, 287
Parade Magazine, 21–23
Park, David, 261n
Parker, Jonathan, 14n
Parks, Daniel, 164n, 167n, 193n
Parks, James, 250n
partisanship: and attitudes toward rich people and poor people, 138–139; and egalitarian values, 133; and perceived tax burdens, 141–142; and policy preferences, 134–135; and support for estate tax repeal, 208–210; and support for 2001 tax cut, 184–186; trends by region and income class, 74–77; and voting behavior, 290
party polarization and voting behavior, cross-national comparison, 96
Paulson, Henry, 18, 29, 61, 296n
Pearce, David, 227n
Pelosi, Nancy, 223, 250
Penn, Mark, 200
Perotti, Roberto, 14n, 27n, 33n, 297n
Persson, Torsten, 14n
Peterson, Peter, 169n
Pethokoukis, James, 195n, 196n
Pew Research Center, 231
Phillip, David (photo), 283
Phillips, Kevin, 24–25, 66, 284, 294–295
Pierson, Paul, 27n, 173–175, 287, 291n
Piketty, Thomas, 1n, 10–13, 63
Plato, 298–299
political economic cycle, 52–54
political parties and economic inequality, 29–63, 289–294; and

macroeconomic performance, 47–50; and state policy, 291–292
Politics, Parties, & Pressure Groups (Key), 126n
polyarchy, 286
Pontusson, Jonas, 296n, 297n
Poole, Keith, 26n, 67, 95n, 96n, 233–234, 255, 265n
Porter, Eduardo, 18n, 194n
presidents and income inequality, 31–63; and macroeconomic performance, 47–50
productivity growth, 17–18, 20
Progressive Era, 284, 285, 294–295
"public mood" and public policy, 293
Putterman, Louis, 31n
Pytte, Alyson, 235n

Quinn, Jane, 195n

race and inequality, 298
Rangel, Charles, 167, 169, 194–195
Rational Public (Page and Shapiro), 287
Rawls, John, 14
Reagan, Ronald, 20, 78, 107n; and Earned Income Tax Credit, 246; economic policies, 46–47, 54–55
religion and voting behavior, 90–94
religious fractionalization and voting behavior, cross-national comparison, 96
Remnick, David, 13n
Republic (Plato), 298–299
Responsible Electorate (Key), 126n
retrospective voting, 100
Richard, Scott, 26n
Riedl, Brian, 194
Riker, William, 175n
Ringsmuth, Eve, 297n
Rivers, Douglas, 244n
Rivlin, Gary, 301n
Roaring Twenties, 13, 24, 284, 294
Rodriguez, Francisco, 27n
Rodrik, Dani, 14n
Roemer, John, 26n, 31n, 64–65n
Rogers, Diane, 291n, 292n
Rogers, John, 291n, 292n

Rohde, David, 70–71n
Roosevelt, Franklin, 94
Roper Center, 174n, 215n, 229
Rosenbaum, David, 168n
Rosenstone, Steven, 252n
Rosenthal, Howard, 26n, 52n, 67, 95n, 96n, 233–234, 255, 265n
Rove, Karl, 65

Sachs, Jeffrey, 31n
Saez, Emmanuel, 1n, 10–13, 63
Safire, William, 250n
Samuelson, Paul, 43
Samuelson, Robert, 128
Santorum, Rick, 237, 238
Schattschneider, E. E., 176, 290
Schlozman, Kay, 116n, 252n, 253, 276n, 280
Scholz, John, 247n
school vouchers (opinion) and voting behavior, 87–90
Schultz, Kenneth, 105n
Schumer, Charles, 249
Schumpeter, Joseph, 287
Schwab, Charles, 167
Schwabish, Jonathan, 15n
Scott, H. Lee, 248n
Scott, Janny, 15n
security issues and voting behavior, 87–90
Seelye, Katherine, 65n
segregation and inequality, 297–298
Senate Appropriations Committee, 207
Senate Finance Committee, 165, 207, 218
senators' responsiveness to public opinion: on abortion, 265–267; on budget votes, 262–265; on Civil Rights Act amendment, 262–265; by income level, 257–265, 275–280; on minimum wage, 244–245, 265; by party, 267–275; on roll call votes, 255–257
Service Employees International Union (survey), 231
Seymour, John, 257n
Shani, Danielle, 157n
Shapiro, Ian, 197–198, 205, 214–218

Shapiro, Robert, 253n, 287
Shea, Christopher, 19n
Silvestre, Joaquim, 31n
Simmons, James, 55n, 224n
skills and economic inequality, 16–17, 25
Slemrod, Joel, 208, 214, 246n
Sloan, Allan, 168n
Smeeding, Timothy, 15n, 148n, 297n
Smoot, Reed, 218
Snow, John, 18
Snowe, Olympia, 165, 168, 237
Snyder, James, 281n
Sobel, Russell, 228
Social Security privatization (opinion) and voting behavior, 88–90
Social Security versus tax cuts, 173–174
Solid South, 75, 94, 98
Solomon, Deborah, 207n
Solon, Gary, 16n, 297n
Solow, Robert, 44
Southern Politics in State and Nation (Key), 289, 291
Specter, Arlen, 166, 237
Springer, John, 163n
"stagflation," 46–47
Stanig, Piero, 95–96
Starobin, Paul, 235n
Stein, Ben, 29, 61
Steinfels, Peter, 296n
Stenner, Karen, 149n
Stevens, Allison, 236n
Stevenson, Adlai, campaign spending, 119
Stimson, James, 127n, 253n, 265n, 293
Stoker, Laura, 212n
Stokes, Donald, 253, 260n
Stonecash, Jeffrey, 67, 68, 150n
"sun-setting" provisions of 2001 tax cut, 164–165, 193, 196
Sununu, John, 235, 238
Swindell, Bill, 167n, 193n

Tabellini, Guido, 14n
Talent, Jim, 250
Task Force on Inequality and American Democracy, American Political Science Association, 2, 30, 252

tax burdens, perceived, 139–141; social bases, 141–143; and support for Bush tax cut, 179–181; and support for estate tax repeal, 202–204, 209–211

tax cuts, 27, 46, 55; and budget deficit, 191–192; Bush administration (*see* Bush tax cuts); and domestic spending, 190–191; ideological rationale, 54

Taylor, Andrew, 164n, 165n

technology and economic inequality, 17

Temin, Peter, 13

Temporary Assistance for Needy Families (TANF), 246

Tester, John, 250

Thomas, Bill, 167

Tilove, Jonathan, 300n

Tobias, Andrew, 21, 22n

Tobin, James, 44, 54n

Tocqueville, Alexis de, 23

Torricelli, Robert, 165, 166

"trickle-down" income growth, 14–15, 41–42

Tufte, Edward, 43, 63, 99n, 104–105

turnout and senators' responsiveness, 276–279

Twain, Mark, 24

Uchitelle, Louis, 13n, 18n

unemployment, 46–47; and income growth, 50–52; partisan differences, 48–50

unions, labor, 20; and minimum wage, 240

"values voters" in 2004 election, 65

Van Dongen, Rachel, 220n, 221n, 239n

Ventry, Dennis, 246n

Verba, Sidney, 5–6, 23–24, 116n, 135, 252, 253, 276n, 280, 284–285

Vieregge, Dale, 298n

Voinovich, George, 168

Waldman, Steven, 65

Wallace, George, 293

Wall Street Journal, 227

Wal-Mart, support for minimum wage increase, 247–248

Warner, Charles, 24

Wayman, Frank, 281n

Wealth and Democracy: A Political History of the American Rich (Phillips), 24

wealth and political power, 283–286

Weidenbaum, Murray, 54n

Weisman, Jonathan, 214

Weisman, Steven, 195n

Weissberg, Robert, 288

What's the Matter with Kansas? (Frank), 65, 66

Why Americans Hate Welfare (Gilens), 298

Wilensky, Harold, 297n

Wilfore, Christina, 249

Will, George, 168n

Wills, Garry, 65

Wilson, Bret, 100n

Wilson, Pete, 257n

Winters, Richard, 291n

W-NOMINATE scores, 255, 258

Wolfe, Kathryn, 238n

Wolfinger, Raymond, 252n

women's role (opinion), 82–83; and voting behavior, 84–94

Woods, James, 93n

working class: party identification, 74–77; voting patterns, 67–74

Wright, Gerald, 260n

Yakovenko, Victor, 19

Yogo, Motohiro, 14n

Yoon, Robert, 166n, 281n

Zaller, John, 99n, 128, 153n, 156–157, 175n

Zellner, Arnold, 38